A Practical Guide to
Security Assessments

OTHER INFORMATION SECURITY BOOKS FROM AUERBACH

Asset Protection and Security Management Handbook
POA Publishing
ISBN: 0-8493-1603-0

Building a Global Information Assurance Program
Raymond J. Curts and Douglas E. Campbell
ISBN: 0-8493-1368-6

Building an Information Security Awareness Program
Mark B. Desman
ISBN: 0-8493-0116-5

Critical Incident Management
Alan B. Sterneckert
ISBN: 0-8493-0010-X

Cyber Crime Investigator's Field Guide
Bruce Middleton
ISBN: 0-8493-1192-6

Cyber Forensics: A Field Manual for Collecting, Examining, and Preserving Evidence of Computer Crimes
Albert J. Marcella, Jr. and Robert S. Greenfield
ISBN: 0-8493-0955-7

The Ethical Hack: A Framework for Business Value Penetration Testing
James S. Tiller
ISBN: 0-8493-1609-X

The Hacker's Handbook: The Strategy Behind Breaking into and Defending Networks
Susan Young and Dave Aitel
ISBN: 0-8493-0888-7

Information Security Architecture: An Integrated Approach to Security in the Organization
Jan Killmeyer Tudor
ISBN: 0-8493-9988-2

Information Security Fundamentals
Thomas R. Peltier
ISBN: 0-8493-1957-9

Information Security Management Handbook, 5th Edition
Harold F. Tipton and Micki Krause
ISBN: 0-8493-1997-8

Information Security Policies, Procedures, and Standards: Guidelines for Effective Information Security Management
Thomas R. Peltier
ISBN: 0-8493-1137-3

Information Security Risk Analysis
Thomas R. Peltier
ISBN: 0-8493-0880-1

Information Technology Control and Audit
Fredrick Gallegos, Daniel Manson, and Sandra Allen-Senft
ISBN: 0-8493-9994-7

Investigator's Guide to Steganography
Gregory Kipper
0-8493-2433-5

Managing a Network Vulnerability Assessment
Thomas Peltier, Justin Peltier, and John A. Blackley
ISBN: 0-8493-1270-1

Network Perimeter Security: Building Defense In-Depth
Cliff Riggs
ISBN: 0-8493-1628-6

The Practical Guide to HIPAA Privacy and Security Compliance
Kevin Beaver and Rebecca Herold
ISBN: 0-8493-1953-6

A Practical Guide to Security Engineering and Information Assurance
Debra S. Herrmann
ISBN: 0-8493-1163-2

The Privacy Papers: Managing Technology, Consumer, Employee and Legislative Actions
Rebecca Herold
ISBN: 0-8493-1248-5

Public Key Infrastructure: Building Trusted Applications and Web Services
John R. Vacca
ISBN: 0-8493-0822-4

Securing and Controlling Cisco Routers
Peter T. Davis
ISBN: 0-8493-1290-6

Strategic Information Security
John Wylder
ISBN: 0-8493-2041-0

Surviving Security: How to Integrate People, Process, and Technology, Second Edition
Amanda Andress
ISBN: 0-8493-2042-9

A Technical Guide to IPSec Virtual Private Networks
James S. Tiller
ISBN: 0-8493-0876-3

Using the Common Criteria for IT Security Evaluation
Debra S. Herrmann
ISBN: 0-8493-1404-6

AUERBACH PUBLICATIONS
www.auerbach-publications.com
To Order Call: 1-800-272-7737 • Fax: 1-800-374-3401
E-mail: orders@crcpress.com

A Practical Guide to
Security
Assessments

Sudhanshu Kairab

AUERBACH PUBLICATIONS

A CRC Press Company
Boca Raton   London   New York   Washington, D.C.

Library of Congress Cataloging-in-Publication Data

Kairab, Sudhanshu.
    A practical guide to security assessments / Sudhanshu Kairab
        p.   cm.
    Includes bibliographical references and index.
    ISBN 0-8493-1706-1 (alk. paper)
    1. Business—Data processing—Security measures—Evaluation. 2. Information
technology—Security measures—Evaluation. 3. Computer networks—Security
measures—Evaluation. 4. Data protection. 5. Computer security. 6. Electronic data
processing departments—Safety measures—Planning. I. Title.

HF5548.32.K345 2004
658.4′78—dc22   2004052842

Visit the CRC Press Web site at www.crcpress.com

© 2005 by CRC Press LLC
Auerbach is an imprint of CRC Press LLC

No claim to original U.S. Government works
International Standard Book Number 0-8493-1706-1
Library of Congress Card Number 2004052842
Printed in the United States of America   1 2 3 4 5 6 7 8 9 0
Printed on acid-free paper

About the Author

Sudhanshu Kairab has over ten years of experience in audit and security. He started in public accounting at a Big Four firm, where he conducted financial audits in a range of industries including financial services, utilities, and healthcare. He has also worked as an internal auditor for a major pharmaceutical company. At this company he was also involved in an ERP rollout, where he focused on security and internal controls. Over the past six years, he has focused on information security and audit. Specifically, he has been involved in conducting security assessment and providing other security consulting services.

Mr. Kairab earned his bachelor's degree from Bucknell University, Lewisburg, Pennsylvania and an MBA and Masters in Accounting from Northeastern University, Boston, Massachusetts. He has obtained the CISA (Certified Information Systems Auditor) and CISSP (Certified Information Systems Security Professional) certifications. He is also a member of the Information Systems Audit & Control Association and the Information Systems Security Association, where he is a member of the Professional Ethics Committee.

Preface

Writing this book has been a wonderful experience for me and was not something I ever anticipated. After writing a chapter on security assessment methodology for the *Information Security Management Handbook* a few years ago, I was asked if I would be interested in writing a comprehensive book on the same topic. The task presented a very exciting opportunity and, as I finished the book, the experience has been both challenging and rewarding.

As the information security field becomes more prominent, with more companies paying increased attention, it is important to be able to properly address security concerns and develop cost-effective security solutions. A security assessment is a key component of any information security program and is something that helps companies proactively address security, prioritize security initiatives, and develop solutions commensurate with risk. This book emphasizes that information security is not a technology but, instead, a process that should be incorporated into a company's operations. In fact, this book is technology-neutral and is more focused on security processes and the methodology for conducting security assessments.

For many companies, a comprehensive security assessment is the first step in building an information security program. The assessment provides a roadmap to a more secure company. Using a structured methodology, which appropriately considers both the business and supporting technology together and incorporates effective methods for gathering and analyzing information, is important for conducting quality security assessments.

For people newly entering the information security field, this book will hopefully provide a structured methodology and other useful content to help in conducting security assessments. The expectation is that this book establishes some structure around security assessment methodology that will help you conduct assessments using a standard yet flexible approach. The questionnaires in the Appendix can be customized and used in conjunction with security assessments.

This book was possible because I was fortunate to work with good people throughout my career. I have learned an invaluable amount from colleagues, particularly over the last few years, as I delved deeper into information security.

I would like to thank my friends and family for their support and words of encouragement, all of which made this process much easier. I would also like to thank the people at Auerbach Publications, including the editors and those involved in producing the final product. And my thanks go to Rich O'Hanley for providing this opportunity and being supportive and flexible as I tried to balance work and family demands while writing this book.

For readers of this book, I hope you find the content useful as you conduct security assessments. I would appreciate any feedback about where improvements can be made and how this methodology works for you, whether you use it or have incorporated elements into your existing methodology. You can reach me at skairab@ureach.com.

Table of Contents

1 Introduction

Over the past few years, information security has evolved from a technology issue to a boardroom issue. Companies are affected every day by security-related incidents such as network intrusions, viruses, or denial-of-service attacks. Some of these incidents are reported but many probably are not. Business is becoming increasingly dependent on technology and the Internet to the point where some businesses would come to a screeching halt if they did not have it. This is particularly true in larger companies, where the ability to communicate and access information is the lifeblood of the business.

For example, if you ask a manager in a multinational Fortune 500 company how long the company could remain productive without having e-mail service or being able to access critical data, you will likely be told that it is not very long. If you ask that same manager what the impact would be if unauthorized persons gained access to the company's critical data or electronic mail, you will get an answer ranging from "not good" to "significant embarrassment to the company or legal troubles." What would happen if critical data was changed without anyone's knowledge? If this happened, the company might be working with erroneous data that could affect operations. Even this fairly simplistic example illustrates why it is critical to secure information to ensure its confidentiality, integrity, and availability.

The need to secure information is becoming greater all the time as we leverage technology to automate functions, as more data becomes electronic, and as companies become increasingly reliant on the Internet as an integral part of their information technology (IT) infrastructure. Businesses are becoming increasingly connected because business-to-business relationships are helping companies drive efficiencies and shorten the supply chain. E-commerce is gaining acceptance as more people buy goods and services online, resulting in an increasing number of companies having a presence on the Web. With these relationships, a host of security issues must be addressed.

Today, solutions that address specific security risks are available. For example, companies have a firewall or a network-based intrusion detection system in place to address perimeter security. The architecture of the intrusion detection system may have been designed to protect a certain network segment and some critical machines. For many companies, intrusion detection and firewalls are solutions that have been implemented without thinking about them from a business perspective. Take the case of a company where intrusion detection is in place, but no one is looking at alerts or updating the system to reflect the latest attack signatures, and the company did not involve people from the business to identify what data warranted protection, so no assurance exists that the intrusion detection system is even protecting critical data. In this case, the intrusion detection system is doing very little to secure critical assets or the perimeter of the network. If the business issues were examined, the same company might have designed the solution differently and considered an outsourcing option or having additional resources. This example is an illustration of security solutions being implemented without considering the business — i.e., security is not always considered a business issue. For many companies, information security is an IT issue and something to which people on the operations side of the house do not really pay attention. This is the case even though operations personnel "own" critical data and are the ones who are dependent on IT systems. Our dependence on the security and availability of information and systems necessitates a more holistic view of information security — one in which personnel from both operations and IT are actively engaged to find the best use of resources to secure critical data and ensure that mission-critical business processes are secure. We must look at risks and develop cost-effective security solutions that are commensurate with risk. As the information security discipline evolves, it must be considered in light of the business and the associated risks. As we implement security solutions, we need to take a step back and ask questions such as:

- Does the security solution address what are we trying to protect?
- What is the value to the business of what we are protecting?
- Does the security solution mitigate identified security risks?

With budgets as tight as they are today, security spending must deliver good ROI (Return on Investment) and adequately protect the information assets of the company. Spending on security, like spending on other areas of the business, must be justified.

To look at information security in terms of delivering good ROI and protecting against identified risks, a risk-based approach to information security is required, which is a slight change for many companies. The first steps in taking such an approach are to understand what the risks are and developing solutions to address those risks — i.e., conducting a security assessment. The purpose of this book is to present a methodology for conducting a security assessment. The central aspect of the methodology is the importance of understanding the business and using that as the basis for determining the security risks. The methodology is vendor and technology neutral. It is process focused and can be used in any environment.

Security assessment methodology is a topic that deserves attention because it is arguably the most important element of a successful information security program. Without a quality security assessment, no assurance exists that the true security risks a company is facing have been identified. As a result, any information security program that is implemented will provide little assurance that the company is secure. In addition, any money invested in an information security program without having a good understanding of the business and the security risks it is facing is a potential misuse of resources.

Figure 1.1 illustrates the relationship between the security assessment process and the overall information security program. As shown, the security assessment process drives the rest of the information security program. The security assessment is basically an analysis of the organization's security risks. The results of the assessment drive the other components of the information security program — i.e., policies,

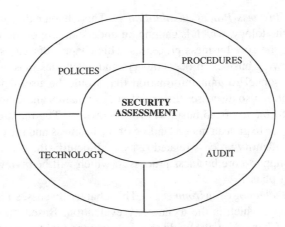

FIGURE 1.1 Components of an information security program.

procedures, technology, and audit. Because these components are all based on the security assessment, it is critical that the results of the security assessment accurately represent the security risks that an organization is facing. The methodology presented in this book will provide information security practitioners a structured methodology for conducting a security assessment as well as some questionnaires (in the appendices) to help facilitate the security assessment process.

This book goes through each step of the methodology and is divided into two sections, including the methodology and the questionnaires, to help facilitate security assessments. Below is a brief chapter-by-chapter summary:

Chapter 1. Introduction

Chapter 2. Evolution of Information Security — This chapter provides some background on information security and historical perspective before discussing security assessment methodology. The chapter discusses some trends and events that have made information security a significant issue.

Chapter 3. The Information Security Program and How a Security Assessment Fits In — This chapter focuses on the critical elements of an information security program and the role of a security assessment in that program.

Chapter 4. Planning a Security Assessment — This chapter discusses Phase 1 of the methodology, which comprises all aspects of the planning phase including developing the scope of an assessment, obtaining support from stakeholders, and setting expectations of the client whose environment will be subject to the assessment.

Chapter 5. Initial Information Gathering — This chapter discusses Phase 2 of the methodology, which includes different ways to research an organization before the fieldwork phase of an assessment occurs. This chapter references some free and publicly available sources of information that can be used to gain familiarity with the company. In this phase, you will also discuss the preparation of question sets to be used when you meet the client, which occurs during the next phase.

Chapter 6. Business Process Evaluation — This chapter discusses Phase 3 of the methodology, which is gaining an understanding of the business and evaluating the core business processes. This chapter discusses the process of interviewing business process owners and what questions you should be asking personnel to gain information that would be useful in a security assessment. It also discusses the use of questionnaires and other techniques to gain information from business process owners. The main objectives of this phase are to gain an understanding of the business and the core business processes, identify process-related risks, and identify the critical technologies that support core business processes, which will be reviewed in detail in the next phase.

Chapter 7. Technology Environment — This chapter discusses Phase 4 of the methodology, which is the technology evaluation. Based on the material covered in Chapter 6, you should now have a good feel for what technology is critical to the business. This chapter walks the reader through the process of assessing the technology that is critical to the business along with some of the associated techniques. Similar to the last chapter, this chapter discusses the use of questionnaires and other techniques to gain information from technology owners.

Chapter 8. Risk Assessment and Final Presentation — This chapter discusses the final phase of the methodology, which is to perform the formal risk analysis, develop recommendations, and present the final report. The chapter discusses a process for performing the risk analysis by calculating a risk score. This calculation takes into account a number of factors related to risk, including potential impact to the business, the probability of a security breach, and the existing controls to mitigate the risks. This chapter also discusses the importance of the final report, as it is the only tangible work product resulting from the assessment.

Chapter 9. Information Security Standards — At this point, the discussion of the methodology is complete. This chapter discusses some key standards that are relevant for information security. Some of the standards discussed include International Standards Organization (ISO) 17799 and COBIT.

Chapter 10. Information Security Legislation — This chapter contains short descriptions of key recent legislation that has a bearing on information security. It is important to be well informed about these laws, as they might affect the company where you are conducting a security assessment.

Appendices. Security Questionnaires — The Appendices contain questionnaires to help information security practitioners in conducting security assessments. Questionnaires for key areas of information security are included, as well as generic questionnaires designed to help you gather information in the early stages of a security assessment. These questionnaires are structured to provide "guidance" so that practitioners understand the relevance of a given question. They can be modified to meet the needs of the specific company where a security assessment is being performed.

2 Evolution of Information Security

INTRODUCTION

In many companies, information security has traditionally been part of the information technology (IT) function. In the days of the mainframe, system administrators were responsible for ensuring that it was secure. Security was centrally controlled and typically, only a few people did anything related to security. This worked because of the tight control on security.

In today's environment, with highly distributed systems, things have significantly changed from a security perspective. We are much more dependent on technology — from standard business applications such as Microsoft Office to complicated communications infrastructures leveraging the Internet. Applications are developed for many purposes, and IT infrastructures can be scaled to meet the needs of thousands of employees. Changes to technology have been rapid, and it seems that this will continue.

These changes and the growing dependency on technology have had a major impact on information security and are a major reason for making it a central issue today. Some of these changes have been quite significant and have resulted in information security becoming a major concern. Major changes that will be discussed in subsequent sections include:

- Distributed systems and the Internet
- Business-to-business (B2B) relationships
- Remote access
- Enterprise Resource Planning (ERP) applications

DISTRIBUTED SYSTEMS AND THE INTERNET

The information technology infrastructures of companies are becoming more distributed and the control of these systems more decentralized. This decentralized control has allowed companies to leverage the technology infrastructure to meet their specific business requirements related to communication, collaboration, and other functions.

This is a far cry from the days of the mainframe, when information and control were much more centralized. Unlike today's distributed environments where computing is decentralized, all computing activity took place on the mainframe. Dumb terminals were the mechanism by which people gained access to these systems. The mainframe was critical because all valuable information was stored there. The mainframe was also designed with security in mind. If it was secured properly, a good administrator could adequately secure it as long as that person was trained properly. Mainframes are still very secure today, and perhaps that is one of the reasons why they are still in use.

In today's distributed environment, critical information is all over the place, and several entry points into local and wide area networks exist. Bring in the Internet, which connects all of these networks together, and you can see how open and complicated the situation becomes.

Today, technology is much more complicated than before and its distributed nature has made it decentralized; both of these factors make information security a significant challenge. It is difficult enough to keep up with the latest advancements in technology, not to mention how to secure it. Information security practitioners have to gain expertise and work with other IT professionals to really understand security risks and the best way to address them with minimal effect on end users.

BUSINESS-TO-BUSINESS (B2B) RELATIONSHIPS

Company systems used to be contained within the boundaries of single companies. Interaction between companies was verbal, and information exchanges were not performed electronically except for electronic data interchange (EDI) transactions. Although these business processes might have been slow and inefficient by today's standards, security concerns related to companies interacting with one another were minimal.

Today, B2B relationships are becoming common and can take many forms. It could be companies buying and selling with each other online, as is the case with an "extranet," where many companies can engage in buying and selling. Companies are also using B2B to gain significant business process efficiencies by shortening the supply chain. For example, some manufacturing operations have their vendors not only supply raw materials but also manage the raw material supply by accessing their relevant systems. The efficiencies come as a result of quicker access to information and the elimination of processes that do not add value. Along with these positive aspects of B2B, a number of security concerns have arisen, particularly with respect to confidentiality, integrity, and availability of information. Company systems are not contained in defined boundaries because people and companies from the outside are accessing the company's systems. A lack of proper access control can result in unauthorized access to some potentially critical and competitive information. Companies are now starting to notice these security issues and as a result, newer B2B relationships are slowly being formed with security in mind.

REMOTE ACCESS

Remote access — the whole concept of accessing IT resources from other locations — and the resulting increase in remote workers is another example of the significant changes we have seen over the past few years. At one time, very few people accessed systems remotely and many who did could not access networks at a speed that allowed them to work effectively. Although much of remote access is done today using phone lines, increasing numbers of people are using high-speed access, making telecommuting and working from remote sites such as hotels and other remote locations more feasible than before. Many companies today advocate telecommuting because of the savings realized by not having to pay for office space. This has made virtual private networks and other remote access solutions very popular.

Although this is very positive, high-speed remote access has introduced new security concerns not present before. With high speed, concerns exist about the security of information transmitted across the Internet and how remote access could potentially allow unauthorized access. These security considerations must be taken into account in an information security program.

ENTERPRISE RESOURCE PLANNING (ERP)

On the application side, ERP has become very prevalent, starting with larger companies and slowly filtering to smaller ones. At a high level, ERP has replaced disparate business systems and consolidated many of the typical functions such as finance, accounting, and production. All of these functions work off centralized information, so fewer disparate systems are talking to each other. ERP has enabled significant efficiencies in these functions and helped reduce the supply chain time for companies. Thanks to ERP, more time is now spent analyzing information instead of gathering it, reconciling it, and creating reports.

When a single system that has all the financial and operational data for a company is used, user access must be carefully assigned. Some of the potential user access issues include segregation of duties, causing a lack of checks and balances, and users being able to see too much information. The information that can be accessed via these applications is very valuable, and companies must ensure that people have access to only the information they need and those transactions required to do their jobs. For example, depending on how it has been implemented, an ERP system may have a company's fully consolidated financial data. This information is very sensitive in the case of a publicly traded company, where the information is released to the financial community as well as regulatory bodies such as the Securities and Exchange Commission (SEC). Companies are obligated to control access to this information to ensure that relevant financial data is released to the public properly. If the wrong people gain access to financial information before official release and use it to their advantage, there could be legal issues related to insider trading. According to the U.S. Securities Act of 1933, "Insider trading is illegal when a person trades a security while in possession of material nonpublic information in violation of a duty to withhold the information or refrain from trading."[1] In pre-ERP days, consolidated financial information presented to the financial community might have been developed manually or using a separate system from data from a variety of systems making it easier to control who has access to it. With ERP, much of this information is generated by a single system, where the necessary information already resides. Although this has made processing information more efficient, access control and proper segregation of duties have become more of a focus for companies.

drug for them. This information is competitive in nature and very critical to their business. Drug companies must employ appropriate security measures to protect this information.

However, companies have always had critical information, and securing this information has always been a concern. Several factors have made securing data a more significant issue today. Some of the factors driving this include:

- The Internet and the availability and accessibility of information
- The shift from information on paper to information in electronic format
- The integration of systems
- New legislation and the legal environment
- Cyber-related threats

THE INTERNET AND THE AVAILABILITY AND ACCESSIBILITY OF INFORMATION

Technology and the Internet have made information more accessible and available than ever before. Through the use of electronic mail, the Internet, and other electronic means, information is widely accessible. Sensitive and confidential information is exchanged by electronic mail, which has become a standard and acceptable form of communication. Much of the information sent over e-mail is confidential in nature. Anyone using electronic mail on a regular basis knows how easy it is to share information this way — e.g., with a simple "Forward" command, information can be disseminated to countless people with the press of a button. Some also know how inherently insecure electronic mail is and how the confidentiality of e-mail can be breached. Someone who is technically savvy can intercept mail or employ social engineering techniques to gain unauthorized access to a person's mail account.

Besides electronic mail, the accessibility and availability of information have been promoted in other ways, including company Web sites, Internet bulletin boards, and message boards. Information about companies is out on the Internet and there for the taking. By doing some simple searches and researching a company using freely available tools on the Internet, one can find out quite a bit of information about a company and its systems. This type of company-related information combined with software tools has made hacking a front-page issue. Hacking has evolved considerably and is now a risk for any company with a presence on the Internet or connected electronically in some way. Insiders can also use this information along with what they already know about a company to hack into a company's systems. Although companies can benefit significantly from having information about their business on the Internet, minimizing any sensitive information that can eventually be used for malicious activities is a challenge.

Access and availability of information have made sharing information very easy and efficient. As a result, considerable security implications exist including access control, protecting information in transit, Internet-related security, etc. Determining whether controls to secure these processes exist is one aspect of a security assessment. How to determine and quantify these risks will be discussed in greater detail later in this book.

Shift from Paper-Based to Electronic-Based Information

In the past, many business functions were paper based; for example, mail was in the form of memos written on paper, and many financial records were on paper. On paper, information was tangible, and people who were responsible for safeguarding it could secure it physically and not worry about it. Sensitive information was locked up in file cabinets, which remained secure because few people had the keys to them. Critical information could be physically secured in such a way that only those who needed it could access it. The question of electronic access was not as prevalent. Today, a significant amount of information exists in electronic format. Everything from documents to mail to pictures is in electronic format, including some things that people do not normally think of as having security implications, such as employee photos used in creating IDs or other sensitive employee information. The distributed environment and the Internet coupled with sensitive documents, pictures, etc. in electronic format have made sharing and communicating this information very easy, to the point where it is now in the mainstream.

With this ability to share and communicate information electronically, people and companies have less control over its distribution. Companies must take measures to protect the confidentiality of information through sophisticated access control measures, which are more complicated than the measures to physically protect information. Controlling access to information, with today's companies, can be internal (e.g., employees) and external (e.g., business partners). Besides access control, security measures are required to ensure the integrity and availability of electronic information. The security measures required are a moving target as both business and technology are changing at a rapid pace.

Companies have generated significant efficiencies in their business processes by having information in electronic format, and at the same time, have introduced new security concerns into the equation.

Integration of Systems

Another key difference today is the integration of systems. Today's systems are very integrated internally (e.g., local and wide area networks, company intranets) and externally (e.g., business-to-business). To keep up with business today, systems must be able to talk to each other and process information quickly. With today's business requirements and stiff competition, companies want the most up-to-date information at their fingertips so that they can make the best decisions possible. Having systems talk to each other and centralizing information provides executives with this type of information.

Integration has happened at the network and application levels. Networks are linked all around the world through wide area networks and the Internet. The Internet is leveraged to connect a company's network to other companies' networks. For example, virtual private networks (VPNs) are commonly used to create secure tunnels of traffic between two parties. On the application side, there is ERP, which includes packages such as SAP and Peoplesoft, which have significantly changed how companies do business. ERP systems by nature are integrated, and if used to full functionality, systems such as accounting systems and their components (e.g., accounts receivable, accounts payable) are tightly integrated with manufacturing-related systems and all are integrated with financials. These integration aspects have provided considerable benefits that have resulted in better information and operating efficiencies in areas such as finance and the overall supply chain.

Integration of networks and applications has given companies the ability to share information across wide area networks and the Internet, enabling cost-effective communication between employees in multiple locations around the world. Also, the integration of business systems (e.g., financial, accounting, production) and currently, e-business integration, have made information processing much more efficient. Based on a report from Nucleus Research reported in *Computerworld* magazine "...e-business integration software such as Microsoft Corp.'s BizTalk Server and BEA Systems Inc.'s WebLogic Integration have helped companies leverage existing investments in their IT infrastructures through both internal links and business-to-business connections. Many of the returns from such projects result from a streamlining of data flows between applications and access to a broader set of information for end users."[3]

Although system integration has yielded benefits, some security concerns have arisen as a result of it, which are discussed below:

- *Confidentiality of data* — With much information in electronic format and the ease with which information can be distributed, management has little control over the distribution of information if proper access controls are not in place. Information such as consolidated financial data or pricing information is very sensitive, and access to it should be controlled through a process where individuals are given access to only what they need to do their jobs. Giving the appropriate level of access can be time consuming and requires a documented process both for giving access to employees and taking away access from terminated employees or employees who have changed jobs. Enforcing strict access rules is critical in these cases, considering the sensitivity of the information being processed.
- *Integrity of data* — As systems are integrated, a risk exists that information may be unintentionally changed. The reliability of data from systems is based on the integrity of the data. Proper validation steps to ensure the integrity of data should be in place. Some of these steps may include manual or automated verification of data at different stages of processing.
- *Availability of data* — Information is needed in real time for mission-critical applications. Systems need to be available so that critical functions such as e-mail and business applications can run properly. Some specific systems, such as e-commerce systems and those systems that provide services to the general public, have significant high availability requirements. If these mission-critical systems are down, loss of productivity and potential financial impact in the form of lost revenue may follow.

LEGISLATION

Another aspect that is different today is legislation that has information security implications. Although some legislation, such as the Computer Security Act of 1987, existed in the past, no specific pieces of legislation forced companies to implement security measures to protect the privacy and confidentiality of information.

Two well-known laws that require information security are the Health Insurance Portability and Accountability Act (HIPAA) and the Gramm–Leach–Bliley Act (GLBA). HIPAA and the GLBA (both discussed in greater detail later in this book) are applicable to health care–related entities and financial services companies, respectively. Each of these laws has an information security component, which mandates companies to have certain information security measures in place to protect sensitive personally identifiable information. In both industries, there is a public interest in maintaining the privacy of people's personal information. Review of the information security requirements in both laws indicates that they are essentially requiring companies to implement sound information security programs. This legislation recognizes that only a comprehensive information security program consisting of people, processes, and technology can effectively secure the information assets of a company and specifically, consumers' personally identifiable information. One of the key parts of the legislation is the requirement to perform a risk analysis or a security assessment to determine the security risks, so that appropriate measures can be put in place.

In addition to these regulations, the Federal Trade Commission (FTC) is becoming influential in enforcing good information security practices. One of the functions of the FTC is to "enhance the smooth operation of the marketplace by eliminating acts or practices that are unfair or deceptive."[4] The FTC is taking a very active role in ensuring that companies live up to any claims they make regarding how they secure consumer information.

> **Example.** In the summer of 2003, the FTC launched an investigation against a pet supplier, PETCO, because of a security incident that left approximately 500,000 credit card numbers exposed and accessible from the Internet. The basis for the investigation was PETCO'S privacy claim, which stated, "At PETCO.com our customers' data is strictly protected against any unauthorized access." In the case of PETCO, an independent programmer had discovered that a database with sensitive information had a structure query language (SQL) Injection vulnerability.

The FTC has been a leading force in trying to enforce companies' claims regarding how they safeguard information. They consider information security an element of fair information practices, which are defined as companies taking "steps to protect the security of the information they collect from consumers." Based on this, the FTC has quite a bit of latitude in being able to enforce good information security practices.

To help achieve compliance, consulting firms and law firms have created offerings around helping organizations achieve compliance with these laws. The laws have led to the development of assessment software and variants of existing security architecture components such as firewalls and intrusion detection systems, which claim that their products help achieve compliance with these regulations.

The laws have helped develop awareness of information security issues. HIPAA, for example, receives a decent amount of exposure in the media. As consumers see that the government is stepping in to force health care companies to properly secure electronic patient information, consumers are beginning to understand that there are potential security issues related to the privacy and security of their personal information, resulting in greater awareness. This legislation, to some extent, has led consumers to understand the implications of their personal health information being compromised.

In most cases, these regulations essentially call for good, solid information security programs. They call for the key elements of information security programs such as risk assessments, security policies and procedures, and enforcement. Each has its particular nuances, but in the end, it is about protecting data, critical systems, etc.

CYBER-RELATED THREATS

The final major difference today is the cyber-related threat. Before the Internet and networking became pervasive, the main threats were of a physical nature. Although physical threats have not disappeared, cyber-related threats are very prevalent today. New attacks are constantly developed and are becoming more sophisticated every day. The Internet has enabled "script kiddies" to download tools and scripts to launch attacks. Hacker tools are readily available on the Internet. Companies must be vigilant to guard against threats that can cause harm, ranging from attacks such as a denial-of-service attack, where systems are unavailable, or individuals breaking into systems and stealing credit card information. These are but two examples that can have significant effects on a company's well being. The results of these types of attacks can directly impact revenue and the bottom line. For example, some companies that are heavily dependent on their e-commerce activities, such as Amazon, which generates significant revenues from online activities, could sustain permanent damage if people's credit card information was compromised or if the site was unavailable for an extended period of time. A recent case of cyber crime involved PayPal, a company that handles online payments for e-commerce sites.

> **Example.** Unsuspecting users were sent an e-mail asking them to go to another Web site to confirm that they are authorized PayPal users. The e-mail sent to PayPal users said, "To confirm that you are an authorized PayPal member, authorization is needed. The New SSL 4.0 Secure Socket Layer has been updated to the PayPal servers. To be authorized, please visit https://www.paypalauthorization.com/. After completion, you will receive [sic] and [sic] e-mail confirmation within 24 hours of reciept [sic]. Thanks for using PayPal!, PayPal Security Team."[18] Once users went to the fake Web site, they entered personal information about themselves including credit card information. Some users were victimized as their credit card–issuing banks called soon after the scam to say that suspicious activity in their accounts had occurred.

For many consumers, security is one of the most significant concerns when purchasing online. To some extent, it is holding back the growth of business-to-consumer activity. In a survey conducted by the Center for Communications Policy at the University of California, Los Angeles (UCLA) and published in the UCLA Internet Report, "92.4 percent were either somewhat or very or extremely concerned about the security of their credit card information when purchasing online in 2002."[5] Some consumers will not purchase online for that reason. Others may stop buying from an e-commerce site completely if a security incident has occurred.

In the case of a denial-of-service attack, if a consumer goes to a Web site and has a bad "user experience," that consumer may think twice about going to that site in the future. These are only a few of the specific risks that fall into the "cyber-related" risks category.

At a higher level, key concerns related to cyber threats include:

- *Damage to reputation* — e.g., security incidents receiving significant press
- *Loss of revenue* — e.g., inability to sell a product or service because the consumer goes to a competitor
- *Permanent loss of customers* — e.g., consumers so displeased that they do not buy from the company again
- *Regulatory concerns* — e.g., if the security breach affected compliance with certain laws such as HIPAA or GLBA
- *Legal liabilities*—e.g., if the security breach causes someone harm and they decide to sue the company

All of the items listed above can be devastating for a business and, if significant enough, can destroy a business. Although loss of revenue is the only item on this list that can be easily quantified into a dollar amount, the other items represent much more lasting and long-term effects on the business.

GROWING ROLE OF INTERNAL AUDIT

Another aspect in the evolution of information security is linked to the internal audit function. The internal audit function plays a key role in larger companies and is now receiving a significant amount of press in the wake of the Enron scandal. At a high level, internal auditors look at certain processes within a company and ensure that proper internal controls are implemented. By the nature of their jobs, internal auditors learn about a company and its processes. They learn the best and worst ways to do something. Some companies have their auditors act like watchdogs, looking for internal control weaknesses, providing recommendations, and following up to make sure they have been implemented. In other companies, auditors are viewed as business partners who find internal control weaknesses, suggest process improvements, and also actively transfer knowledge about best practices around the company — i.e., effectively serving as internal business consultants.

The internal audit process is very much like the security assessment process, which is part of the bigger picture of information security. However, internal audit departments have mostly focused on operational and financial processes, and there has not been widespread focus on technology and its related processes — i.e., IT audit. As IT audit becomes more prevalent, information security will continue to have importance through company internal audit departments.

Although security assessments are not exactly the same as internal audit, many similarities exist — with the main similarity being evaluating systems from an internal control/security perspective. Each of these processes examines how systems function within an organization and whether or not the organization is secure. This includes reviewing the critical data transacted by the various systems and its dependencies from both the process and technology perspectives.

The differences between security assessments and IT audits are really quite subtle. Essentially, the focus of an IT audit is broader. In a security assessment, the process is very focused around the security aspects of information, such as storage, transmission, and access. In an IT audit, the focus also includes ensuring that systems function as intended from a business perspective. This clearly goes beyond the realm of information security.

Today, traditional operational auditors must be more knowledgeable about technology and system-related controls, as most mission-critical business processes are dependent on technology. As a result, IT auditors are an integral part of the process of securing information assets. Similar to what internal auditors have been doing for years — providing an independent opinion of the quality of internal controls around business processes — IT auditors now provide that same independent view of technology and associated controls. The overlap between IT audit and security assessments can be seen with internal controls related to technology — access control, configurations of systems, etc., which are critical to the confidentiality, integrity, and availability of information.

Besides the increased use of technology, laws are also raising the stature of IT auditors. "While heightened concerns over security and terrorism accounts for some of IT auditor's new sheen, there's also another reason: the freshly minted law known as the Sarbanes–Oxley Act puts more pressure on upper management to vouch for 'internal controls,' with specific sections related to information auditing."[6]

The other key aspects of internal auditors are their independence and their reporting structure. From an organizational perspective, internal audit is separate and has limited ties to any operational unit of a company. Internal auditors have access to senior management and often report directly to the board of directors. From a security perspective, as security assessments are incorporated into audits, internal audit departments can provide independent judgment and help drive security initiatives.

From an evolutionary perspective, internal audit continues to give legitimacy to the information security discipline as it becomes integrated into the function of internal audit. The dependence on technology and laws such as the Sarbanes–Oxley Act, HIPAA, and GLBA are expediting this process.

SECURITY STANDARDS

One of the driving forces behind information security has been the proliferation of different information security standards (key standards will be discussed in detail in Chapter 9). Similar to other competencies, companies are looking for guidance as it relates to information security both at an operational level and from an assessment perspective. For example, from an assessment perspective, the accounting profession has guidelines for auditing financial statements, the Generally Accepted Auditing Standards (GAAS). These standards provide guidance that should be taken when auditing certain areas of the financial statements. At an operational level, certain standards for internal controls are considered best practices that companies follow.

As information security has become more important, companies are looking for standards they can use in implementing information security measures. Information security experts, companies, and government agencies have come together to share information and develop standards for information security. Different organizations have cropped up recently to develop best practices for the information security discipline. Although some information security standards have been around for some time, most have not received much attention until recently. Companies are using three types of standards:

- Best practice standards
- Technical standards
- Marketplace standards administered by third parties

BEST PRACTICE STANDARDS

"Best practice" standards or information security guidelines are used by companies to develop and monitor their information security programs. Two of these standards are Generally Accepted System Security Principles (GASSP) and the International Standards Organization (ISO) 17799 standard, which was based on the BS 7799 (British Standards 7799) standard. These standards are vendor neutral and do not focus on specific technologies. Both of these standards are focused on policy and the different elements of an information security program that companies should have in place. Although technology is mentioned in broad generic terms, the standard is focused on the process of information security.

The ISO 17799 standard, which is widely recognized as an information security best practice standard, was developed by a consortium of companies and is based on companies' best practices and input from industry experts. This consortium represented a cross section of companies to bring out best practices that can be applicable to a wide range of companies. These standards are meant to help companies create an information security program addressing a wide range of topics that fall under the umbrella of information security. The ISO 17799 standards provide high-level guidance on information security topics including:

- Security policy
- Organizational security
- Asset classification and control
- Personnel security
- Physical and environmental security
- Communications and operations management
- Access control
- Systems development and maintenance
- Business continuity management
- Compliance

The ISO 17799 standard provides guidance in each of the above areas. The standard can guide the development of security policies and can serve as the foundation of an information security program. One thing to note is that the guidance provided by the ISO 17799 pertains to "what" should be in an information security program. This standard does not provide much guidance on process or how a specific security requirement can be achieved. The ISO 17799 is one of several standards (some of which will be discussed in detail later in this book) in use by companies.

One of the earliest sets of standards was the GASSP. GASSP was developed as a result of a recommendation from the U.S. National Research Council's 1990 report *Computers at Risk*. The first recommendation in this report was "To promulgate comprehensive generally accepted system security principles" using input from information security practitioners in the private and public sectors from the United States and abroad.

These technology-neutral best practice standards serve a very important purpose when the overall information security program in a company is developed. They help set the foundation of the program, which is then used to develop the rest of the program including technology, processes, people with the appropriate skill sets, etc. From a security assessment perspective, these standards can be used as a basis for evaluating a company's security posture. In a security assessment, one of the first things to look for is a solid foundation — i.e., a security strategy including policies and procedures and ongoing assessments to ensure that the information security program is up to date.

TECHNICAL STANDARDS

Technical standards are published by information security practitioners and vendors. For example, many information security professionals utilize the Microsoft Technet Web site (www.technet.com) to access best practice security standards for Microsoft products. Many of the major vendors, such as Cisco and Microsoft, have a wealth of information that can be used to help lock down the respective technologies. These standards can come in the form of case studies or as checklists that can be used with some minor customization to reflect a specific company's business requirements. The checklists tend to be very technical in nature, actually recommending specific system settings. An example is the Windows 2000 Server Baseline Security Checklist[7], which is published on the Microsoft Technet Web site. This checklist contains a comprehensive list of security measures that system administrators should take to adequately lock down a Windows 2000 server. Some of the items in this checklist include:

- Disabling unnecessary services
- Disabling and deleting unnecessary accounts
- Disabling the guest account

Not all of the items on the checklist have to be complied with because the checklist is only meant to provide guidance. It is probable that some of the items on these checklists cannot be complied with because of certain business requirements a given company might have. These checklists are designed to help you consider all of the alternatives in locking down a company's systems. When used, they should be modified based on the specific client. Because of the rapid pace of change with technology, these guides should be checked frequently, as they are constantly updated.

In addition to material supplied by vendors, significant material is available in the public domain relating to best practice technology standards contributed by security practitioners. Some of the technical standards used by companies today include the National Institute of Standards and Technology (NIST) Standards, Center for Internet Security benchmarks, and the SysAdmin, Audit, Network Security (SANS) Top 20 list. These can be helpful documents, as they often reflect real world scenarios. People who are out in the field actually trying the recommendations on these checklists typically prepare these documents. The sources of these documents should be considered, and you should make sure that you trust the document before using it. All checklists should be modified as required to reflect the client's business requirements before using them.

MARKETPLACE STANDARDS

The third type of standards is marketplace standards. These standards are independent standards that signify a certain level of security. They are like certifications in that companies must meet certain criteria to be certified. This has become somewhat prevalent in the business-to-consumer space, where consumers want to see that companies who conduct business online have met certain standards related to privacy and security. In the business-to-consumer space, these standards go a long way in providing credibility related to security and privacy for companies with an online presence. Based on a Harris Interactive survey dated February 19, 2002, "…most consumers still do not trust companies to handle their personal information properly. However, independent verification of company privacy policies is the single business action that would satisfy almost two out of three consumers (62 percent). In fact, 84 percent think such verification should be 'a requirement' for companies today."[8] Consumers are clearly demanding some minimum standards related to security. Three examples of these standards are:

- Better Business Bureau (BBB) Online Privacy Seal
- American Institute of Certified Public Accountants (AICPA)/Canadian Institute of Chartered Accountants (CICA) WebTrust Program

Each of these programs is discussed in greater detail below.

Better Business Bureau (BBB) Online Privacy Seal

The BBB has several programs that companies may apply for, one of which is the Online Privacy Seal. This program is for companies that conduct commerce online. These companies know the value of giving consumers confidence that their personal and credit card data is secured and that their online transaction will be secure. Based on a Greenfield Online survey performed in 2001 cited by BBB *OnLine*, "almost 90 percent of online shoppers would feel more confident shopping on a site that displays the BBB *OnLine* Privacy Seal, than from an online company that does not."⁹ To receive the BBB *OnLine* Privacy Seal, companies must apply and meet requirements in the following general areas:

- *Threshold requirements* — These requirements lay out some general conditions for the organization completing an application for the BBB *OnLine* Privacy Seal. They also detail the eligibility requirements for organizations — one of which is having a good standing with the BBB.
- *Privacy notice requirements* — These are detailed guidelines for the content of privacy notices. Some of the key requirements include having to describe "...all the types of personally identifiable information or prospect information that may be collected through the Web site or online service (including e-mail correspondence)"¹⁰ Other key requirements in this section include a stated commitment to online data security and an "opt-in or opt-out" provision for consumers, so they can decide whether or not their personal information can be shared. A number of other specific requirements related to the Privacy Notice can be found on www.bbbonline.org.
- *Sharing information* — This section outlines rules regarding when and how consumers' personally identifiable information can be shared with third parties. Sharing information is specifically prohibited when the party with which information is being shared can take that information and use it for its own marketing efforts.
- *Choice and consent* — These requirements provide consumers with an explicit choice of whether to "opt in" or "opt out" when deciding whether they want their personally identifiable information used in a company's direct marketing efforts. The choice and consent requirements also provide guidance on how information should be transferred to outside parties and the choice that is required to be given to consumers.
- *Access and correction* — This section requires organizations to have a policy and process in place so that consumers can have their personally identifiable information corrected if they find it to be factually incorrect. This section also obligates companies to have personally identifiable information available in retrievable form so that consumers can readily access this information.
- *Security* — The security requirements essentially say that a company must take "reasonable steps to ensure that personally identifiable information or prospect information is safe from unauthorized access, either physical or electronic. These steps include at least the following:
  - The organization maintains logs to properly track information and assure that authorized individuals only access data.
  - The organization maintains a written data security policy.
  - The organization performs at least an annual review of its written data security policy.

- The organization provides adequate training for employees, agents, and contractors.
- The organization stores information in a secure environment (using features such as doors, locks, and electronic security)."[11]

The security section also requires the use of encryption when certain personal information such as credit card numbers or social security information is transmitted or received online.

- *Additional staff determinations* — The additional staff determinations deal with providing proper measures for screening out children when the Web site content is inappropriate for children under the age of 13. The requirement also provides guidance for where the BBB *OnLine* Privacy Seal may be used when there is content inappropriate for children under 13.

The BBB *OnLine* Privacy Seal is prevalent today and, based on the requirements listed above, is quite comprehensive. Two of the security-related requirements are that the company must have a data security policy and an annual review of that policy. As with some of the regulations that have been discussed so far, the developers of the BBB *OnLine* Privacy Seal recognized the need to look at information security in terms of a comprehensive program and the need to perform regular assessments — in this case, there are requirements for a policy and an annual review, which is very similar to doing a security assessment.

AICPA/CICA WebTrust Program

The American Institute of Certified Public Accountants (AICPA), along with the Canadian Institute of Chartered Accountants (CICA), developed the WebTrust Program to address security and privacy concerns that consumers have with companies conducting business over the Internet. The WebTrust Program provides a seal for companies that can pass an audit against the WebTrust standards. Although companies conducting electronic commerce over the Internet do not have to have the WebTrust seal, it is a recognized standard that gives some consumers confidence in the integrity of transactions and some assurance that their personal information is secure — very similar to the BBB *OnLine* Privacy Seal. The value of this kind of program is significant, considering all of the press about consumers being hesitant to do business over the Internet for fear of having their personal information compromised. Similar to the BBB *OnLine* program, the WebTrust program attempts to allay fears that some consumers have by providing an independent certification to companies. The program is only offered by Certified Public Accountants (CPAs) and Chartered Accountants (CAs), who are appropriately trained and licensed. The independence aspect is very important to note here. Notwithstanding some of the scandals that the CPA profession has seen recently, the profession is known for its independence.

The AICPA's WebTrust Seal program is a set of best practice standards for electronic commerce sites. Separate standards and programs exist for fundamental areas defined by the AICPA and the CICA. The specific programs were released in 2003 and are listed on the AICPA Web site.[12]

Below is a detailed discussion of one of the WebTrust Seal programs — WebTrust Security. This standard is an example of what the requirements of an information security program specific to business to commerce could be. It is an example of a standard that looks at information security as a program that is built on a foundation of policies and with ongoing monitoring and enforcement to ensure that the program is functioning as intended and is updated as necessary.

From a security assessment perspective, this is relevant because the things described in the standard below are similar to those you would look for when conducting a security assessment.

WebTrust Security

The WebTrust Security certification has some similarities to the other WebTrust certifications, but the focus here is on restricting access to the electronic commerce system and data to authorized individuals.

The criteria used in performing a WebTrust Security examination are divided into four distinct areas:

- *Disclosure* — Disclosure requirements obligate companies to disclose their security practices regarding:
  - Access to information collected during electronic commerce activities.
  - Access to systems used and how it is controlled.
  - Consumer recourse and third party resolution processes — Consumer recourse is an important aspect of electronic commerce, and there is a common interest for customers and companies in ensuring that disputes are resolved quickly without costly litigation, which many consumers cannot afford and in which companies do not want to engage.
- *Policies* — The requirement related to policies obligates companies to have security policies in place to address roles and responsibilities related to information security including user access and administration, change management (ensuring proper testing before migration to the production environment), physical security for systems used in electronic commerce activities, incident handling, and dispute resolution. In addition, requirements exist related to security awareness training and ensuring that the company has allocated adequate resources to security initiatives.
- *Procedures* — Procedures are the next step after policies. Although the policies describe "what" has to be in place, the procedures describe "how" a company becomes compliant with those policies. For example, there are specific user ID access requirements or policies related to who can access systems. The procedures lay out the specific steps taken (e.g., giving network access to employees) to ensure that those requirements are met.
- *Monitoring* — The monitoring requirements help ensure that systems and processes are in place to make certain that companies can monitor the security of their e-commerce systems, react to events, and make changes as required to ensure an adequate level of security. The monitoring component of this standard is the enforcement aspect of the policy, which is

a key component of any information security program. A lack of enforcement can be interpreted as a lack of commitment to security, and personnel may therefore not take security very seriously.

Another aspect of the monitoring component is ensuring that updates to the policies and procedures and the information security program in general are made. Organizations tend to be dynamic, and as changes to the organization occur, adjustments are required from a security perspective. For example, there may be changes to the business related to new processes, changes in technology, or organization structure. These changes may require adjustments to the overall information security program. Considering the speed of change in today's companies and the fact that much of it is fueled by technology, security processes can become obsolete quickly.

The final aspect of the monitoring component addresses noncompliance with security policies. Noncompliance can happen in two ways.

First, despite the security polices being feasible, personnel do not follow policies for a variety of reasons including a lack of understanding of security policies, resource constraints, or a lack of awareness. In this scenario, there should be compliance and it should be enforced.

The second type of noncompliance is when a policy is not feasible or it does not make business sense to adhere to a policy. It may not be possible because the cost related to compliance far outweighs the benefits. In these cases, the risks must be understood, and mitigating controls must be put in place to the extent possible. Management should also formally acknowledge that they are accepting risk. This process ensures that management understands the risk and takes ownership of the decision to accept the risk.

The WebTrust Seal programs are a good standard by which to measure e-commerce companies. As evident from the descriptions of the WebTrust security program, the standards are technology neutral and can be incorporated into an information security program to address e-commerce operations.

ORGANIZATIONAL IMPACTS

Another aspect of the evolution of information security is the organizational changes that have taken place as information security has become more important. Before information security became a central issue for many companies, security was just a part of someone's job in many cases. This meant that one of the people in IT had information security in his or her job description. There was no concept of conducting a formal risk analysis, determining what the risks are, and determining recommendations to address those risks. Enforcement related to security was not really a concept either.

In today's market, information security is becoming a more important issue. Many companies recognize that one of their most important assets is their data. With all of the different security vulnerabilities that exist today and the government regulations related to security, it is no wonder that companies are taking steps to adequately secure these assets. This recognition has resulted in companies making a number of changes in their businesses — specifically at the organization level. Some of the changes that have occurred and are discussed in detail in the next few sections include:

- Rise of the Chief Security Officer (CSO)
- Separate organizations dedicated to information security

The organization is a critical part of a security assessment. Organizations speak to roles and responsibilities and ownership of the security function. How information security is handled from an organizational perspective is based on several factors including budget, personnel, and most important — how to best align security personnel and organization so that security risk is managed effectively. An information security program with the best processes and technology can be completely ineffective without the right organization structure and clearly defined roles and responsibilities. One of the challenges when conducting a security assessment is a company's tendency to focus on technology when talking security. The organization aspect and clearly defined roles and responsibilities are critical for the success of an information security program.

RISE OF THE CHIEF SECURITY OFFICER

One of the major shifts that the industry has seen is the coming of the Chief Security Officer (CSO). This would typically be an executive- or management-level position with overall responsibility for security. The CSO's role will vary from company to company but in general is very broad because it touches virtually every piece of the company including technology, critical business processes, physical security, investigations, and executive protection. The CSO must be aware of security, operational, and financial risks and issues facing a company and have the ability to communicate and build relationships across organizational boundaries.

The advent of the CSO is a new trend that is a very positive step in realizing the importance of information security. In a survey performed by *CSO Magazine* in September 2002, where approximately 1,000 security professionals were surveyed, 37 percent said that they were in that position for less than one year and over 60 percent were in their positions less than two years.[13] Clearly, it is a new trend but a very positive one. It is possible that many of these positions came to be in the aftermath of the 9/11 tragedy in the United States, because that brought on a heightened awareness of security.

Although having someone with the CSO title or having someone with overall ownership for security is becoming more common, it is still an uphill battle to justify security and show its value. This is largely because of the mentality — "since nothing has happened, nothing is wrong—so why fix it?" This mentality gives senior management a false sense of confidence. A security officer with a global financial firm recently commented, "The greatest threat we face is the belief of senior management that there is no threat. So we don't get funds, money, or resources, and without those things, you can never address security threats and risks."[14] There is a lack of education within many companies at all levels from management on down about the importance of information security. At this stage of the evolution of information security, one of the CSO's main tasks is to educate employees and instill a culture where information security is integrated into business processes. The key messages that CSOs should focus on today include:

- *"Evangelize" the importance of information security* — The CSO must educate people about what information security is, where it fits into the business, and why it is important. CSOs also must educate company executives about the impact of security risks in terms of dollars, damage to reputation, and other relevant impacts. The CSO must "evangelize" to the right people and build a culture where information security is viewed as being important. Information security should be integrated into business processes, and employees should understand their responsibility as it relates to information security. It must be stressed that information security is something for which all personnel have responsibility. This culture change is very important for CSOs as they try to succeed in their mission to secure the assets and information of a company.
- *Align security measures with business risks* — It must be understood that security measures help manage risk and are a business issue — not a technical issue. Best-of-breed technology and complicated business processes to ensure that internal controls are built in are not always the answer. The financial and resource commitment required for information security measures can be significant and must be considered. The ROI (Return on Investment) for security must be demonstrated, which can be difficult because a cost-benefit and ROI analysis for security is not always possible due to the unknowns and intangible aspects of security. However, showing ROI is absolutely critical for information security to go to the next level and be viewed more strategically in an organization. As information security professionals, we need to think like other parts of a business and think in terms of ROI and cost-benefit when it comes to security spending. Security expenditures face the same level of scrutiny as other expenses when it comes time to budget. In one way, security expenditures might face even more scrutiny because it is sometimes difficult to quantify the benefit. By its nature, security is preventive, like an insurance policy. For some security measures, people do not see the value until something happens — e.g., the value of intrusion detection is not seen until there is an intrusion. It is important, particularly with financial decision makers in an organization, to show how security measures help manage risk, how they are aligned with key business processes, and how they make sense from a cost perspective.
- *View security as a revenue enabler* — As stated earlier, security is like an insurance policy. No one really likes the idea of spending lots of money on something that "might" be useful. For many companies, spending on security is viewed as a "necessary evil" at best, or it is done because there is some other compelling reason to spend on information security such

as legislation (e.g., HIPAA or GLBA) or a requirement from a business partner. Although these are good reasons for having information security in place, a better way to view security is that of a "business enabler." An example is the business-to-consumer space, where security is very important. Numerous surveys cite security and privacy of personal information as one of the primary concerns that consumers have when shopping online. In the case of business-to-consumer, information security measures and some type of security certification might provide consumers with the assurance they need before they shop online and thereby enable revenue. In any business, it is a much more powerful argument if you can show that information security is not so much a cost as something that will help a company enhance revenues and reach financial goals.

Some other key findings from the survey of approximately 1,000 security professionals (referenced above):

- 60 percent had a CSO or someone dedicated to IT security.
- 45 percent report to either the chief information officer (CIO) or the Information Systems (IS) director.
- 80 percent reported that the security budget was part of the overall IT budget.

What do these statistics mean? First, security is still considered an IT issue because of where the position sits in the organization. Because the security budget is part of the overall IT budget, it competes with other IT initiatives in terms of priority. As a result, security is still not being viewed as something that is different from IT in many companies.

Ideally, the CSO should not report to IT, as the goals of a security organization can conflict with those of an IT organization. In fact, having information security not reporting through IT creates a mechanism for helping to ensure that security issues surface and are addressed.

When conducting a security assessment and reviewing the organization and roles and responsibilities, the existence of a CSO is significant because it shows some level of commitment to information security. Ownership, accountability, and having dedicated resources for security immediately diminish some of the security risk related to the lack of ownership of security. Although the CSO will not perform every security task, this individual does have the ability to instill a culture where information security becomes pervasive and to establish an information security program complete with policies and procedures, security technology, and a mechanism for monitoring and compliance. The CSO also has the opportunity to be a part of the executive team and make security a consideration as new business initiatives are developed. During a security assessment, it is important to understand what authority the CSO has — budgetary authority, dedicated staff reporting to this individual, etc.

AUTONOMOUS DEPARTMENTS DEVOTED TO INFORMATION SECURITY

Separate autonomous departments devoted to information security are a strong indication that security is taken seriously at a company. Typically, information security responsibilities from a technical perspective fall into the IT department and other security-related responsibilities are dispersed among various departments. For example, system administrators might have information security as part of their jobs, where they are responsible for log review and ensuring that certain security-related configuration settings are in place. With the recent reductions seen in IT, system administrators are especially stretched thin, and because their security-related responsibilities might not be seen as critical or as a key priority in their job responsibilities, it is sometimes questionable whether they are able to devote the proper time to this function.

It is not black and white as to where information security responsibilities should fall. Some information security responsibilities fall on end users and different departments, such as human resources (for personnel-related security issues), IT, and management. However, a separate department dedicated to information security shows a real focus in this area. For some companies, a dedicated group makes sense in the short term, because the group can build an information security program and try to ingrain it into the culture of the company. An ideal scenario is where security is a separate department outside of IT with authority to enforce good security practices and make decisions as they relate to information security.

What does having a separate group devoted to information security tell you about a company when conducting a security assessment? Two key aspects are worth noting.

Independence and the Ability to Escalate

A separate department devoted to security, depending on how it sits organizationally (i.e., is it separate from IT?), allows the information security function to be independent. Similar to an internal audit–type function, a separate department will not have any conflicts in implementing security measures or escalating security-related issues to management when necessary. The ability to do this is very important from an enforcement perspective. Without enforcement, it can be very difficult to ensure that security policies and procedures are followed in a company where security has been lax.

When conducting a security assessment, give enforcement of security policies and the ability to escalate significant consideration. If information security policies are being enforced and there is a track record of management requiring employees to address information security issues, the overall security posture of a company is significantly enhanced. From a security assessment perspective, this attitude from management would indicate that security is not an afterthought. In these organizations, information security personnel are probably abreast of changes in the organization and have the opportunity to raise security concerns before those changes are implemented.

Expertise

A separate group devoted to information security probably implies specific expertise in the area of information security. With the advances that have been made in technology and in how business is conducted, it is becoming more difficult to rely on people being "jacks of all trades." In the past, security was viewed as a technology issue, and IT departments would deal with security issues. Technology, related business processes, and functionality relative to business requirements are complicated enough without thinking of all the related security considerations. Attacks are being developed all the time using vulnerabilities existing in all parts of the IT environment including the network, operating systems, databases, and applications. Those who subscribe to alert services or newsletters where vulnerabilities and attacks are published know the sheer number of vulnerabilities and attacks out there. In fact, one of the significant areas of the information security industry is that of providing security intelligence services to help companies take the necessary measures to protect themselves from these attacks. The bottom line is that security is very significant, and someone or some group should own the responsibility if possible. It can cost a company dearly if the company does not have the security expertise to react to security incidents and security risks facing it. Besides these incidents, companies face many security issues related to their internal staff, such as segregation of duty issues and users with inappropriate system access. Although a separate security function may not be appropriate for some small companies, the value can be seen in mid-size and large companies.

From a security assessment perspective, dedicated security staff probably means that specific security tasks, such as reviewing logs, applying security patches on a regular basis, keeping up with the latest vulnerabilities, and applying mitigation strategies, are potentially performed. Also, it is more likely a company is employing a proactive approach to security as opposed to a reactive one. Some examples include:

- Security patches are applied before the related security vulnerability is exploited.
- Potential intrusions are detected and appropriate adjustments are made to perimeter security measures as needed before an intrusion actually takes place.
- Security-related logs are reviewed on a regular basis.

These are only a few examples of where security procedures are performed proactively instead of reactively.

Companies that do not have dedicated security staff do not necessarily see the value if they have never suffered a security incident. The argument can be made that a dedicated staff cannot prevent security incidents, and that is true. Dedicated staff can, however, minimize the risk of security incidents taking place. At the end of the day, information security is about managing risk in a cost-effective manner. Companies need to go through the exercise to determine whether the cost of having dedicated staff is worth it based on what is being protected. It is also worth noting that other options exist, such as outsourcing the security function. Some companies have recognized the importance of security and decided that they do not have the staff to do it, so they outsource some portion of the security responsibilities to experts in the area for a reasonable price.

SECURITY CERTIFICATIONS

One of the major forces in the evolution of information security is that a "body of knowledge" is slowly being carved out. This is being driven by a number of factors including industry certifications such as the CISSP (Certified Information Systems Security Professional) and CISA (Certified Information Systems Auditor), which have defined a body of knowledge that someone needs proficiency in to become certified, and employers who are trying to fill security-related positions and advertising for these skill sets. The information security profession itself has, to some extent, led the way in defining what information security is. International organizations have played a role. For example, Information Systems Security Certification Consortium, Inc. (ISC)², the body that administers the CISSP certification, has defined a common body of knowledge that security personnel are tested on before they can receive the CISSP certification. This body of knowledge includes operational, management, and technical concepts related to information security.

As the body of knowledge has become more defined, there has been a proliferation of certifications in the information security profession. The certifications have, to some extent, established standards of knowledge for the profession similar to those of other professions such as accounting and IT. As some of the certifications have gained in popularity, the demand for them has also risen. Some employers now either require a certification or a commitment to obtain a certification within a specified period of time as a condition of employment. Employers are having their own employees with security responsibility obtain relevant security certifications to help them in their jobs. These certifications are establishing minimum standards of knowledge for information security professionals. Although certifications today are differentiators or "nice to haves" for security professionals, they will become requirements in the future.

As more security professionals become certified, certification should be kept in perspective. For the information security profession, security certifications establish minimum standards of knowledge that security professionals should have. Like other certifications, security certifications are mostly based on examinations. Candidates must be able to take a test reasonably well. A certification does not necessarily mean that a person has mastered the subject material. Conversely, someone without a certification can be an expert.

From a security assessment perspective, certifications show a certain level of competence in information security or a specialty area of security, depending on the certification. In addition, some of the certifications have minimum experience requirements, which can give an indication of the level and type of expertise a security professional has. It must be stressed, however, that a certification does not take the place of real world experience, as is true in other professions.

On the whole, security certifications have been positive for the profession and have contributed to defining the information security "body of knowledge." The bodies that administer the certifications will have to continue keeping up with changes in the industry in order for the certifications to remain relevant.

As stated earlier, there has been a proliferation of the number of security certifications. We will discuss some of the more popular and sought-after security certifications. These certifications can be divided into two broad categories:

- Vendor-neutral certifications
- Vendor-specific certifications

VENDOR-NEUTRAL CERTIFICATIONS

The vendor-neutral certifications are independent certifications that can include testing on high-level broad-based security knowledge as well as knowledge of technical security processes. The maintenance of these certifications can usually be satisfied by taking a certain number of continuing professional education (CPE) credits. Four popular vendor-neutral certifications are currently sought after:

- *CISSP* — Certified Information Systems Security Professional
- *CISA* — Certified Information Systems Auditor
- *SANS (GIAC)* — Global Information Assurance Certification
- *CISM* — Certified Information Security Manager

Certified Information Systems Security Professional (CISSP)

The CISSP is administered by (ISC)^2 and is considered the premier information security certification. The CISSP certification signifies a minimum level of expertise in a variety of areas of information security, ranging from technical security to operational and management aspects of security. The certification exam tests candidates on the ten domains of knowledge referred to as the CBK or Common Body of Knowledge (the information below on the CBK is based on (ISC)^2 guidance on its Web site)[15] by (ISC)^2. The exam comprehensively tests information security and is ideal for people who have worked in operational and management roles in security. The exam content is mostly nontechnical and deals with security organization and process issues such as change management, organizational practices, law, and business continuity/disaster recovery. The ten domains of the CBK are discussed briefly below:

- *Security Management Practices* — The security management practices domain focuses on the overall information security program. The focus is on what the best information security program for a given environment is and how to keep it up to date. The key items in this domain include:
  - Identification of critical information and assets
  - Security policies and standards
  - Risk assessment

- *Security Architecture and Models* — This domain of knowledge covers security architecture concepts from the network infrastructure to the application level. The overall security architecture, how it ensures the confidentiality, integrity, and availability of the information, and some of the standards and methods used to achieve it are discussed. Some of the key items in this domain include:
  - Security architecture and associated technical controls
  - Security issues related to system designs
  - Security standards
- *Access Control Systems and Methodology* — This domain covers principles relating to access control and the "least privilege" principle, where a person's access is limited to what that individual needs to perform his or her job. This domain requires knowledge of access control and what is appropriate based on different factors a given environment. Some of the key items in this domain include:
  - Access control methodology, administration, and techniques
  - Value of information
  - File and data ownership
- *Application Development Security* — This domain covers security at the application level. It covers the application development process and how security and controls should be considered early and built into applications. It covers the risks associated with the development environment and why the process of moving code to production needs to be properly controlled. Some of the key items in this domain include:
  - Application controls
  - Systems development controls
  - Change management
- *Operations Security* — Operations security consists of the internal control structure of the IT infrastructure, access controls related to these resources, and monitoring. Some of the key items in this domain include:
  - Computer operations
  - Administration and operational controls
- *Physical Security* — Before electronic security became a significant concern, physical security was the main component of security. As a result, it is perhaps the most developed area of security. Today, physical security is still a critical part of the overall information security program, partly evidenced by it being one of the ten domains of the CBK. This domain covers all aspects of physical security including perimeter security, inside security, environmental controls, and other physical security–related concepts.
- *Cryptography*— The cryptography domain covers basic concepts of cryptography and how they are used to ensure the confidentiality and integrity of information. This domain covers the use of public and private key algorithms, digital signatures, key distribution and management, and other cryptography-related concepts.
- *Telecommunications, Network, and Internet Security* — This domain is probably the most technical of the ten domains. It requires an understanding

of security concepts related to telecommunications and network security including firewalls, routers, and protocols such as Transmission Control Protocol/Internet Protocol (TCP/IP). Different types of networks such as local area and wide area networks along with the seven-layer Open System Instrumentation (OSI) model and related security concepts are also discussed in this domain. On the telecommunications side, security concepts related to Private Branch Exchange (PBX) and Integrated Services Digital Network (ISDN) are discussed.

- *Business Continuity Planning* — Business continuity planning and disaster recovery are discussed at a high level. The overall methodology for developing and maintaining a business continuity plan are covered, including identifying mission-critical processes, contingency planning strategies, offsite storage, and plan testing and maintenance.
- *Law, Investigations, and Ethics* — This domain covers the (ISC)²'s code of ethics and the expectations for a CISSP holder from a legal and ethical perspective. The other two key areas of this domain are investigations and relevant laws in the information security arena.

In addition to passing the exam testing the topics listed above, a candidate for the CISSP must also comply with an experience requirement and agree to follow the (ISC)² code of ethics. As is evident by the contents of the CBK above, the certification is for the information security generalist with experience in the information security profession. The exam tests everything from technical network security to security management practices. The CISSP certification is one of the most sought-after certifications in the information security profession and indicates a proficiency in a broad set of concepts related to information security.

Certified Information Systems Auditor (CISA)

The CISA certification is very similar to the CISSP but with more of an emphasis on auditing. The CISA has seven domains, which are very similar to those of the CISSP and include:

- Management, Planning, and Organization of IS
- Technical Infrastructure and Operational Practices
- Protection of Information Assets
- Disaster Recovery and Business Continuity
- Business Application System Development, Acquisition, Implementation, and Maintenance
- Business Process Evaluation and Risk Management
- The IS Audit Process

Although the CISSP exam content is related more to the operations side of security — i.e., security management practices, physical security, and the methods used to secure (e.g., cryptography, networking security), the CISA exam content deals more with how to ensure that these practices are functioning as they should based on a specific company's business requirements. Each of the domains of the

CISA exam emphasizes auditing the processes and ensuring that appropriate controls are in place and that the process is in compliance with the company's own standards.

System Administration and Network Security Certifications (SANS) — GIAC (Global Information Assurance Certification)

The GIAC certifications are administered by SANS (SysAdmin, Audit, Network, Security), which is one of the premier information security organizations in the world. SANS offers training in a number of security "tracks," and its courses are considered among the best offered. The different tracks include areas of information security such as intrusion detection, firewalls and perimeter protection, auditing, and others. Students can attend the classes for a specific track and then seek the GIAC certification. For most tracks, a corresponding certification exam exists. SANS offers a fairly wide range of choices, resulting in a variety of students with expertise ranging from nontechnical management to technical system administrators. Individuals with a GIAC certification have gone through a rigorous process including submission of a practical and passing an exam. An individual with one of the GIAC certifications typically has hands-on real world experience. The individual tracks (as posted on the GIAC Web site) are:

- GIAC Security Essentials Certification (GSEC)
- GIAC Certified Firewall Analyst (GCFW)
- GIAC Certified Security Leadership (GSLC)
- GIAC Certified Intrusion Analyst (GCIA)
- GIAC Certified Incident Handler (GCIH)
- GIAC Certified Windows Security Administrator (GCWN)
- GIAC Certified UNIX Security Administrator (GCUX)
- GIAC Information Security Officer (GISO)
- GIAC Systems and Network Auditor (GSNA)
- GIAC Certified Forensic Analyst (GCFA)
- GIAC IT Security Audit Essentials (GSAE)

The contents of the individual tracks are self-explanatory, and further information is available on the GIAC Web site.

CISM (Certified Information Security Manager)

The CISM is a relatively new certification that was developed by ISACA (which also administers the CISA examination). The CISM, unlike the CISA, is geared towards security management personnel who are involved in security operations. The focus is on the business side of security rather than the technical side. Based on the Information System Audit and Control Association's (ISACA) own description, the CISM is designed to assure employers that those who have the CISM designation have the ability to manage a security function as well as provide consulting services pertaining to security.

The CISM exam is based on content from the following practice areas (this information is from the CISM brochure on the ISACA Web site — www.isaca.org):

- *Information security governance* — Assurance that alignment exists between the business and the specific information security strategies
- *Risk management* — Managing information security risks to manage the business
- *Information security program management* — Design and development of an information security program that aligns information security measures to security risks that the business is facing
- *Information security management* — Oversight of information security activities
- *Response management* — Essentially, incident management — ability to react in the event of a security incident

As the exam is relatively new, there was an opportunity for people with the right experience to be grandfathered the certification. This ended in January 2004. To obtain the CISM, you must pass the CISM exam, have at least five years work experience in information security (three years must be in information security management), and adhere to a Code of Ethics.

VENDOR-SPECIFIC CERTIFICATIONS

Many of the security vendors offer a certification to show a level of expertise in the particular technology. An example is the vendors in the firewall and intrusion detection space, who have certification programs for security professionals. The vendor certifications do not typically have an experience requirement as the vendor-neutral certifications do, and they are usually obtained by simply taking an exam or multiple exams. Unlike with the vendor-neutral certifications, security professionals must take exams periodically to ensure they remain up to date with the changes in the technology. Certain vendor certifications are very marketable, but others are considered "paper certifications" because they can be obtained by studying from a book and involve little hands-on experience. Nevertheless, product certifications show a minimum level of proficiency with a given product and are adding to the security body of knowledge.

TRENDS IN INFORMATION SECURITY

As the business environment and the technologies that support it change, changes in information security also occur. It is worth noting some of the trends the information security industry is facing today. As we do security assessments, we have an opportunity to see what security issues companies are facing today and how these companies will be affected from a security perspective as the threats change and evolve. Security professionals should always consider trends as they review business processes, supporting technologies, security architecture, and other aspects reviewed in a security assessment. The task of staying up to date with information security trends and determining how they affect an organization can be daunting.

When performing a security assessment, being up to date on what is happening in the information security world helps in providing good recommendations to clients. Understanding some of the trends in the information security space is critical to being able to provide this guidance to clients when performing security assessments. The trends in information security today are being driven by economic factors, government regulation, new technology, and new information security threats companies are facing. Some of the key trends include:

- Focus on the overall information security program as opposed to disparate point solutions
- Tight budgets — justifying security initiatives and the importance of showing ROI
- Growing awareness of information security
- Outsourcing security functions
- Legislation — e.g., HIPAA, GLBA

FOCUS ON THE OVERALL INFORMATION SECURITY PROGRAM

An information security program is the set of measures taken by a company to secure its information assets. It is a comprehensive approach to information security, where business requirements and risks are considered in formulating what measures should be taken to protect the confidentiality, integrity, and availability of information and systems in a cost-effective manner. This is a very broad definition, and it represents a holistic approach to information security. The important aspect here is that security is being driven by the business and not the other way around. Security technology and processes should not be used unless a clear understanding exists about what business risk they are mitigating. Without the business justifying security, it is difficult to show its value and justify the expense. As a rule of thumb, the cost to adequately secure assets and information should not exceed their value.

As information security has evolved, companies are looking at it as something that should be incorporated into the company processes. Companies with good information security programs understand that all employees have roles in information security and that it must be built into all processes. This holistic approach to information security has resulted in security at many companies being viewed as a comprehensive program and not a disparate set of technologies or point solutions.

However, many companies today do not really have an information security program containing the necessary components. They have some pieces of an information security program in place but have not really integrated it. Some of the characteristics you might see at companies with a piecemeal information security program include:

- *Fragmented security policies* — A fragmented set of policies consisting of some of the bare minimum policies such as Acceptable Use and User ID administration might exist but are not typically followed. Employees are often not even aware of any policies that are in place. If they are not sure about something security related, they find out by asking someone they work with. These policies might have minimal value because they might fulfill some compliance requirement. From an operations perspective, however, they are essentially ineffective.

- *Security point solutions* — Security point solutions such as firewalls, intrusion detection systems, and other technologies are in place to protect the company's IT infrastructure. These technologies are often put in place without any consideration of the company's business risks, and as a result, the security technology in place may not be appropriate for the environment. In addition, the technologies are probably not being used properly because processes have not been developed to maximize the value of the technology.

- *Lack of enforcement* — Lack of enforcement weakens the security posture because no one takes security seriously. Although there may be exceptions to this rule, such as companies where security is ingrained in the culture of the company, by and large, security tends to be weak where it is not enforced. One reason for lack of enforcement is that there is nothing to enforce. When there are no security policies or other standards in place that employees are required to follow, it is very difficult to enforce good security practices. Another reason is that companies do not have dedicated security staff to actively enforce critical security functions.

- *Reactive versus proactive security* — Security is performed in many places in a reactive mode. Unless a security incident takes place, the status quo remains — i.e., there is no process to proactively try to find vulnerabilities and address them before something happens. One of the questions during a security assessment on the topic of intrusions is "Has there been an intrusion?" The answer is often "no." In most cases, the person providing the answer really does not know because there is no mechanism for knowing whether an intrusion occurred in the first place. People have a feeling that it is not worth spending the money on the resources to take a proactive approach to security and that they will take care of anything when it happens. The problem is that, with the types of vulnerabilities and attacks out there today, by the time a company can react to a security incident, the damage has already been done. An example is where an e-commerce company has consumers' personal information on its systems and someone gains unauthorized access to the system and steals consumer credit card information. In this case, by the time the company finds out about the attack, the damage has already been done. The reputation of the e-commerce company has already been hurt, and potential legal troubles related to not properly safeguarding consumer information are on the horizon. One major security incident can sometimes show the value of taking a proactive approach to security.

All of the characteristics above are the signs of a piecemeal information security program. As the risks and attacks become more significant, the piecemeal approach does not adequately manage risk. The trends are pointing towards a more holistic approach to information security, which can be difficult. It requires cultural change, where information security is an integral part of business processes and where all employees understand that they have some responsibility towards it. This change is tough for security management personnel trying to build effective information security programs. For CSOs, it has been a tough battle to build successful information security programs with the lack of funds and support. In an article that appeared in *Computerworld* magazine about the difficulty that CSOs are having in trying to build information security programs, David Foote of Foote Partners LLC stated, "They see the risks in trying to build in the next phase of security — moving from fragmented delivery of security technology to a coordinated, aggressive, well-conceived security program. They understand how long it takes to build attention and change the culture to make this next step, but they're not getting the support they need to brand and build this next level of security."[16]

To develop recommendations for creating a holistic information security program when conducting a security assessment, you must have a good understanding of the business and the security risks it is facing so that appropriate cost-effective recommendations can be made. Although short-term recommendations might be made with regards to locking down systems or changing certain processes, the information security program as a whole must be considered as part of the long-term recommendations. A holistic approach to information security addresses the specific security risks for a company and can help decide how to allocate information security resources. This holistic approach allows companies to have a more integrated information security management process.

SECURITY SPENDING IS TIGHTENING

As most IT professionals today know, budgets are tight. Many companies are fighting to just survive, and as a result, they have renewed their focus on how money is being spent. Regardless of whether something was budgeted for, expenditures still face significant scrutiny. In the IT world, the key criteria in determining whether funds will be spent on an initiative are:

- General questions
  - Does it support mission-critical operations?
  - Is there a compelling return on investment (ROI)?
  - What is the total cost of ownership (TCO)?
- Security-related questions
  - Is the security initiative fulfilling a legal or compliance requirement?
  - What risk is the security initiative addressing and how critical is the risk — i.e., is it cost beneficial to spend the money?
  - What is the potential impact to the business if this security risk is not addressed?

In making a decision on whether to spend on security, the basic questions above along with some other questions related to the risks the security measure is addressing are asked. When security spending is judged against the criteria above, it is sometimes very difficult to justify security spending.

Some executives have the attitude that as long as they have not had a security incident, nothing is really wrong — so why spend on it? For an executive to spend money on security, the spending must be justified by the answers to the questions in the criteria above.

The bottom line is that overall security spending is tight, as is true for other areas of IT. What is different about security is that its benefits are not always apparent and as a result, justification of security is difficult. Usually, events such as a security incident will open people's eyes and provide some level of awareness of information security. However, security professionals must constantly understand what they are securing and do it in a cost-effective manner. As you develop new security initiatives, you must ask the same questions above.

GROWING AWARENESS OF INFORMATION SECURITY

Information security–related incidents are happening all the time, and some cases are receiving significant publicity. The range of incidents varies greatly and can include events such as a high school student breaking into a system to change a grade, personal credit card information being compromised from an e-commerce operation, or a worm causing significant network outages. These types of incidents will continue to happen even though security measures are becoming better all the time. As security at every level becomes more sophisticated, so do the attacks. All of this has made the public more aware of information security.

With this rise in awareness, consumers are scrutinizing how business is done as they try to determine whether their personal information is safe. Many consumers will not shop on an Internet site if they do not believe that their information is secure. This awareness has resulted in consumers becoming concerned about their personal information in areas other than e-commerce. For example, at one time, people rarely questioned giving a credit card to a waiter to pay a bill. Today, some of those same people question whether their credit card information is safe when they give it in a restaurant. Although the restaurant scenario is the same as it was years ago, the heightened awareness of security concerns has raised questions in people's minds. Companies are also more aware of potential information security issues as they become more aware of what can happen.

The result of all this awareness is that companies are slowly becoming more interested in looking at security as a program and at a strategic level. Executives from all areas of companies are becoming interested in security. As a result, there is a growing trend for companies to focus on security risk and how to manage it effectively and in a cost-effective manner. This approach helps ensure that the company is using funds wisely in securing its information assets.

OUTSOURCING SECURITY FUNCTIONS

Outsourcing security functions is following the same type of trend that IT outsourcing has been following over the past few years. IT outsourcing is something that companies have been doing for some time now. Many companies have outsourced part or all of their IT functions to companies such as IBM or EDS. The outsourcers handle a wide range of IT activities including (but not limited to):

- Infrastructure administration
- Asset management

- Application development
- Help desk
- Ad-hoc projects

Outsourcing contracts tend to be long term and have the following benefits for customers:

- *Cost savings* — This is probably the biggest reason to outsource. The work that outsourcers would do is their core competency, so the argument is that they can do it better, more efficiently, and cheaper because they have skilled professionals who do this type of work for a number of companies already. For many mid-size to large companies, the cost savings can be significant enough to make the case for outsourcing. However, all outsourcing agreements and outsourcers are not created equal. Companies must negotiate contracts that are in the best interests of both companies and with which both companies are ultimately happy — otherwise, outsourcing has the potential of becoming an operational nightmare for everyone.
- *Leverage someone else's infrastructure* — This is one of the reasons why IT outsourcing is cost effective. From a company's perspective, the infrastructure cost can be expensive. The general concept is that you can use an outsourcer's facilities and infrastructure and essentially pay only for the piece that you use. Outsourcers spread the cost of many components of the infrastructure across multiple clients resulting in lower costs to each client.
- *Companies want to concentrate on their competencies* — Managing IT can require significant incremental staff and overhead. Besides the management of IT, there are certain support functions that are required for it to run including:
  - *Accounting and finance* — IT projects have certain accounting regulations that an accounting staff must be up to date with to properly record IT activity in the accounting records.
  - *Vendor management* — There might be multiple vendors (hardware, software, etc.) that must be dealt with.
  - *Software maintenance* — Software upgrades need to be performed on a timely basis to ensure operations run smoothly.

For a company whose core competency is not IT, the functions listed above can be difficult to manage. Many companies are now moving towards focusing on what their core competencies are and letting someone else handle the rest of it. Although this is a compelling reason by itself, it becomes even more compelling when cost is factored in.

For many of the same reasons above, security-related functions are beginning to be outsourced. Security infrastructures are becoming very complicated. With the complicated nature of security architectures and related processes and the number of vulnerabilities that are being found, security must be given attention at every level. The number of regular day-to-day security activities that should take place can be daunting. Examples of some of these activities include:

- Security administration — firewalls, other security devices
- Log review — firewalls, intrusion detection systems
- Security patch application
- Signature updates for anti-virus, intrusion detection
- Software version updates
- Responding to new threats
- Compliance reviews

The list above represents some of the major tasks for people responsible for information security. These tasks, if done correctly, take significant time, which may not exist among a company's staff. As discussed earlier, companies can and do survive without paying attention to security and some of the tasks listed above. However, one security incident can do major damage and cause enough pain that they may feel compelled to perform these activities. Security for most companies can then become expensive very quickly. When looking at the cost of security, consider three key components:

- Security technology — firewalls, intrusion detection system, etc.
- Security processes
- Qualified security personnel

The above components can vary in cost but will still be expensive. Add in another complication, which is that security incidents occur on a 24/7 basis and do not follow the same work schedule as people do (i.e.. attacks do not just occur from nine to five on Monday to Friday), and outsourcing begins to make more sense.

Also, consider that attacks have become automated and very sophisticated. Anyone from practically anywhere in the world can attack a company at practically any time. Although some of the larger companies have the resources such as security operations centers and qualified security staff to provide 24-hour security, this is not the case for most companies. As a result, companies are facing two issues that are making the idea of outsourcing security a viable one:

- Companies do not have the manpower nor is it cost effective to monitor security on a 24/7 basis.
- It is difficult and expensive for companies to hire and retain qualified security-focused personnel.

These are the problems that outsourcing solves for companies. Clearly, the cost of 24/7 coverage can be staggering. Companies can outsource security to managed security service providers (MSSPs), who can provide the 24/7 coverage and the qualified personnel who are focused on security. MSSPs also have the expertise to work with a customer to ensure that the security infrastructure and technology are updated as the customer's business and environment change.

MSSPs work in much the same way as traditional IT outsourcing where there is a contract and a service level agreement (SLA) detailing the service. They offer a wide range of services, which can include:

- Managed firewall
- Managed VPN (Virtual Private Network)
- Managed intrusion detection
- Risk assessment services
- Other security monitoring–related services

Clients need to understand the best combination of services for them and negotiate a contract and SLA that are in the best interests of both companies. It is important to remember that outsourcing contracts with MSSPs are not turnkey solutions and that these relationships have to be managed. The SLA has to be managed and updated as business requirements change. This is even more important when a company is governed by security-related laws, such as HIPAA or GLBA, where the MSSP is sharing in the responsibility of safeguarding the company's data. Keep in mind that the company is ultimately responsible in ensuring that the outsourcing solution is compliant with relevant legislation.

Companies must be very selective when selecting a MSSP. It is critical for clients to do proper due diligence on any MSSP which includes (but is not limited to):

- Checking client references
- Walking through facilities
- Understanding how network architecture is going to work
- Determining whether MSSP is financially sound

A MSSP, like a traditional IT outsourcer, provides mission-critical services to a company, so it behooves clients to do their homework. In particular, it is critical to determine whether a MSSP is financially sound. Two well-publicized cases where MSSP customers were left high and dry involved MSSPs — Salinas Group and Pilot Network Services — who shut down operations with little or no warning to their customers. In each of these cases, insufficient contingency plans for their customers were in place. One of the affected companies was a West Coast health care provider, which kept its identity anonymous and said, "When Pilot went out of business, the health care provider went scrambling for other resources. Employees using the virtual private network (VPN) system to connect from outside the company were disconnected for up to four days."[17] MSSPs can be a wonderful solution for companies, but clients must do their due diligence when selecting the MSSP that is the best fit.

Outsourcing is a very important concept when performing a security assessment. If a client is already outsourcing, this should be reviewed in detail (this will be discussed later in this book) — e.g., review security of connections, SLAs, and contracts. If a client is not outsourcing, it is something that the information security professional should be aware of when assessing security and making recommendations. In some cases, it might be appropriate to make a recommendation to outsource some portion of information security, in which case the concept of conducting thorough due diligence should be stressed.

GOVERNMENT REGULATIONS

Another trend driving information security today in the United States is laws that are mandating companies to implement information security measures. Much of this legislation is being passed at the federal level in the United States. The security measures being mandated protect the confidentiality of consumer information.

Two pieces of legislation that are prominent today are HIPAA and GLBA, which affect health care–related companies and financial services companies, respectively. In each of these industries, a tremendous amount of information is collected about people, and much of it is sensitive. Examples include illness, medication, and personal financial information. If proper measures are not taken to keep this information confidential, consumers can be significantly harmed. Although some companies have strong information security programs that safeguard the information, others do not. This legislation is forcing companies to implement information security measures to protect sensitive consumer information.

An interesting aspect of the legislation is that it is not technology focused. In fact, the legislation calls on companies to implement comprehensive information security programs, which include security policies and procedures, risk analysis, awareness programs, and certain technical security measures to protect personally identifiable information. Companies are taking a holistic approach to security, which is the end result of the methodology suggested in this book

The major pieces of information security legislation are discussed in more detail in Chapter 10 — Information Security Legislation.

NOTES

1. U.S. Securities Act of 1933 — http://www.sec.gov/about/laws.shtml
2. 2003 CSI/FBI Computer Crime and Computer Survey — http://www.gocsi.com
3. Computerworld Magazine — September 9, 2002 — Online Training, E-Business Integration Yield Big Returns — http://www.computerworld.com/managementtopics/roi/story/0,10801,74061,00.html
4. FTC Web site — http://www.ftc.gov/ftc/mission.htm
5. CSOONLINE.COM — "Most Online Buyers Worried About Credit Card Data," by John Sumarcz; February 13, 2003
6. Network World Fusion — January 13, 2003 — Auditor's Ascension by Ellen Messmer, http://www.nwfusion.com/careers/2003/0113man.html
7. Microsoft Technet Web site — Windows 2000 Server Baseline Security Checklist, http://www.microsoft.com/technet/treeview/default.asp?url=/technet/security/tools/chklist/w2ksvrcl.asp
8. WebTrust press release — First major post-9/11 privacy survey finds consumers demanding companies do more to protect privacy — http://webtrust.org/abtpress.htm#feb19_02
9. BBB OnLine — http://www.bbbonline.org/privacy/priv_EN.asp
10. BBB OnLine — http://www.bbbonline.org/privacy/threshold.asp

11. BBB OnLine — http://www.bbbonline.org/privacy/threshold.asp—Privacy Program Eligibility Requirements
12. AICPA Web site — WebTrust v3.0 Principles and Criteria—http://www.aicpa.org/assurance/webtrust/princip.htm
13. *CSO Magazine* — "The Evolution of the Chief Security Officer"—September 2002, http://www.csoonline.com/csoresearch/report35.html
14. *Computerworld* — "Chief Security Officers Run into Hard Times" by Deborah Radcliffe, June 10, 2002 http://www.computerworld.com/careertopics/careers/story/0,10801,71866,00.html
15. International Information Systems Security Certification Consortium Inc. — http://isc2.org/cgi/content.cgi?category=19
16. *Computerworld* — "Chief Security Officers Run into Hard Times" — June 10, 2002 — http://www.computerworld.com/careertopics/careers/story/0,10801,71866,00.html
17. *Interactive Week* — "Shakeout Threatens Managed Security Clients" — by Brian Ploskina — August 27, 2001 http://www.landfield.com/isn/mail-archive/2001/Aug/0181.html
18. *Computerworld* — "PayPal Users Targeted by e-mail scam — again" — by Linda Rseucrance, October 25, 2002.

3 The Information Security Program and How a Security Assessment Fits In

An information security program is the umbrella heading for all security measures a company has in place. An information security program can contain many elements including physical security, system security, and internal controls that can touch virtually every part of an organization. Information security programs can vary significantly by organization. Some companies might have an extensive and formalized information security program based on a well-thought-out information security strategy, but another organization's idea of information security might be some physical security and password management. It varies greatly, and you will likely run into different scenarios as you conduct security assessments. This chapter will discuss the key elements of information security programs and how security assessments fit into the overall security picture. Understanding what an information security program is will develop a good foundation for discussing security assessment methodology, as much of what you will evaluate during an assessment will be the information security program. The recommendations you make at the end of the security assessment will be to enhance the overall information security program. Therefore, it is important to understand the key elements of an information security program before discussing the methodology.

WHAT IS AN INFORMATION SECURITY PROGRAM?

An information security program has seven key elements, as illustrated in Figure 3.1. The security strategy is the focal point; it drives the rest of the program. Each of the areas is critical to the success of the information security program and will be discussed in greater detail in subsequent sections. After discussing these key elements, we will discuss how the security assessment process fits in with the concept of the information security program.

SECURITY STRATEGY

At a high level, the security strategy is what drives the rest of the information security program. It consists of understanding the security risks a company is facing and developing the most cost-effective way to protect the company's information assets.

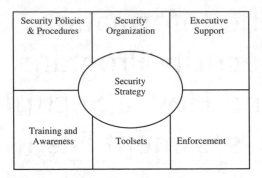

FIGURE 3.1 Information security program.

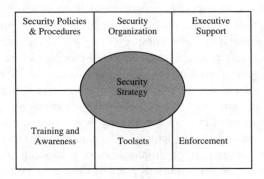

FIGURE 3.2 Security strategy.

Cost-effective implies evaluating the risks and impacts and then determining the best way to address those risks.

In Figure 3.2, the security strategy is in the center because it represents the basis for everything that is done from a security perspective. The security strategy should be well thought out by key stakeholders in an organization and driven by the needs of the business — i.e., the business requirements of an organization should be the basis of the security strategy. Security measures should be aligned with an organization's risks to help ensure that information security resources are allocated appropriately.

Some examples of things to consider when developing a security strategy include:

- Identifying critical data and determining the impact to the business if it is compromised (e.g., data is destroyed, unauthorized individuals gain access to data)
- Identifying critical applications and determining the impact if the application was not available
- Ensuring that any regulations with information security requirements are properly addressed

These and a host of other areas should be discussed when developing the security strategy of an organization. The key aspect of the security strategy is alignment, which is essentially determining the security risks facing a company and developing cost-effective security solutions to address them. The aim of the information is not to mitigate 100 percent of the security risk; rather, it is to reduce the risk to an acceptable level where the company is effectively managing the risk.

As with the other areas of the business, funds are limited, and part of the challenge in developing a security strategy is to determine the best use of the available funds. In these tough economic times, spending is scrutinized, so risks and potential impacts to the business must be clearly articulated when determining what security measures a company is going to take. Risks should be quantified if possible, and financial measurements such as ROI (Return on Investment) for potential security measures should be calculated.

As you consider these points when developing a security strategy, remember that there is some element of risk that the organization will have to accept. The challenge is to achieve the right balance between security and an acceptable level of risk.

SECURITY POLICIES AND PROCEDURES

Once the security strategy is developed, the first step in implementing it is to develop security policies (Figure 3.3). Policies are high-level requirements that are designed to meet the goals of the information security strategy. They are management's representation of what security measures need to be in place for effective information security.

Although the security strategy was a very high-level set of requirements that set the direction for the information security program, security policies are the first step in implementing the security strategy. As a result, developing good security policies requires a more detailed understanding of business processes, critical technologies, and

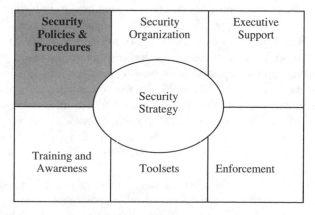

FIGURE 3.3 Security policies and procedures.

critical data. Good security policies are tailored to address the specific security risks facing the company. These risks are the starting point for developing the security policies.

Security policies should be developed with input from both business process owners and technology owners. The input from the business side is critical because the business will play a significant role in driving what is done from an information security perspective. Depending on how a company is organized, this input is important also because it is the business units that may be ultimately responsible for funding the implementation of security policies and other security initiatives. Security policies are generally developed with input from both business and technology owners to ensure that the policies are both feasible and reasonable with respect to addressing the specific security risks the company is facing.

Some standard security policies that almost every company has include Backup and Recovery, Data Retention, Acceptable Use, etc. There are also some policy areas such as Business-to-Business and Business-to-Consumer that many companies do not have. The policies you end up developing will depend on the business process and technology analysis of the company.

Once security policies are developed, they must be implemented by developing procedures. This is an important concept and it brings us to the distinction between policies and procedures. Where policies tell "what" needs to be done, procedures tell "how" to do it. To clearly understand what policies and procedures are, it is valuable to highlight some of the key differences:

- In the same way that policies were the next step after the development of the security strategy, procedures are the next step after development of policies.
- Policies tend to be global in nature, but procedures may be at a more granular level in the organization (e.g., at the department or business unit level).

Security policies by themselves do not tell users how to implement that policy. For example, a monitoring policy might say, "system logs should be reviewed periodically." Based on this policy, users do not necessarily know "how" to review logs or what "periodic" review means. In this case, there may be a procedure that goes through the step-by-step process of how to review the logs, what to look for, and how frequent the review should be. Notice that the policy can leave a fair amount of latitude for interpretation. This is necessary because different groups within a company may implement policies differently based on their specific requirements. For example, one group might review system logs on a daily basis, but another group might review them on a weekly basis. Both frequencies, daily and weekly, are interpretations of "periodic."

Policies will tend to remain relatively static, although procedures will vary based on technology, organization, resources, and other requirements. For example, procedures related to ID administration will vary depending on what technology is used (e.g., Microsoft, Novell), but the ID administration policy requirements should not

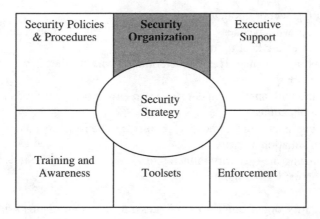

FIGURE 3.4 Security organization.

really change. The policy might say that users must change passwords on a regular basis. The "procedure" for making users change passwords periodically will differ for each system.

Policies only tend to change when there are fundamental changes to the business or some external driver exists, such as new legislation that might mandate certain things. For example, companies that have just begun to engage in commerce over the Internet will have to make additions to their security policy to reflect the risks of doing business in this way. Procedures, on the other hand, are much more dynamic in nature and can change more often. Changes in the organizational structure, technologies used, and business processes can potentially result in modifications to procedures.

One of the key benefits of both policies and procedures is that they clearly define roles and responsibilities and thus bring some accountability to security processes. Without documented policies and procedures, it is difficult to hold someone accountable for a process.

The other key aspect to remember with security policies and procedures is that someone (or a group of people) must own the responsibility of maintaining them. The value of these documents diminishes significantly once they become out of date.

SECURITY ORGANIZATION

The security organization (Figure 3.4) is the group that ensures that the information security program is followed and maintained. The "security organization" does not necessarily mean that a separate group ensures that security requirements are carried out; rather it means that there are people who are assigned in different capacities to ensure that the information security program is followed and maintained.

Typical people in a security organization could include a Chief Security Officer (CSO), security analysts, and system administrators with some security-related responsibilities. Some of the key responsibilities of the security organization include the following:

- Updating security policies as required
- Working with business process owners to ensure that security-related procedures are kept up to date
- Evaluating new initiatives and determining whether they have any security implications
- Working with application developers to ensure that security is being built into applications
- Working in an "enforcement" type of role to help ensure compliance with the information security program
- Monitoring new security vulnerabilities and determining steps to protect the company from them

For a security organization to be successful, it is important to have someone who is high enough in management so that potential issues can be properly escalated and so that the security organization has some clout. The CSO position, which many companies now have, sometimes has the required level of influence. It depends on whom the CSO reports to in upper management and where the CSO sits in the overall organizational structure. There is a huge difference between having a CSO who reports to a Chief Financial Officer and a CSO who reports to an Information Technology (IT) Manager. Where management level positions of security fit in the overall management chain has a bearing on how influential the security organization is. This factor is related to executive support, which is discussed in the next section.

Another factor that influences the success of the security organization is the culture of the company. Some companies are very security conscious; all employees understand the importance of information security, and the level of compliance with security policies is high. In these companies, upper management tends to be very security conscious and there tends to be a strong security organization. In other cases where security is not necessarily a priority, you might find the lack of a security organization or one that has little authority or influence. In these companies, the security organization must continually show why security is important to the business.

EXECUTIVE SUPPORT

Executive support (Figure 3.5) refers to upper management and their general attitude towards information security. When upper management is supportive of security and related initiatives, the security environment tends to be strong because that same attitude trickles down to all employees. Without executive support, any effort, whether information security or any other initiative, is very difficult. With executive support, activities are driven from the top versus from lower levels. From a security perspective, it is very difficult if not impossible to drive information security initiatives from lower levels in the organization. Remember that security does not make the typical employee's life easier. In fact, security initiatives tend to create more work for people. Some employees may even feel that security processes that create more work are more of a nuisance than anything else. Without executive support, it is difficult to convince someone that security processes are important. After all, how

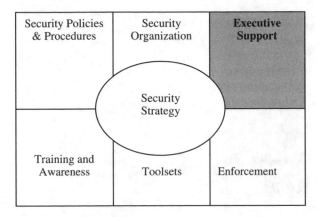

FIGURE 3.5 Executive support.

do you answer someone who tells you, "My manager doesn't have to do this, why do I?"

If employees of a company see that executives do not care about security, they probably will not care about it either. Even if there are policies and procedures, they are not followed because there is no management support for them. If employees do not "have" to do something, they will not — i.e., if they do not have to perform a process in a secure way, they will not. Strong executive support can change this attitude. Executive support for information security helps to instill a culture where information security is considered important and people know they have to do their part or else face some negative consequence. Without this support, there is a risk of noncompliance and difficulty in enforcing existing security policies because employees will not take information security seriously.

Executive support can be demonstrated by participation in training and awareness programs, where a company executive speaks to employees about the importance of information security. Executives can also support information security efforts by serving as a point of escalation in cases of noncompliance with security policies. Managers and other employees will be much more apt to follow security policies if they know that noncompliance might result in a reprimand from an executive of the company. Escalation ties back into the CSO concept and where security management sits in an organization. There is a better chance of security being taken seriously if the management responsible for it has access to people at the executive level. This type of access allows security issues to be escalated to levels where significant decisions can be made.

TRAINING AND AWARENESS

Regardless of what security policies and procedures are documented, employees will not necessarily be compliant with them unless they are aware of them and are provided training as necessary (Figure 3.6). Besides providing the initial communication of the information security program, training and awareness on a regular basis

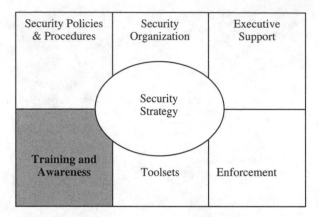

FIGURE 3.6 Training and awareness.

help to ensure that people are constantly being reminded of their responsibilities from an information security perspective. Remembering that information security is "everyone's" responsibility, it is critical to provide training and awareness so that average employees understand what they need to do and so that they have an opportunity to ask any questions if they do not understand. The chances of success of the information security program can be significantly enhanced by a good training and awareness campaign.

Training and awareness can be very challenging based on the number of people in the organization and the organization's complexity. Keep in mind that all employees do not need all of the training and awareness. Employees should be given training on the various aspects of the information security program that impact them. There will be some cases where training might be appropriate for everyone (e.g., importance of having strong passwords, acceptable use) and other cases where it might be appropriate only for a select group of individuals (e.g., training related to backups and offsite storage might only be relevant for IT personnel and a few business unit personnel who are data owners). A targeted program is an effective way to provide training and awareness in a cost-effective manner.

Some training and awareness delivery methods to consider include instructor-led training, manuals, online training, and documented processes. For instructor-led training, it is critical that qualified people deliver the training. A bad instructor can ruin a course and turn people off, but a good instructor can make people understand and motivate them. There are also some "regular" opportunities to give training and awareness — e.g., acceptable use policies related to Internet, e-mail, etc. could be discussed with employees when they first start as part of their orientation and then on an annual basis as a reminder. Another method to promote awareness is to provide employees easy access to security-related information such as policies and procedures. An easy way to provide this type of access is to leverage the company intranet. If the content is kept current, employees will refer to it if they have any questions regarding security, which will lead to greater levels of compliance.

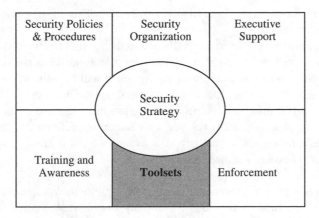

FIGURE 3.7 Toolsets.

TOOLSETS

IT environments are very complex, and security vulnerabilities are numerous. Systems must be checked on a regular basis to ensure that they are in compliance with best practice standards — e.g., servers should be checked to ensure that they have certain security settings in place and the appropriate patches. For most companies, checking manually to the level of detail required is just not feasible. It is virtually impossible to maintain a secure environment without having the proper toolsets (Figure 3.7) to automate some of these enforcement functions. Toolsets are emphasized as a separate element of an information security program because in today's environment, it is very difficult to enforce technical security manually. Some of the functions must be automated.

One of the areas where tools are critical is ensuring that servers and other systems are properly hardened. Although manual procedures can be used in some cases to check compliance, it is far more efficient to use tools to automate some tasks. This technical compliance effort, which the proper toolsets facilitate, is a critical part of the overall information security program. Some of the key compliance areas where tools are important include:

- Vulnerability assessment tools for the IT infrastructure
- Tools to check patch levels
- Tools that check password strength
- Vendor-specific tools to check specific systems (e.g., Microsoft Baseline Security Analyzer used to audit Windows machines)
- Application security assessment tools to ensure that applications do not have vulnerable code
- Tools to parse through logs to facilitate easier analysis

The list above is by no means all-inclusive; it does, however, show the need for tools. The work that the tools listed above can accomplish would be virtually impossible for an average IT staff to do manually. This clearly underscores the importance of toolsets.

Tools are available both commercially and in the form of freeware and shareware. In some cases, companies might have the expertise to develop their own custom tools. The type of tools you use in your environment will be influenced by a number of factors, some of which include what is being run on the network, existing security policies, budget (for purchasing tools), and the level of expertise of the people who will be using the tools. The tools you use are a matter of preference. The trend today is to use some combination of commercially available tools, custom-developed tools, and freeware/shareware, for three reasons:

First, some wonderful tools that are free and community supported provide much of the functionality that a company would want. Some of the most widely respected security tools, such as Nmap and Nessus, are available for free.

Second, most companies have budget constraints, and so if some good tools can be had for nothing, companies will certainly take advantage of it. Some companies do take a hard line on downloading tools from the Internet because there is no assurance that they are not corrupted. Also, with freeware, there is no recourse — freeware is taken on the basis of "try at your own risk." It all depends on the company.

Third, companies want to protect themselves against people who would potentially break into their systems (i.e., hackers). In most cases, hackers are using freely available tools to do most of their work. Using these same tools helps companies simulate what a hacker would do and use that to protect themselves.

ENFORCEMENT

Enforcement (Figure 3.8) is the final yet critical component of an information security program. Enforcement in the context of an information security program consists of actively ensuring that information security policies and procedures are followed. Enforcement can take place using manual procedures or can be automated using functionality available in existing systems (e.g., strong password policies can be enforced automatically in systems such as Microsoft Windows 2000). To the extent that enforcement can be automated, it should be because this results in greater compliance. Manual enforcement of security policies and procedures is a bit more difficult. The security organization, as discussed earlier, would have people carry out these enforcement activities. Besides these individuals, the IT audit part of an internal audit department would likely conduct some enforcement-related activities as well. For enforcement to be successful, strong upper management support for good security practices is necessary. Without management support, enforcement has no "teeth." Auditors or other members of a security organization may try to enforce security policies and procedures and not get very far because no repercussions for noncompliance exist. Conversations with people in different companies have uncovered numerous stories of where business groups are given a report that documents

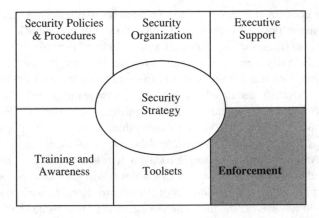

FIGURE 3.8 Enforcement.

security concerns as a result of a security audit. When a follow-up is done, it is found that none of the recommendations were ever implemented and thus, it is clear that the report was not taken seriously. If management support for enforcement is lacking, business groups can easily get away with not addressing issues raised during a security audit. Ideally, management should openly support enforcement efforts, and noncompliance should have repercussions.

Following the internal audit model, reports with findings are normally distributed to senior management. This method demonstrates the support from management, and then the individual groups are compelled to address the findings.

Without enforcement, which is very closely tied to executive support, the whole information security program suffers because people do not care.

HOW DOES A SECURITY ASSESSMENT FIT IN?

Now that we have gone over the key elements of the information security program, we can discuss how a security assessment fits into the overall information security picture.

Companies are dynamic in nature, and different aspects of the company are constantly changing. Everything from how the organization is set up to what the company does changes over time. Few companies in today's environment stay the same — there is always some element of change, and changes have implications from an information security perspective. For example, if a company restructures its operations and outsources its IT operations, there are security implications because data and systems are now under the control of a third party. Other examples include a company beginning to offer goods and services on the Internet or implementing a wireless environment. These changes have significant security implications that must be considered up front and on an ongoing basis.

In many cases, changes and initiatives are made without considering the security implications. In addition, no ongoing compliance effort exists to ensure that no security vulnerabilities result from these changes to the environment. For example, a business considering an e-commerce initiative is primarily concerned with the best way to offer goods and services on the Internet so that sales are maximized and consumers have a positive experience so that they will come back. While implementing these services, security is not always considered proactively; rather, it is an afterthought. Security personnel may be brought in after the fact to review the implementation, which is not the best way to ensure that the environment is secure. In some cases, security personnel may come to know about it well after the fact — after the service has been operational for a significant time period. This scenario is more common in large Fortune 500–type companies where decentralized and autonomous groups have the authority initiate these types of e-commerce–type implementations. Another common example today is wireless networks. There are well-publicized and known security issues with wireless. Wireless networks are, however, very easy to put up and can provide major benefits to users. In some companies, IT departments do not even know that wireless networks are attached to their network because business groups just decide to put them up without considering the security implications. When these networks are found, even the minimal level of security that is provided is not implemented. These are only a couple of examples out of many. The bottom line is that if security personnel are not aware of changes in the environment, it is difficult to provide the assurance of a secure environment.

This is where a security assessments fit in. A security assessment is the process of looking at the business and supporting technologies and determining what security risks are present. It is a process that management can use to determine whether the existing information security program is adequately addressing a company's security risks. It is also something that should be done on an ongoing basis to make sure that any security implications resulting from changes in the environment or new initiatives are addressed. In the cases of the two examples discussed in the last paragraph, a comprehensive security assessment would likely have discovered the changes and provided recommendations to address the risks.

Security assessments are broad in nature and cover people, processes, and technology. Assessments at a high level can be performed using the following methodology:

• Evaluate business processes and identify related security risks.
• Evaluate critical supporting technologies and perform testing to determine security vulnerabilities.
• Perform risk analysis and provide cost-effective recommendations to manage the security risks identified.

In the process outlined above, which is a high-level version of the assessment methodology discussed in this book, it is important to note that the business processes are the starting point. Without understanding the business processes, it is difficult to determine what the risks are. The key driver for the information security program is the list of risks identified when reviewing the business processes and critical data, which is basically what is done in a security assessment. Once the information security program is developed, all information security measures taken should clearly map back to a risk that was identified in this analysis. Recommendations from a security assessment should also map back to security risks related to business processes.

Depending on the type of business and the related business processes, the security risks can vary widely. For example, a company that is highly dependent on revenues from online commerce activities will be much more sensitive to any risks related to its Web site and in guarding the privacy of customer information. A company like this will probably see its Web site and the related business processes as the key risks. On the other hand, a manufacturing company would view the systems that support its manufacturing process and the systems where key manufacturing data reside as the key systems. This company might not really care that much about its Internet site.

The security assessment is essentially the process of evaluating the information security program and determining what is important to the business and whether it is adequately secured. Done on an ongoing basis, it is the process of periodically looking at the business in a holistic way to determine whether the existing information security program is properly addressing the security risks the company faces. With the dynamic nature of businesses today and the speed at which technology is changing, new security vulnerabilities surface all the time. It behooves companies to try to address these risks in a proactive manner rather than dealing with them after the fact. These risks range from organizational issues such as not having a strong termination policy where terminated employees' access to systems is properly revoked to technical system vulnerabilities. A regular security assessment process uncovers these issues so they can be addressed appropriately. In the context of the information security program, the security assessment process is what keeps it current — i.e., it is the constant evaluation. The security assessment process also helps to instill a culture where security is taken seriously. If personnel know that a regular security assessment is done, they will naturally become more aware of security issues.

One important aspect of security assessments is that they are dependent on the key elements of the information security program, which were discussed in the preceding section. In particular, executive support for security assessments is critical to their success. By its nature, the security assessment process will uncover security risks and potentially raise issues about how employees are doing their jobs. Using the example from the previous paragraph regarding the employee termination process, this is a weak process for some companies because no one owns it. If you look at your own company, you might find that after an employee leaves, it might be weeks or months before that person's access is removed from the company's systems. In some cases, IT may not even know of employee terminations on a timely basis. A successful termination process requires ownership and communication between multiple groups including human resources (HR), finance, IT, and others. In the context of a security assessment, raising an issue about terminations could make people feel uncomfortable, and as a result, you may not receive the cooperation necessary during an assessment. In these cases, executive support is critical so personnel know that they must be forthcoming and cooperative during the security assessment process.

The other important element of an information security program that is very helpful is security policies. If the company has a set of up-to-date security policies, they can be used as the basis against which to conduct the assessment. Although a lack of policies can be worked around by using publicly available best practice standards, policies are better because they reflect the specific risks facing the company and thus are a better standard against which to measure the company.

WHY CONDUCT A SECURITY ASSESSMENT?

In the previous section, we explained how the security assessment fits into the overall information security program. However, you may encounter cases where an executive or member of management might say that the company has a handle on security and that a security assessment is not necessary. You may encounter other companies that tell you that they feel secure and that nothing has ever happened to them before so why would it happen now. For any company, there are a number of reasons why a security assessment is important regardless of the environment, culture, size, etc. This is important to understand because there are times when you will have to convince management of the value of assessing the environment from a security perspective.

Reasons for conducting a security assessment include:

- Obtaining an independent view of security
- Managing security risks proactively
- Determining measures to take to address any regulatory concerns
- Justifying funds

OBTAINING AN INDEPENDENT VIEW OF SECURITY

Like a third-party audit, similar to how public companies are audited (notwithstanding some of the scandals that have surfaced as of this writing — e.g., the Enron debacle), an independent assessment of security is a valuable tool for management. A third party can be an outside company or an independent party within a company such as an internal audit department. If the party assessing is an internal audit department, you must ensure that they were not actively involved in the development or ongoing functioning of the security operations so that they can be independent.

Security assessments, if performed correctly, are an independent view of security, which validates whether security measures are properly aligned with the security risks a company is facing. The assessment process also uncovers vulnerabilities and leads to recommendations to remediate those vulnerabilities. A qualified independent third party conducting an assessment has several advantages including:

- *Objective and unbiased feedback* — Because of their independence, third parties have the ability to offer honest feedback about the information security program and how it stacks up. The recommendations that third parties make are objective and unbiased. Although you may receive the same information by not having a third party conduct the security assessment, you will not have the assurance that the assessment was objective.

- *Expertise and best practices* — Some companies do not have the expertise to conduct a security assessment. A qualified independent third party can provide the expertise and knowledge of best practices that will make the security assessment process more meaningful. If you engage the right third party with the appropriate skill sets, they can provide a different perspective because of their experience with other companies or groups. Remember that for a third party, security is their area of expertise and they have probably seen a variety of ways that environments are secured. If you use a third party, this experience and knowledge can be leveraged to improve your own information security program.
- *No politically motivated inhibitions* — Independent third parties do not tend to have any friends or enemies or relationships that might cloud their judgment during the security assessment process. As we discussed earlier, security assessments potentially uncover information about how securely your business is run. Some findings might embarrass someone or make someone defensive. Internal parties who do not have the required level of independence can be influenced by their relationships. Independent third parties, on the other hand, do not have these concerns. As a result, their results will be objective and unbiased.

MANAGING SECURITY RISKS PROACTIVELY

Ideally, security assessments should be performed on a regular basis because doing them often allows you to leverage what you already know about the business and just look at changes to the business on an ongoing basis. Basically, the first assessment is the "baseline," and all subsequent assessments address changes to the business based on the "baseline." This is an efficient and effective way to manage security risks. The security assessment process is a way for companies to look at the information security program and ensure that security risks are managed in a cost-effective manner. By conducting security assessments, companies have the ability to know what their risks are and what the associated impacts of those risks are. Based on this knowledge, companies can then make informed decisions on how to allocate funds and resources to manage security risks in a cost-effective manner. Without this process, resources for information security, including staffing and funds, may not be allocated properly. Stepping back periodically and evaluating the information security program provides a fresh perspective on whether the information security measures in place are appropriate.

One of the classic examples in recent years is intrusion detection. These systems can require significant administration time because of tasks related to updating detection signatures, reacting to alerts, and fine-tuning the system to minimize false alarms. Some companies have implemented intrusion detection systems without considering whether they have the resources to properly administer them or whether they really need them. In the end, many of these companies do not end up using intrusion detection. The result is a very expensive system on the network that is not managing any risk or providing any benefit to the company. In this example, a security assessment would have determined whether a need for intrusion detection exists. If the need were determined to be valid, the assessment would have also flagged the need for additional resources to administer the system or the possibility of outsourcing the function.

DETERMINING MEASURES TO TAKE TO ADDRESS ANY REGULATORY CONCERNS

Unlike the financial statements of publicly traded companies, which have to be audited by a third-party firm and where certain statements are filed with the Securities and Exchange Commission (SEC), most companies have no such regulatory requirement related to having their information security evaluated. For some industries, however, the government has felt compelled to pass laws to protect individuals' personal information. Two such laws that have been touched on already are the HIPAA (Health Insurance Portability and Accountability Act) and the GLBA (Gramm–Leach–Bliley Act).

HIPAA applies to health care–related companies, and part of this regulation is focused on information security. At a high level, this law mandates that health care–related companies have information security programs in place that reasonably protect patients' personally identifiable information (in electronic form). All aspects of an information security program, ranging from security policies and procedures, risk analysis, and awareness at the foundation level to different technologies that support the security policies, must be present.

GLBA does something similar for financial services companies. GLBA requires financial service companies to have adequate security measures in place to protect the privacy of customer information. The regulations also cover what institutions may and may not do with customer information. Also, similar to HIPAA, the law, at a high level, essentially requires a sound information security program.

The potential liabilities that health care and financial services companies face are enough in themselves to make them want to put good security measures in place. Legislation and the related threats are a clear justification for ensuring that related security requirements are in place.

The Federal Trade Commission (FTC) is taking a very active role in holding companies accountable for claims they make regarding security and privacy. The FTC has gone after many companies that have not provided a reasonable level of security based on claims companies have made.

With these laws in place, one of the challenges companies are having today is that it is not clear what is required to be in compliance — i.e., they do not know, from a governmental audit perspective, what is necessary to be compliant with legislation. As the U.S. government does more audits against these laws, the interpretation will become clearer. More importantly, empirical data related to the sizes of the fines will also be established making quantification of risk easier. A security assessment with a focus on meeting the requirements of these pieces of legislation is a useful tool in determining where the gaps are and what needs to be done to achieve compliance.

Besides these two laws, a number of other pieces of legislation affect companies from an information security perspective. Information security professionals can bring this type of expertise to the table to help ensure that companies are in compliance with legislation that affects them. Information security legislation is discussed in greater detail in Chapter 10 of this book.

JUSTIFICATION FOR FUNDS

In many companies, information security is perceived to be an expensive proposition. Information security programs often introduce new processes, which many perceive as being cumbersome or not worth doing. Information security programs also introduce security-related technology that could be very expensive to purchase, implement, and manage.

In today's environment, obtaining funds from shrinking budgets is no easy task. With information security–related spending, it is even worse because people do not necessarily see the value of it. For management, information security measures are sometimes viewed as "nice to haves" instead of "must haves."

Security assessments can provide this justification and demonstrate the value of information security. Remember that recommendations are developed as a result of the security assessment process and that recommendations should link back to security risks identified. The negative impacts associated with those risks can help demonstrate the value of implementing information security measures. This link between business process, risk, impact, and recommendation can help show management why it is important to provide funds for security measures. In this scenario, information security can be viewed as a way to control potential costs related to security incidents.

Another aspect to consider is looking at information security as a "revenue enhancer." An example of where security is a revenue enhancer is e-commerce. Companies that generate revenues through e-commerce activities know that one of the main considerations for consumers when shopping online is the security of their personal information — e.g., name, address, and credit card information. Security as it pertains to e-commerce can be viewed in two ways:

First, inadequate security measures can lead to a security breach where consumers' information is compromised resulting in short-term loss of revenue because consumers would be hesitant to shop with that company. More importantly, it would also result in some permanent loss of customers leading to a long-term negative impact on revenue. This, by itself, is a compelling case that justifies strong information security measures for e-commerce.

Second, a security certification (e.g., BBB *OnLine*) might be worth spending money on because it is something that might bring customers to an e-commerce site. Customers might look for some third-party certification, and it might be the criterion that determines whether a consumer will shop at a site. The e-commerce company would suffer against its competitors if it did not have the third-party seal that its competitors have. In this scenario, spending on information security can be viewed as a "revenue enhancer."

Companies often perform security assessments because IT management is looking for a third party to help justify information security initiatives. Revenue enhancement as a reason is very compelling and in that case, the questions will center around what would happen if those measures were not taken and how quickly the investment in the information security initiative will pay off. Return on Investment (ROI) is something to think about when proposing a security solution and is something that can be difficult when trying to demonstrate the probability that something might happen.

Risk analysis and the concept of ROI are discussed in detail in Chapter 8 — Risk Analysis and Final Presentation.

THE SECURITY ASSESSMENT PROCESS

We now have an understanding of information security programs and how security assessments fit in. We also know some reasons why companies would potentially conduct a security assessment. As with other processes, it is critical to have a methodology for conducting a security assessment to ensure that:

- Assessments are performed in an efficient manner.
- The process facilitates the gathering and analysis of all relevant information.
- Assessments provide the client with a "security roadmap" that can be used to improve the information security program.

Assessments can take time and require the time of staff from the client. Because client personnel are busy people, the assessment methodology must be adequately refined to use time efficiently. Assessments are intrusive to some degree because employees from the client who are involved must take time from their daily responsibilities to provide the information necessary for an assessment. Therefore, its important that time with them is efficiently used to gather the information required.

The next five chapters will provide a detailed discussion of a methodology for conducting security assessments. Figure 3.9 illustrates that methodology. The diagram details each of the phases along with the specific steps in each phase. The methodology is meant to be followed so that each of the steps in each phase is completed before beginning the next phase (with some exceptions). The approach is flexible and provides a structure around conducting assessments.

The five key phases and key tasks in each phase are:

- *Planning* — Define the scope, logistics, and scheduling.
- *Initial Preparation* — Gather publicly available information; prepare initial documentation.
- *Business Process Evaluation* — Gain understanding of the key business processes; meet with business process owners; identify critical supporting technologies.
- *Technology Evaluation* — Test critical technologies.
- *Risk Analysis and Final Presentation* — Quantify risks and develop recommendations.

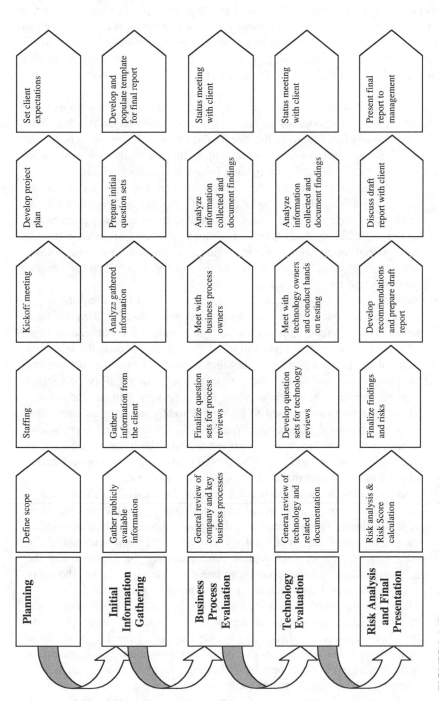

Planning
- Define scope
- Staffing
- Kickoff meeting
- Develop project plan
- Set client expectations

Initial Information Gathering
- Gather publicly available information
- Gather information from the client
- Analyze gathered information
- Prepare initial question sets
- Develop and populate template for final report

Business Process Evaluation
- General review of company and key business processes
- Finalize question sets for process reviews
- Meet with business process owners
- Analyze information collected and document findings
- Status meeting with client

Technology Evaluation
- General review of technology and related documentation
- Develop question sets for technology reviews
- Meet with technology owners and conduct hands on testing
- Analyze information collected and document findings
- Status meeting with client

Risk Analysis and Final Presentation
- Risk analysis & Risk Score calculation
- Finalize findings and risks
- Develop recommendations and prepare draft report
- Discuss draft report with client
- Present final report to management

FIGURE 3.9 Security assessment methodology.

Many readers of this book have probably carried out some or most of this methodology. The presentation here will put that methodology into a structured format, where each step of the assessment is clear and where it is easy to see exactly where you are in the process at any given time. The discussion of the methodology will also show why each of the steps is important. As you go through the next five chapters and read the details of the methodology, keep these key points to in mind:

- *The methodology is flexible.* Security assessments will rarely go exactly the way the methodology is laid out, so you need to be flexible. The methodology is meant to be flexible to allow for such things as scheduling conflicts or resource issues. For example, the client may ask you to do the first two phases, Planning and Initial Information Gathering, in a compressed time frame in which some steps may not be performed as thoroughly as you like (or maybe not at all). In this case, the other phases might take longer because you were not able to do as much preparation as you would have liked. The methodology is meant to provide a framework within which you can work, and at times you will have to be flexible with the steps, which is acceptable, as long as you stay within the general framework of this methodology.
- *Steps can be combined.* In cases, you may be able to combine steps. If this can be done and it makes the process more efficient, then it should be done. For example, consider a security assessment for a small company, where you only conduct a handful of interviews. In this case, the last three steps of the planning phase — holding the kickoff meeting, developing the project plan, and setting client expectations — might all be performed together because the scope of work might be very limited. Part of the kickoff meeting can be used to go over a rough project plan consisting of interviews and system testing. You can also set the client's expectations regarding the assessment in the same meeting. The point is that each of the steps should be addressed. You should take advantage of opportunities to combine steps and make the process more efficient.
- *Understanding the business is fundamental.* The basis for this methodology is that a security assessment starts with having a solid understanding of the business. You will read this time and again in this book. A fundamental aspect of this methodology is that you cannot understand the criticality of security risks without understanding the business and the mission-critical business processes. The methodology stresses the point that the business drives security and not the other way around.
- *Communication with clients should be emphasized.* One of the common steps in each of the phases of the methodology is communication with the client. Clients should always be kept aware of the progress of the assessment and of the findings that have been uncovered. This is important for two reasons. First, clients have the opportunity to provide additional information that might change the nature of a finding. Second, the client is prepared to talk about it when the final report is presented to management.

Clients should not feel blindsided by anything in the final report resulting from the assessment.

- *Preparation should be emphasized.* In each of the first four phases, there is some element of preparation, which is a key concept in this security assessment methodology. Preparation is in the form of doing research on companies and preparing question sets for meetings with clients. Preparation is important because it enables you to ask more informed questions during the assessment. Instead of wasting time on things you could have learned by preparing, you can spend the time in interviews talking about more meaningful aspects of the business. In addition, people are busy, so it is in everyone's best interest to use time with the client efficiently. Good preparation allows you to do this.

EXECUTIVE SUMMARY

This chapter was a discussion of the definition of information security programs and their key components, how a security assessment fits in, why companies would conduct a security assessment, and the high-level security assessment methodology.

An information security program consists of people, processes, and technology and is essentially the conglomeration of all steps a company takes to protect its information assets. The key components of an information security program include:

- *Security strategy* — Central component of an information security program; overall information security strategy based on the security risks the business is facing
- *Security policies and procedures* — Security requirements and processes to implement the security strategy
- *Security organization* — Personnel who ensure that the information security program is up to date and who conduct enforcement activities related to information security
- *Executive support* — Support from management that is critical in helping to ensure that employees take the information security program seriously
- *Toolsets* — Tools to automate tasks that are necessary for enforcement of good security practices but are virtually impossible to perform manually
- *Enforcement* — Proactively checking for compliance with security policies and procedures to ensure that the information security program is effective

Due to the dynamic nature of companies, security risks are always changing. Consequently, the information security program should be constantly evolving to address current risks. The security assessment process is essentially the process for ensuring that the information security program is addressing the security risks a company faces. It is a constant evaluation of the information security program to ensure that security measures are aligned with the security risks facing a company.

Companies conduct security assessments for a variety of reasons. Some of the key reasons include the following:

- *Obtaining an independent view of security* — Companies want an independent assessment of how well their information security program is addressing the risks facing the company.
- *Managing security risks proactively* — Constant evaluation of the information security program helps to effectively allocate resources for information security.
- *Determining measures to take to address any regulatory concerns* — Many companies are regulated by information security legislation or regulations promulgated by the government such as GLBA, HIPAA, and requirements set forth by the FTC; a security assessment can help them determine what measures they need to take to achieve compliance.
- *Justification for funds* — Some companies have security assessments conducted to help justify funds for information security initiatives; a security assessment can help show how information security can enhance revenues or reduce the risk related to security vulnerabilities and thus demonstrate the value of making investments in information security.

Once the business drivers for an assessment are identified and a need for a security assessment is established, it is critical to conduct it using a sound methodology that ensures that all relevant aspects of the assessment are covered in an efficient manner. In the methodology detailed in this book, the five key phases of the security assessment methodology are:

- *Planning* — Define the scope, logistics, and scheduling.
- *Initial Preparation* — Gather publicly available information; prepare initial documentation.
- *Business Process Evaluation* — Gain understanding of the key business processes and identify critical supporting technologies.
- *Technology Evaluation* — Evaluate and test critical technologies.
- *Risk Analysis and Final Presentation* — Quantify risks, develop recommendations, and present the final report to the client.

4 Planning

Once the decision is made that a security assessment will be performed, careful planning must be done to ensure that it is smooth and efficient. Good planning will save time and yield better results. Planning for the security assessment refers to logistic aspects such as scheduling with the client, specifically the subject matter experts who will participate in the security assessment. The key task in this phase, which will influence the scheduling and resources, is the scope definition process. You must be able to define what you are going to do in the security assessment so that you can properly plan the time and resources to complete the assessment.

The key activities in the planning phase of the security assessment are listed below and will be discussed in detail in this chapter:

- Defining the scope
- Staffing
- Kickoff meeting
- Development of the project plan
- Setting the expectations of the client

DEFINING THE SCOPE

The scope should define and put some boundaries around your work. Defining the scope (Figure 4.1) is one of the most important steps in a security assessment because it influences everything else you do. This is especially the case in larger organizations where there is much to review but less so in smaller companies where virtually every part of the business will be part of the scope. Developing the scope should be a two-way conversation between yourself and the client. Although the client might have some ideas about the scope, you should also use your own expertise to offer advice to the client on defining the scope.

Implications that you must think about as the scope is being developed include:

- *Time and resources required to complete the assessment* — You will need to schedule the right number of resources with the right skill sets.
- *Upcoming changes to the business that might affect the scope* — If certain changes in the business are upcoming, they might affect the scope and thus, should be considered.

Being clear on the scope of the security assessment is ultimately beneficial for everyone. From the perspective of the party performing the assessment, it is important in planning and also in meeting the expectations of the client. From the perspective of the client, it provides a clear idea of the work to be performed.

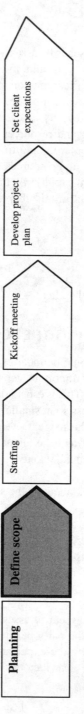

FIGURE 4.1 Define scope.

If the scope of the security assessment is not clearly defined right in the beginning, it can be very detrimental to the entire assessment process because of the gap between the work performed and the client's expectations. How do we close the gap and ensure that everyone is on the same page as it relates to the security assessment? Essentially, the scope has to be defined in enough detail so that everyone understands it. One major mistake that is sometimes made is to define the scope at such a high level that there is too much room for interpretation, resulting in inconsistent views of the scope of work.

To properly define the scope, you must first understand what the business drivers are for the security assessment. This will probably not be clear until you discuss with the client why a security assessment is desired in the first place. Security assessments may be conducted for a variety of reasons. By having a clear understanding of the reasons for the assessment, you will be able to work with the client to develop the scope and set their expectations. You will find that you end up guiding the client in the scope definition process by discussing the business drivers.

Business drivers can vary and can include such things as regulatory concerns or significant changes that have taken place in the environment. Using business drivers, you can help the client "put a box" around what needs to be in the scope of work. This is probably the most critical aspect of defining the scope and where the actual scope is defined.

Once the scope is defined, the next step is to agree to a set of standards or benchmarks that will be used in the assessment. These can be the clients' own security policies and procedures, specific laws such as the Health Insurance Portability and Accountability Act (HIPAA), or a set of external standards such as International Standards Organization (ISO) 17799. It could also be a combination of standards. You should offer your expertise in helping to determine what standard would be appropriate.

Once the scope is defined and the standards are agreed to, you must manage to the agreed-upon scope. One of the most significant issues you deal with is "scope creep," which is essentially changing the scope of the work once it has begun. The changes can include increasing or completely changing the scope. Both of these problems can lead to an unsuccessful assessment.

Four important aspects of scope definition are:

- Business drivers
- Items to include in the scope
- Standards
- Managing the scope

In the subsequent sections, each of these aspects of scope definition will be discussed in greater detail.

BUSINESS DRIVERS

As stated earlier, understanding the business drivers or reason for the security assessment is critical in defining the scope. It will not only affect the scope from a coverage perspective, it will also affect the approach in terms of what standards are selected as benchmarks and the nature of the content of the final report. Business drivers can vary greatly and are dependent on a number of factors including:

- Management's attitude on the importance of information security
- The risk environment in which the company operates
- Changes happening in the business (e.g., significant employee turnover, merger or acquisition)
- Security-related events that may have taken place — e.g., an incident in which systems were compromised

The business drivers for the assessment will help determine how wide or narrow the scope is and what type of information the client is seeking. The main business drivers you will see when conducting security assessments include:

- The client is taking a proactive approach to security.
- Regulatory concerns have prompted the assessment.
- The client wants to justify additional funds for information security initiatives.
- A security incident has occurred.
- Disgruntled employees have been terminated.
- Changes have occurred in the information technology (IT) environment.
- A merger or acquisition is under consideration or has occurred.

Each of these business drivers is discussed in detail below.

Proactive Approach to Security

This is the ideal scenario for any company. Companies that are proactively looking at their information security programs probably have some part of an information security program already in place, but because of changes in the business or because they have not reviewed security in some time, they want to determine how well their information security program is addressing the risks facing them. In this scenario, clients want to know where they can improve and what steps they need to take on a short-term and long-term basis to ensure their environment is secure — i.e., a security roadmap that will help them identify and prioritize security-related initiatives. These clients are likely to have an assessment done on a regular basis, where each assessment builds on the one previously performed. These clients will also likely want to look at most of the environment in the first assessment and then focus on specific areas in future periodic assessments.

From a scope perspective, these clients want to look at everything. They tend to be cautious and want to make sure that their information security program is adequate. As a result, it can be challenging to effectively scope this type of assessment.

Regulatory Concerns

HIPAA, the Gramm–Leach–Bliley Act (GLBA) and other laws have forced companies to have information security programs. Companies can face significant fines if these requirements are not adequately addressed. With the breadth of some of these requirements, companies often do not know where to start, so an assessment is performed to determine what needs to be done to become compliant with a given law or regulation. In fact, for both HIPAA and GLBA, part of the legislation includes a requirement to conduct a risk analysis. Clients having an assessment conducted based on regulatory concerns want to know the specific steps to take to achieve compliance. You will definitely use the law or regulation to help define scope and as a standard against which to measure the information security program.

The deliverable resulting from this type of security assessment should be a set of findings, risks, and recommendations that will identify security initiatives to help achieve compliance with the law or regulation that is relevant to the client's industry. Because the client is most concerned with achieving compliance, the findings should map back to specific parts of the law or regulation and the recommendations should help ensure compliance. This type of document is also useful to show to government auditors who audit for compliance with a given law or regulation.

Justification for Additional Funds for Information Security Initiatives

In companies today, budgets are very tight and most expenditures are questioned, particularly those for which a solid return on investment (ROI) cannot be shown. With information security, it is sometimes difficult to justify money because of the perception that information security initiatives are not necessary. The attitude "nothing has happened, so why spend money for security" often prevails.

Management does not always understand the risks associated with a security weakness and that spending money proactively to fix something is far cheaper than letting a security incident take place and dealing with the aftermath. In these cases, a security assessment can highlight areas of concern and demonstrate what risks are present in a given environment. The security assessment can also look at the risks in aggregate and show management the potential impacts of potential security incidents. This type of exercise helps management see where it might be smart to invest in securing the assets of the company. Clients who are looking to justify funding probably have an idea of where they want to spend the money. In these cases, the assessment may be focused on one or a small set of areas. One thing to keep in mind is that you should always provide input on where it makes sense to include or not include items in the scope of work.

Security Incident Has Occurred

For some companies, the importance of information security is not always apparent. For these companies, if security is not tied to avoiding something tangible, such as loss of revenue, additional cost, or negative publicity, they do not necessarily see the value of information security. It sometimes takes a security incident to make them notice the importance of information security. An incident such as a Web site being defaced or a network being compromised can immediately raise security awareness. After the realization that a security incident took place, the next questions from management are "what other security weaknesses do we have and how do we prevent another incident like the one we had from happening again?" They want an overall picture of where they have security weaknesses and they want to secure the environment so a similar security incident does not take place again. A security incident is a very common reason to have an assessment done because companies do not know what other weaknesses exist in their environment or whether the same security incident can happen again. In this scenario, a security assessment is perfect for determining those security weaknesses that need to be addressed. Clients who want an assessment because they had an incident are looking for a comprehensive set of findings and recommendations to help them lock down their environment as soon as possible. These types of assessments can be very technical or very process focused depending on the nature of the security assessment and the nature of the recent security incident. As with the other business drivers, you should advise the client in defining the scope so that the risk of another security incident is minimized.

These assessments also tend to have a certain sense of urgency about them. The urgency becomes more significant depending on the type of business environment the client operates in and the severity of the incident that occurred. For example, companies that operate in a regulated environment where a security breach could mean a penalty of some sort might be very anxious to get the assessment done quickly.

Disgruntled Employees

As of this writing, the country is in the midst of an economic downturn, which has resulted in layoffs in companies across the board. Many of these employees are not let go under the best of circumstances. In a 2002 survey of approximately 500 information security professionals performed by the Federal Bureau of Investigation (FBI) and Computer Security Institute, 75 percent of those surveyed said "disgruntled employees were the most likely source of insider attacks during the preceding 12 months."[1] Companies face tremendous risks from these employees, especially from those who worked in IT and who are technically savvy. Individuals with IT skills who are laid off can wreak havoc on a company's IT systems, depending on their level of technical competence. With the distributed environment we work in today, the risk related to disgruntled employees is greater than ever because control is not very centralized, unlike the mainframe days where everything was happening in one place.

If the driver for the assessment is a terminated disgruntled employee, the assessment can become a fire drill of sorts. The typical scenario would be that some very good technical person who had all the administrator and root authorizations and knew the company inside and out was let go under negative circumstances. This type of employee poses a significant risk because of the individual's knowledge and level of access. In this case, the security assessment is performed after the environment is immediately locked down — critical passwords are changed, access is removed, etc. Clients having a security assessment done under these circumstances want to know how to secure the environment from a process and technology perspective. They are also probably very concerned about the insider threat. The client will expect some emphasis on process in the security assessment, especially as it pertains to access administration.

Defining the scope in these cases will focus on the processes that the disgruntled employee was engaged in. Clients will be interested in how key processes such as ID administration work. They will also want to know how to keep systems locked down — e.g., system hardening measures, vulnerability management.

Changes in the IT Environment

When the IT architecture is overhauled, issues arise related to performance, administration, and security. Changes in architecture can bring about process changes and technical changes as well as changes in overall roles and responsibilities. All of these changes potentially have security implications. When IT architecture changes are being made, security should be an integral part of the design effort before anything is actually executed. However, that does not always happen. It is very possible for the IT architecture to be designed and implemented before any thought is given to how secure the changes will be or what security risks may have been introduced as a result of the changes. Once someone from the company realizes that security was not adequately considered during the design and implementation phases, they may want a security assessment done to determine what (if any) security risks exist. Managers who want assessments done under these circumstances tend to be focused on the security implications of the new architecture and what adjustments need to be made to the information security program. The assessment should focus on the new design, how it supports the business, and related security implications. This scope can be defined easily with clear boundaries.

When changes in the IT environment are the reason for the assessment, you will need to have someone with expertise in the systems that the client is using. The final report resulting from the assessment will also have to identify any security weaknesses related to the changes in the environment and ways to specifically address those security weaknesses.

Mergers and Acquisitions

Security assessment can occur at two different times with regard to mergers and acquisitions. First, when a company is purchasing or merging with another company, there is normally some due diligence to validate details about the potential acquisition. This due diligence, at the minimum, includes a financial review. As companies realize the IT integration and security challenges of merging companies, IT and security representatives are becoming involved in the due diligence process. The impact of IT and security can impact the actual cost of an acquisition, which if significant enough, can affect a decision about whether or not to acquire. A security assessment as part of the due diligence process can provide information on what the potential security issues might be once the merger or acquisition takes place and what measures can be taken to mitigate those risks. This proactive approach to security ultimately leads to better security. Also, because the information security measures are determined before the merger or acquisition, the risk of re-work is minimized.

The second scenario related to mergers and acquisitions occurs after the merger or acquisition has taken place and the companies have been integrated. The security assessment at this stage is to determine how secure the combined environment is. The security assessment process will entail reviewing what the new risks are as a result of the merger or acquisition and determining whether there are adequate security measures to mitigate the risks. If security was not addressed during the integration process, the security assessment will help determine the risks and mitigation strategies and provide a roadmap outlining specific security initiatives for securing the combined entity.

In either case, security implications relative to processes and technology are present when dealing with mergers and acquisitions. Information security programs have to be extended and modified to address business requirements of the newer and larger company. Cultural, organizational, and technical challenges must be dealt with in fairly short order to minimize significant security risks.

The scope of a security assessment in these cases will be focused on the areas of integration between the companies. It will cover business processes, technology, and the subsequent integration of the company's technologies, as well as roles and responsibilities from a security perspective. As an example, one of the typical areas that will be covered is the integration of the security architectures of the two companies.

In developing the scope, you should try to tie the scope back to the areas of integration between the two companies (unless the company wants a more comprehensive review for other reasons).

Scope Definition

Once you understand the business drivers of the security assessment, it is much easier to define the scope. Although the client might understand what needs to be in the scope at a high level, you should now define the scope in more detailed terms.

The purpose of clearly defining the scope is so you can properly plan and execute the assessment. The scope should be expressed in terms of the areas of the business or some specific aspect of the business that you would cover — e.g., a specific business unit, activities related to a legislative requirement (HIPAA security requirements). The scope should also define the number of interviews you will conduct and a high-level idea of what technology will be tested. This is important because the real drivers of how much work will be involved in the security assessment are the number of interviews you will be conducting and the amount of technical testing you will be doing. The more you can specify up front, the better you can plan the assessment. Keep in mind that there will be some changes because it is very difficult to know exactly what you will do in the assessment. For example, during the scoping stage, you may have some high-level idea of what technology you will be testing. However, this will not be confirmed until you gain an understanding of the business and what the critical business processes are. The key is to define the scope in a way that allows you to effectively plan and execute it.

To find out the number of people you will need to talk to, you need to ask some questions about the company's business processes. Depending on the business driver for the security assessment, the client may or may not know what business processes are relevant. To develop the scope, you will have to determine at a high level what the key business processes are.

When developing the scope, you will face two situations. In the first case, the client may just say, "look at everything." You will find this in cases where a client is proactively looking at security or there have been significant changes in the company's IT environment and the client does not really have an idea of where the company is from a security perspective. The other case is where a client has a very good idea of scope and knows exactly what needs to be looked at. An example of this is when an assessment is done after a disgruntled employee leaves.

Let us take the first case where the client is not sure what needs to be looked at and is looking to you to provide guidance on what is relevant. A good place to start is to have an open discussion about what the company does. From here, the discussion can turn to a number of topics including:

- How are the goods and services delivered?
- What are the key processes involved in delivering these goods and services?
- What are the key supporting technologies upon which these processes depend?
- Who are the key individuals and organizations involved in the process?
- What other processes with security implications are there?

With the general questions listed above, you should get a sense for developing the scope. As you will see later, these questions are asked in much more detail once you start the assessment. For this stage, however, we only need to know enough information to help us define the scope. Consider the example below of going through a scope development exercise.

EXAMPLE — MANUFACTURING CLIENT SCOPE DEFINITION

A manufacturing client is going to have a security assessment done. This client has tripled its user base over the past three years and has made significant upgrades to the IT environment. For this client, let us take the questions above and use that process to help determine the scope:

Information Gathering

- How are goods and services delivered?
  - Goods are manufactured at a plant.
  - Key customers are large discount department stores.
  - The company uses a business-to-business (B2B) application to communicate with suppliers and procure materials.
- What are the key processes involved in delivering these goods and services?
  - Customers place orders through a customer care department.
  - Customer care interfaces with the shipping department and finance area.
  - Manufacturing uses order data to help them forecast operations.

- What are the key technologies in place?
  - The client is running a network with 30 servers that include Windows 2000 and UNIX servers.
  - There are approximately 200 users on the network.
  - Order entry, shipping, and finance are all running off one application (finance) and manufacturing is on another application; the finance application interfaces with the manufacturing application.
  - Besides the finance and manufacturing applications, there are only general office (word processor, spreadsheet) applications.
  - The finance application and manufacturing application are on the same server; the database for both systems are on separate servers.
  - There is an Oracle database that contains all information in different tables.
  - Citrix thin client is used as a solution for remote access and for access in manufacturing locations.
- Who are the key individuals and organizations involved in the process?
  - Five system administrators manage all of the systems.
  - An IT Manager is in charge of the IT function.
  - Three IT support personnel handle help desk calls.
  - Customer care consists of 10 people including a supervisor.
  - The shipping area consists of five individuals including a supervisor.
  - The finance area consists of 10 people in the different areas including accounts receivable.
- What other processes/information with security implications are there?
  - No formal security policies or procedures are in place.
  - Physical security is handled by facilities personnel.
  - Adding and deleting users is done by a combination effort between human resources (HR) and IT.
  - An incident handling process is in place.

All of the information above is gained through a discussion with the client. In some cases, you may have a history with the client and thus already know much of this information.

Analysis

The next step is to take this raw information and break it down into a format where you can define the scope and related work effort. The key facts we can glean from the information above include:

- The scope in this case could be a general security assessment of the company's operations because the client is looking at everything. It is evident that the client does not really have a handle on how the company is doing from a security perspective.
- The company is a pure manufacturing company.
- The finance and manufacturing systems are critical to the business.
- The B2B application is important from a supply chain perspective.
- The company is running a Windows 2000 network.
- The key departments or groups within the company include manufacturing, finance, customer care, shipping, and IT.

Based on the information above, the scope of work involves a general review of the entire business and associated security exposures.

Define the Scope of Work

From an organization/business perspective, the scope will cover the company's entire operation. The next step is to define the activities that will be performed during the course of the assessment based on the information obtained. This process, which is in line with the methodology discussed in this book, is a way to help us plan the work and determine what type of resources will be required to complete the assessment.

As you will see when we start discussing the assessment process at the client site in subsequent phases, the main items that drive the work effort include interviews with key individuals to gain an understanding of business processes and associated security exposures and the detailed technology testing. The technology you actually test will be determined from interviews with the business process owners, which will primarily happen in the Business Process Evaluation phase.

During this process of defining the scope and determining the work effort, some guesswork is necessary. Keep in mind that this process is for estimation purposes for determining the appropriate time and resources to complete the assessment. Because this scope will be shared with the client, this process will also help set expectations with the client about the specific activities to take place in the assessment.

The four items to work through during the scope definition process include:

- Interviews with management and process owners
- Interviews with security personnel
- Technical testing
- Determination of standards

1. Interviews with Management and Process Owners

The purpose of these interviews is to gain a good understanding of business processes and identify potential security risks. The list of individuals below is based on the initial discussion of the company, what it does, and how it is organized. The time spent for each interview is an estimation based on a number of factors including how much information was gained during the initial preparation and how complicated you think the processes will be. As a standard estimate, you should try to budget approximately one to two hours with each interviewee to make sure you have enough time to obtain the necessary information. For each of these individuals, you will have to prepare the appropriate question sets, as discussed in the next phase. In this example, the people to meet include the following:

- IT manager
- One system administrator
- IT help desk personnel
- Order entry process owner
- Shipping process owner
- Manufacturing application owner

- Finance application owner
- B2B application owner
- System administrator for servers running finance and manufacturing applications and database(s)
- Human resources personnel handling addition of new users, termination of users, and orientation-type issues such as educating users about acceptable use

The list above represents the key areas of the business to help us understand the business and determine where some of the security vulnerabilities might be. From a time perspective, you can estimate that these interviews will take probably 18 to 24 hours total to be safe.

2. Security Personnel

As part of this effort, you must cover the essential areas of security that might not be covered with the appropriate process owners such as the following:

- User ID administration
- Physical security
- Backup and recovery
- Change management
- Incident handling

3. Technical Testing

The technical testing in this case includes a combination of automated testing using tools and manual testing. The client has identified the critical systems, which include the network, the finance and manufacturing systems, and the B2B application, which requires Internet connectivity. The time estimate for this work depends on the skill sets you have in place (or will get for the assessment) and the tools you have in place. For this particular assessment, you should perform some combination of scans on the network, running specific tools on the database and the B2B application, and some manual testing. Note that this is a preliminary list of technologies to test, which is all right for scope purposes. The list will be finalized after business processes are analyzed and critical technologies to be tested are identified. Below is the preliminary list:

- Network
- Finance application
- Manufacturing application
- Database
- B2B application

Time estimates for doing the technology evaluation will vary based on what you can do using automated tools and what you will have to do manually. Someone technical should probably estimate the time for doing this testing.

4. Standards

The final aspect of developing the scope is deciding on standards to use. Standards could mean internal standards such as company security policies and procedures or external standards such as ISO 17799. With this client, no security policies and procedures are in place. You should talk about best practice standards such as ISO 17799 and technical standards such as the National Institute of Standards and Technology (NIST) standards. In this case, the client is probably expecting you to make some suggestions about standards to use. As an independent party, you should suggest what standard would be appropriate to use for the assessment.

At this point, the scope of work for this security assessment is defined. You should also have a fairly good sense for the timing and skill sets required to do the assessment. Keep in mind that this is an estimate at this point. It is very possible that some things might change as a result of information you uncover during the assessment. Minor changes should be expected. For more significant changes, there should be a process for changing the scope.

POTENTIAL SCOPE ISSUES

Arguably, properly defining the scope is the most critical aspect of a security assessment. This is especially the case in large environments, where there is potentially so much to review. Because scope definition is very important, it is valuable to go through some of the common problems you might face when you go through the exercise of defining the scope and as you conduct the security assessment.

Scope Creep

Scope creep is a typical problem in consulting engagements where the original agreed-upon scope is significantly changed or expanded. As you discover security problems, they will naturally lead you to other areas that you did not necessarily plan for or have the right skill sets for. Scope creep is managed by sticking to the agreed-upon scope of work to the extent possible. Through the regular status meetings, you must educate the client right from the beginning about staying within the scope. Clients must understand that any significant changes to the scope will be handled through a change control process to allow for the potential changes in timing and resources. As a security consultant (or internal employee) performing the assessment, if you do not manage scope creep, you run the risk of not having the time or the appropriate skill sets to handle the security assessment and thereby not meeting the client's expectations. As you go through the evaluation, it is important to keep referring to the scope so you can stay focused.

Incorrect Assumptions

As you plan the work based on the scope, you make certain assumptions about the company based on what the client is telling you. There will be cases where certain key assumptions will be made that are incorrect and will impact your work. For example, the client might tell you that there is a network topology diagram that can be reviewed. During the assessment, however, you may discover that the diagram is two years old and was not updated to reflect significant changes made during the last six months. In this case, because the network diagram is essentially useless, you will be forced to spend time mapping the network to understand what is on the network and what it looks like. Depending on the size of the network, this can take a significant amount of time.

Another example is where the client has taken on the responsibility of arranging interviews with the business process owners. You are completely dependent on the client to set up these meetings, but you still are accountable for certain work to be completed in a given time frame. If the client does not handle these logistical responsibilities properly, your work will be impacted.

The point is that key assumptions that can impact your work should be documented and agreed to up front. These assumptions should be discussed in detail with clients, who should understand their role and the dependencies.

Lack of Standards

The client might tell you that the company has security policies and procedures in place and that they should be used as standards. When you start conducting the assessment, you might realize that the policies are so high level that they really cannot be used as a standard and the procedures are mostly nonexistent. You are now faced with a situation where you have nothing to use as a standard. In this case, you must talk to the client about using another standard or trying to "interpret" the existing security policies with enough detail so that they can be used as a standard. If you take the route of interpreting the high-level policies, it can involve a very significant amount of additional work. You must agree to a standard at the outset of the assessment in any case. As a security practitioner, you should present the client with options for standards. Chapter 9 of this book discusses some of the more recognized information security standards.

Staffing

At this point, the scope of the security assessment is defined and the type of skill sets required is known for the most part. You are ready to start thinking about staffing (Figure 4.2).

There are two aspects to staffing. First, the party performing the assessment must assemble their team. Second, the client has to decide whether to use internal employees or a third party.

Note: For purposes of this methodology, we will generally assume that a third-party consultant is conducting the security assessment. If there are differences in how an internal resource and a third-party consultant might approach something, the difference is stated.

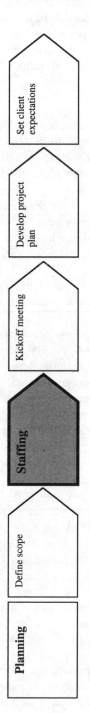

FIGURE 4.2 Staffing.

As a result, you will notice throughout the rest of the book references to "client," which will be the company being assessed. In this section, however, we will discuss staffing from both the consultant's perspective (i.e., gathering the right skill sets) and the client's perspective (i.e., internal versus third-party consultant). Clearly, the client would have made their decision well before this stage of the assessment.

CONSULTANT'S PERSPECTIVE

From a consultant's viewpoint, assembling the right resources is critical in having a successful assessment. You will need to determine the staff based on what you have defined in the scope in the last section. At this point, you should have done a fair amount of pre-sales activity to give you a good sense for what the company is all about.

The first step is to inventory all of the different skill sets you need to conduct the security assessment. Use your knowledge to write down the different skill sets with a rating of how strong the resource has to be in a given area. When creating this inventory, consider the industry, technology in use, and what tools you might use in conducting the assessment.

Based on that knowledge and how you defined the scope, you must assemble a staff. Some considerations to think about when putting a staff together are as follows:

- *Maturity* — Assessments by their nature find weaknesses, and at times this can become sensitive with clients. People conducting these assessments should have a certain maturity level to handle adverse situations, uncooperative clients, etc. and get the job done. If you turn off a client once or offend them, it can make the entire assessment difficult.
- *Industry experience* — Different industries have their own nuances (e.g., regulations, unique business processes), which are useful to know about. For example, if you are doing an assessment on a company in an industry with regulations, you may want to find someone with that particular experience. Note that not everyone on the team needs to have that experience. As long as there is one person, that is of great help.
- *Process experience* — As you will see in this methodology, security is very much about process and the nuts and bolts of how things are done. A person with process experience can be helpful in interviewing business process owners (this will be discussed in Chapter 6 — Business Process Review).
- *Technology experience* — You should get a sense of the technology that the client has in place and ensure that you have people on the team who are familiar with those technologies. Depending on how critical a particular technology is, you may want to find someone with significant experience in a given technology. The other aspect of technical experience is based on what tools you think you might run on the client's IT environment.
- *Ensuring that all areas are adequately covered* — This consideration is really a catch-all. Go back and look at the inventory of skill sets and make sure that all the skill sets are covered.

Staffing is somewhat dynamic, and you may need to make some changes as you go further into the assessment. However, if the staffing exercise at this stage is thorough, the modifications you will need to make later will be minimal at best.

CLIENT'S PERSPECTIVE

The client must choose between going to an outside firm to conduct the assessment or using internal resources. The client's choice of who does the assessment is driven by a number of factors including:

- *Funding allocated for the project* — Money always plays a big part in these projects and depending on the funding or lack thereof, this can have an impact on this decision. If funds are used for an assessment, they must be justified, particularly if there are internal resources that can do the job.
- *Business driver for the assessment* — As discussed in the previous section, the business driver for the assessment will play a part in determining who will ultimately perform it. For example, when dealing with an assessment prompted by a disgruntled employee situation, it might be a good idea to have outside consultants involved because of the sensitivity. The client might not want people inside the company to know too much, and the use of internal resources might involve a conflict of interests.
- *Resource availability* — If the decision is made to have internal employees perform the assessment, they must be able to take time away from their regular jobs. For example, if everyone is stretched to the limit and cannot afford the time, it might be difficult to have internal employees conduct the assessment. On the other hand, if the decision is made to go to a third party, you might find that the third party you want does not have availability for a significant period of time. In either case, the client must look at availability for qualified people to come in and do the assessment.

Besides the considerations above, a number of advantages and disadvantages should be considered when determining who does the assessment. The client has to choose between using internal resources or outside consultants. In smaller companies, it will probably be an outside firm because it is difficult to find any internal employees who would not have some conflict of interest. In large companies, however, there are independent groups such as the internal audit group.

The next sections discuss the advantages and disadvantages of using internal resources versus outside consulting firms.

Internal Employees

When using internal resources, the employees' knowledge of the company can be leveraged. Internal employees, especially those who have had exposure to many areas of the business, can provide a significant amount of the knowledge required in a security assessment. One of the main points in this book is that the foundation of an effective security assessment is that security must be evaluated in the context of the company's business. The security assessment methodology must begin with understanding the business. To take it one step further, it is also important to know how the various business processes tie together and ultimately, how these processes accomplish the goals of the company. Employees may know how they tie together and what dependencies exist among the different processes. In addition, employees may also have knowledge of some of the company's security issues based on their experience. These issues may be process related, technology related or both. All of this knowledge is critical when performing a security assessment; with an employee conducting the security assessment, this knowledge can be leveraged.

In addition to the business process, employees on the technology side are also intimately familiar with the systems in place and how they support critical business processes. Some internal IT professionals might have a good knowledge of the infrastructure, the information flows between systems, and what security issues exist (if any). Their knowledge of the technology supporting the business processes can be wide ranging and can include many aspects including functionality, performance, and security. Similar to the process owners, technology owners have a significant amount of knowledge that can be very useful in the context of a security assessment.

The main problem with internal employees conducting a security assessment is the potential lack of independence. Aside from groups such as internal audit, it is difficult to find employees who can be independent when conducting a security assessment. If the internal audit staff has the expertise to conduct a security assessment, they are a good choice because of their combination of independence and knowledge of the business. If any other group does the assessment, their independence must be scrutinized; otherwise, the results of the assessment may lose credibility with management. Independence is a tricky concept in that it is all about perception — i.e., if the perception is that someone is not independent, it does not matter whether or not the person is independent because the perception is already set. For a security assessment to be taken seriously, management has to believe that it came from a credible source.

Another potential issue with internal employees conducting a security assessment is that they potentially lack new ideas that a third party might be able to provide. Qualified third-party consultants have the advantage that they work with a variety of companies in different industries, which allows them to learn about what works, what does not work, best practices, and new ideas that the company might not necessarily consider. Internal employees may or may not have that kind of experience; it is something to consider when assembling the team to conduct the security assessment.

Third-Party Consultants

Many companies prefer to work with third-party consultants when doing any type of assessment or study. In terms of a security assessment, consultants bring a few important items to the table.

First, qualified consultants bring a wide variety of experience as a result of working with many clients and knowledge of security best practices. Qualified and experienced consultants have typically done security assessments and/or security-related consulting work at other companies. These experiences have allowed them to see a variety of methods for securing a company's assets and as a result, they have a good idea of what works and what does not work. If they have worked with companies across many industries, they have a breadth of experience that internal employees might not have. The experience of conducting security assessments in a variety of environments trains them to find security weaknesses that are not apparent, which could be significant when evaluating the overall security posture. This experience includes knowledge of information security best practices.

Having said that, consultants do not always have more knowledge or better recommendations. Companies must evaluate and screen consultants to ensure that they hire the right type of experience and skill set. The quality of the assessment and the final deliverable are only as good as the people who conduct it and the information they receive from the client's personnel.

When hiring consultants, besides finding people through word-of-mouth reference, there are some aspects of consultants you should think about during the selection process that will help you in making the right choice:

- *How much industry experience do they have?* Depending on what industry a company is in, industry experience can be very important. Consultants with industry experience can add tremendous value to an assessment. In the case of highly regulated industries, it is critical to hire a consultant who is familiar with the relevant laws and regulations. For companies that have to adhere to federal laws such as HIPAA and GLBA, significant risks are associated with not being compliant with security requirements. Consultants with HIPAA or GLBA knowledge not only know the industry but also are familiar with the requirements. They can evaluate security in light of the legal requirements and offer recommendations that can help the company achieve compliance. Consultants without industry experience may not have a good idea of the industry-level risks facing a company. Depending on the company and how unique their industry and business processes are, there may be significant value in having a consultant with industry knowledge.
- *How much technical experience do they have?* The technical component of an assessment is very important. Ensuring that security vulnerabilities from a technical perspective are uncovered is an important aspect of the security assessment. Depending on how sophisticated the company's IT environment is, a consultant's technical competency in a given area may be important. Without technical expertise, the value of a consulting team diminishes. The consulting team should have people versed in the technologies that the company uses. You will find that depending on the technology in use, it may or may not be easy to find consultants with the right expertise. For example, if a company is a heavy user of Microsoft, it may not be difficult to find consultants with the right expertise. This

might not be the case if you are looking for expertise in mainframes or UNIX.

- *Do they have a methodology?* Any consulting firm that is hired should have some type of methodology they use to perform the assessment. They should be able to articulate the methodology and translate it into a project plan. The risk of not having a methodology is that the assessment might become a "free for all." Interviews with company personnel might not be fruitful because the consulting team performing the assessment does not have a methodology guiding them on what they need to do. The result is that the client's expectations are not met and people's time is wasted. A proven methodology that makes sense provides some assurance that the security assessment process will be efficient and complete.

- *Who will ultimately do the work?* When consulting firms sell security assessment services (or any services for that matter), this should be one of the first questions asked. Although highly qualified individuals may be there during the selling process, they may not be there when it comes time to deliver the services. Before agreeing to have a consulting firm perform a security assessment, it behooves companies to know exactly who will be doing the work and what skills they bring to the table.

- *What is their reputation?* It is critical to find out about a consultant's reputation by checking references and looking at sample deliverables that they have provided to other clients. A consulting firm hired to conduct a security assessment should be subject to the same level of scrutiny as an employee being screened. The quality of the assessment is directly dependent on the qualifications of the people conducting the assessment.

- *What is the final deliverable going to look like?* Regardless of what consulting firms say during the selling process, reviewing sample deliverables is important. The final deliverable is one of the most important components of the assessment. If its done correctly, the deliverable should be the "security roadmap" to be used in planning security initiatives for short and long term. One of the pitfalls a company might face with a security assessment is not receiving a quality deliverable once the assessment has been completed. The last thing you want to do is to receive some computer-generated report that is either not very readable or has information that is not relevant or on the flip side, a high-level document that does not provide any meaningful details. Ideally, a consultant should be able to give you a report that can be given to multiple levels of individuals in the organization. The deliverable should contain a range of information from an executive-level summary, which management can read to understand high-level results, to technical-level details, which business process and technology owners can use. The deliverable should also contain specific recommendations that have sufficient detail and can be implemented.

The considerations above are very important when evaluating consulting firms. Remember that the security assessment and the recommendations resulting from it will act as the foundation for improving the information security program. The recommendations will drive the security initiatives that a company undertakes to secure the company's information assets. Therefore, it is critical that qualified personnel perform the assessment.

The second important aspect of having a consultant perform the security assessment is independence. Because a consultant is not a part of the company, the consultant is in a position to provide management with an independent view of security. Similar to internal audits being performed by employees who do not have any ties to what they are auditing, consultants also do not have ties to what they are reviewing. One thing to look out for is working with a consulting firm that has performed consulting services for the client in the past. Depending on what they did, there might be a conflict of interest. For example, if a consulting firm designed and implemented the current network, it probably is not a good idea for that firm to do an assessment on something they designed, as that will be a conflict of interest. For internal employees who are directly involved with security-related functions, it is virtually impossible for them to be completely objective and independent.

There is great value in having an independent party conduct the security assessment, but you must have qualified people conduct it, otherwise it is a waste of time. The time taken in selecting the right consulting firm is more than worth it.

KICKOFF MEETING

At this point in the process, you have defined the scope and determined who is going to do the work. From a time perspective, it is now from a few days to a few weeks before the start of the actual fieldwork, depending on the client. Until now, there has been involvement from only a few people from the client for scope development and staffing. The next step is to begin the security assessment with a kickoff meeting (Figure 4.3).

The kickoff meeting is the beginning of the assessment. It is the first opportunity for the team conducting the assessment and the key stakeholders from the client to get together and discuss the engagement. This meeting covers logistical items such as scheduling and goes over how the assessment process is going to work. For the key stakeholders, it is an opportunity to ask any questions and meet some of the people who will conduct the assessment.

The kickoff meeting should be scheduled before the commencement of interviews and the technology review. There should be enough of a gap between the kickoff meeting and the interviews to allow the client time to schedule the interviews. As long as it is before the on-site interviews, it is acceptable.

To ensure a successful kickoff meeting, the following key players should be present at the meeting:

- *Executive sponsor for the assessment* — Executive support for a security assessment gives it credibility and value. Having the executive who championed the security assessment present shows that management is taking it seriously. It helps set the right tone for the assessment, where everyone understands the importance of supporting the effort to determine where the security gaps are. The value of executive sponsorship will become

FIGURE 4.3 Kickoff meeting.

evident during the interviews with client personnel. Executive support for the assessment will help ensure that client personnel are forthright and take the process seriously, which makes the assessment go much more smoothly. On the other hand, if executive support is lacking, personnel may not be cooperative or take the assessment seriously enough. For example, you might walk into a meeting where someone starts by saying that he or she does not have much time because of a need to go to another meeting or the person's mannerisms clearly indicate that this individual does not want anything to do with the assessment. As part of the group conducting the assessment, you must work with the executive sponsor to show the importance of the assessment so that the same attitude trickles down. It should also be clear that you have the ability to escalate any issues to the executive sponsor if you are not getting the cooperation you need.

- *Key stakeholders* — The key stakeholders include people who have an interest in the security assessment. These people should include high-level business process owners and technology owners who will potentially be affected by the findings and recommendations of the security assessment. As these individuals have an interest in the assessment, they should have a good understanding of the nature of the assessment, how it will be conducted, and the importance of their support in the process. During the kickoff meeting, you can set their expectations of what is to come and how they fit in. These stakeholders will be instrumental in helping to identify the subject matter experts to interview during the assessment. The advantage of having them at the kickoff meeting is it gives you a chance to explain what is happening so you can avoid the comment, "What is the purpose of the assessment? Why are we doing this?" The stakeholders' support is critical to the success of the security assessment.
- *Personnel or consultants who will conduct the assessment* — It might seem obvious that the personnel conducting the assessment should be at the kickoff meeting. The reason for highlighting these individuals separately is that the kickoff meeting is probably the first time when all members of the team conducting the assessment will have a chance to meet the client. Until an assessment becomes final, it is typically being discussed at a senior level and as a result, the entire team is never introduced. Keep in mind that some portion of the team from a technical perspective may change based on what you determine to be the critical technologies. These introductions are important so that the client and the consultants (or internal personnel) conducting the assessment can meet face to face and understand what some of the specific roles and responsibilities are. It is also an icebreaker for everyone so they can become more comfortable with each other.

Each of the parties listed above has an interest in the security assessment. It is important to ensure that they are all on the "same page" when conducting the assessment.

Once you round up the key parties for the kickoff meeting, you must decide what to cover in this meeting. Depending on the client, there may be a range of topics you want to cover. Key topics that should be covered at a minimum are:

- *Introductions* — This is the first time that all of the key players are together. To make everyone feel comfortable, it is worthwhile to introduce everyone and talk about roles and responsibilities. This is a good icebreaker and allows you to begin the fieldwork phase smoothly.
- *High-level assessment process* — You should also take the opportunity to stress that the security assessment process will be as nonintrusive as possible and that you are reviewing the information security posture of the company to find opportunities for improvement. You should go over the methodology from a high level and discuss how you will first review business processes and supporting technologies and then perform a risk analysis. You should also talk a little about the final deliverable and what the client can expect. You should stress the consultative approach you are taking in assessing the security posture of the company. The interviews during a security assessment delve into what people do in their jobs, and for some people, this can make them nervous. You must work with the client to allay any fears they might have regarding what you are doing.
- *Scope* — By the time the kickoff meeting takes place, the scope should be fairly well documented and some time and resource allocations would have already been made. During the kickoff meeting, the scope should be discussed and the client should be given the opportunity to ask questions and clear up any confusion about what the assessment will cover. The scope discussion should include the boundaries around what is going to be done and what type of deliverable the client can expect at the conclusion of the assessment. You should also discuss change control — i.e., changes in scope should be handled through a change process where clients and the group conducting the assessment can determine if the change is appropriate and what effect it will have on the project from a timing and pricing perspective.
- *Logistics* — Logistics refers to potential meeting schedules with client personnel and housekeeping details such as having proper access to facilities and most importantly, having a single point of contact (SPOC) from the client side. Up until now, you have been working with someone from the client on an informal basis to set up the kickoff meeting. Going forward, you will need a SPOC to ensure that the assessment runs in a smooth and efficient manner. The SPOC is a tremendous help because this person is your interface with the client. Depending on the size of the company and familiarity with the people in the organization, a SPOC can make life a lot easier for the people conducting the assessments. The SPOC can make sure that meetings are happening per the schedule and that any other logistical matters are given the attention required. Some of the logistical matters that are often taken for granted but that can waste time if not done properly include ensuring that the appropriate facilities

are available and having access to phones or a meeting area. For example, conference rooms or some place to meet sometimes need to be scheduled far in advance. Another task is providing access to phones and the Internet so that you can check e-mail and make phone calls as necessary. Tremendous amounts of time can be wasted if these things are not coordinated. If meetings are not properly coordinated, clients run the risk of the assessment being done in a rushed manner to meet a deadline. Client representatives may not be as forthright as they should be if it appears that the assessment is being done in a haphazard manner. It is important to note that the quality of the assessment and the related findings is directly dependent on the quality of the information received. The value of having someone in this role cannot be stressed too much. One way to ensure that there is a single point of contact is to make that one of the assumptions going into the assessment — i.e., the client must provide a single point of contact as part of the assessment. In most cases, as with other consulting projects, clients are happy to provide someone in this role because it is a win-win situation for everyone.

- *Identification of key business and technology owners* — As stated earlier, the quality of the assessment is directly dependent on the information received from the client's subject matter experts. Therefore, it is critical to identify who the key business and technology owners are who should be interviewed as part of the security assessment. In smaller organizations, this is not as critical because the number of people is small and most of those people are likely to be involved in the assessment. In larger organizations, such as a multinational corporation or a company with many different sites and departments at scattered locations, identifying the right people for a security assessment can be a daunting task. The main risk of not finding the right people is that it is possible to receive inaccurate information or just not receive information necessary to perform the security assessment. For example, a business process owner who is involved in only an ancillary capacity to a given business process may give information that is not totally accurate or relevant to the assessment. Based on the information gathered in the initial preparation phase and at the kickoff meeting, you should work with the SPOC to identify who should be interviewed as part of the assessment. For your part, you should be able to tell the client the specific items you want to discuss and based on that, the client should be able to identify the subject matter experts. The sooner these individuals are identified, the better it is. Scheduling in a security assessment can be difficult, so getting an early jump on this will make the whole assessment process much more efficient. You do not want the assessment process to be long and drawn out, as one of the selling points of an assessment is that it is a relatively quick effort. As for scheduling the meetings, one organized way of having the meetings with the subject matter experts is to have them over a concentrated period of days (depending on the number of people to meet). The advantage of this method is that most of the information, other than the detailed system testing, is gathered at one time, which facilitates easier and better analysis of the information. One thing you will find is that if meetings with subject matter experts are spread out over a long period of time, you will constantly have to refresh your knowledge, making the process inefficient and drawn out.

DEVELOP PROJECT PLAN

As a result of the kickoff meeting, you will have a good understanding of the subject matter experts you will need to talk to and a sense of how the timing will work. Based on this information, you should develop a project plan to help manage the project (Figure 4.4). The longer the timeline for the project, the more important it is to have a project plan in place. For smaller projects where time tends to be limited, the project plan may be a simple list of tasks.

One thing to note is that developing the timing of the assessment is a joint effort between the client and yourself. The input from the kickoff meeting will help in developing a reasonable project plan that satisfies everyone. It is important that the project plan is reasonable so that people will take it seriously and it will be used as a tool to manage the assessment. If the project plan has unrealistic timelines, no one will take it seriously. You then run the risk of the project not being managed properly and not being completed on a timely basis.

Some of the key elements that should be included in a project plan are:

- Specific tasks
  - Documentation
  - Meetings with process and technology owners
  - Hands-on system testing
- Status meetings
- Deliverable presentation

The list above represents some of the high-level tasks. The specific tasks for each of the phases will be discussed in detail in subsequent chapters. For each of the tasks, you should also include the resources that are assigned to it. The resources should include both the members of the team conducting the security assessment and the specific subject matter experts from the client. This type of information can be captured in a simple spreadsheet format such as Microsoft Excel or using more advanced software such as Microsoft Project.

Having this type of information in a project plan creates accountability for all parties involved. With the responsibilities documented in the project plan, people understand the importance of ensuring that they fulfill their responsibilities.

Once the specific tasks are developed in the project plan, you should work with the SPOC to put dates around the meetings with business process and technology owners as well as the other tasks. It is critical that the SPOC share the project plan with the client personnel so that they also understand their responsibilities and that they are accountable. Once the plan has been communicated, it should be used to manage the project. Ideally, the project plan should be a tool that is used to facilitate

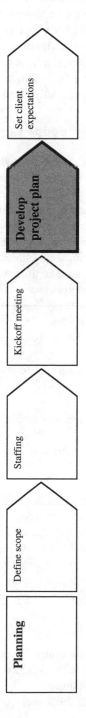

FIGURE 4.4 Develop project plan.

status meetings and ensure that the assessment is on track. The plan will help you identify any areas where progress might be slipping. In addition, as you discuss the findings (this is discussed in depth in later chapters), you may uncover information that might prompt you to do further investigation into an area.

Also, someone from the project team must own the responsibility of updating the project plan so that it remains an effective tool. The project plan is an evolving document. If it is not kept up to date, its value will diminish considerably.

SET CLIENT EXPECTATIONS

What will happen in the security assessment and what can a client expect once it is all over? To ensure that the answers to these questions do not surprise clients, you must set clear expectations of what the security assessment is (and is not) and what they will receive at the end of it. Keep in mind that this is something that you are doing throughout the assessment. At this point, however, it is important for you to make sure that the client understands what comes with the security assessment (Figure 4.5). Even though you have discussed the methodology and gone through a scoping exercise, it is a good idea to clear up any potential confusion before the fieldwork phase begins. If the client's expectations are not properly set and managed, even the best security assessment will be deemed a failure. This concept is not specific to security assessments; it applies to any consulting engagement. The gap between the client's perception of what is being done and what is actually being done should be minimized.

The purpose of setting the expectations at this stage is to ensure that the following is communicated with the client:

- Meaning of a security assessment — what a security assessment is and is not
- Communications during the security assessment — via status meetings
- Format of the final deliverable

The list above will bring final clarity to what the assessment is and is not and also provide some insight about the client communications aspect of the security assessment.

Communication with the client is very important because it will make the client much more comfortable with the whole security assessment process. Many clients who deal with consultants complain, "I don't exactly know what they are doing" or "They never explained exactly what they are doing." By providing clarity about the assessment and regular communications, you can avoid these comments.

UNDERSTANDING THE MEANING OF A SECURITY ASSESSMENT

One of the reasons for clarifying the meaning of a security assessment is that different people have different ideas of what it is. Based on the methodology this book is suggesting, a security assessment is defined as an evaluation of a company's information security program to determine how well information security measures are

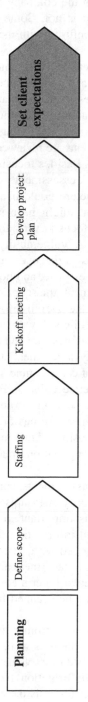

FIGURE 4.5 Set client expectations.

aligned with the security risks facing the company. Equally important as this definition is what a security assessment is not. Some other types of services that a security assessment should not be confused with include:

- *Network assessment* — A network assessment focuses on how well a network (local area networks and wide area networks) is meeting business requirements. A network assessment looks at network performance, network traffic patterns, usage patterns, and other metrics such as downtime to determine whether a network is functioning as it should be. In a network assessment, business requirements are reviewed from a different perspective than in a security assessment. Besides focusing on network performance, a person performing a network assessment would also determine whether the current network infrastructure could handle future business requirements. A security assessment might have some commonalities with a network assessment, but the focus is very different.
- *Vulnerability assessment* — A vulnerability assessment is a technical assessment, where the goal is to discover vulnerabilities in the IT environment, what kind of risk they pose, and how the risk can be mitigated. Unlike with a security assessment, the scope of a vulnerability assessment does not include a review of the overall information security program or how security measures are aligned with security risks. Vulnerability assessments are more technical in nature and do not have as strong a focus on the business as a security assessment does. These assessments are typically done using tools that can examine security settings and configurations very quickly and generate vulnerability reports. The reports must then be interpreted by qualified personnel to determine which vulnerabilities are legitimate for the environment. Some of the tools used in vulnerability assessments generate "false positives" that must be weeded out. For legitimate vulnerabilities, risks and mitigation strategies are typically developed.

Before conducting vulnerability assessments, companies should ensure that they have already taken appropriate security measures such as applying patches and closing ports that are not used. It is important to remember that a vulnerability assessment is only part of an overall information security strategy and is another layer of security that should be integrated with security policies and procedures and other information security measures. In fact, there are firms that now offer managed vulnerability assessments where a network perimeter, a demilitarized zone, or some other part of the IT infrastructure can be scanned for vulnerabilities automatically on a regular basis.

Although security assessments differ from network and vulnerability assessments, there are similarities between them as well. They are related and synergies exist that can be capitalized upon to add more value to a security assessment. When conducting a security assessment, information from a network or vulnerability assessment can be invaluable. One example is the concept of availability, which is one of the three key objectives of security (confidentiality, integrity, and availability). If during a security assessment, you discover that personnel are suffering from significant outages where the network and shared resources are not available, results of a network assessment may be valuable in determining what the reasons might be. You may be able to review some of those same network assessment reports for the security assessment.

In the case of a vulnerability assessment, there are significant overlaps with security assessments. As stated earlier, vulnerability assessments are basically technical reviews using some automated scanning tools and some manual hands-on testing of critical components of the IT environment. You can think of a vulnerability assessment being a subset of a security assessment. In almost any security assessment, some level of vulnerability testing is done on critical systems.

KEY COMMUNICATIONS

To continuously keep the client informed and manage the expectations of the client, communication is critical before and during the engagement. The essential communications, aside from the kickoff meeting, at this stage and once the fieldwork has commenced can be characterized as follows:

- *Status meetings* — during the engagement
- *Deliverable template* — sets client's expectations for what the final document is going to look like

Status Meetings

Status meetings are a standard part of any consulting project. The purpose of these meetings is to go over status and discuss findings during the assessment. Status meetings should be held on a regular basis to keep clients informed. Keeping clients informed entails going over basic logistic information such as whether meetings are happening as scheduled, whether the assessment timing is on track, and whether any changes in the scope are anticipated. However, the most important piece of communication during status meetings is what issues have been uncovered. This is important for a couple of reasons.

First, the client may have additional information about an issue that could change your opinion of it. For example, an internal control issue might be uncovered, but there might be mitigating controls that you were not aware of — this would surface during a status meeting. Discussion of issues during a status meeting allows the client to follow up on findings so that all relevant information is considered. Remember that most of the information gathered during the assessment is through conversations with various individuals in the client's organization. The assessment is not a perfect process and you may not always receive all the information necessary for a number of reasons. It is possible that the questions were not asked correctly or the person from the client's organization did not understand them correctly. It is also possible that you spoke to the wrong person. By sharing the issues with the client early in the process, you cover your bases in terms of seeking all of the relevant facts before coming to a conclusion on a given finding.

Second, as issues are presented to the client in the status meetings, the deliverable is actually being shared with the client as it is developed because the bulk of the final deliverable consists of the issues that are uncovered. Although there will certainly be cosmetic changes to wording in the final deliverable, the issues will mostly remain the same. The advantage of sharing this information throughout the course of the assessment is that when final document is presented, there are no surprises. The last thing you want to do is blindside the client with issues that have not been discussed before. By doing this, there are risks to the client as well as to the people performing the assessment. For the client, it can be an embarrassing situation in the final meeting, where all of the key players are assembled, if they cannot effectively talk about the issue. For the group conducting the assessment, it can be embarrassing if it turns out that there was some critical piece of information that was overlooked and the finding is really not legitimate. Either of these situations reduces the credibility of the security assessment process and the resulting information.

Note that status meetings do not have to be a formal process. It all depends on the client and how the assessment is going. The bottom line is that some type of status update should be happening throughout the security assessment process.

Deliverable Template

One of the main expectations of the client is the content of the final deliverable. This document represents the results of the assessment, and the client probably has an idea of what is desired in terms of content and the level of detail. As part of this step of setting expectations, it is valuable to share the template of the final deliverable so they have a good idea of what they are going to get at the end of the assessment. It is important to obtain the client's buy-in on the deliverable early in the process. As you will see in later phases of the assessment, you will document as much as possible straight into the report to be more efficient and save time. Having the client approve the deliverable provides significant assurance that the document will be acceptable to the client at the end of the assessment.

Gaining client approval on the format of the final deliverable is a critical component of the security assessment because the deliverable is the finished product representing what was done. The final deliverable will contribute significantly to how the client perceives you. The security assessment can be done in the most professional way, and some very pertinent findings may have been discovered. However, if the results of the assessment are not delivered to the client in the way they are expecting or are delivered in an unsatisfactory way, the perceived quality of the assessment can be significantly diminished. Consequently, setting expectations for the deliverable with the client is critical in ensuring a successful assessment. The first step in determining what the deliverable should look like is to determine what the client is seeking. One of the main things to consider when preparing the final deliverable is who the audience for the report is. Another consideration is how much detail the client wants in the report.

An effective way to have a dialogue about the final format of the deliverable is to show the client "scrubbed" deliverables (i.e., names and any other pertinent customer-specific information is taken out of the document) from other security assessments. Clients can use these templates as a starting point in determining the format of the deliverable. Based on this discussion with the client, you should provide at least a high-level format of what the final deliverable is going to look like at one of the status meetings during the assessment. This is the client's chance to say that they are happy with that format or they want something different. Based on past experience, a suggested format for the report should contain the following information:

- Executive summary
  - High-level description of what was done
  - Business drivers for the assessment
- Scope — definition of scope as defined
- Methodology
- Current state
  - Description of core business processes
  - Significant initiatives that are either underway or planned in the near term
- Findings, risks, and recommendations
  - Comprehensive prioritized list of all findings, associated risks, and recommendations categorized by severity

Some characteristics that should be considered when preparing the final deliverable include:

- *Length of the final report* — When preparing the final report, length should not be a factor. Most clients prefer a report that is succinct, provides a summary of what was done in the assessment, and clearly articulates findings, risks, and recommendations. In other words, clients do not want a novel when they receive the final report. They typically want something that they can go through relatively quickly and extract the information they need.
- *Audience of the final report* — Audience is a very important factor when preparing the final deliverable. You can have everyone from executive managerial types to hard-core technical employees who might be interested in the report, in which case you must accommodate them. Because of the range of people that you deal with in an assessment, the deliverable must have something for the different groups that are reading it. The suggested format above is designed to address the different groups. For example, executives are probably interested in a summary of what was done, which is covered in the executive summary, scope, and methodology sections. A security officer, who already is familiar with what was done, might only be interested in critical findings, which are in a separate section. Finally, a technical person might only care about what was found; these individuals would go straight to the detailed findings section. The main point is to ensure that the different audiences for the report have the information they are looking for in the report.
- *Inclusion of the notes from meetings* — Including the notes from meetings is a pitfall that should be avoided. Some clients might ask for an electronic version of the notes so they can see who said what during the assessment. There are two problems with including the notes as part of the deliverable:

- Meeting notes were probably recorded by hand during meetings with the client. To create an electronic version of these notes is a very time-consuming task that probably is not very valuable.
- If meeting notes are voluminous and included in the deliverable, the notes will overshadow the actual report.

Some clients will ask for this information. Unless there is some really good and compelling reason to provide these notes, they should not be provided.

EXECUTIVE SUMMARY

The planning phase of a security assessment is vital in ensuring that the security assessment is successful. Spending the time to effectively plan a security assessment will eventually save you time later.

The key steps in planning the security assessment include the following:

- Defining scope
- Staffing
- Holding kickoff meeting
- Developing project plan
- Setting client expectations

DEFINING SCOPE

Once the decision is made to conduct a security assessment, the scope of the assessment should be clearly defined. Scope definition depends on the following four key factors:

- *Business drivers* — Business reasons for the client to have a security assessment done are established.
- *Scope definition* — Scope is defined in terms of what is covered and what processes will be performed.
- *Standards* — Benchmarks that will be used to determine the security posture are established.
- *Managing scope* — It is important for the group conducting the assessment to ensure that the scope is not changed and if it is, that there is a good reason and that the change goes through a change control process.

STAFFING

Clients must then decide who is going to actually conduct the security assessment. They can have it done using either internal resources or third-party consultants. Some of the drivers that will influence their selection include:

- Funding allocated for the project
- Business drivers for the assessment
- Resource availability

Both internal employees and consultants have their advantages and disadvantages. Third-party consultants bring the following advantages to the table:

- Independence
- Specific technical skill sets
- Methodologies
- References
- Industry expertise

Internal resources often have the right skill sets to perform an assessment. The major hurdle with using internal resources is whether they can be independent in performing the assessment. A good internal resource is the internal audit department, which has the independence, the access to senior management, and significant knowledge of the company business processes.

KICKOFF MEETING

The kickoff meeting should occur prior to the commencement of fieldwork at the client site. The kickoff meeting should have the following people in attendance:

- *Executive sponsor* — The executive sponsor's presence is important because it shows management's commitment to the security assessment.
- *Key stakeholders* — The key stakeholders will be involved in helping to identify the business and technology owners who will be involved in the assessment; the key stakeholders' support is critical to the success of the assessment.
- *Team conducting the assessment* — Until this meeting, the client has probably not met the team that will conduct the assessment; this is a good time for them to meet so the client understands the roles and responsibilities of team members.

The goals of the kickoff meeting include:

- *Introductions* — The team conducting the assessment and the key players from the client are introduced to one another.
- *High-level assessment process* — The assessment methodology is discussed.
- *Scope* — What will and will not be covered is established.
- *Logistics* — The client will assign a single point of contact who will be responsible for scheduling meetings and addressing other logistical concerns such as work space, phones, and Internet access.
- *Identify business process and technology owners* — The key business process and technology owners who will take part in the assessment are identified.

DEVELOP PROJECT PLAN

The project plan should be developed and reviewed with the client so that the client has the opportunity to provide feedback and then approve it. The project plan creates accountability both for the team conducting the assessment and the client personnel involved.

Creating a project plan serves several key purposes:

- *Documented plan* — The plan, which is a translation of the scope into tasks, is documented and can be used to run the project.
- *Accountability* — Because resources are specified in the project plan, a sense of accountability is created for everyone involved including client subject matter experts and the people conducting the assessment.
- *Management tool* — The project plan can be used to manage the dates and tasks of the assessment

It is important that someone owns the responsibility of updating the project plan to ensure that it remains an effective tool to manage the assessment.

SET CLIENT EXPECTATIONS

The final aspect of planning is to clearly set the expectations of the client — i.e., articulate how the assessment is going to work and what the client can expect. Communications should take place before, during, and after an engagement. Clients should understand what is done as part of the assessment and what exactly they are receiving. One of the problems today is that there are security services similar to a security assessment. If the client is confused, the differences between a security assessment and the other related security services (e.g., vulnerability assessment) should be clarified.

Once the fieldwork commences, there should be different communications at different stages of the assessment process. At this stage, the two key communications to discuss are:

- *Status meetings* — These meetings occur during the assessment.
  - Discuss findings and risks so that the client can provide any additional information that might have been overlooked.
  - Obtain buy-in for the format of the deliverable.
  - Resolve any logistics issues.
- *Deliverable template presentation* — Sharing the deliverable template will allow the client to review and approve what the final document is going to look like. This will enable you to gradually complete the deliverable throughout the course of the assessment.

NOTES

1. *Computerworld*—Managing Financial Services Security: An Internal Affair—by: Lucas Mearian—August 5, 2002 http://www.computerworld.com/securitytopics/security/story/0,10801,73167,00.html

5 Initial Information Gathering

At this point in the process, the project scope has been defined and the subject matter experts have been identified. You are now waiting for the client to schedule meetings so you can begin the fieldwork phase of the project. In the meantime, you should start the initial information gathering process.

The purpose of the initial information gathering phase is to gather information and become knowledgeable about the company so you are better prepared once you begin the assessment at the client site. The information gathered at this stage comprises some independently gathered information and some basic information gathered from the client. During this phase, the information is gathered off site (i.e., not on the client's premises), and minimal interaction with the client occurs.

The time you have to complete this phase can vary depending on scheduling. Regardless of the amount of time you have, it is in your best interest to do the research in this phase, so you will be better prepared once at the client site.

The more thorough the initial preparation, the better the whole security assessment process will go. However, if time for the security assessment is limited, use your time wisely and do the preparation that will give you the most benefit during the assessment. With experience, you will be able to determine what information is worth learning about during this phase and useful for the assessment.

BENEFITS OF INITIAL PREPARATION

Learning general information about a company provides a strong foundation for interviews with business process and technology owners. Knowing general information about a company, such as its core operations, locations, and general demographic information, allows you to be better prepared and thus get more out of the interviews. Two key advantages of obtaining this preliminary information are:

- Credibility with the client
- Ability to ask better questions

CREDIBILITY WITH THE CUSTOMER

If an internal group is performing the security assessment, obtaining preliminary information may or may not be useful because much of it may already be known. For a third party doing the security assessment, this process of initial research is invaluable. The concept here, and stressed throughout this book, is that understanding the business is a critical prerequisite to understanding how it is to be secured. Having a general understanding of the business and some current events involving the company gives you a tremendous amount of credibility with the customer. From a customer's perspective, it shows that you are taking the security assessment seriously and it starts the security assessment on a very positive note. It is worth noting that this is really true for any consulting assignment one does with a company. Taking the time to learn about a company before walking in the door helps establish credibility, which has a positive impact throughout the course of the engagement.

ABILITY TO ASK THE RIGHT QUESTIONS

Once the assessment starts, having this basic understanding allows you to tailor your questions for the client. In the initial questionnaire (discussed later in this chapter) that is sent to the client, the questions can be tailored to reflect what you have learned about the company. Based on knowledge you gain during the initial preparation, certain events might give rise to or place emphasis on specific questions or generate questions you would not have otherwise thought to ask. For example:

- *The company has announced layoffs.* If the company has just announced layoffs, personnel security and the issue of ensuring that employees' access is properly terminated would be an area of concern. Questions geared around the termination process would be important in this scenario because of the need to reduce the risk of what former employees can do. In addition, if layoffs occur, it could mean that the company might be suffering financially. If this is the case, other projects or initiatives may have been placed on hold — this too could have security implications.
- *The company is involved in the acquisition of another company.* Acquisitions can have significant impact on a company from a security perspective. Questions will need to be asked about how the new company will be integrated into the information technology (IT) environment as well as into the overall environment from a business perspective. You may also want to find out about how the organization structure is impacted by the acquisition, as that will impact roles and responsibilities. These are all important pieces of information for a security assessment.

Uncovering information during this phase allows you to ask the right questions during the interviews. One thing to note regarding interviews with client personnel is that if you do not ask about changes to the business, they may not volunteer the information. This is not being done because they are trying to withhold information; instead, they just do not understand the importance of it from a security perspective. Once you put the information out to client personnel and engage them in a conversation about it, you are likely to find out how the change to the business impacts the security assessment.

Obtaining this information up front gives more credibility to the process and makes the security assessment a more efficient process. Initial preparation will give you knowledge about a company that you will not have to learn when you go on site. Consequently, the interviews with the client personnel can focus on security.

As for the time spent on the initial preparation, it is a judgment call based on the time that is available to you. Although heavy-duty preparation might not be necessary, some level of preparation, where you at least know what the company does and some of the geographic demographics and the financial condition of the company, is very useful and can go a long way. Initial preparation can be time consuming; however, most of this preparation probably saves time in the security assessment over the long term.

Overall, the main purpose of this phase is to conduct research on the client using publicly available information and prepare for the fieldwork phase of the assessment. The amount of initial preparation depends on how much you already know about the client and the time constraints under which you are working. The five key components in the initial information gathering phase are:

- Gather publicly available information
- Gather information from the client
- Analyze gathered information
- Prepare initial question sets
- Develop and populate template for final report

GATHER PUBLICLY AVAILABLE INFORMATION

Gathering publicly available information before the interviews in the next phase is very helpful in performing a security assessment (Figure 5.1). This process will yield many kinds of information about a company that might be relevant for a security assessment, including such details as:

- How the company is doing financially
- Significant management changes
- Merger or acquisition activity
- Security breaches
- Expansion or reduction plans
- Regulatory activity that might be affecting the company

All of the events listed above as well as others not included in the list have security implications and should be considered if conducting a security assessment. The list above represents some of the events to look for when conducting initial research. As explained in the previous section, having this information and being able to ask about it during the interviews gives you a tremendous amount of credibility. If you know some basic information about events such as the ones listed above, you have the opportunity to spend time during the interviews talking in depth about the security implications of the events.

WHERE IS THIS INFORMATION FOUND?

During this initial research phase, the more information that can be found in a reasonable period of time, the better. The key is to find information in the most

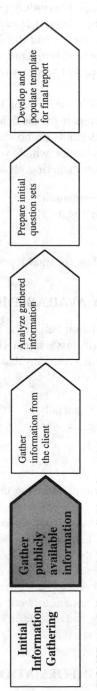

FIGURE 5.1 Gather publicly available information.

efficient manner possible. With this in mind, there is no better source of information than the Internet. Besides some of the obvious sites to visit such as the company's Web site (if one exists), a good search engine is the fastest way to search for news articles in newspapers, magazines, trade journals, and other publications. Search engines can be used to conduct searches about a company's operations and management team, as well as other aspects of a company.

When researching a company on the Internet, there are many places to look. You must make the most of the limited time you have to conduct initial research, so you must have some guidelines about where you are going to look. Based on experience, the best places to find out information about a company where you get the most "bang for the buck" are the following:

- Company Web site (if one exists)
- Public financial statements (if they exist)
- Trade journals
- Other articles found on the Internet

COMPANY WEB SITE

The company Web site, if one exists, can provide a tremendous amount of information about a company. Many organizations are becoming increasingly dependent on their Web sites to provide information as well as to offer services over the Internet. The company Web site name can be provided by the client or it can probably be obtained through searching the Internet. Some of the basic information that can be taken from a Web site includes general company-related information and operations-related information. In conducting a security assessment, Web site review can yield the following types of information:

- General company news
- Operations-related information
- Planned initiatives
- Management team
- Financial information
- Web-based offerings
- Sense of dependency on Internet presence

Although this sounds like a significant amount of information to look for and review, the intention is only to familiarize yourself with the company, so the amount of time spent should be chosen with that in mind. The purpose of reviewing this information is to become familiar with the company, not to learn everything possible about it. The next sections contain discussions about the specific items listed above.

General Company News

Many company Web sites have a section that is devoted to current events relevant to the company. This section may contain company-related press releases as well as other items that might have been in newspapers. Although no assurance exists that the company's news is completely up to date, the general news found on a company's Web site can be useful.

Operations-Related Information

Operations information is basically what the company does, including the following:

- *Products and services provided* — This is perhaps the most important piece of information that can be obtained from the company Web site. Based on the products and services being offered, you can gain a sense for what some of the mission-critical business processes are.
- *Locations* — The number of locations is significant for a security assessment when discussing the network infrastructure and connectivity issues as well as general operations. The various locations will normally have to communicate with each other, so you will probably have to learn about the infrastructure and how the different sites are connected. It will be crucial to build on this information later when planning and conducting the technology review (Phase 4 of the assessment). There may be some potential issues related to security of communications between sites, firewall configuration, and the overall security architecture. The discussion around locations will also naturally lead to how employees are given remote access to the company network. Knowing the locations provides invaluable information that can be built upon.
- *Number of employees* — The number of employees coupled with other information including revenues, number of locations, and other statistics can provide some sense of the size of the company. It is important to note that the size of the company does not necessarily reflect the complexity of the company's operations or how complicated the related security issues might be.
- *Business unit information* — The business unit information is, in some ways, an extension of the information on what products and services are offered by a company. Details about what the various business units do and where they are located are invaluable when performing the security assessment. Another aspect of business units that has security implications is how the company was formed in the first place. If business units became part of the company via acquisition, there are potential security implications related to how well the new company was integrated into the existing infrastructure.
- *Business-to-business (B2B) relationships* — B2B relationships have made many processes very efficient. Supply chain activities are a case in point; B2B relationships have streamlined these processes. Suppliers, for example, sometimes now manage inventory for their customers. They have a view of inventory and are charged with maintaining certain levels. Although this process is very efficient, areas of security risk exist and should be reviewed. Some of the risks with B2B relationships include (full list can be reviewed using the questionnaire provided in the appendices):

- – How is the B2B partner's access to the company's information limited to only the information required for that partner?
- – How is access controlled at the B2B partner level when an employee is terminated?
- • *Regulatory environment* — Sometimes, companies may have information regarding certain regulatory requirements to which they are subject. If the regulatory requirements have any information security components, it would be important to know this as early as possible in the assessment process. Some of the more recent legislation that has information security components includes the Health Insurance Portability and Accountability Act (HIPAA; health care), the Gramm–Leach–Bliley Act (GLBA; financial services) and the Sarbanes–Oxley Act, which affects publicly traded companies.

Planned Initiatives

It is critical to understand what the customer is planning for the future and what type of security implications that might have. Planned initiatives can significantly change recommendations you might make in a security assessment. These initiatives can range from simple changes, such as adding to an existing network, to very complicated changes in the overall network architecture, acquisition or disposal of a business unit, or a major change to the products and services offered. Depending on the nature of the initiative, the company Web site might provide details about it. Recommendations in the security assessment should take planned initiatives into account, as both the content and the criticality may be affected.

Management Team

The management team is often listed on a company's Web site. Although this information will not necessarily allow you to ask better questions, a name might "ring a bell." Someone may be familiar to you based on other places where you have performed security assessments or someone in management may be known from other companies. If you skim the bios of the management team, you might gain a sense of where they previously worked; this might be useful information when trying to gauge management's attitude about security. Also, if a management overhaul has taken place, that could mean changes in the focus of the business, changes in business processes, or other changes to the business that could potentially affect the outcome of a security assessment.

Financial Information

Financial statements (discussed in detail in the next section), especially in the case of publicly traded companies, are often published on the company's Web site. If the company is not publicly traded, information on how they are funded and how much funding they have may be available. Financial information can give some indication as to how the company is doing and what their financial position is. A company that is doing well might be more proactive when it comes to security. Conversely, companies that are not doing as well tend to cut corners wherever possible and are completely focused on generating revenue and keeping expenses down.

The financial situation of a company should viewed in conjunction with other available information about the company. It is just one more way to help understand the company before diving into the details regarding processes and technology in place.

When conducting a security assessment, you not only have to consider the financial condition of the company, you must also consider the financial condition of any companies with whom there is a dependency. Consider the example of a company that outsources its IT operations to an outsourcing provider. The outsourcing provider is now charged with providing an adequate level of security for the company's data residing on machines inside the outsourcer's data center.

Web-Based Offerings

Web-based offerings are becoming more common every day, with many companies now either offering or planning to offer goods and services over the Internet. In terms of a security assessment, any type of Web-based offering should raise a flag and will probably warrant further detailed testing. Web-based offerings can come in a number of forms, with each carrying its own level of risk. One thing to look for is if the Web site is certified by "BBB *OnLine*" or other similar bodies; this provides some level of assurance that the company has taken steps to have an independent assessment performed to assess the security of their Web site. When evaluating Web-based offerings and determining the extent to which they will be reviewed in the security assessment, the following should be kept in mind:

- *Sensitivity of information used in the Web-based offering* — i.e., are users entering any of their personal information?
- *Whether Web site users will be able to buy something from the site* — i.e., will they be providing sensitive credit card information?
- *Does the Web-based offering provide content only?* — i.e., users will not enter any personal information.

Based on the criteria above as well as other criteria that will become evident as you obtain more information about the operations, you can determine how Web-based offerings will impact the scope of the security assessment (e.g., the potential need for additional process reviews and hands-on testing of the systems supporting the Web-based activity).

Sense of Dependency on the Web Presence

One of the questions we will ask as we go through different areas of the security assessment will be, "How important is it to you?" or "How dependent are you on a certain system and how long could you tolerate its unavailability?" As far as the Web presence, you can gain a sense for the company's dependency on their Web presence just by looking at the Web site and what it offers. The importance of the Web site, how it integrates into the key business processes, and where it is in the overall network architecture will drive the extent and type of testing that will be done.

As is evident above, a company's Web site can provide a plethora of information and make you better prepared to talk with the client. When evaluating information that a company posts on its Web site, keep in mind that it is the company that is posting the information. Although some of the information, such as financial data, is objective, some data on a company's Web site may be subjective in nature. This subjective information should be viewed with "healthy skepticism," as it is not independent. Subjective information should be questioned and not taken at face value, and to the extent it affects a finding, you should consider verifying certain information.

FINANCIAL STATEMENTS

In the previous section, we discussed financial statements, which sometimes reside on the company's Web site. In addition, the financial statements for publicly traded companies are public documents that are filed with the Securities and Exchange Commission (SEC). Links to SEC filings are normally available on financial-related Web sites such as the Yahoo! Finance Web site or http://www.secinfo.com/. A number of different parts of the statements provide a wealth of information that is useful in learning about a company. Some of this information is objective in nature and has been attested to by an independent auditor, but other information is more subjective. The subjective information must be viewed with a "healthy skepticism" and to the extent that it is relevant for the security assessment, some level of independent verification should be performed. Some of the key statements to look for in preparation of a security assessment include:

- Form 10K — Annual Report
- Form 10Q — Quarterly Report
- Form 8K — Report of Unscheduled Material Events

Form 10K — Annual Report

The 10K is essentially the company's annual report, which is filed with SEC soon after the end of the company's fiscal year. If you have limited time to become familiar with a company, the 10K is the best document to review. The 10K is very comprehensive and probably one of the best sources of information for a company. Note that the 10K form is only required for publicly traded companies; other companies might still have an annual report that the client can provide if needed. The Annual Report and the 10K are the same document. Some of the information that the 10K provides can include:

- *Description of the business* — The 10K provides a description of the company in a narrative-type format explaining what the company does and the products or services it sells. This is high-level information, which you have probably seen from other sources.
- *Business unit information* — Business unit information provides more details about the business. The 10K might go into detail about what each

division or business unit does and how the business unit is doing. This information can be evaluated to identify potential areas of concern from a security perspective. Although the 10K will probably not go into process-level detail, it might give enough information to allow you to have a high-level understanding of the different business units. The business unit information can also be used in conjunction with the financial information to understand the focus of the business. In some cases, the 10K might contain a breakdown of revenues at the business unit level providing some indication about which business units are more or less critical to the business. This information becomes more important as the business becomes larger and more complex. For smaller businesses, there may be only one business unit, and this type of information might be a moot point.

- *Management discussion and analysis* — The Management Discussion and Analysis (MD&A) is management's discussion of the business, which includes a review of the year's results as well as an idea of what is to come in the future. This discussion goes through some of the financial details of the company and typically includes a comparison with the numbers from the prior year. Any significant variances in the results from the prior year are explained, which can provide information regarding changes in the business. Keep in mind that the MD&A is prepared by the company's management, so it is not objective and independent. Even so, the information is valuable because it might give a sense of what the company views as important in the business. Note that the numbers referenced in the MD&A are audited, but the overall content of the MD&A is management's view of the business today and where they see it going in the future.

- *Merger or acquisition activity* — Merger or acquisition activity is an important consideration for a security assessment. Mergers and acquisitions potentially introduce new processes and technologies into a company. The degree to which a company can integrate processes and technology infrastructure as a result of a merger or acquisition can have an impact on the overall security posture of the company. Questions regarding security policies, security infrastructure, and security ownership all become more relevant when mergers or acquisitions occur. The significance of the merger or acquisition depends on how large the new business is and how it is going to be integrated. Companies sometimes will integrate new acquisitions over a period of time and let them function "business as usual" for a short time before beginning the integration process. If a merger or acquisition has occurred, it should definitely be covered in the interviews with the client.

In addition to the information listed above, the 10K also contains financial statements and supplementary data. The statements include the balance sheet, income statement, and cash flow statement, as well as other summary statements and the notes to the financial statements — all of which are worth looking at.

TABLE 5.1
Balance Sheet Ratios

Ratio	Calculation
Current ratio	Current assets/current liabilities
Quick ratio	Quick assets[a]/current liabilities
Net working capital ratio	Net working capital[b]/total assets

[a] Quick assets is current assets less inventories.
[b] Net working capital is the current assets less the current liabilities.

Balance Sheet

The balance sheet represents the financial state of a company at a specific point in time — the end of the fiscal year for the company. Reviewing the financial statements can give you a sense of how financially strong a company is. No standard benchmarks exist to indicate whether the financial position of a company is strong. However, there is value in looking at numbers in comparison with the prior year and over a few years (if that information is available). The information from the balance sheet can be analyzed using ratios shown in Table 5.1.

The ratios in the table are ratios used for liquidity analysis, which is a way of measuring the company's ability to meet its current obligations in a timely fashion. These ratios should be analyzed over a period of time. Any downward trend in the ratios could potentially be a cause for concern. The numbers used in the ratios are readily available from the balance sheet, and the calculations are relatively quick.

The relevance of reviewing liquidity is that if a company is struggling with current obligations, a tendency to cut corners may be present. Depending on the severity of the situation, the company may be in "survival" mode, where only mission-critical operations are happening and everything else is on the back burner. In a "survival-mode" scenario, it is very possible that information security is not being given much attention.

The other impact of the financial condition on a security assessment is in the recommendations. When making recommendations, the company's financial situation must be considered. Although cost-effective recommendations should always be made regardless of the situation, extra attention must be given to ensure that recommendations make sense based on the current financial condition. Sometimes, it is appropriate to provide clients with recommendations containing different options that range in cost. It is then the client's decision to choose the most comfortable option for them.

Income Statement (Also the Profit and Loss [P&L] Statement)

Unlike the balance sheet, which represents the company position at a point in time, the income statement represents the activity over a period of time — e.g., during the company's fiscal year. As with the balance sheet, the numbers should be compared over at least two years; this information is available in the 10K. The numbers that make up the operating income and the changes in these numbers from the prior year are worth reviewing when preparing for a security assessment, as those variances might indicate changes to the business or other relevant events. The high-level line items that make up the operating income include revenues, cost of goods sold, and selling, general, and administrative expenses.

The revenue number might be broken up into more granular components based on the type of business it is. Significant fluctuations in the revenues over time should be explained. Trends can be due to market conditions and be completely expected or they may be due to other conditions in the company. For many companies affected by the economic downturn in 2002, reduction in revenues was expected and forecasted at that time. The key is that the trend and its effect on the business should be explained; from the explanation, you can determine whether any impact on the security assessment is likely. For example, if a company is continuing to have less revenue in a particular division, there may be a plan to discontinue certain products and services. This will certainly impact a security assessment because those processes and the technology that specifically support that business might be discontinued, and thus you might not spend significant time on it during the security assessment.

Similar to revenue, the cost of goods sold can be presented in a more granular fashion depending on the company and its reporting requirements. The cost of goods sold represents those costs directly associated with goods or services sold by the company. Like revenues, the cost of goods sold should be reviewed over a period of time, with any significant fluctuations explained by the client. These fluctuations may be explained by economic conditions or by specific issues that the company might be facing. An example of a case where differences in cost of goods sold might impact the security assessment is if there is an unusual rise in cost of goods sold. This could result from changes in the cost of materials (resulting in little impact on the security assessment), changes in processes, or other changes in the organization. If the changes resulted from changes in processes or further use of technology, this could impact what you look at in the security assessment.

Selling, general, and administrative expenses (SG&A) generally include support costs such as sales, back office operations such as accounting and finance, and other support costs. SG&A should be reviewed over a period of time. Fluctuations in the components of SG&A such as accounting, finance, and human resources (HR) could have security implications depending on the reason for the fluctuation.

Notes to the Financial Statements

Glancing through the notes to the financial statements is valuable. The notes contain details about line items on the financial statements that might need further clarification. The notes also contain other information that is not reflected in the financial statements but that companies are required to disclose. The notes are part of the financial statements and they are audited — i.e., a third party has audited the content of the notes and the numbers referenced in the notes. Some important pieces of information that would be helpful in the security assessment can be extracted from the notes. Notes vary from company to company, but some examples of important information from the notes include mergers, acquisitions, and divestitures; contingencies — potential litigation; alliances with other companies; and details on specific line items on the financial statements.

Form 10Q — Quarterly Report

The 10Q is very much like the 10K but with two significant differences:

- The 10Q reflects activity over a three-month period.
- The 10Q, unlike the 10K, is not subject to a full audit by a third party.

For the purposes of a security assessment, these two differences are not that significant. Remember that the review of these statements is for the purpose of gaining initial information and to be better informed when asking the questions. The 10Q is worth reviewing during the initial preparation phase of the security assessment if it is taking place well into the client's next fiscal year and the 10K is not completely current. The 10Q should be reviewed in much the same manner as the 10K, as they both include much of the same information.

Form 8K — Report of Unscheduled Material Events

The 8K is used to report "unscheduled material events." These events have a material (i.e., significant) impact on the business; publicly traded companies are obligated to inform the public about such developments. Classifying an unscheduled event as a "material" event is the decision of management and the board of directors of a company. However, certain events such as the following will probably be reported via an 8K:

- Merger or acquisition
- Significant changes to management (e.g., new chief executive officer [CEO], etc.)
- Major litigation settlement

Events reported using an 8K also appear in the 10K and 10Q statements. When preparing for a security assessment, you should look at any 8Ks filed since the last 10K or 10Q. If any type of material event has occurred, there is a chance that it can impact the security assessment.

To reiterate, the statements listed above are an invaluable resource in obtaining information about a company in preparation for a security assessment. The review of these statements, however, must be kept in perspective. The time spent on reviewing the financial statements depends on how much time is available for completing the security assessment and how much knowledge you already have about the company. If you are new to the company or have only superficial knowledge of it, a cursory review of the statements, at a minimum, is warranted. For an internal employee doing the assessment, the level of review depends on how complex the company is and how much of the operations is familiar as a result of the employee's current role. In any case, reviewing the statements is important, and the time spent is a judgment call for those conducting the security assessment.

Reviewing the financial statements normally clues us in to areas of the business where potential security concerns exist. This supports the notion that information security is an integral part of the business and not a set of disparate technologies that is not integrated with the business. Security is a business issue, and it is the business that drives the security requirements, which is the basis for this security assessment methodology.

TRADE JOURNALS

Another good source of information is trade journals. Besides providing information about the company being evaluated, trade journals provide information about the industry in general. Going through trade journals provides a sense of what is happening in the specific industry, as well as some of the issues facing the industry as a whole. Some items that might be of interest in the context of a security assessment include:

- *Regulatory requirements facing companies in that industry* — When performing a security assessment, it is important to understand any regulatory requirements with security implications that affect a company. With regulatory requirements, management must comply and specific steps should be included in the security assessment to determine compliance with regulations. If you are working with a company subject to regulations, it is important to review the regulations in the scope development process to determine what parts of the regulations are in the scope. Some regulations are very extensive, so it is wise to be granular with what is in scope and what is not. Besides some of the better-known security related requirements such as HIPAA (for health care) and GLBA (for financial services), other security-related regulatory requirements exist in other industries. One example is the Family Educational Rights and Privacy Act (FERPA), which requires most schools to secure student information. Besides identifying regulations, trade journals can also provide information about how similar companies are addressing regulatory issues.
- *Use of new technology that is changing how business processes are performed* — Technology has impacted virtually every industry by streamlining business processes and changing how things are done. Trade journals can provide information on industry-standard technologies, emerging technologies, and potential security issues with these technologies. If the company for which the security assessment is being done is using these technologies or is planning to use them, this information can be valuable.
- *Security-related issues facing the industry* — With the dependence on technology and the level of connectivity of today's networks, security is a major issue that affects almost every industry. Security issues can be technology specific and also industry specific because certain technologies are specifically built for certain industries. Trade journals can provide

information related to industry-specific risks, which can be valuable information in preparing for the security assessment.

- *Issues that the company's alliance partners are facing* — Alliance partners, as noted in the earlier section, can be third parties that are connected with the company. Specifically, if business-to-business (B2B) or application service providers (ASPs) are having problems, this can affect the company being assessed. For example, consider a situation in which an ASP is providing an application that is a core business process for a company. If the ASP has financial troubles to the extent that it could be on the verge of bankruptcy, this can have a very significant impact on the company.

Reviewing for all of the information outlined above can seem to be a daunting amount of work. As with the financial statements, this should be done based on time constraints and the knowledge that an individual has about the industry. Its important to remember that this review is done in the "Initial Preparation" phase, and the purpose is to gather information to create good question sets and be able to talk to the client armed with as much information as possible. Also, obtaining information from trade journals or any other source discussed here is an iterative process. During the security assessment, information can be uncovered that would warrant revisiting some of the sources already reviewed. Additional reviews would obviously be more focused on specific topics.

OTHER ARTICLES ON THE INTERNET

The final place where you can seek information about a company is the Internet, using traditional search engines such as Google and Yahoo! Aside from the sources identified in the sections above, the Internet in general can provide a wealth of information. Searches on the Internet can yield all kinds of information about the company, its competitors, and the industry in which they operate. These articles might be from traditional daily newspapers and magazines. This category of information rounds out obtaining publicly available information from the Internet.

Myriad information can be gathered in the initial information gathering phase. How much or how little information can be obtained depends on how well known the company is, whether it is publicly traded, and other factors. If the company is publicly traded, a host of information is available through the SEC filings. In any case, the more information that can be gathered, the more prepared you will be for the assessment.

GATHER INFORMATION FROM THE CLIENT

Once the publicly available information is reviewed, information should be obtained from the client if possible (Figure 5.2). If an internal employee is conducting the assessment, that individual might already have access to much of the information that can be used in preparation for the security assessment.

FIGURE 5.2 Gather information from the client.

An initial questionnaire like the one in Appendix A can be used to gather general information about the company being assessed. The questionnaire in Appendix A, like all of the other questionnaires, is generic in nature and should be modified based on:

- Information obtained from reviewing the publicly available information.
- Industry-specific risks.
- Any other knowledge about the company. If an internal employee is doing the assessment, that person may be privy to information that might be relevant for the security assessment.

In this phase, you should have a conversation with the client to go over the questions. Your single point of contact should set up a meeting between you and some management-level person from the client who knows the business and can talk at a high level about virtually any aspect of the company. This type of person is perfect for this meeting because you are not looking to get detailed at this stage. You are only seeking general information to lay the foundation for the rest of the security assessment.

When discussing the questions with the client, there might be some instances where there is a temptation to start digging further into topics. Assuming you are talking to a management-level person, that individual will probably not be prepared to talk at a technical level. In addition, you should avoid doing this because you will not be fully prepared with questions, knowledge, etc. Time is already allotted for doing the proper research and developing solid question sets. The risk of delving too deep into the topics on the questionnaire is that you probably will not obtain information at the level you want, and you will waste time because you will have to go through this again.

Depending on how the scheduling for the assessment works out, you may or may not get time with the client to obtain the answers for the questionnaire. You should do your best to go over these questions, as it will help immensely in preparing for the fieldwork phase. You should explain the value of going through the questions with the client before the major fieldwork starts. If the questionnaire is not completed in this phase, you will need to spend the first part of the next phase going over questions from the questionnaire.

Using the questionnaires in the appendices, much of the basic foundation type of information about the company can be obtained. This information coupled with the publicly available information gives a sense of the size, operations, and complexity of the organization. The goal is to be prepared with information before beginning the fieldwork phase. Another thing to keep in mind is that some of the information listed in the questionnaire might already be known and if so, the questions can potentially be taken out. Internal employees should already know some of the information because of their familiarity with the company.

Another important point to remember with the initial questionnaire is that if the client provides any documentation, you should properly safeguard it. Although this might sound obvious, there are many instances where sensitive information, such as network diagrams with Internet Protocol (IP) addresses or other confidential documents, is not properly handled. Your credibility as a security professional can be undermined if you do not ensure that this information is properly safeguarded.

Although the initial questionnaire to use in this step is in the appendices, it is worth highlighting some key areas that are addressed in this questionnaire:

- *Demographic information* — The purpose of the demographic information–related questions is to begin understanding the size and complexity of the company. The high-level items that should be requested include the number of employees and number of contractors. With respect to contractors, you can also request information regarding procedures related to how contractors are screened and how access control is handled (i.e., how do contractors gain access to the company systems).
- *Number of locations* — The number of locations and what happens at each location will give you a sense of size and help you plan your fieldwork. This information will give an indication of the overall operations, as well as alert you to potential IT infrastructure issues, such as connectivity between sites and how IT is run — e.g., centralized versus decentralized models.
- *Information technology environment* — Information about the technology environment is critical in developing a preliminary understanding of the company. Using this information, you can start to gain a high-level understanding of the technology environment and begin to think about some of the hands-on testing that might be required. The detailed testing is a significant component of the assessment, and knowing this information in the initial stages allows you to think about how the detailed testing will be done (e.g., can automated tools [proprietary as well as freeware and shareware tools] be leveraged? what checklists do I need to have? is there any research that should be done about their systems?) and how long it will potentially take. Keep in mind that this discussion is still high level; the purpose is to gain an initial understanding. A more detailed discussion will occur during subsequent phases of the assessment. Your understanding of the IT environment and the specific system-level testing will be finalized only after meeting with subject matter experts and finding out more information about the company's critical processes and supporting technologies. In the meantime, this questionnaire does delve into some of the IT details including:
  - *Network topology diagram* — The network topology diagram, if available, gives a layout of the network as well as the security architecture (if any) in place. The diagram should show the placement of security devices such as firewalls, intrusion detection systems, and authentication mechanisms, which should provide some preliminary understanding of the company's view on security and what they are trying to protect. Placement of devices such as firewalls and intrusion detection systems may give an indication of where their critical information is. The extent of the security architecture can also give an indication of how security conscious the client is.
  - *IT infrastructure and critical applications* — The specific information that should be requested regarding the IT infrastructure includes operating

system information, number of desktops and servers, and critical applications. The IT infrastructure details provide two very important pieces of information. First, the infrastructure details along with the network topology will provide some basis for deciding what system testing will be required. Second, the infrastructure details, particularly the operating systems and critical applications information, will allow you to plan the right resources for detailed testing of those systems if appropriate. If a variety of systems are deemed critical, you can start to plan the correct resources to perform this testing. You can also determine whether any testing tools are warranted.

- *Information security program* — With questions in this area, the goal is to see what elements of an information security program are present in the client's environment. The key elements were discussed in Chapter 3 of this book. The discussion as it relates to the information security program will focus on these elements, which include security strategy, security policies and procedures, security organization, executive support, training and awareness, toolsets, and enforcement. This discussion will give you only an initial feel for what is in place today and you will have the opportunity to build on this once you begin the fieldwork.

Other documentation should be reviewed prior to the assessment if possible. These documents, which include existing security policies and procedures, technical documentation, internal audit reports, and external audit reports, provide information about the current and historical internal control and security environment at the company. By reviewing these documents, you can begin to learn about what is in place and what issues or risks the company has faced. Below is a more detailed discussion of the various types of documentation to review:

- *Existing security policies and procedures* — Security policies and procedures are the foundation of any information security program. Having this information beforehand can provide insight into how extensive the information security program is, what the company is trying to protect, and some of the high-level roles and responsibilities related to information security.
- *Technical documents* — Certain infrastructure-related documents such as firewall rule bases and other security-related configuration information from the various components of the infrastructure could provide some excellent detailed information about the technical security measures in place. This is very sensitive information, which security or network personnel might not feel comfortable giving out. If this information is provided, it can give you an idea of what types of risks the company faces. For example, the firewall rule base configuration, which contains rules regarding traffic into and out of the network, can provide insight into the client's activities and business requirements and some risks they face. This is still going to have to be reviewed with the client, but having the opportunity to review the information first makes the review with the client much more meaningful.

- *Internal audit reports (if any)*— Internal audit reports can provide information about what types of internal control issues the client has had in
  the past. Internal controls, which are process-related measures that play
  a part in achieving security objectives, are a significant part of the overall
  information security program. Depending on the company, internal audit
  reports have different meaning and impact. Some companies take internal
  audit very seriously — i.e., audit reports are sent to senior management,
  and the expectation is that findings will be addressed in a timely fashion.
  In other companies, internal audit is not taken very seriously — i.e.,
  findings are not necessarily addressed, and internal audit does not have
  much visibility with senior management. Although you will not know this
  until the on-site visits, how internal audit is viewed in the company might
  be analogous to how information security is viewed. In either case, past
  reports are very helpful because they cite specific control weaknesses that
  were acknowledged by management and hopefully addressed.
- *External audit reports* — External audits are normally more focused on
  financial statements, but some element of IT review that deals with general
  IT controls and systems that generate the numbers in the financial statements is present. Sometimes the reports from external audits might cite
  some type of internal control or security weakness that is worth examining.

Keep in mind when requesting the information above that it is sensitive information
and some clients may want it handled it a certain way. You should make a judgment
regarding the client's comfort level and ask accordingly.

One factor that will impact how much information can be obtained during the
initial preparation is whether internal or external resources are performing the assessment. If internal resources are performing the assessment, they may already have
access to the information required during this initial phase. Some of the information
might be available on the company intranet, and they may know specific people who
can provide access to the right information.

With third parties performing the security assessment, the information received
is completely dependent on the client. Different clients have different views on what
information is appropriate to make available. To make things easier, access to this
information in the context of the overall security assessment methodology should
be discussed during the kickoff meeting. Clients then have the opportunity to say
what they will provide access to during this time. For your part, the value of the
initial preparation should be explained to the client so they understand the value of
reviewing the documents listed earlier at this stage of the security assessment. Clearly
defining the initial preparation phase and what information is required from clients
will be beneficial for everyone involved in the assessment. This information can be
used to develop questions and to help allocate the proper amount of time for the
different aspects of the security assessment.

Initial preparation is very important, and some amount should be done on any
security assessment. At the minimum, you should gather the publicly available
information, as that is under your control. The amount of information that is obtained
from the client during the initial preparation phase is really dependent on the client.

If the client does not provide information during this phase, more time will have to be spent on "learning" during interviews with client personnel. Although time constraints or other external factors may not allow the proper amount of initial preparation, every effort should be made to devote a reasonable amount of time to it. As part of setting expectations with the client, you should explain the mutual benefit of the initial preparation phase and how good preparation will increase the overall quality of the security assessment.

ANALYZE GATHERED INFORMATION

At this point, you have enough information between the client meeting and the public information to do some initial analysis. Although the knowledge is fresh, it is best to analyze the information and determine whether you have any findings or other pertinent information to be aware of for the rest of the security assessment (Figure 5.3).

The first thing you should do is document the key points of the conversation. If you document it electronically, you might be able to use it when developing the final deliverable. Also, the notes from the conversation are easier to share with other members of the team if they are documented electronically. One of the areas where significant time is wasted is when notes are taken by hand and you must spend time two weeks later trying to make sense out of them. If you are not diligent about documenting what you learn, you can become confused later in the process. If your notes are good, this is not a problem, but for many this can waste significant time later when conducting analysis. Remember that the notes from client meetings are the justification for your analysis. If you are questioned later about why you came to certain conclusions, you should be able to go back and say what the basis of the conclusion was.

Once you document the conversation, you should do a quick analysis of the information and further refine your planning for the fieldwork phases of the security assessment. If you were able to have a good discussion with the client, it is possible that some findings already have begun to surface and if so, they should be documented. When documenting the potential findings, try to also determine the risk. This documentation is preliminary and will be refined in later stages of the assessment. Anything you can document now will be a big help to you later.

In summary, the main goals for this step include:

- Document the conversation with the client.
- Document any relevant information gained by searching publicly available information.
- Document any potential findings.
- Determine how the information you have learned can be used to modify the question sets, which are prepared in the next step.

PREPARE INITIAL QUESTION SETS

Question sets (Figure 5.4) will be used to facilitate meetings with business process owners in the next two phases of the assessment — business process review (Chapter 6) and technology review (Chapter 7). At this point in the assessment, you

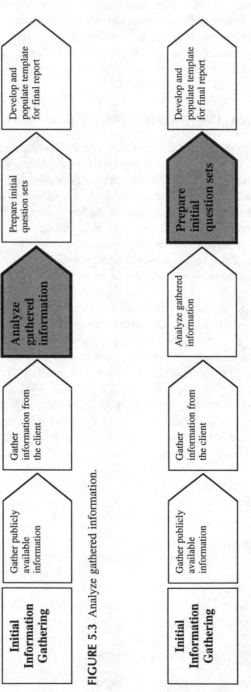

FIGURE 5.3 Analyze gathered information.

FIGURE 5.4 Prepare initial question sets.

have enough information so that you can develop a good initial set of questions because you have researched the company and a have an understanding of what they do. There are some areas of the question sets that you will not be able to address, such as things that are organization specific or about any specific business processes. These more specific items will be addressed in the next phase, where time is allotted to finalizing the question sets. For now, however, you can complete a very substantial part of the question sets.

The question sets should be based on the answers to the initial questionnaire, client documentation review, and the general research about the company, all of which should have been done in the initial preparation phase of the assessment. The main rule when developing the question sets is "don't reinvent the wheel." You should start with sample questionnaires and questions you have used in the past and then modify them based on the initial research performed in this phase and as you go through the rest of the assessment. The appendices contain some sample question sets that can be used as a starting point in developing the questions for the assessment. Remember that the time to perform these assessments is usually limited, so you should take advantage of any efficiency that can be gained in the process.

As you develop the questionnaires, keep in mind that the question sets are there to guide the conversation with the client and they should not be used as a strict checklist. When you discuss these topics with clients, the conversation can be all over the map depending on how it goes. The purpose of the question sets is to help bring structure to the conversation and to help you ensure that all relevant questions are asked.

The question sets will include two types of questions:

* Business process–related questions
* Traditional security process–related questions based on the interviewee's job function

The question sets developed in this phase will be generic, and the same ones can be used for all interviews. In the next phase (Chapter 6 — Business Process Review), the question sets will be modified to include questions specific to business process owners.

BUSINESS PROCESS-RELATED QUESTIONS

When developing the initial question sets, some standard questions for each of the areas listed above can be used as a starting point and can be modified in the next phase. These standard questions or topics should be used for all the people you interview because these topics are general and applicable to anyone you talk to during the assessment. The following list includes the general categories as well as questions for each category:

* Significant business processes and supporting technologies
  – Describe how the business process works.
  – What are the critical roles in the process, and do backups exist in the event that key individuals are not present?
  – What technology supports this business process?

- Who is responsible for managing the supporting technology?
- If the supporting technology was unavailable and this business process could not occur, what are the impacts related to revenue, operations, legal or regulatory concerns, and reputation damage?
- What is the tolerable downtime for the technology supporting this business process?
- Are there any manual or other workarounds that can be done while the technology is unavailable? For how long can the workaround be done?
- What critical data is generated as a result of this process and where does it reside?
- Integration with other departments
  - Dependencies between departments
  - System integration and determination of single points of failure
  - Transmission of information
- Past security incidents (questions for each incident)
  - What was the nature of the security incident?
  - How soon did you become aware of the incident? Did you find out because of a documented process or by accident (e.g., happened to be talking to somebody)?
  - What was the reaction?
  - What was the impact of the incident?
  - What has been done to prevent such incidents from happening in the future?
- Planned initiatives
  - Some examples of initiatives that can be asked about include:
    - Offering services via the Internet — e.g., e-commerce, content
    - Change in location
    - Outsourcing processes or technology
    - Use of Application Service Providers for key business processes
    - Deployment of a major application
    - Will the company be required to comply with certain regulations in the future (HIPAA, GLBA, etc.)?
- Other interviewee-specific questions
  - Questions can be added here that are specific to the business based on what you have learned about the company so far.

The topics and questions above are generic in nature and are there to serve as a guide for the conversation. You might already know some of the information related to what is listed above and if so, you can modify the questions accordingly. They are also applicable to almost any business process owner to whom you talk.

In the next few sections, we will discuss the specific questions listed above. The entire set of business process–related questions is in Appendix B.

Significant Business Processes and Supporting Technologies

The significant business processes will drive the rest of the security assessment. They will help determine where to focus your efforts relative to process analysis and supporting technologies in determining security weaknesses. Note that some of the significant business processes should already be known at least at a high level based on the information gathered thus far. For each of the significant business processes, you should have a structured discussion with the appropriate subject matter expert to help ensure that you are capturing the relevant information. Below is a detailed discussion of specific questions you can ask related to significant business processes and supporting technologies. These questions are generic and can be used for any business process subject matter expert. To the extent that you can customize the questions for the specific people you will interview, you should do so. In the next phase, time is allotted for finalizing the question sets, so modifications can be made up until that time. As you discuss the processes, some or all of the questions might be answered during the course of the conversation. These questions will help ensure that you gain a comprehensive level of knowledge about the different business processes.

As with the other questionnaires contained in the appendices, the questions are there to serve as a guide and help ensure that all pertinent questions have been answered. Below are questions and topics that should be addressed for each of the significant business processes:

- *Describe how the business process works* — This is a general question to start the discussion of specifics about the business process. Here, process owners can talk about what they do and how they do it. This is a good way to start the discussion because it provides you an understanding of the process as well as other aspects, which will be discussed in the next questions.
- *What are the critical roles in the process and do backups exist in the event that key individuals are not present?* — Understanding the roles and responsibilities as they relate to the business process is important for a few reasons. First, you can determine whether any segregation of duties issues exist, and if they exist, whether any mitigating controls are present. Second, you can determine whether there is a dependency on specific people to ensure the process is running. You should be particularly interested if there is a dependency that has a security implication (e.g., only one person can administer a particular application or only one person has a particular skill set that is critical). Third, you can determine whether someone owns the key responsibilities related to the business process. Ownership is a fundamental concept in information security — without ownership, there is no accountability or assurance that tasks will be completed.
- *What technology supports this business process?* — Understanding the supporting technology to determine what warrants further examination is the purpose of this question. In this question, technology refers to critical servers, applications, infrastructure, and any other technology that supports the process. In addition, things like general network connectivity, Internet connectivity, printing services or the availability of a third-party ASP (Application Service Provider) should be considered. When determining the key technologies that support the process, it is best to document

the process flow and look at where the various technologies fit into the process. One of the dangers when determining the critical technology is that there is a tendency to just focus on a particular area. It is important to look at all of the technologies that make the process work because a failure in any one component could potentially bring down the process or cause a security breach.

- *Who is responsible for managing the supporting technology?* — The purpose of this question is to determine whether someone owns the technology — i.e., is someone charged with the responsibility of ensuring that the technology is working as intended? For example, are there system administrators in charge of administering the servers or application owners who have responsibility for the application? If ownership is lacking, it should raise a red flag immediately because a potential lack of accountability is present.

- *If the supporting technology was unavailable and this business process could not occur, what are the impacts related to revenue, legal, or regulatory concerns, reputation damage, or any other impacts?* — This question will give you a good feel for how important the different pieces of technology are. The level of security required for the technology is based on how critical the technology is to the business process. If you discover a security weakness with the technology, this information related to business impact will influence your recommendation. For example, assume that you discovered security vulnerability on a server. Your recommendation to fix the vulnerability might be different based on the potential impact — e.g., there is a big difference between the impact being some users not being able to log on and the impact being that the company might not be in compliance with a regulation that can result in fines.

- *What is the tolerable downtime?* — Tolerable downtime is the amount of time that systems or processes can be down and the company can tolerate it. It is after the tolerable downtime that companies begin to "feel the pain." At what point does the downtime really affect someone's ability to do his or her job? The answer to this question will give a sense of the criticality of the process (similar to the previous question). Tolerable downtime will also influence some of the recommendations you make. When analyzing the tolerable downtime, keep in mind that it might vary based on when it occurs. At some times during the year or even at particular times during the day, the tolerable downtimes might be different. For organizations that are cyclical in nature such as universities, tolerable downtime varies based on the time of year (i.e., the tolerable downtimes for systems during the beginning of a semester and the period when prospective student applications are being processed are lower than other times). Another example is typical for-profit companies, which have a financial closing at the end of the month. During the one to two weeks when the financial closing activities are taking place and companies are trying to meet financial reporting deadlines, the tolerable downtime is significantly less than during the rest of the month.

- *Are there any manual or other workarounds that can be done while the technology is unavailable? For how long can the workaround be done?* — This is related to the previous question on the tolerable downtimes because workarounds must be considered if technology is unavailable. Whether some workaround exists can have a significant impact when determining the risk and recommendations. A good workaround can potentially change a high-priority risk to a medium- or low-priority risk simply because if the technology is not available, there is still a way to get the job done. As will be discussed later, the recommendations must reflect the associated risk and be as cost effective as possible.
- *What critical data is generated as a result of this process and where does it reside?* — In any critical process, critical data is probably generated. Information regarding where critical data resides will be important to know when you begin to determine what systems are critical and will be reviewed in detail.

Integration Points with Other Departments

Integration points with other departments are instances where different departments work together as part of a business process. Different departments working together can range from a simple verbal information exchange to different systems communicating together. Integration points are important to understand because it is at these points where processes do not always work. Roles and responsibilities are not always clear because everyone has a different idea of who is doing what. In some cases you might find that no one owns a specific task because everyone thinks someone else is responsible. Some of the typical areas to consider when evaluating the integration points between departments are listed below:

- *Dependencies between departments* — One key area to look at with critical business processes is dependencies that can be single points of failure. Dependencies may include providing information for a transaction, being another step in a process that spans many departments, or in general any process where there is a dependency between different groups. One example of dependencies between departments as it pertains to a business process, which is prevalent in companies today, is user terminations. When an employee leaves a company, many companies do not have a good process for ensuring that all relevant parties know that someone is leaving the company. The IT department, which is responsible for removing the employee's network access, is often the last to know. Application owners who are responsible for application-level access are often never told. In addition, often no method exists of definitively knowing what company assets the person might have. An overall lack of communication between groups and a lack of ownership of key parts of the process are present. In this process, there are dependencies on all the departments to communicate with each other to ensure that terminations are handled properly. Significant risks may occur if terminations are not handled properly (See

Employee Terminations Questionnaire in Appendix I), and a single point of failure can result in a significant security incident.

- *System integration and determination of single points of failure* — Different departments might have different systems, which might exchange information. The security implications of the integration of the two systems should be reviewed. Some of these implications can include ensuring the integrity of information and reviewing people's level of access. An example is the creation of financial statements in some companies. Where no enterprise-type system is in place, financial statements might be created by having a general ledger system obtain information from other systems that record specific functions — e.g., accounts receivable, accounts payable. For the creation of the monthly or quarterly financial statements, the integrity of the data from the legacy systems must be accurate. In light of some recent scandals, companies (publicly traded) have a vested interest in ensuring that their financial statements are accurate. Another example that you might see on the infrastructure security side relates to Internet connectivity. Take the case of a company that is dependent on Internet connectivity as part of a critical business process. This company might have all inbound and outbound traffic to and from the Internet go through a single firewall. The firewall is a single point of failure because if it goes down, no Internet connectivity is possible. As part of the security assessment, it would certainly be appropriate to ask what type of redundancy the company has for the firewall.

- *Transmission of information* — The transmission of information can have significant implications depending on the nature of the information. With this question, you need to determine where information transmission needs to be secured. In particular, the transmissions of sensitive information such as personally identifiable information, sensitive employee-related information, certain operations-related information, competitive proprietary information, and other information could have security implications. These security implications can affect the business from a legal or operational perspective as well as damage the reputation of the company. For example, when employees face some kind of disciplinary action, managers might send sensitive information about the person over electronic mail to human resources. Someone who is technically savvy can potentially intercept this information, which can result in potential legal problems for the company.

Past Security Incidents

Past security incidents are very useful to know about because they demonstrate potential security weaknesses. Also, past security incidents are hard evidence about how a company reacted to the security incident and how severe the impact was. If the client had any security incidents recently, below are some questions to ask regarding them:

- *What was the nature of the security incident?* The nature of the security incident will probably highlight some area of weakness from a security perspective. For example, a disgruntled employee who was terminated but who still had certain access to systems because his access was not properly terminated could have caused the incident. This issue could lead to findings in the areas of how terminations are handled and general user ID administration, if these topics were not addressed after the incident.

- *How soon did you become aware of the incident? Did you find out because of a documented process or by accident (e.g., happened to be talking to somebody)?* How soon the client became aware of the incident is an indication of whether the company has proper mechanisms in place to find out about security incidents. "Proper mechanisms" can refer to employees being aware enough to alert the right people or having the right systems in place to alert the company to incidents. During the security assessment, if you ask whether the client has had a security incident and the response is "no," the next question is "how do you know?" For many companies, no mechanism is in place to ensure knowledge that an incident had occurred. Although security incidents can occur with any company, how quickly the incident is detected can make a big difference. Good detection methods and a strong incident response process can significantly reduce the damage resulting from an incident. A perfect example is Web site defacement. Some companies will know immediately, but other companies will find out about it by accident. How quickly the Web site can be fixed can make a big difference in the impact of the defacement.

- *What was the reaction?* Once the incident occurred and the client found out about it, did all the people involved understand what they needed to do in reacting to it? Questions related to whether proper communication took place, whether the right people were involved in restoring systems, and a host of other items (which are covered in the Incident Response checklist) should be asked. If the reaction was less than adequate, a weak incident response process should be flagged as an issue.

- *What was the impact of the incident?* The impact of the incident provides empirical evidence of what the true risk of an incident is. It can help you quantify the impact, which is important because it helps determine cost-effective steps for mitigation that are commensurate with the risk. For example, if an incident occurs where a business-to-consumer Web site is taken down, you can quantify the immediate impact related to revenue and the long-term impact related to a loss of customers. Here, you can look at the real impact related to an incident and how it affected the business, which will be helpful when doing the risk analysis.

- *What has been done to prevent such incidents from happening in the future?* With any security incident, companies should at least go through the process of assessing what happened and determining whether any additional security measures should be taken to prevent it from happening again. Whether or not management does anything gives some indication about management's attitude about security. If nothing was done, there is a chance that management did an analysis and determined that there were no measures to take that were cost effective. It could also mean that they just did not do anything about it. As part of the security assessment, you should find out about this, as it will potentially lead to a finding. The answer to this question may also result in recommendations related to deploying new technologies such as intrusion detection systems or additional security-related procedures.

Planned Initiatives

A critical component of a security assessment is to determine what steps need to be taken long term to secure the company's processes and related environment. To determine long-term information security recommendations, you have to know what kind of initiatives the company is planning for the future. Initiatives can vary from company to company and can include such things as:

- Offering services via the Internet — e.g., e-commerce, content — See Business-to-Business and Business-to-Commerce questionnaires in Appendices K and L.
- Change in location.
- Outsourcing processes or technology — See Managed Security questionnaire in Appendix O.
- Use of Application Service Providers for key business processes — See Externally Hosted Services questionnaire in Appendix G.
- Deployment of a major application.
- Will the company be required to comply with certain regulations in the future (HIPAA, GLBA, etc.)? — See HIPAA questionnaire in Appendix Q.

The initiatives listed above are common initiatives for companies. For each of these initiatives, specific questions can be asked. In some cases, questionnaires in the Appendices can help you develop specific questions.

Other Interviewee-Specific Questions

This section is for any questions that you have developed as a result of your knowledge of the company. It is based on the initial research you have done so far and the questionnaire that was discussed with the client. These questions in this area will be added in the next phase — business process review — when the question sets are finalized.

TRADITIONAL SECURITY-RELATED QUESTIONS

The other major area of the generic questionnaire for business process owners is traditional security-related processes that affect or involve them. Some of these topics might have been discussed during the business process discussion. To the extent that they have not been discussed, this is the time to address them.

Listed below are traditional areas of security that are relevant for most employees. Most of the topics listed below are addressed in ISO 17799 (the Information Security best practice standard). For each of the topics listed below, most employees have some involvement in them. Although a good majority of the tasks related to these areas are performed by IT, all employees have some role in them. For each of the areas listed below, some questions would be appropriate to discuss with business process owners. You can use these questions as a starting point and build on them based on the person you are interviewing. To the extent that a person you are interviewing is heavily involved in any area listed below, use the specific question-naires for the given area to develop additional questions to ask:

- User ID administration
  - What is your role in users gaining access to systems, e.g., approval authority?
- Employee termination
  - What do you do if an employee reporting to you is terminated?
  - For what are you accountable?
  - Is there a documented process for terminations that you follow?
- Data retention and classification
  - Are you aware of any policies related to data classification or data retention?
  - Are you the "owner" of any data?
  - Do you specify retention or classification requirements for data for which you are responsible?
- Backup and recovery
  - For data that you own, do you specify any backup requirements for that data?
  - In the event of a disaster, what data would need to be restored for you to become operational?
  - Is that data readily available?
- Business continuity and disaster recovery
  - Are you aware of any business continuity or disaster recovery plan?
  - What is your involvement in business continuity or disaster recovery?
- Incident handling
  - Do you know what to do in the event of a security incident?
  - To whom would you report an incident?
  - Are you aware of any documented procedures for incident handling?
- Change management
  - Do you follow a change management process for changes?
  - Are you aware of a documented process for change management?
- Acceptable use of IT resources
  - Is there documented Acceptable Use policy?
  - Has HR or management ever discussed what is considered acceptable use of IT resources?
  - Have you ever signed an Acceptable Use policy?
- Physical security
  - What physical security measures are in place for the areas of the facility you access?
  - Do you have any sensitive information in your desk or office and if so, how is it secured?

- Do you practice a "clean desk" policy when you leave the office?
- Do you use screensavers on your computer?
- Do you shred sensitive documents before throwing them away?

The questions above are generic and all generally apply to most business process owners. You need to customize them for the people you are talking to. For example, if you already know that the company does not have any security policies, you need not ask any questions related to the existence of policies. Similarly, if you know that someone you are interviewing is one of the main people to handle incident response, you may ask that individual additional questions that are specific to incident response (see Incident Response questionnaire).

For more details about the questions listed above, you can review the specific questionnaires in the appendices. The questionnaires in the appendices are more comprehensive and are meant to be used when interviewing business process owners who are very involved in those functions. The questions in this section are for the business process owners who have ancillary involvement in those processes.

DEVELOP AND DOCUMENT TEMPLATE
FOR FINAL REPORT

Unlike product implementations or technology projects, where something tangible can be given to the customer, the result of a security assessment is information. A good deliverable document is critical to the success of the assessment. At this point, you should begin that process by developing and populating the template of the final report (Figure 5.5; format is discussed later in this section). As you will see, you can already begin to complete some sections, such as the Executive Summary. The advantage of getting an early jump on the report is so you are not rushed in the end. In addition, you can also document your findings for the security assessment straight into the report.

The importance of the final report is that it allows you to convey the results of the assessment in a tangible way. Ultimately, the final report resulting from a security assessment is a "security roadmap," which a client can hopefully use as a list of prioritized action items to improve the company's security program. The quality of your work will be largely measured by the quality of this document. It is therefore critical to start preparing the final document early in the process.

The basic structure of this document, which was discussed in the last chapter, consists of the following:

- Executive Summary
  - High-level description of the assessment
  - Brief discussion of the business drivers for the assessment
  - Highlights of the results of the assessment
- Scope
  - Description of the agreed-upon scope
- Methodology
  - Description of the methodology, including interviews, testing, and tools

FIGURE 5.5 Develop and document template for final report.

- Current State
  - High-level description of what the company does, the key issues that the company faces, and where the company is headed
- Comprehensive list of findings, risks, and recommendations

Before you even go to the client site to begin fieldwork, you can start working on the deliverable. You should already know part of the executive overview, the scope, the methodology, and some of the information for the current state section, so those sections can be populated now. The contents of the final report will be discussed in further detail in Chapter 9.

By populating the final report with the information early on, you are ahead of the game. At this stage, you should focus on the content you are putting in the document. It is not important to focus on grammar or making the content sound just perfect, as this can be taken care of later. At this point, it is only important to start putting down your ideas of what will potentially be in the final report, keeping in mind that it will probably be modified.

As with the other components of this phase, starting to work on the final report is something that will save you time later and if you have the time, it is definitely worth doing.

EXECUTIVE SUMMARY

The initial information gathering phase takes place after the kickoff meeting with the client and before the commencement of fieldwork. The main purpose of this phase is to prepare for fieldwork and do as much up-front documentation as you can.

Gathering initial information about a company will give you a better understanding about the company and will result in a better assessment.

The key tasks of this phase include the following:

- Gather publicly available information.
- Gather information using an initial questionnaire.
- Analyze gathered information.
- Prepare initial question sets.
- Develop and populate the template for the final report.

Note that the completion of the tasks in this phase is dependent on a number of factors including:

- *Publicly traded company versus private company* — If the company is not publicly traded, the amount of information from publicly available sources might be limited.
- *Time constraints* — It is possible that time for thorough initial preparation might be insufficient; at the minimum, some research should be done on the Internet to obtain information from the public domain.
- *Information provided by the client* — The amount of information provided is influenced by a number of factors including timing, availability of client

personnel, and how much information the client was comfortable giving at this point. Clearly, the more information provided, the better.

Below is a description of each of the steps in this phase.

GATHER PUBLICLY AVAILABLE INFORMATION

Publicly available information is easier to obtain in the case of publicly traded companies, as their financial statements are publicly available. In addition to the financial statements, you can explore the company's Web site and the Internet in general using search engines. You should look for any information about the company's operations and how they are doing as a company. Other good pieces of information include any significant changes to the business that have either occurred or are planned for the near future.

Much of this information is potentially useful once you have your meetings with the client's subject matter experts. Having knowledge about the company makes you more credible in the client's eyes, and you will likely obtain better information.

GATHER INFORMATION USING AN INITIAL QUESTIONNAIRE

Appendix A of this book contains a general questionnaire that can be given to clients at the start of a security assessment. This questionnaire should be modified for the company you are assessing. The questionnaire itself has general questions about the demographics of the company, general IT information, and general security-related questions.

You should use this questionnaire (or something similar) to talk with a client representative and go over general information about the company. If the client is willing to spend the time with you, it can be of significant help for when you begin your fieldwork. Some clients might not do this because it can be time consuming, and some redundancy exists because some of the same questions might be asked again. However, the value of this process at this stage is that will help you develop better question sets for the meetings with the client's subject matter experts and ultimately result in a more thorough review.

ANALYZE GATHERED INFO

The information gathered to this point should be documented and analyzed so you can understand the company's business, what kind of security issues the company might have, and other information. The main goals for this phase include:

- Document conversation with the client.
- Document any relevant information gained by searching publicly available information.
- Document any potential findings.
- Determine how the information you have learned can be used to modify the question sets, which are prepared in the next step.

Prepare Initial Question Sets

Question sets, as you will see in the next chapter, are used to facilitate meetings with the client's subject matter experts. In this phase, the generic questionnaires to be used for the interviews with business process owners are developed. The generic questions can be customized based on the research done thus far and the answers to the initial questionnaire discussed with the client. In the generic questionnaire, there are two types of questions — business process and security-related questions. These questions are a starting point that can be augmented by questions from the appendices as well as your existing knowledge about the client. These question sets will be finalized in the next phase, once you have a more detailed understanding of the business from meeting with management.

Develop and Document Template for Final Report

The final report is going to be the product resulting from the assessment. It is important to ensure that the proper time is spent on producing a document that can be used by the client as a "security roadmap" for the future. One of the ways to have more time at the later stages of the assessment to focus on the document is to get some of the document done early. At this stage, you know several of the components of the final report so it is best to complete those now.

The final report can be set up with the right headings and can be populated with some information you already know such as part of the executive overview, scope, methodology, and current state. If this document is started, you can continue to populate it once you begin fieldwork so that the final report is completed efficiently.

6 Business Process Evaluation

The third phase of the security assessment is the Business Process Evaluation, which marks the beginning of the substantive portion of the security assessment. Before going into the details of this phase, it is worth discussing the overall progression of information gathering that will take place beginning with this phase, why the process is important, and some of the reasons why the process may not go as smoothly as we would like. This is relevant because the business process evaluation phase is arguably the most critical phase of the security assessment. The work in this phase will drive the rest of the security assessment, including what technologies you review and how you classify the findings.

The main information gathering happens in this phase and the next (Business Process Evaluation, Technology Evaluation). In these two phases, you will evaluate the business processes and supporting technologies from a security perspective. You will meet with management, business process owners, and technology owners to gather the necessary information.

The progression of information gathering will start with the business and then move into technology. We first start with the where the business is today and where it is heading from a strategic perspective. Based on this, we will determine the high-level security requirements of the business. The strategy discussion is high level, and the discussion is mainly about the core business processes, the organizational structure, and other topics that might affect the direction of the company.

As a result of this discussion, we will determine the core business processes of the company. In addition, other business processes that are relevant from a security perspective might be worth exploring.

The final area to review is the information technology (IT) environment. At this stage, the key technologies have been identified. Interviews with technology owners and certain hands-on testing of critical systems are performed.

The point of the progression of information gathering is that each step of the process builds on the previous step. Doing the steps in the wrong order may result in focusing on processes or technology that are not very important to the business, resulting in an assessment that is not accurate. If you start with the core business processes and supporting technologies from a security perspective, your analysis will have the right focus. This approach will also help you prioritize your efforts in the security assessment. This flow of information gathering is in line with the fundamental concept of this methodology, which is that the business drives security and not the other way around.

One mistake that is often made when doing a security assessment is immediately focusing on the technology; this sometimes happens because IT groups often initiate security assessments. The security assessment is viewed as a technical process instead of a process where business and technology are intertwined. Depending on how much the IT person you are dealing with interacts with users and their management, security assessments tend to be very technical-focused and have minimal focus on the business.

An example of how you can immediately fall off track is a security assessment where you immediately begin the engagement by discussing the security architecture, which then leads to a lengthy technical discussion about the merits of the security architecture and whether it makes sense. Although some aspect of the business might be discussed, there is no assurance that the core business processes of the company — i.e., those most important to the business — have been identified. As part of the discussion, you might even gain access to certain systems to start looking at what security measures are in place. Security configurations such as the firewall rule base and security settings on servers might be reviewed. The fundamental problem with this approach is that you cannot really determine how good or appropriate the security posture is without knowing what it is that is being protected. At this stage, even with the initial research that has been done, your knowledge about the company is still fairly minimal so you are evaluating security without really knowing what risks you are dealing with. By not following the methodology, and more specifically, by not starting with the business process, you run the risk of making incorrect conclusions related to findings, risks, and security measures in place.

How does the security assessment fall off track? Below are some typical reasons and how these situations can be avoided:

- **Reason:** *Security assessment ownership* — From the client's side, someone from the information technology group often owns the security assessment — i.e., it was initiated by IT and they are responsible for it. This ownership is often the result of management labeling security as an IT problem, when it is really something that cuts across all parts of the business. The IT person who is responsible for the security assessment may or may not be versed in what is important to the business and also may not have strong relationships with people from the business side. One thing for sure is that people from the IT group are probably focused on technology because that is their job. They probably have some idea of how the technology supports the business, but they cannot definitively answer key questions related to how the business would be impacted if critical information is compromised or what the tolerable downtime is if systems are not available. Even if the IT person can provide an answer, it should really come from the business process owners, who can provide the definitive answer. IT personnel should not be speaking for the business. If the security assessment is exclusively owned by IT, you will probably do the assessment without having any substantive conversation with anyone from the business. Consequently, if you start with technology, you risk having an inaccurate security assessment.

- *Remedy:* During the initial phases of the security assessment, from the kickoff meeting on, you must educate the client on the methodology and insist on working with people from both the business and the technical sides of the company. You can also talk to the executive sponsor of the assessment about the importance of following the methodology. The argument for the approach is that the final document resulting from the security assessment will be a "security roadmap" to help improve the security posture of the company. If the assessment is not performed correctly, the results could overlook key risks and incorrectly prioritize future security initiatives. This in turn leads to an ineffective allocation of funds for security initiatives. The long-term impact of not conducting the security assessment in the right way should be stressed.

- *Reason:* *Scope was not properly defined* — With some assessments, the scope of work is very vague and not clearly defined. Sometimes, the prefieldwork steps, as defined in this methodology, are rushed due to time constraints and other factors. You might have been developing the scope with someone from the company who did not have a good grasp on the business, or the scope definition might have seemed obvious so you did not spend much time on it. As discussed earlier, the scope development process can take some time; if it is rushed, there is a chance that it can cause problems later.
  - *Remedy:* The process of gathering information and the business process owners you need to speak to should be mentioned in the scope and then covered in the kickoff meeting. If this was not done, you must address this quickly with your single point of contact and potentially, the executive sponsor. As with the previous reason, the importance of following the methodology and the consequences of not following it should be stressed. Specifically, you should stress that if the assessment is not done correctly, the "security roadmap" from the assessment might overlook key risks and incorrectly prioritize security initiatives for the short and long term. This can result in an ineffective allocation of funds for future security initiatives.

- *Reason:* *Lack of cooperation from key individuals* — Some security assessments are done under circumstances where not everyone is necessarily on board with the process. The assessment might not have been presented in the right way to the people in the organization and as a result, employees may be fearful about the results of the assessment. By their very nature, security assessments will uncover security weaknesses with processes and technology. Some of these weaknesses will point back to individuals in the organization, and that causes some level of discomfort, which can result in people being less than cooperative during the assessment. This does not mean that an employee will not talk to you or answer questions as part of the security assessment process. It does mean that this is all the employees will do. In other words, they may *only* answer the question. They will not volunteer other information that may be related and relevant to the questions you ask. These other bits of information are often valuable. This lack of cooperation can potentially lead to not uncovering issues and to providing inappropriate recommendations.

- **Remedy:** If you are not receiving the cooperation you need and you have done what you can to make people feel at ease, you must escalate to your single point of contact. If that does not work, you must escalate to the executive sponsor. Escalation is critical here. Keep in mind that you are ultimately accountable to the executive sponsor, who is responsible for making the assessment happen in the first place. Do not fall into the trap of feeling bad and not wanting to get the client personnel into trouble. Remember that you have a limited amount of time to do the assessment and you cannot afford to have time wasted due to people not cooperating. The quality of the assessment is only as good as the information you receive from client personnel, so their cooperation is critical.

To ensure that the security assessment follows the proper methodology, you must ensure that you properly define the scope and that you are clear with the client about the methodology you use.

GENERAL REVIEW OF COMPANY AND KEY BUSINESS PROCESSES

In this step (Figure 6.1), you will meet with management to gain a "big picture" view of the company. Before you can really start looking at detailed business processes, you need to have a good overview of the company and what it does. At this stage, you may know some general information based on your initial research and the questionnaire that you went over with the client representative. That information is useful, but you still need to learn about the company from the people who are actually running it on a day-to-day basis. The information being sought at this point is a high-level understanding that goes a level deeper than the initial questionnaire that you discussed with the client. The purpose is to lay the groundwork for the rest of the assessment.

In gaining an understanding of the business, the first step is to understand what it does and what the strategic direction of the company is. At this point, you should give minimal attention to technology, as that will come later. You are really trying to come away with an idea of what the company does and how it is done at a high level. You want to know the core business processes of the company — i.e., how does the company make money? From a security perspective, you should also try to learn about the company's information security program and the various elements discussed in Chapter 3.

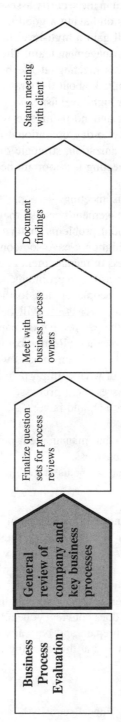

FIGURE 6.1 General review of company and key business processes.

This phase is absolutely critical in the security assessment process, as the success of the rest of the assessment rests on having a good understanding of the business. In this step of the phase, you will gain a high-level understanding of the business by meeting with members of the management team. The single point of contact from the client's side should set up this meeting at the beginning of this phase with members of management who can talk about the strategic direction of the business, organizational structure, and other high-level aspects of the company. It is important that you meet with management and not someone who is more tactical — i.e., someone who is in more of a day-to-day operational role. Management can offer insight, particularly about the organization, strategic direction, and a "big picture" view of the company. This first meeting is important because it will set the tone for the rest of the security assessment.

Because of the nature of this meeting — e.g., "big picture" view, strategic direction, you should talk to management because they can best provide this type of information. One of the potential problems that you may run into is that your point of contact in the company might not have someone from management for this meeting because of a lack of access to management or a failure to see the necessity of involving management. Either reason is a problem and if that happens, you should insist on speaking with the right people or talk to the executive sponsor for the project. This meeting is important because it will help you determine what the core business processes are from the perspective of management — the people who are ultimately responsible for the business. Remember that the ultimate audience of your work product will probably be decision makers with budgetary authority who have their own "big picture" view of what is important. It is important to understand this at the outset of the security assessment process.

As a result of this meeting, you should have:

- A good understanding of what management perceives as being the core business processes of the business.
- Additional information that can be used to refine the question sets developed in the last phase

When you do have this meeting with management, you must be fully prepared. You should have done the proper research and be prepared to ask questions. This meeting also helps establish (or hurts) your credibility with the company. The person from management you talk to is probably someone who will be interested in the final product resulting from the assessment. Making a bad impression with this individual will create a negative perception, which might impact the assessment long term — especially if management does not view you and your team as being credible. Consequently, it is imperative to prepare and be ready for this meeting.

Key topics that should be covered at this meeting include:

- Critical business processes
- Business environment
- Planned changes that may impact security

- Organizational structure
  - Placement of the security function
  - IT organization
- Management's concerns related to information security

Each of these is discussed in detail in the next sections.

CRITICAL BUSINESS PROCESSES

The first thing you should discuss with management is basically what the business does to earn money and how they do it. You need to understand what goods and services they sell and how they are produced and delivered. You also want to know what the key dependencies are, which can include certain suppliers, certain individuals, etc. To illustrate this point, review the example below:

EXAMPLE

Consider a manufacturing company that produces and sells products through certain distributors. This particular company makes money by manufacturing and selling a few different products. For this company, the manufacturing process is a critical process, which looks something like the one in Figure 6.2.

The figure is a very simple illustration of a typical manufacturing process that outlines the key steps at a high level. This technique of flowcharting is an effective way of documenting processes and is something you should consider if you have flowcharting tools such as Microsoft Visio.

Based on the information above, we can ascertain the following:

- Manufacturing, order processing, and billing and collections are core operations of the company.
- Integrity of inventory information is important because it is used to determine what the company needs from the raw material supplier.
- The physical security of the manufacturing plant where the goods are manufactured is important.
- Good internal controls should be in place for the process of shipping product to the third-party packaging company to ensure that all product sent was received.
- Critical systems include:
  - Accounting systems that record inventory (raw material and final product)
  - Finance and accounting systems
  - Systems that support the shipping process

The example above is a fairly simplistic example in which we identify core business processes and critical systems. This information is at a high level, but it is enough so that we can go to the next level when we talk to the business process and technology owners and get into the nuts and bolts of how this is all done. Besides this process, you might find out about other processes as a result of your discussion with management.

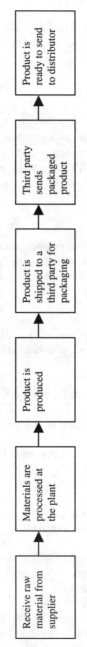

FIGURE 6.2 Manufacturing process.

One thing to stress here is that you are talking to management, and it is not appropriate to try to talk about detailed processes, as they will probably not be conversant with them. Note that in smaller and mid-size companies, this might not be the case. In smaller companies, you might be able to talk about details. This will require that you adjust the methodology and potentially combine some steps.

At the end of this discussion, you want to come away with an understanding of what business processes are important to the company — i.e., what does management consider mission critical to their business. This understanding will guide the rest of the security assessment. The information security program for the company must minimize any security risks to these business processes and ensure that they can be performed in a secure manner. In other words, the information security program must be aligned to ensure that mission-critical business processes and data are adequately secured.

BUSINESS ENVIRONMENT

The business environment includes the company and the environment in which it operates. The company's environment includes various aspects such as the industry, competition, geography, and regulations to which the company is subject. The security implications associated with these aspects should be considered in an assessment. One characteristic of the environmental forces a company is facing is that the company has no control over them. This is important to understand because security risks associated with these environmental forces normally must be addressed. Companies have a certain amount of latitude in how much they do to address these security implications, but they must address them.

Two of the most prevalent forces from a business environment perspective are:

- *Regulatory requirements* — Laws such as the Health Insurance Portability and Accountability Act (HIPAA), the Gramm–Leach–Bliley Act (GLBA), and the Sarbanes–Oxley Act have forced companies to address information security. Companies have the opportunity to interpret the requirements for their own businesses but they must be compliant.
- *Industry* — One example is e-commerce, where an increasing number of companies have some type of security certification. As a result, some e-commerce vendors are now feeling the pressure to have a similar certification because they either have not really addressed security or they want to have a certification to provide confidence to consumers who shop at their site.

The best way to approach this topic with the client is to ask open-ended questions based on the research you have done. You should leverage any knowledge gained from reviewing trade journals, the Internet, and other sources to ask these questions.

PLANNED CHANGES THAT MAY IMPACT SECURITY

Planned changes or initiatives in a company can impact the results of a security assessment. Planned changes are significant events coming up for the company that will potentially have some sort of a security impact. Planned changes vary and can include:

- *Merger or acquisition* — If one has taken place, how will the different businesses be integrated? If a merger or acquisition is pending or has already occurred, what are the plans for integration? The information you receive on this topic may be limited because of confidentiality issues.
- *New technology implementation* — Major new technology initiatives — e.g., new remote access methods using clientless virtual private networks (VPNs) — will certainly impact the security posture of a company.
- *Location changes* — The company might be expanding into new locations or consolidating locations.
- *Outsourcing* — To save money, more companies are turning to outsourcing activities, including certain business processes and the management of parts of their IT organization. If this is in process, all kinds of security issues exist related to how the company's data will be secured and how information security activities are integrated into the outsourcing service.

The examples listed above are not an all-inclusive list, but they can be used to spark discussions with clients. The examples are also sensitive areas, some of which might still be in the initial discussion phases, so it is very possible that clients will not divulge this type of information. However, you should go through this process and see what information emerges.

Planned changes are brought up in this meeting because management will likely have a better sense of them. Although some things will be confidential and thus not divulged, management probably has a wealth of other information that would be useful for the security assessment. One key message that management should receive is that as these initiatives are planned, information security should be considered, particularly with changes in technology. You can provide significant added value by demonstrating how these planned initiatives impact the security posture of the company and why it is important to consider security early in the process.

ORGANIZATION STRUCTURE

The high-level organization structure was discussed in the initial questionnaire with the client. If those questions were answered, this discussion is merely to confirm the results of the questionnaire and drill down a little deeper, if necessary, to gain further information regarding the organization structure. The organization structure is important in a security assessment because it deals with people's roles and responsibilities. This leads to ownership and accountability, which is a fundamental concept in information security. Unclear roles and responsibilities and a lack of ownership and accountability of tasks lend themselves to an insecure environment.

When discussing the organization, some of the more specific items you should focus on for the security assessment include:

- *Ownership of the security function* — In any of the best practice standards for information security, one of the key components is accountability and ownership. Some companies have individuals who are officially responsible for the information security function, but in other companies, it is part of someone's responsibilities. When looking at overall ownership of information security, there are two main things to look for:
  - *What level position does the person responsible for information security report to?* — The reporting aspect is important because it will give some indication as to how seriously information security is taken. There is a big difference between a junior staff-level person with security-related responsibilities reporting to a manager-level person in IT and a Chief Information Security Officer (CISO) reporting to the chief information officer (CIO) or some other C-level executive of the company. If security is recognized at the C-level, greater assurance exists that the company is giving security importance. This is not a rule but it does provide a fairly strong indication. Another aspect to consider is how the security organization has evolved. Most CSOs, for example, have not been on the job for very long. In a survey that was reported in *CSO Magazine* in September 2002, 37 percent of CSOs surveyed had been in that position for less than one year and 25 percent had been on the job for one to two years. In other words, if a CSO who reports to a C-level executive is in place, it could mean that security is something that has recently been recognized as a concern. It could also mean that a security incident occurred that prompted the company to take security more seriously. The bottom line is that you should not only understand who is in charge of security and where that person reports, you should also understand how the structure evolved to its current state.
  - *Security organization* — This question is sort of an extension of the previous point and speaks to what someone in charge of security has at his or her disposal. Recall that the security organization is one of the key elements of an effective information security program. Ideally, the person in charge of security should have some people who report to him or her and who can implement and enforce good security practices. One of the things you might see is an organization where there is a person who is responsible for security but has no organization or authority. Such individuals are in a position where they are trying to convince other organizations to implement certain security measures. In companies where there is a strong security culture, this works. Otherwise, this structure is not very effective. During this discussion, you should also gauge management's attitude about ownership of the security function. Ownership is one of the most critical aspects of an

information security program, so it is important to understand how management sees the ownership of the security function.

- *Key roles and responsibilities related to information security* — As an extension to the above points regarding the ownership of information security, the next step is to understand the key roles and responsibilities with respect to information security. For the discussion with management, you need to determine whether the necessary building blocks for an information security program are present, as discussed in Chapter 3. The key roles and responsibilities related to each of these elements should be discussed at a high level with management. The seven elements and the associated roles and responsibilities are:
  - *Security strategy* — Security management in collaboration with business representatives responsible for developing strategy
  - *Security policies and procedures* — Security personnel responsible for working with various groups to update policies as the business changes
  - *Security organization* — Security personnel responsible for carrying out tasks related to information security
  - *Executive support* — Management responsible for providing support for information security initiatives
  - *Training and awareness* — Security and business unit personnel responsible for delivering appropriate training to ensure awareness of the importance of security
  - *Toolsets* — Management who have the authority to procure the right tools to automate certain security tasks
  - *Enforcement* — Security or audit personnel responsible for enforcing security measures and management providing the appropriate backing
- *IT organization* — The IT organization is a significant component of the overall information security posture of a company. The way in which the IT organization is set up will have implications as you perform the security assessment. In smaller companies, it could be a traditional IT staff with some work being done by consultants. You may even see certain parts of IT or all of IT being outsourced. In larger companies, you may see IT set up like a shared services organization, where one organization services the IT needs for various business units or each business unit has its own IT staff. It might be a combination of the two. A typical scenario for a company is having the management of the overall network as a centralized function and the typical system administration, application development, and other IT functions managed by the specific business units. Both types of environments (centralized and decentralized) have implications relevant for a security assessment. In a decentralized environment, the implications include potentially inconsistent security standards across platforms, inconsistent application of security policies, and a potential lack of ownership of security-related responsibilities at integration points between groups — i.e., each group thinks the other one is responsible for functions such as termination of users or change management. In a centralized environment, the implications include more controlled ownership of security and consistent

security processes related to information technology. For smaller companies, there is often one organization, in which case the issue of centralization versus decentralization does not make much of a difference.

MANAGEMENT CONCERNS REGARDING INFORMATION SECURITY

In most cases, the audience for the security assessment is management. Assuming that they are on board with the security assessment and understand the value of it, they will have certain expectations. They also have some of their own expectations and concerns when it comes to information security in their own environment. These expectations and concerns might be based on security incidents that might have occurred in the past, what they are reading in the trade magazines, regulatory concerns, and other issues. It is in your interest to understand what management's expectations and security-related concerns are. Although this may not substantively change what is done in the assessment, it does help you ensure that management is satisfied with the final outcome of the assessment because you can set their expectations accordingly. If something in particular concerns them from a security perspective, you can accommodate their concern by addressing it in the assessment or explain to the client that it is not really a concern or that it is not part of the scope. In any case, you have an opportunity to let the client know how you are going to handle their concerns so that they are not surprised in the end.

Remember that the success of the security assessment is partly driven by whether management sees the value in the final deliverable — i.e., the findings, risks, and recommendations. If key members of management feel that their concerns have not been addressed in some way, the value of the final product can be diminished no matter how good it is simply because some member of management was disappointed. Taking the time at the beginning of the assessment to listen to management's concerns is useful, and what you discover in this way should be kept in the back of your mind during the assessment. This knowledge will give you additional guidance when gathering information and making recommendations.

FINALIZE QUESTION SETS FOR PROCESS REVIEWS

In this step of the assessment (Figure 6.3), you will use your existing knowledge to finalize the question sets in preparation for the meetings with business process owners. At this point in the security assessment, you have had the initial meeting with management and you have a good "big picture" view of the company. Your next meetings will be with business process owners, where you will get into the details of business processes and the key supporting technologies. In preparation for your meetings, the question sets that were begun in the last phase need to be modified to reflect what you have learned about the company. Using the Generic Question Set for business process owners from the last chapter (in Appendix B), you now have to build on that question set based on what you have learned about the company since developing those questions. Finalizing the question sets is really a process of developing specific questions for the people whom you will be interviewing. For example, if you are interviewing someone who has responsibility for facilities, you

FIGURE 6.3 Finalize question sets for process reviews.

would add more specific questions related to physical security. Similarly, if you are talking to someone who handles all application service provider (ASP) relationships, you would ask more specific questions related to externally hosted services. If you are meeting with a business process owner who is responsible for an area for which a specific questionnaire is provided in the appendices, use that particular question-naire in addition to the generic questionnaire.

To finalize the question sets, you essentially have to take the generic question set that has been developed and add in the specific questions for the people whom you will interview. These updates may or may not be extensive, depending on how much you learned from your meeting with management and how many additional questions it raised. When you update question sets, you will certainly add questions, but equally important, you will be able to take some questions out because they have been answered or are not applicable. One thing to avoid is asking questions that have already been answered unless there is some value in confirming the answer or hearing another perspective.

The process of updating the question sets can be daunting, considering the amount of information you are learning. You must document the information you learned from the meeting with management and determine what updates are required. Going forward, you should get used to documenting your meetings in a way that is most efficient for you.

As you update the question sets, ask anything you feel is necessary for you to conduct a successful security assessment. On the other hand, keep in mind that you should have a reason for asking your questions. There is a good chance that at some point, the client might say, "Why are you asking me that question?" If you cannot provide a response and tell the client the reason for the question, you will lose credibility with the client. Conversely, being able to clearly explain the reason for a question will enhance your credibility with the client. For the questions in the appendices, note that all questions have a section called "Guidance." This section articulates why certain questions are asked and why they are relevant for a security assessment. You should have something similar for the questions you develop so you are prepared when questioning the client.

The other value of understanding why you are asking a question is that it can help you frame the question to the customer. If the person being interviewed under-stands why the question is being asked, the response will probably be more mean-ingful. The client will also start to see you as an expert and might open up with other information.

The value of the question sets cannot be emphasized enough. Being prepared when talking to the client's subject matter experts is critical. It represents one of the fundamental concepts of this methodology, which is preparation. A common com-plaint with customers is that consultants either ask questions that are irrelevant or they are just using a checklist without giving any thought to the particular circum-stances of the company. This approach indicates that you have done little preparation and immediately diminishes your credibility. Remember that when a company wants security assessment done, they are looking for independent expertise. Being pre-pared, asking the right questions, and demonstrating knowledge about security and the client's business demonstrate the expertise that clients expect.

MEET WITH BUSINESS PROCESS OWNERS

Now that you have finalized the question sets, you are ready to meet with the business process owners (Figure 6.4). These meetings are one of the most important parts of the security assessment because it is in these meetings where you will learn the business of the client in detail. Before you begin the meetings, certain steps should be taken.

PREPARATION FOR MEETINGS

First, the business process owners must be "prepared" so that they are aware of the security assessment. Until now, you and the team performing the assessment have not met the business process owners. At the kickoff meeting, you met the stakeholders, who were probably managers of the business process owners with whom you will now be working. Even if some of the stakeholders are also the business process owners, the security assessment might not be something that is in the forefront for them. It is for these reasons that you should ensure that your single point of contact from the client personally informs the process owners before you meet with them. The one thing you do not want to hear when you walk into a meeting is, "What are we doing? I don't know about any security assessment." If people are not told in advance, this type of response is very possible. If this does happen, it creates a problem for two reasons. First, you have to waste a portion of the meeting time having to explain the security assessment, why it is being done, and other details about it. Second, if the people you are interviewing are surprised about the assessment, they might be suspicious about the whole process, and as a result, they may be less than forthcoming with information.

To prevent this from happening, you can do two things. First, you can insist that your single point of contact inform the interviewees prior to you meeting them to ensure that they know that you are coming. Second, you can provide the question set to them in advance of the meeting. This enables business process owners to prepare for the meeting. In addition, if there are topics that they cannot discuss effectively, they can bring in the people who can.

INTERVIEWS WITH PROCESS OWNERS

Once in the meeting, you must ensure that you are prepared for the meeting and that you run it in an efficient way. Remember that the people you are talking to are taking time out from their jobs to talk to you. They might be on tight schedules, so you should make the most of the time you have with them.

To facilitate the conversation, use the question set that you have prepared and hopefully given them prior to the meeting. If you can follow the order of the questions from the question set, then definitely do so. More likely than not, the conversation you have will jump around a little based on how the question set is structured. This is all right as long as you stay within the intended topics. If the conversation goes off on a tangent, you will have to make a judgment call as to whether the topic is relevant.

FIGURE 6.4 Meet with business process owners.

One issue for many people during these meetings is taking notes. This may seem trivial, but when you consider the amount of information that you are obtaining, it can be a challenge to document the information. The challenge is knowing what to document and then organizing the information afterwards so the proper analysis can be done. In these situations, people use a variety of methods to make sure everything is captured. You can use a white board and document key facts as the client says them so the client also sees the documentation and can confirm that the right information is captured. You can also bring a person to the meeting whose job is to be the scribe and make sure that the information is being captured. Ensuring that these meetings are properly documented is critical because the information derived from the meetings will be used in the analysis.

If process owners seem confused when you are asking something or are uncertain about the relevance of the question, you should explain the relevance. In the question sets in the appendices of this book, the questions have "Guidance" sections to help in understanding the relevance of questions.

POTENTIAL PITFALLS

When you get into this phase of the security assessment and particularly with the business process owner meetings, you should be aware of and try to avoid several potential pitfalls.

One that has already been touched on is an interview going off track. To avoid this, use the question sets to help you remain focused on the topics relevant to the assessment. You should stress that in the interest of time, you have to address the topics in the question set, which the client should have received prior to the meeting. The question sets will be of great help in this scenario because you can see what has to be discussed. Without the question sets, there is nothing in writing to help you focus the conversation.

Another potential pitfall is the uncooperative client. These cases are difficult because you must handle them delicately. Again, the question sets help you at least in obtaining the listed information. Depending on how the meeting goes, you may or may not get any additional information from these individuals, but you must at least address the items on the questionnaire. If you are not getting the cooperation you need and you have exhausted diplomatic ways to deal with the situation, you should talk to the single point of contact or preferably, the executive sponsor. This can be difficult, but keep in mind who the customer is — the executive sponsor. You are accountable to that person. If issues arise that you cannot resolve, you should escalate to the executive sponsor. This can be done in a separate conversation with the executive sponsor or it can be done during a status meeting, depending on the severity of the situation.

ANALYZE INFORMATION COLLECTED
AND DOCUMENT FINDINGS

Once your meetings with the business process owners are complete, it is important to analyze and document what you have learned, particularly the findings (Figure 6.5).

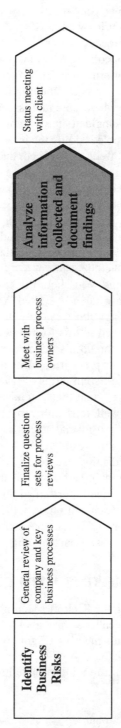

FIGURE 6.5 Analyze information collected and document findings.

Using the raw data collected during your meetings with the client, you must now perform the analysis to identify security weaknesses. At this point, whatever findings you have are primarily business process related.

Analyzing the information you collected will take some time. Flowcharting can be used to help you analyze the information. This method enables you to visualize the process, along with where in the process the different systems are used; thus, it will make it easier for you to see where potential issues exist.

When analyzing the data, you should do it as a team. This is important, especially in assessments where a team of people is doing the interviewing because it facilitates information sharing between the different people conducting the assessments. Information sharing is critical during the analysis because it is likely that information that someone else collected may help you better understand the business processes. Also, significant integration points probably exist between the various business processes, thus increasing the importance of information sharing.

The data used in the analysis and the basis of any findings you make are important to have. You need them to help explain the basis of the finding. It is also possible that when you present a finding, the client might ask for its basis.

As you document your findings, you should document them straight into the final report, which you should have already started. You can gain significant efficiencies by formatting your findings the way they are going to look in the final report. They will have to be arranged in this format at some point anyway.

Along with the findings, you should also document the associated risk. When documenting risk, do your best to express it in terms of impact to the business. To the extent that you can quantify the risk in terms of revenue or potential costs to the company, you should do so. To the extent that you have formulated a recommendation, you should document that as well. Remember that this is an evolving document, so it is not a problem if it is in rough format at this stage. The key is to have your thoughts on paper while they are still fresh.

One of the pitfalls when conducting security assessments is not documenting throughout the process. If you are saving all of the documentation until the end, you risk leaving information out of the final report. In addition, the more time you spend developing the report during the assessment process, the more time you can spend at the end refining the report. Conversely, it can take significantly more time to document the report at the end just because your thoughts are no longer fresh.

STATUS MEETING WITH CLIENT

One of the topics discussed during the Kickoff Meeting during the first phase of the security assessment was communications throughout the course of the assessment. Now is a good time to have a status meeting (Figure 6.6) because you are about to complete this phase. As you near the end of this phase, you should have a status meeting with the client to go over a few items including:

- Findings
- Status based on the project plan
- Discussion of critical technologies you plan to test

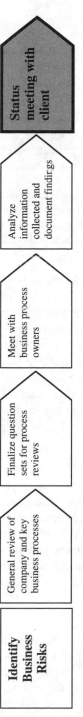

FIGURE 6.6 Status meeting with client.

FINDINGS

Discussing the findings at this stage is important for two reasons:

- *Clients have the opportunity to provide feedback* — Although you may think you have a valid issue, you might not have considered all of the facts or there might be some mitigating controls related to a finding of which you were not aware. The status meeting provides the client an opportunity to respond to the issue and provide you with additional information that might be relevant. In the following example, the client was able to provide feedback indicating that the risk related to a finding was lower than anticipated.

Example: You may cite a critical finding because there is no real process for ensuring that terminated employees' access is removed. You might not have considered the fact that user access lists are reviewed every two weeks, allowing the customer to find out which terminated employees still have access. With this mitigating control, the risk is reduced.

- *Clients are not surprised when they see the final report* — When management reviews reports, there is usually a focus on security weaknesses, which is reasonable because the purpose of the security assessment is to discover weaknesses in the security posture of the company. The client should not be surprised by these findings for two reasons. First, it makes business process owners uncomfortable because they might not know how to answer questions posed by management regarding the security weaknesses identified. Second, the client may point out something that you did not catch, and the finding either has to change or be taken out altogether. Either situation is not good for any of the parties involved.

STATUS BASED ON PROJECT PLAN

You should now use the project plan you developed to track where you are relative to the original timing. This is also the time to discuss any scheduling issues you might be having. It is good for the client to see progress or lack thereof. Tracking against the project plan is especially critical because you are very dependent on the client to coordinate all of the meetings and facilitate the process from a client perspective. If things are not going as planned, there should be clear accountability for it. Project plans help establish that accountability.

DISCUSSION OF CRITICAL TECHNOLOGIES

One of the outcomes of this phase of the security assessment is to finalize what critical technologies you plan to test during the next phase of the assessment. It is useful to discuss these technologies with your point of contact so the required scheduling can begin. Depending on the testing, there might be a potential for disrupting service, or you might need certain people to be with you while you do the testing. The client can begin making these arrangements to help ensure that the technology evaluation phase of the security assessment is done in an efficient manner. Depending on the size and complexity of the organization, scheduling the resources from a systems perspective can be challenging. This is especially true because you will be reviewing systems that are critical to the business.

Having a security assessment status meeting at the end of this phase is critical. However, the first phase may have taken a couple of weeks. If that is the case, you should have a quick status meeting with the client at least on a weekly basis to discuss findings and determine how progress is going according to the project plan. If you go too long without giving status information to the client, you risk not meeting the expectations of the client.

POTENTIAL CONCERNS DURING THIS PHASE

Concerns that you should be aware of as you progress through this phase include:

- *Lack of cooperation from the client business process owners* — Business process owners may not be forthcoming with information for several reasons. First, they may not have been forewarned about the security assessment, so they may be caught off guard. In this case, you should inform your point of contact, so that this person can educate the business process owners about why the security assessment is being done. Another reason is that the security assessment might not be a welcome process for people in the company. Again, in this case, you should ask your point of contact or the executive sponsor to educate client personnel.
- *Your findings do not reflect accurate information* — If you document a finding and do not discuss it with the client early in the process through a status meeting or some other means, the client will not have the opportunity to let you know about any facts you might have missed. The remedy for this issue is communication with the client. If you have an important finding, you need not wait for the status meetings.
- *The client feels that you are not well informed about the company or the assessment* — This is an issue of credibility that you may have with the client. One of the reasons is a lack of research about the company, which is the second phase of the security assessment methodology. In talking with the business process owners, you should already have a good idea about the company and thus, you should not be asking general questions that have been covered. Another reason this issue with the client might occur is a lack of communication among the team performing the security assessment. It is possible that someone else from the team already asked the information you are asking about. Consequently, communication within the team is important, just as communication with the client is.

EXECUTIVE SUMMARY

Business process review is the third phase in the security assessment methodology. It is also the first time when significant interaction with the client occurs. In this phase, the focus is to gain a good understanding of critical business processes at a fairly detailed level. Another result of this phase is determining the key technology dependencies, which will be reviewed in the next phase.

The key steps in this phase are:

- *Generally review the company and key business processes* — The purpose of this step is to learn about the company, what it does, and how it does it. In this step, you are trying to identify the mission-critical business processes and their technology dependencies. In addition, you should also learn about the strategic direction of the company and whether any changes are planned that may have an impact on the existing information security program. This is important, as it will affect the recommendations. To obtain this information, it is essential that you meet with someone from management who has a good "big picture" of the company and the direction in which it is heading.
- *Finalize question sets for process reviews* — The question sets that are used to facilitate the meetings with business process owners should have been started during the last phase, initial information gathering, based on initial research about the company. During this phase, after you identify the critical business processes and gain other strategy-related information about the company, you should modify your question sets as necessary to reflect the new information learned. These modifications can include addition, deletion, or modification of questions.
- *Meet with business process owners* — Using the question sets developed, meetings with business process owners should take place next. In these meetings, business processes and related security implications are discussed. An effective technique to capture process-related information is to create a flowchart. Some of the items you should capture out of these meetings are the criticality of the business processes, critical data and how it is stored, access control, and tolerable downtime — i.e., how long the client could withstand not being able to perform a given business process. You should also be determining what the technology dependencies are and whether any workarounds exist if the technology is not available.
- *Analyze information collected and document findings* — With the data collected from the business process owners, the next step is to analyze the data and determine whether you have any findings. The findings should be documented along with the associated risk and the recommendation (if one has been formulated) straight into the report template that was developed in the previous phases. Documenting this way is efficient and leaves more time for reviewing and refining the findings and recommendations.

- *Hold a status meeting with the client* — The final step in this phase is to have a status meeting with the client to communicate the findings and discuss the project status based on the project plan. Status meetings are important because they give the client a chance to provide feedback on findings that have been discovered and to ensure that you are meeting the client's expectations regarding the security assessment. Status meetings should be held as often as necessary, or at least once a week so that the client is aware of what is happening with the assessment. In some cases, you might even have informal meetings with the client to go over project status or a significant finding. The key is to always make sure the client is well informed.

7 Technology Evaluation

The evaluation of the technology environment is the last part of the information-gathering phase. The approach for the review of the technology environment is the same as that for the business process. It starts with looking at the technology in place from a "big picture" perspective and then drilling down and examining the critical technologies in more detail. Based on where you are in the methodology, you should know what the critical technologies are based on the interviews in the last phase and the business process analysis.

At this point, most or all of the business process–related interviews should have occurred. Per the methodology espoused in this book, it is critical that the business process discussions happen before the technology discussions take place. The reality is that schedules do not always go as planned, though, and as a result, some of the activities from the business process analysis phase will probably carry over into the technology review phase. This will usually happen to accommodate schedules of the participants in the security assessment. As long as the number of business process interviews not yet completed is small, you can proceed with the technology evaluation. However, some technical reviews will have to wait until the outstanding meetings from the last phase are completed. In approaching the security assessment, you must be flexible in your approach.

The purpose of this phase is to evaluate the technology environment and assess how secure it is based on the business processes it supports. All components in the technology environment do not have to meet the same standard. Components that support mission-critical business processes will clearly have higher standards to meet. You will know the appropriate level of security based on what you learned during interviews with business process owners. For example, if a mission-critical application requires Internet connectivity, the security of the connection to the Internet will be considered critical. Conversely, a server that is used to provide remote access to users in an environment where the vast majority of workers do not work remotely will not be very important from an availability perspective, but you might look at who has administrative rights on the machine. It all depends on the business process that the technology is supporting and the potential impact to the business in the event of a security incident.

In evaluating the technology environment, you should be looking for security measures that are commensurate with the degree of risk and the criticality of the technology. Although we want to err on the side of conservatism by having more security than required, you should try to ensure that the level of security is "appropriate" — neither too little nor too much. This idea of an "appropriate" level of security ties into the concept of risk analysis and employing security measures that are cost effective. In the next chapter, we will discuss the concept of "risk score," which will delve deeper into risk analysis.

The reason for bringing this up at this stage is to help frame your thinking as you start to assess the technology. When reviewing the various security measures, think along the lines of how the technology supports the critical business processes and protects critical data and whether the level of security is appropriate.

We will now discuss the specific steps of this phase, which include the following:

- General review of technology and related documentation
- Finalizing question sets for technology reviews
- Meeting with technology owners and conducting detailed testing
- Analysis of information collected and documentation of findings
- Status meeting with client

Note that the steps in this phase are similar to the business process review. The similarities include starting with a general review, drilling down into specifics, analysis, and communication with the client. This approach of starting general and then conducting detailed reviews in specific risk areas provides the opportunity to get the "big picture" as well as a detailed look into critical areas.

The next sections discuss each step of this phase in detail.

GENERAL REVIEW OF TECHNOLOGY
AND RELATED DOCUMENTATION

The first step in this phase is to conduct a general review of the technology the company is using and what the company's plans are for future changes in technology (Figure 7.1). This step has two components:

- Receiving an overview of technology from someone who has a management role in information technology (IT)
- Reviewing any technology documentation

One problem you might run into is that there might not be any IT people who are considered management. This is especially true in small companies where there might be a very small number of users. In these small companies, the office administrator might be the person who is charged with IT. Even in these cases, it is good to get this individual's perspective on technology, its current use, and what the plans are for the future.

As you speak to IT management, you will find that you know some of the information already from speaking with the business process owners. It is still worth going over this information again for two reasons. First, IT management might give you some general information that the business process owners did not give. For example, IT management might have insight into certain technology selections and why they were made. This is good background information in helping you understand how the different technologies are supposed to support the business. The second reason is that it allows you to determine whether IT management and the business process owners are on the same page as it relates to technology. If business process owners and IT management do not have a common understanding about

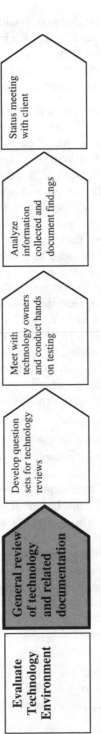

FIGURE 7.1 General review of technology and related documentation.

technology, this is a potential finding that you should discuss with the client because it could indicate a disconnect between IT and the business process owners.

To make the most of your time with the technology owners, you should first review some key technology-related documentation that the client might have. You should request the following documentation and review what is given:

- *Network topology diagram* — The topology diagram is the first thing you should review because it will give you a good overview of what the technology environment looks like. You should be able to look at this diagram and see it how it relates to the business — i.e., how the technology is supporting the business. Reviewing the network topology might uncover potential single points of failure or raise other questions about the environment that you can ask the technology owners when you interview them.
- *Copies of configurations, logs, and other operational documents* — These are miscellaneous documents that you can review to look at what kind of activity is going on. Some of these logs may include security and event logs from servers, intrusion detection logs, or other operational documents. You may find that some of this review is more appropriately performed online. If you do decide to review this information online, make sure the client knows and provides limited access for you to perform your job.
- *Recent audit reports* — Some companies have had previous security audits performed, or some clients might have some level of security review based on their financial audits. If any recent audit reports exist that provide any information about the company's security posture, it is good to have them as they might provide you with information about security issues that the company might have had.

When asking for documentation, such as the items listed above, remember that it is confidential information. You must ensure that you are treating the documents appropriately.

Once you have reviewed this documentation, you are in a position to have a meeting with IT management. As stated before, it is very important to speak with someone in a managerial capacity who can give you the "big-picture" view of the technology environment and show you how everything fits together and how it has evolved to what it is today. This information should be especially meaningful now that you have learned about the business in some detail. Note: You might have gone over some of this information during the Initial Information Gathering phase when you went over the questionnaire with the client. Some of this information is worth going over again with IT management.

The topics that you should discuss during your meeting with IT management include:

- Describe how the network and the general IT environment are set up.
  - Discuss the network topology diagram.
  - Gain a historical perspective as to how the environment evolved to where it is today.

- Describe what security architecture is in place.
  - Are there security technologies such as firewalls, intrusion detection systems, or other devices in place?
  - Who administers these devices?
- Describe any security-related procedures that are in place.
  - Examples of security-related procedures include log review and change management.
- Where does the critical data reside?
  - Based on your meetings from the last phase, you should be able to identify what data is critical and have IT management tell you where it resides. You might know this already; even if that is the case, it is worth confirming.
  - What security measures are in place to protect the critical data?
  - How is access to this data controlled?
- Where do the critical applications reside?
  - Based on your meetings, you should be able to identify the critical applications and have the client tell you where they reside.
  - How is access control for the applications handled?
- Describe the high-level roles and responsibilities within IT.
  - Is there ownership for key systems?
  - Who owns security from an IT perspective — e.g., duties such as log review, ensuring that servers have the appropriate security settings, anti-virus administration?
  - Who owns the responsibility for the information security program (if one exists)?
  - Does someone in the company have the ultimate responsibility for security?
- What are your key vendor relationships?
  - Determine who the key vendors are and how those relationships are managed. This is important because of the technical and other support a vendor can offer.
  - Does someone own the responsibility of managing the key vendor relationships?
  - What warranties and service contracts do you have in place with key vendors?
- Where does the security function fit into the IT organization?
  - Are there any positions dedicated to security?
  - Is security incorporated into people's job responsibilities?
- Have there been any security incidents? What mechanisms do you have in place to detect security incidents?
  - How was the incident handled?
  - Is there a documented incident handling process?
  - What measures were put in place to prevent similar incidents from happening again?

- What initiatives are being planned for IT? Are any security related?
  - Examples of potential initiatives include e-commerce, outsourcing, use of ASPs (Application Service Providers), and business-to-business (B2B).
- What concerns does IT management have relative to information security?
  - Is IT management concerned about any specific security issues? If there are any, what is being planned to mitigate the potential risks?
- How is the communication between IT and the rest of the business?
  - Are there any liaisons that facilitate communication between IT and everyone else?

The questions above are a generic set of questions to get you started. You can add to these questions or take away items that you might already know about. If you are adding questions, keep in mind that you are dealing with someone from management — i.e., you are better off keeping your questions high level.

With the information learned in this meeting, you are ready to begin developing question sets to use when meeting with the specific technology owners. By this time, you should also have finalized which technology owners you will need to meet with. Based on how long you will need to develop the question sets, you should tell your single point of contact to begin setting up the meetings with the technology owners.

DEVELOP QUESTION SETS
FOR TECHNOLOGY REVIEWS

Now you are in a position to develop and finalize the question sets for your meetings with technology owners (Figure 7.2). Similar to the list of topics and questions developed for the business process subject matter experts, a similar list should be developed for the technology owners. The question sets for the technology owners are as important as the last set. They will help you prepare for the meetings and help you ensure that all relevant topics are covered.

The structure of the suggested question sets for the technology owners is similar to that of the question sets for the business process owners. There will be a set of generic questions that can be asked to all of the technology owners. To develop the specific questions, you must leverage what you learned from the business process evaluation, the meeting with IT management, and any information you learned from the initial research about the company. The answers to these questions along with the detailed technical review later in this phase will provide you with what you need to properly evaluate the technology environment from a security perspective.

The generic questions that will be used in the meetings with technology owners will focus on what technology they are responsible for, how they manage it, how they secure it, and various other aspects. In addition to that, there will be some specific questions for the person you are talking to based on that individual's job

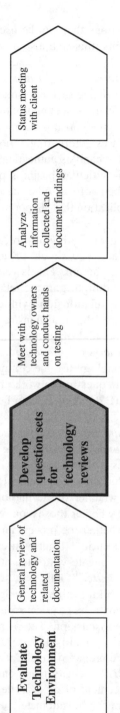

FIGURE 7.2 Develop question sets for technology reviews.

function. Below are generic questions that can be used as a starting point, which can be used in security assessments (this will also be included in the appendices):

- *What technology are you responsible for and what business process does it support?* With your knowledge of the business, you should have some perspective on how the technology supports the business. However, the IT person will be able to give you a different angle on how it supports the business. In some cases, there might not be a specific business process — e.g., a server that handles authentication into the network does not necessarily support a particular business process — it is providing access so users can do their job. In other cases, the technology owner might be managing an application that supports a mission-critical business process.
- *Where does it fit into the overall architecture?* Assuming that a network topology diagram is in place, you should be able to see where the technology fits into the IT environment. This is very helpful because it gives you a visual perspective and highlights the relationships with other parts of the IT environment. The relationships with other parts of the IT environment will likely generate other questions regarding integration points, transmission of information, and other topics.
- *What are the key dependencies for the technology you manage?* The key dependencies for any technology are the components that must be functional for the technology in question to work properly. A simple example is business to commerce (B2C). For B2C to be functional, access to the Internet is required.
- *What are the security requirements from a security perspective — e.g., confidentiality, integrity, and availability? Are these requirements being met?* From the discussions with the business process owners, you should have a good sense for what these requirements are. The purpose of this question is to determine whether the technology owner is aware of the security requirements and whether those requirements are being met. One thing to look for here is whether the process and technology owners have the same perspective on security. If not, you can delve further into how the different groups communicate with each other.
- *How is the technology secured?* This is a follow-up on the previous question. When you are talking about how it is secured, a number of aspects including access controls, physical security, and integrity controls should be included in the discussion. The methods depend on the technology. This question will probably lead to a technical discussion, for which it is important to be prepared to talk at a technical level.
- *How is security enforced?* If security is not enforced, its value is diminished significantly. Enforcement efforts can be automated or manual. To the extent that enforcement can be automated, it should be. Other methods of enforcement include periodic reviews and audits.
- *Does critical data reside on any system you manage? If so, how is it secured?* From your business process interviews, you should know what

critical data exists. This is an opportunity to get the perspective of the IT person, which should hopefully be in line with what you know already. Once you learn how the information is secured, you can determine whether the level of security is appropriate based on the criticality of the data.

- *If the systems you manage were not available, how quickly could they be functional?* With this question, you will have to go through several different scenarios because all system failures are not the same. The goal with this question is to get a range of times for how long the systems can be unavailable and whether these ranges are acceptable based on the availability requirements that the business has. This is one of the areas where there is often a disconnect between IT and the business. It is both a communication and a budget issue. For example, there is a big difference in guaranteeing four-hour maximum downtime and one business day maximum downtime on a given system. A classic example is e-mail. Many people will tell you that they cannot do any work without e-mail and that half a day is about all they can tolerate. When you start looking at what it costs to meet a half-day maximum downtime requirement, the tolerable downtime will likely change and other methods of communication such as the telephone might become more of a viable option.

- *What type of logging and monitoring activities do you perform?* For key machines or devices, some level of logging and monitoring should be taking place. For example, for critical servers, does anyone review any of the event logs or any of the other relevant logs? How much log review and monitoring activity occurs provides some indication of how proactive or reactive the company's security measures are. The level of logging and monitoring is often a function of how many people the client has to do the work and the risks that the company faces.

- *Is a formal change management process followed for any changes to the technology managed?* Whether or not a change management process is followed is an indicator of how controlled the environment is. If no change management process is followed, it can lead to more questions depending on the technology. At a minimum, a lack of a change management process should be flagged as an issue.

- *Have there been any security incidents with any of the technology you manage?* This question is the same as what was asked to the process owners. This is good information because it provides some clues about what vulnerabilities might exist, what the impacts are, and what management did to ensure that it does not happen again. If an incident occurred, find out the details and ask about how it was handled and what subsequent steps were taken to prevent it from happening again.

- *Are there any changes planned for the technology you manage? If so, have the security implications been considered?* Planned changes can affect your evaluation depending on what they are. Some examples include a major overhaul of the technology, change in architecture, changes in organization, merger or acquisition activity, and outsourcing. If any new initiatives are planned, you should find out if security is (was) considered in the planning process. Any changes that the technology owner can talk about are worth discussing because they will affect your evaluation.

- *Other questions as a result of the information gathered:* These are the customized questions you will generate based on what you have learned so far. Some of the specific questions should be detailed questions about the configuration of the technology being managed and the activities required to administer it.

The questions above should be modified to the extent you feel necessary. You can add to these questions and use the question sets in the appendices as a guide. Although the questions above are general, you might have already gone over much of this from your other interviews. This is particularly true in smaller environments where everyone knows what everyone does. In larger environments, it is definitely worth asking the questions, as you will find cases where little communication occurs between IT and the business. As a result, there is a gap between what the business is expecting from a technical security perspective and what is actually being done.

MEET WITH TECHNOLOGY OWNERS
AND CONDUCT DETAILED TESTING

Meeting with the technology owners (Figure 7.3) is the second set of meetings where you will gather significant information for the security assessment. At this point, you have a good understanding of the business, what some of the key risks are, and what the critical technologies are. You are ready to go deeper into the technology and determine whether the level of security is appropriate. In preparation for the meetings with the technology owners, two key steps should be taken:

- *Developing the question sets for the meetings* — In the previous step of the methodology, we discussed the development of the question sets, so they should be completed. In preparation for meetings with technology owners, questionnaires should be given to the technology owners in advance. This allows them to be prepared for the meeting and bring in any other resources that might be necessary to answer your questions. When developing the question sets, it is critical to customize the questions as much as possible. This will help you in spending more meaningful time with the technology owners. It is important to recognize that technology owners are involved in day-to-day operations, and in some companies, smaller ones in particular, their time is typically stretched very thin. It is therefore critical to make the most of your time with them. It is in everyone's interest to be as efficient as possible.
- *Preparing the technology owners* — Similar to business process owners, technology owners must be educated about the security assessment so that when they are asked questions, they are not caught off guard. One of the worst things that can happen is going to a meeting and having the person say to you, "Why are you here?" or "I don't know anything about

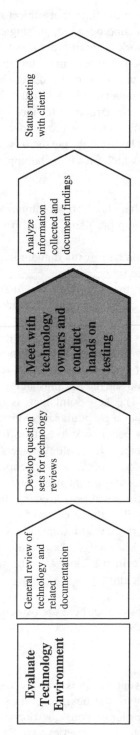

FIGURE 7.3 Meet with technology owners and conduct detailed testing.

what you are doing." From the time that subject matter experts are identified on the business or technology side, the single point of contact should get the message out or work through other management to make sure the message is out. Technology owners must understand what the security assessment is all about, why it is being done, and what their role is. If the participants have that understanding, it makes it that much easier when you talk to them about the particular technology they work with. The other benefit of informing technology owners early is that if anyone is identified who might not be the right person to work with, you will know sooner rather than later, which provides the opportunity to find the right person.

Some of the key messages that should be communicated to technology owners when scheduling interviews to help put them at ease if necessary include:

- Technology owners should be informed about what has been done in the security assessment so far.
- They should realize that the quality of the final deliverable is directly dependent on the quality of the information that the various subject matter experts provide.
- Technology owners (this is also true for business process owners who participate in the security assessment) should know that they will have an opportunity to comment on the findings and recommendations in the report. Ideally, they should see the findings and recommendations as soon as they are developed. The key point here is that they will have the opportunity to say whether a particular recommendation is feasible or if they may perhaps have a better way to address the security issues.
- On a more logistical level, the technology owners should understand that hands-on testing will be done on various machines. In some cases, individuals performing the testing might need temporary access to different machines or devices on the network. Assessing the security related to the key technologies is critical to the success of the overall security assessment. Technology owners can add tremendous value in ensuring this success because of their knowledge. As a result, it is very important that technology personnel are in the loop with the security assessment and understand why it is happening.

For this step of the security assessment, there are two components: interviews with the technology owners and hands-on testing of the critical systems.

INTERVIEWS

The interviews are conducted using the question sets to guide the conversation. As with the interviews conducted with the business process owners, the conversation will not necessarily follow the order of your questionnaire; however, the questionnaire will help ensure that you have covered everything you needed to cover. The interviews with the technology owners will include both process-related questions and technical questions about the technology they specifically manage. You may find that some of the information you receive from the technology owners is information you already know because of your previous conversations. It is still valuable to hear this because it will help you ensure that everyone is on the same page with regards to the technology.

When recording the results of the meeting, it is valuable to document processes through some type of flowcharting method. In fact, you can take any flowcharts that were developed during the last phase, and the technology can almost be overlaid on top of the processes. This is an excellent technique to help you tie in the technology to the business processes. It also helps you identify where the holes or single points of failure potentially exist on the network. This analysis will help you further confirm the technologies on which you have chosen to conduct detailed testing.

When conducting these interviews with technical people, it is critical to have the right people doing the interviewing. People without the right skill sets can lose credibility with the client and not gain the information that is required for the analysis. One of the concerns that the company is going to have is that someone who is not very qualified is going to talk to them using a checklist or questionnaire to gather information. If this happens, it can lead to a loss of credibility for those conducting the assessment.

HANDS-ON TESTING

Hands-on testing requires careful planning with the client's personnel. You also need to understand what you are testing and the purpose of it. In keeping with the methodology discussed in this book, you need to ensure that you are spending the time testing the technologies that support key business processes. These technologies should have been identified based on the business process–related interviews and your meeting with IT management.

When thinking about hands-on testing, you need to consider several factors related to planning, tool selection, etc. In this section, we will discuss all of the relevant facets of hands-on testing, which include the following:

- Reasons for conducting hands-on testing
- Planning considerations for hands-on testing
- Manual vs. automated testing
- Tool selection
- Hands-on testing methodology

Reasons for Conducting Detailed Testing

Before discussing the actual methodology for hands-on testing, it is worth discussing why we conduct hands-on testing and some of the challenges and risks associated with it. Hands-on testing is a critical component of a security assessment for a number of reasons. Up until now, all of the information you have received has been through interviews and has been largely process focused. You might have tested some processes through observation to verify that they were being done the way they were explained to you. Even for the technology, you have conducted interviews with technology owners. On the technology side, you have not looked at anything in detail. For example, you have not reviewed certain configuration settings on machines to determine whether they are secure. To really understand the security posture of a company, you must look at the critical technologies in detail to determine what vulnerabilities exist. These are technical vulnerabilities, which technology owners may or may not know depending on how much they do from a security perspective. Unlike process-focused vulnerabilities, which can be subjective, the vulnerabilities found in the technical testing will tend to be objective with fairly clear fixes. These vulnerabilities are ones that have been exploited in the past by hackers and the like. With these vulnerabilities, the choice is to either fix them or demonstrate that the vulnerability is a result of a required business process.

It is very likely that one of the reasons you were asked to conduct a security assessment was because of the expertise to conduct this type of detailed testing. For customer management teams who have requested a security assessment, the vulnerabilities that exist in the technology are an unknown to which they cannot relate. As a security practitioner, you bring security expertise and the right tools to determine vulnerabilities on systems. You also know what resources to tap into to determine vulnerabilities. This knowledge and expertise make hands-on testing successful.

Hands-on testing is performed for these reasons:

- *Verification* — Up to this point, everything you know is based on what people in the company have told you. Some of the information is critical enough to verify using hands-on testing. This does not mean that you are being misled. It is very possible and probable that what people think is not always the case. IT staffs are stretched very thin and in some companies, no one has any ownership of security. It is perfectly reasonable that some things are going to fall through the cracks. For example, one thing that many companies need to do a better job with is staying up to date with patches. In large environments and even some small ones, this can be a daunting task. Not staying up to date with certain patches can have major security implications depending on the technology and the patch. In this case, even if you are being told that all patches are up to date, it might be worthwhile to scan or manually review some of the critical machines to ensure and verify that patches are up to date. This testing will either confirm or not confirm what you are being told about patches, which will enhance the results of the security assessment. Depending on the results, you might also be able to provide some valuable recommendations. How much or little detailed testing is performed is a judgment call based on what business processes are supported by the given technology, how critical a component the technology is in the process, and the risk associated with the technology and how it is administered.
- *Perception* — Depending on the audience, detailed testing is very important. For many people who understand the vulnerabilities associated with technology, a security assessment without going hands-on into the system

might not carry a whole lot of credibility. For example, in your review of user ID administration practices, you might have been told that users do not have good passwords. Taking that at face value and writing a recommendation where you recite password best practices may or may not carry weight. However, if you take the password file and run a password cracker that guesses 90 percent of the passwords in less than five minutes and use those results as your finding, both the finding and recommendation will carry much more weight. Findings that are backed up with objective hands-on test results are difficult to dispute. The only discussion then is what risk does it pose and whether the associated recommendation is appropriate. The other aspect of perception is that clients will generally expect that some level of detailed testing will be done unless this was specifically taken out of the scope of the assessment via mutual agreement between you and the client. Generally speaking, a security assessment is thought of as having some level of focus on technology, which is understandable as many of the security issues today are due to technology and the related processes. If you do not conduct any hands-on testing of the technology, it is very possible that clients might not be completely comfortable with the results, particularly the technology-related findings and recommendations, thereby potentially reducing the credibility of the whole assessment.

- *Quality of results* — The quality of the results of the security assessment, to a large extent, will depend on the hands-on testing. As alluded to earlier, some of the findings have more impact if technical and objective testing can back them up. For the more significant findings dealing with technical issues, it is almost imperative to have some technical hands-on testing results to back up the finding. Keep in mind the audience of the deliverable when thinking about the quality of the results. For the executive-level person whose focus is the "big picture," these details do not matter much. For the IT director or security officer who might be in charge of implementing some of the recommendations you present in the final deliverable, the hands-on testing details are very relevant. The success of the assessment is largely driven by whether or not the company uses the final deliverable as intended — as a "roadmap" to plan short- and long-term security initiatives. On this basis, it is important to understand the needs of the total audience. Specific to this discussion, detailed testing results as they relate to the critical technologies is very relevant for the IT personnel who are charged with implementing the recommendations you make.

- *Some information cannot be obtained via interviews* — The final aspect of hands-on testing is that some information cannot be obtained via interviews. People just do not know some important technical details off the tops of their heads. An example is security settings in a Windows server. Although a system administrator might know some of the settings, that person probably will not know what all of them are. Another example is a firewall rule base, which dictates what kind of traffic can go through the firewall. Unless the company is a small or mid-size company where the rule base is relatively simple, security or IT personnel will not generally know the rules that exist. In both examples, personnel are usually not familiar with the details, and therefore detailed testing is required. In the case of the firewall, it is probably a key component of the network security architecture. Without reviewing the rule base, it is very difficult to get a clear picture of what the actual rules are. The client might know some of the rules but not know other, more obscure, rules that present significant security risks. In fact, there are rules that the client might not even be aware of. You would not know about this unless you look at the details.

Test Planning and Related Considerations

As you test any type of technology, you should have some plan of what you are testing for. In planning the test, you should consider these issues:

- *Impact on the production environment* — Much of the hands-on testing will be conducted in a client's production environment, which will understandably make some clients very nervous. They do not want their environment to go down because of the security assessment. In consideration of the production environment, you should properly analyze what is going to happen on the network if you run your tests. The impacts could include slowing down the network or generating traffic on an intrusion detection system. Your testing might also have no impact. If an impact on the network's speed is expected, consider conducting the testing during off hours if appropriate. Other considerations related to the production environment include whether or not any agents or similar software will have to be loaded into the production environment. Finally, when testing in the production environment, you may have some type of administrator-type access that allows you access to sensitive information. If the client is nervous about this, you should encourage the client to look over your shoulder as you perform the tests.
- *Sign-off or release from the client* — If you are working in the production environment, you should have the client acknowledge and approve it. This can be done via a separate form or can be covered when the initial security assessment is signed. This process will differ if internal employees are conducting the assessment. There might also be an internal policy that covers this process of auditing production systems. If such a policy exists, it should be adhered to. With the dependency on systems today, you must protect yourself, and the client should also be aware of the responsibility involved in making the right judgment as it relates to any testing being done on the production system.
- *Access requirements* — Many of the tools that are used for testing require administrator-type access on systems to run the test. With proper planning, the client can set up temporary access for you to use. If the client knows of this requirement in advance, the approvals required to set up this access

can be obtained. In many companies, there are strict requirements related
to providing this level of access.

- *Required changes to system settings* — For some of the tests you run,
  temporary changes in systems settings may be required to facilitate the
  testing. For example, you might run a test remotely that would require
  the client to open a port on a firewall. Another example is where a
  particular log might have to be enabled to capture information for the
  tests. If these changes to system settings are not performed properly, you
  could end up wasting some time in your testing.

- *Tool licensing issues* — For the commercial tools that you are going to
  use in testing, look into how you will license them for a particular client.
  Different tool vendors have different ways in which they license. Some
  vendors may license by Internet Protocol (IP) addresses, but others might
  ask for certain information to generate a key to use the product. In some
  cases, you might be using a tool that is supplied by the client, in which
  case the client must be told to take care of any licensing issues beforehand.
  Tool licensing is something that might not seem critical, but if it is not
  handled properly, you stand to lose significant time in working out these
  issues.

- *Resources* — As with any other area of the security assessment, you must
  have the right people performing the hands-on testing. Be very careful
  about this because much of the testing will be performed on production
  systems. People without the right skill set can improperly use the tool and
  negatively impact the production system. Scheduling the right people is
  something that should be addressed early in the assessment process.

The issues above are some of the issues you might face as you plan the detailed
testing. It is best to be proactive and resolve them as quickly as possible to ensure
that this testing phase runs smoothly.

Once the issues above are considered, the process for the test should be developed. The plan should be detailed and include timing, tool selections, resources
required, and any steps (e.g., changes in system settings, off-hours scheduling)
required to facilitate the testing. Because some of these tests can take time and are
potentially disruptive to the environment, it is critical to plan them properly and
communicate the plan to the client. This will help ensure that test objectives are met
and the necessary information is gathered for analysis.

Manual vs. Automated Testing

For most environments, you will do some combination of manual and automated
testing. The combination of manual and automated is required because some tests
cannot be performed using tools and others are performed more efficiently using
tools. When planning the tests, it is useful to identify what tools and related features
are going to be used. It is also useful to identify what manual procedures you will
be performing. Note that these plans are evolving and they will change based on
how the tests progress and what you find.

Both manual testing and automated testing have their uses. Tools can perform tests and gather information that would take significant time if you tried to do the same things manually. In addition, for information gathering that is repetitive, tools are far more efficient. For example, if you wanted to see whether patch levels on servers are up to date, you can use tools that scan servers and provide this information. Another example is application security. There are tools now that can simulate actions that hackers would take to break into an application. These tools can send out many simultaneous commands that simulate someone trying to break in. This would be virtually impossible to do manually.

On the other hand, tools cannot perform some tests. For example, there may be specific checklists (e.g., Windows 2000 server), such as the best practice checklists provided by Microsoft on its Web site. It might be easier to go through such a checklist using manual procedures. This is where manual testing will be necessary. In addition, manual procedures will be required to analyze information that the tools generate. Manual testing is also more appropriate when the testing is a trial-and-error type test where certain commands are executed and results are analyzed. The other key area where manual testing is necessary is when information gathered from automated testing tools needs to be analyzed. Tools are not perfect and as a result, the results they generate sometimes have "false positives." In addition, two different tools performing similar tests might generate different results. To investigate this further, manual testing is required.

Ultimately, you need to start with a clear idea of the test objectives before deciding how to perform the testing. Using this as a basis will help you understand what tools are necessary and what manual procedures are appropriate. As you select tools to use, you should consider several factors. These are discussed in the next section.

Tool Selection

Those who have been in the information security industry know that myriad testing tools are commercially available or in the form of shareware and freeware. All of these tools have their merits, and each is appropriate in certain circumstances. When selecting tools to use in a security assessment, consider these factors:

- *Financial* — Depending on the environment and the funds set aside for conducting the assessment, the cost of tools must be considered. Commercial tools can be expensive, and the reality is that unless you can spread the cost of commercial tools across assessments, you may not get the approval to buy them. In these tight economic times, you must be able to show return on investment (ROI) for tools. Commercial tools obviously make more sense in larger environments or across multiple clients. They also make sense in cases where the tools used to assess can be used as a compliance tool going forward. In smaller environments, ROI for some tools is more difficult to demonstrate. In these cases, freeware tools can be very attractive. Freeware tools are widely used by security practitioners, and many are well supported by the community. Some of the more famous security tools, such as Nmap and Nessus, are very widely used by both consultants and security operations personnel. One of the main differences with commercial tools is the technical support and training that are typically available. Freeware tools, on the other hand, provide significant functionality at essentially no cost. One way to combine commercial and freeware tools is to use one to validate the results of the other. This technique will help you identify potential false positives and areas where more detailed manual testing is required.

- *Real-world scenario* — When assessing security, one of the main concerns is how an unauthorized individual could find vulnerabilities to exploit. Unauthorized individuals with these types of intentions will not typically pay $20,000 for a tool to gather information about a company's systems. The reality is that these individuals will use tools that are freely available on the Internet. For this reason, it is useful to use some freeware tools when performing a security assessment, as this will simulate the real-world scenario. As you perform security assessments, you will see that many clients want this real-world simulation.

- *Reporting functionality* — Reporting functionality is a significant consideration when considering what tools to use. Remember that tools are used in the "Technology Evaluation" phase, which is primarily composed of information gathering. To be able to properly analyze the information generated from tools, you should ensure that the reports are adequate. Some things to consider are whether or not you can take a vulnerability and drill down to obtain more specific information about it. Another consideration is how much detail the reports provide. Commercial tools tend to have good reports; this is part of what you are paying for. Some of the freeware tools also have excellent reporting functionality — e.g., Nessus provides good reporting about vulnerabilities. Reporting is critical because it serves as the basis for analysis and the identification of findings.

- *Source* — Commercial tools come from vendors and a "controlled" environment. One of the issues you should be aware of is where you are obtaining freeware tools. Realizing that these tools will be deployed in a company's production environment, you should be careful in obtaining tools to ensure that they come from reputable sources. Remember that with freeware tools, no recourse exists if something goes wrong.

Tools are absolutely critical to the security assessment process, and the recommendation is to use both commercially available and freeware or shareware tools. If you use caution and clearly lay out the test objectives, the use of a combination of tools provides the best value. The goal is to find the information necessary to perform a quality technical analysis.

Process for Conducting Detailed Technology Testing

The process for conducting detailed testing is largely a logistical matter. The steps include items that were discussed in the previous sections. The key steps require consistent and regular communication with the client's IT personnel. The high-level steps comprising the methodology for conducting hands-on technology testing are:

1. *Inform the technology owners and schedule the test* — The technology owners need to be aware, and you need to schedule the testing at a time when it is appropriate. Potential impacts to the production environment should be considered.
2. *Obtain any signoff or release process* — Depending on what type of testing you are doing and the specific environment you are in, it may be appropriate to obtain official approval for conducting testing. This type of approval could be obtained in different ways including a formal form or an acknowledgment of electronic mail.
3. *Obtain all the necessary access* — Some of the testing that you do will require administrator or user access to certain systems. At some companies, providing access (especially administrator-level access) can take time. Therefore, you should determine what type of access you need and initiate the process of receiving this access as soon as possible.
4. *Conduct testing using tools and manual procedures* — This is the actual testing with the tools as well as the manual testing. In preparation for the manual testing, you should ensure that you have the checklists you are going to use in conducting the tests. When using the checklists, review them beforehand to determine whether some items can be eliminated and whether some things should be added.
5. *Generate information and organize for analysis* — The information from both the manual and automated testing should be gathered and organized for easy analysis. For the automated testing, you will have reports that can be generated. For the manual testing, you should ensure that you have some type of checklist or form that will make it easy to record information.

The process for hands-on testing is fairly straightforward. There might be a tendency to try to rush through this process, but you should ensure that you follow it. In particular, Steps 1 through 3 are critical when doing the testing because they affect the client. If those steps do not happen properly, impacts may include:

- Revision of the timing of the security assessment — e.g., if the proper access is not obtained or if scheduling is not performed
- Legal issues if the client is not aware of the tests or has not approved them

COMMON DETAILED TECHNOLOGY TESTING

Although you will develop the list of what technology will be tested in further detail, this section will discuss, at a high level, some of the common technology testing that happens in virtually any security assessment. These are some distinct areas that are present and tested in many companies:

- *Local area network* — The local area network is critical at almost any company because it is the area that employees access and an entry point

to where critical data and applications reside. An example of an area that is often reviewed is user ID administration, and terminated employees in particular. In the case of terminated employees, network access is often the only access that is removed. As part of the testing on the network operating system, some of the areas that might be tested for include:
– Authentication process
– Audit settings
– Settings related to auditing
– Disabling workstations after certain number of unauthorized log-on attempts
– Machines logging off automatically after a period of inactivity

The items above are only a small sample of items that might be tested. The actual test items will depend on what is deemed critical to the local area network. Based on what is reviewed and the factors listed in the previous section, you can determine whether it is appropriate to use a tool, do manual testing, or use some combination thereof.

- *Critical servers* — With critical servers, where mission-critical data and applications are potentially stored, it is a given that detailed testing will be performed on them. With these servers, the impact to the business would probably be very significant if they went down or if confidential information stored on them was compromised. The testing done on critical servers focuses on a number of areas including (but not limited to):
  - *Access control* — The question here is simply "Who has access to this machine and why do they have it?" Because these are critical machines, it is important to ensure that access is limited to those individuals who require it.
  - *What services are running?* — The rule of thumb is to deny all services and allow only those required for operational reasons. Unnecessary services running provide a way for attackers to get to the machine. Testing for unnecessary services is normally done by a tool, which generates a report of all services running. This report is reviewed with client personnel to determine which services are truly necessary; all other services are turned off.
  - *Security patch levels* — With all of the new vulnerabilities coming out on a frequent basis, keeping up to date on security patches is critical. Manual and automated methods for checking patch levels exist. Some tools actually identify what patches are missing and then automatically install them without user intervention.
  - *Best-practice hardening standards* — Critical technologies often have best-practice hardening standards developed either by the vendor or by the security community. These standards are relatively easy to find on the Internet and are a great resource when testing technology as part of a security assessment. Other excellent resources that can be used are the SANS Top 20 and the Open Web Application Security Project (OWASP) application-related vulnerability list. Both of these resources are freely available on the Internet and widely known. These standards

are checklists that have to be modified for the environment similar to the more process-oriented checklists in the appendices of this book.

- *Firewalls* — Firewalls are a key component of the overall security architecture and will almost certainly be tested in any security assessment. Firewalls are put up to filter traffic that is coming into and out of the network. Firewall testing has three components:
  - *Firewall placement* — There is a review of the overall network topology and the placement of the firewall to determine whether it is optimally placed. In addition, access control to the firewall is also reviewed to determine who has access to the firewall.
  - *Rule base configuration* — The firewall rule base is reviewed with the client to determine whether the rules reflect the client's business requirements with the rule of thumb being "deny everything and allow only what is required." With firewalls, VPN (virtual private network) functionality is often used, and if that is the case, VPN configuration is also reviewed.
  - *Logging and monitoring* — The logging feature is reviewed with the client to determine what is logged and the frequency of the log review.

  The testing related to the firewall can require significant time with client personnel due to the interactive nature of the test.

- *Intrusion detection systems (IDS)* — Along with firewalls, intrusion detection systems are another significant piece of the overall security architecture. Traditional intrusion detection systems are essentially alarms — i.e., they tell you something is happening but you then must validate and research the issue so you can react. Intrusion detection systems can be a significant amount of work to manage. The testing of intrusion detection systems comprises four main areas:
  - *Architecture* — The IDS architecture will be reviewed in conjunction with the network topology to determine whether the IDS sensors are optimally placed — i.e., are the IDS sensors protecting the critical hosts and network segments?
  - *Signature update maintenance* — For an IDS to continue to be effective, attack signatures should be updated on a regular basis. The process for doing these updates will be reviewed.
  - *Incident handling process* — IDS primarily serves as an alarm (it can be configured to take action depending on the software), so the process for responding to these alarms is important. The alert classifications as well as the process for responding to alarms are reviewed.
  - *Optimization process* — One of the most significant issues with IDS is false alarms — i.e., illegitimate alerts. The way to minimize false alarms is to review the IDS logs on an ongoing basis, determine which alerts are false alarms, and make the necessary adjustments so that those false alarms are minimized.

The different intrusion detection systems are similar in some ways but each has its own nuances for how alerts are done. The particular system needs to be thoroughly researched before reviewing the IDS.

ANALYZE INFORMATION COLLECTED
AND DOCUMENT FINDINGS

The analysis done during this phase is based on data collected during the interviews with technology owners and the actual hands-on testing you did. The hands-on testing results consist of notes from manual testing and reports from tests using the various tools. Many of these reports generated from tools have vulnerability information as well as recommendations for fixing the vulnerabilities, which can be used in developing recommendations for the final report (Figure 7.4).

When analyzing the information collected in this phase, you should consult with known guidelines such as vendor-recommended best practices and other technical standards. You should also look at this information in conjunction with the information from the last phase. Much of the information collected from the business side and the technology side should make sense together. One of the things to think about is whether the technology is adequately supporting the business. If certain technologies went down, could the technology recover fast enough to support the business?

> **Example:** Business process owners say that they are extremely dependent on e-mail. When asked how long they could function with e-mail unavailable, the answers ranged from four to eight hours. The business process owners also said that not having e-mail would significantly impact productivity. The technology owners, however, say that depending on the problem, e-mail can be down for up to 16 hours. On average, if there is a "severe" security incident, e-mail will be down for at least 12 hours. The target time of 12 hours will not be acceptable to business process owners. This is an example of a finding that could be in the final report.

In identifying vulnerabilities, keep in mind that some vulnerabilities will exist because they are necessary for the company to do business. For example, certain ports on the firewall may be open because this is required for certain applications the client is running. To validate that they are vulnerabilities and to develop an appropriate recommendation, you must go over the findings from the reports and your manual testing. In this case of open ports on the firewall, you can identify this as a vulnerability but you must validate it with the client. If the ports are required to be open, you might think of other ways to meet the business requirement so that the port associated with the vulnerability could be closed. In other words, if there is a way to close that particular port that will allow the client to still conduct business with no impact, that should be recommended. If not, some other recommendation will be required that will minimize the risk from having the port opened. Remember that the business comes first and any recommendation you make should have minimal impact on it.

As with the last phase, the findings resulting from the analysis of this data should be documented straight into the final report for efficiency's sake. At this point, you should be able to document the findings and the associated risks. To the extent that you have a recommendation (or several recommendations) in mind, you should document that as well. These details will all be ironed out in the next and last phase when you do the risk assessment, quantify the risks, and develop recommendations.

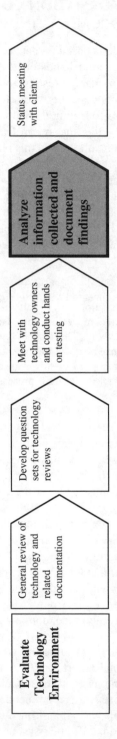

FIGURE 7.4 Analyze information collected and document findings.

As you move into the next phase, the data collected should be kept safe for two reasons. First, if you are questioned about a particular finding, you might need to refer back to your notes and tool-generated reports. Second, the system-related information you collected in this phase probably has specific details about the client's systems that can be deemed highly sensitive. In some cases, the client's own employees may not be privy to some of the detailed system information you have in your possession. If this information were to fall into the wrong hands, it could be used to compromise the client's systems. Therefore, it is critical to guard any data collected in this phase as well as any data collected during the assessment.

STATUS MEETING WITH CLIENT

This status meeting with the client (Figure 7.5) is an important one because it is the first time that the client will see all of the findings from the assessment. To facilitate this meeting, you should present the client with the findings section of the report that you have completed so far. The client will have the opportunity to tell you whether there are any findings where other mitigating factors should be considered or whether some of the findings are simply not valid. On the other hand, based on what the client sees, you might be directed to something else to look at, and as long as it is in scope and worthwhile, you should do so. Because this status meeting will focus on the technology review that was performed in this phase, there should be appropriate representatives from the client side. If you think that certain people should be at this status meeting, you should request it. The value of this particular status meeting is that you can gain buy-in from the client regarding the findings. This is important because you do not want to spend time developing recommendations for findings that may not be legitimate in the first place. In addition, when you present the final report, the client will not be surprised by its content.

POTENTIAL CONCERNS DURING THIS PHASE

As with the other phases, the technology review has a few potential pitfalls that are worth being aware of, including:

- *Client approval for any testing done on their systems* — Ensure that you obtain approval for any testing done on the client's systems. For accountability purposes, this approval is absolutely critical. Avoid the situation where the approval is vague. Ideally, the client should at least acknowledge the testing *procedure.*
- *Spend testing time wisely* — Security assessment methodology is based on risk. Accordingly, you should spend time and effort on systems according to risk. Time is limited for both you and the client technology representatives who will facilitate your testing. Therefore, you want to make the most of your time and use it wisely.
- *Findings need to be specific* — As you develop your findings from a technical perspective, keep in mind that the audience for these findings

FIGURE 7.5 Status meeting with client.

will probably be technical. Therefore, your findings should be documented in a manner that is technical enough so that the technical audience finds it valuable. When developing recommendations, the same holds true.

- *Lack of cooperation from technology owners* — As with the business process owners in the last phase, if you are not receiving cooperation from technology owners, you must escalate to your point of contact for resolution. You might have technology owners who do not want you to test for a number of reasons. Make sure that you are doing the testing that is appropriate for the assessment. Remember that it is these test results that will be the basis of some of the recommendations that you make.

EXECUTIVE SUMMARY

This phase focuses on evaluating the technology environment based on the critical technologies identified in the business process analysis. The critical technologies, which were identified in the last phase by process owners, are those that support critical business processes. Using this list of technologies as a starting point, the following five steps are performed in this phase:

- *General review of technology environment* — The general review is done with IT management and the purpose of this review is to obtain an overview of the technology in place. You should discuss IT from a technical and organizational perspective. Some of the key items to talk about include:
  - Network topology
  - Critical data
  - Critical applications
  - IT organization and high-level roles and responsibilities
  - Vendor relationships
  - Warranties and contracts in place
  - Planned initiatives
  - IT management's concerns

  This topic list is a starting point and should be modified based on the client and the specific circumstances.
- *Development of question sets for technology reviews* — Using the information gained in the overview and the information from the business process interviews in the last phase, you should develop question sets to help facilitate meetings with technology owners. These question sets are a combination of generic-type questions regarding the specific technology, administration processes, etc. and questions specific to the technology being reviewed. The question sets should be customized to reflect the client's specific business requirements. Ideally, the question sets should be given to technology owners before you meet with them so that they are prepared and can get any additional people involved as necessary.
- *Meeting with technology owners and performance of hands-on testing* — Using the question sets, the next step in this phase is to meet with the

specific technology owners and conduct detailed hands-on testing on the systems. Before meeting with the client, the testing should be scheduled and the technology owners should be made aware of the security assessment. The testing will be a combination of interviews and technical hands-on testing. The technical hands-on testing will primarily be done using automated tools and some manual procedures. Testing needs to be carefully planned. Some of the key points in planning include tool selection, obtaining proper access, and obtaining the appropriate checklists for manual testing. Before performing any testing, you should consult with and gain approval from the client to help ensure that you do not do anything that will disrupt operations. Once all of the information is collected, you should organize it in a way to facilitate analysis.

* *Analysis of information collected and documenting of findings* — Information used in this analysis is a combination of notes from the meeting with technology owners and data collected from automated and manual testing. The information in the tool-generated reports and the manual testing should be reviewed with the client to determine which vulnerabilities are legitimate and which are required for business purposes. Once the findings are finalized, they should be placed straight into the final report for efficiency's sake.

* *Status meeting with client* — As was true in the last phase, giving regular status reports to the client is critical so that there are no surprises when the client sees what the final report looks like. Status meetings are used to communicate where you are from a project management perspective and to communicate any issues found thus far. This status meeting is particularly important because the client will see a comprehensive list of findings because all of the information gathering — i.e., business process review, technology review — has been completed.

8 Risk Analysis and Final Presentation

At this point, the entire information gathering process has been completed and you are now set to do the risk analysis and develop and present the final report. This phase essentially takes all of the information gathered and looks at it in totality. The methodology for risk analysis is based on subjective criteria and thus, you will have to use significant judgment in analyzing the risk and articulating it in a way that makes it clear to the client and enables the client to make the company's management understand it.

This phase is critical in that all of the good work in the previous phases can be a wasted effort if the analysis in this phase is not performed and presented properly. Remember that the final report is the only tangible item that comes out of a security assessment. Ideally, the client should use the final report from the security assessment as the list of action items to improve the company's information security program. For this to happen, the final report must address several audiences (technical, management, etc.) and must present the findings, risks, and recommendations so they can be easily be translated into action items.

This chapter will go through the risk analysis and the final presentation–related processes. The specific steps discussed in this chapter are:

- Risk analysis and risk score calculation
- Finalizing findings and risks
- Developing recommendations and preparing the draft report
- Discussing the draft report with the client
- Presenting the final report to management

RISK ANALYSIS AND RISK SCORE CALCULATION

Risk analysis (Figure 8.1) is the final phase of the security assessment. In this methodology, risk analysis is really the impact to the business associated with a given finding. Business impact is something that was alluded to in the interviews in the last two phases and thus, risk analysis is something that happens to some extent throughout the assessment process. As you discover findings, you will naturally assess risk and begin to think of potential recommendations. In some cases, this analysis might be completely obvious.

Example: After reviewing a firewall, you find some ports that are open for no reason. You know from experience that known vulnerabilities are associated with these open ports. These ports are not supporting any business process and closing them will not affect the business. They are open because of an oversight when the firewall was configured. In this case, the recommendation would be to close those ports.

193

FIGURE 8.1 Risk analysis and risk score calculation.

In other cases, recommendations are not as obvious when you consider all of the implications.

Example: You have run a password-cracking tool to test the passwords that employees are using to gain access to the network. Your test revealed that the passwords are very weak. Roughly half of the passwords have never been changed, and a good percentage of them are the name of the company. From a risk perspective, users have extremely sensitive information on individuals' home drives, which are accessed through the network. If this information was compromised, it could severely impact the reputation of the company. Although using strong passwords is an option that would mitigate some risk and one that would make sense given the risk, one must consider the implications of such a recommendation. First, there is the issue of educating users about creating strong passwords and then changing them periodically. Second, such a recommendation could require significant help desk support in the beginning. Third and most important, there may be significant resistance from the employees, which is a battle for management. In this case, risk analysis will result in a few options that will have to be discussed with the client. In this case, the most suitable recommendation for the client is not entirely clear when you consider the dynamics of the company.

The point is that some "informal" risk assessment occurs throughout the assessment, which is important because it lays the groundwork for the formal risk analysis in this last phase of the security assessment.

In the previous phases, any risks and recommendations were documented and saved for further analysis. In this phase, risks will be reviewed based on a formula where a "risk score" will be calculated using specific guidelines. Recommendations will also be developed and modified so that they are commensurate with the associated risk.

Risk analysis involves taking the risks you have identified so far and expressing them in terms of what they mean to the business. It is a holistic look at the findings and involves looking at risks not just individually but also in the aggregate. One risk by itself might not be that significant, but when reviewed with other risks, it could be very important. Risk analysis also means prioritizing risks to help clients prioritize their own security initiatives and use the final report as a "security roadmap."

Doing this kind of analysis requires a good understanding of the client's business. In particular, you should have a good understanding of what the company does, key business drivers, "mission-critical" business processes, and the critical supporting technologies — i.e., all of the things you learned in the previous phases.

Although the risks have been documented to some degree in previous phases, you now need to clearly articulate risks in terms of impact to the business, as this is one of the things in which the client is most interested. In fact, this independent view of risk is probably one of the reasons you were asked to do the security assessment in the first place. If you put yourself in the client's shoes, the first question you will have when seeing a finding is, "Why is this important?" or with clients who are more direct, you might hear the question, "So what?" The answer to these questions is the risk. The risk should clearly articulate how the finding impacts the business. The most powerful way to state risk is in terms of financial impact so to the extent that you can quantify the risk, you should do so (quantifying the risk will be discussed in more detail in the next section). Besides financial impact, there are other impacts such as damage to reputation and regulatory noncompliance, which will be discussed later in this chapter. The bottom line is that the risk must clearly articulate to the client how the business will be impacted.

When thinking about impacts to the business, consideration must be given to how critical business processes are affected and what it that means to the business. Some of these impacts such as an order entry system might have an immediate effect on the bottom line, but other impacts such as electronic employee records being compromised might damage a company's reputation, which is felt over an extended period of time. These are all considerations when determining how to mitigate the risk. The "risk score," which is discussed in the next section, and the recommendations you eventually make will depend on your analysis of the risk.

As risk analysis is done and recommendations are made, it is critical to understand that the goal is not to be 100 percent secure, but rather, to manage security risk in a cost-effective manner.

The actual risk analysis process will be done when you calculate the risk score in the next section. Listed below are some of the factors to start thinking about as you do the risk analysis for the findings identified:

- Value of the critical asset or business process
- Likelihood that a security compromise will take place
- Existing controls in place to reduce the likelihood of a security compromise
- Potential impact if a security compromise were to take place

The items listed above are not the most objective factors. Clearly, risk analysis is very subjective and by no means an exact science. As it relates to a security assessment, the risk associated with a given finding is the potential impact to the business if a security-related incident associated with that finding occurred. When considering risk, there are some fairly standard impacts that you should think about as many of them will fall into one of these general categories. Some of the potential impacts include:

- Financial impacts:
  - *Loss of revenue* — short-term and long-term — e.g., the compromising of sensitive credit card information on an e-commerce site has an immediate short-term impact relative to revenue and a long-term impact related to reputation damage and loss of customers.
  - *Expenses related to remediation* — e.g., if data on systems are destroyed and the backups do not work, there will be cost associated with recovering data.
- *Loss of productivity* — e.g., employees are not productive if they do not have e-mail for a day.
- *Regulatory-related fines* — e.g., Health Insurance Portability and Accountability Act (HIPAA) or the Gramm–Leach–Bliley Act (GLBA).
- *Potential litigation* — e.g., sensitive customer information was compromised.
- *Damage to the reputation of a company* — e.g., defacement of a Web site.
- *Loss of customers* — e.g., e-commerce site was unavailable.

The examples above are not all inclusive, but they do represent the kind of impacts that receive attention. These impacts along with the associated recommendations are what guides decision makers when they are deciding on what resources and funding they are willing to commit for information security. This is how many executives look at security. It is very important to clearly define risk and be able to back up your conclusions. Where risk is quantified, it is not that difficult. Where risk is more subjective, it is more challenging.

Successful risk analysis depends on being able to leverage your knowledge of information security best practices, knowledge of business processes and technology, and industry knowledge to determine the risk. Specifically, you should use the following as benchmarks when determining the risk:

- Information security best-practice standards such as the International Standards Organization (ISO) 17799
- Technology best-practice standards
- Industry knowledge gained through experience and research (performed during the initial research phase)

In addition to the benchmarks listed above and most importantly, you must consider the client's specific business requirements when assessing risk.

From a process perspective, consider each finding separately and then look at them in aggregate. This will give the holistic view that is necessary when conducting a security assessment.

RISK SCORE CALCULATION

Quantifying the risk is an effective way to illustrate the severity of the risks discovered during an assessment. In this section, we will discuss the process for quantifying the risk and calculating a "risk score." The purpose of the risk score is to try to take the subjective ways we think about risk and present them in a way that is objective. Quantifying the risks allows you to prioritize what findings are important based on a standard set of criteria. This is very valuable because it helps clients understand what is important and how security initiatives need to be prioritized. Clients are very interested in knowing what must be done and what can reasonably wait. The risk score provides an objective way to make decisions about what security initiatives to pursue in both the short term and the long term.

The risk score is a tool used collaboratively with clients to help quantify the risk. The calculation, which is done for each finding, considers two factors, "business impact" and "level of control," to determine risk. Business impact related to a finding is defined as how the business is affected if the finding is exploited. The risk analysis associated with a finding considers this impact as well as the level of control, which can be defined as the extent to which security measures are in place to mitigate the risks related to the vulnerability.

In this methodology, both the business impact and the level of control have numerical values assigned based on a criterion. The actual risk score is the product of the business impact and the level of control. One thing to keep in mind is that the process of assigning values to the criteria is not an exact science and that some judgment will be required. The next two sections will discuss each of these concepts in detail and provide criteria for assigning numerical values to each of the variables.

Business Impact

Business impact is a combination of the potential impact to the business if there is a security breach and the probability that a security breach could occur. In this methodology, business impact is calculated without the consideration of any internal controls or security measures that might be in place. The existing security measures and internal controls will be accounted for when the "level of control" is determined. As a result, in determining the business impact, only the probability of a security breach and the potential impacts of a security breach are examined.

To quantify these characteristics, Table 8.1 and Table 8.2 offer guidance for the potential impact to the business and the probability that a security breach could occur. Each table contains guidance for determining a high, medium, or low score for each of the characteristics. The high, medium, and low scores translate to scores of 3, 2, and 1 respectively. This numerical value will be used in the calculation of business impact.

Table 8.1 addresses the potential impacts to the business. This is information that should have been gathered in previous meetings with business process and technology owners. If needed, the client subject matter experts should be consulted with again to thoroughly understand the impacts of the security risks identified. Table 8.1 lists criteria for assigning numerical values for potential impact to the business. Note that this is a guideline — it can be modified if needed for a given client as different clients may have different criteria. Note: When doing this analysis, finalize this criteria first so that all findings are measured based on the same criteria. The examples of potential impacts are there to help you determine the best classification of a given risk.

The criteria above should help you classify impact of your findings in a consistent manner. Note that a given finding does not have to meet all of the items listed in a particular category. For example, you could have a finding that you classify as having a "high" business impact because of the cost to address the security breach even though an effective workaround exists. You might also classify this risk as a "medium" because there was an effective workaround. This is where your judgment comes in and why there is a fair degree of subjectivity to this process. The key is to apply your judgment as consistently as possible.

Table 8.2 defines the criteria for assigning values to the probability that a breach could occur. In this methodology, probability is thought of as a high, medium, or low likelihood that the vulnerability associated with a finding can be exploited. Like the last one, this is a highly subjective calculation and will require judgment and a good knowledge of the business. Also, you must apply your judgment consistently across all findings. This probability combined with the potential impact will be used to calculate the business impact.

As you can see, both components that determine the business impact are highly subjective and require judgment. The second component, the probability of a security

TABLE 8.1
Potential Impact to the Business

	Score	Potential Impacts
High	3	Significant revenue impact
		No effective workaround
		Core business processes adversely affected
		Permanent loss of customers
		Potential litigation
		Regulatory fines can result from a security breach
		Significant damage to reputation — to the extent that it might cause a loss of customers
		Significant expense to address security breach — e.g., outside consultants required, major expenses related to data recovery
		IT systems unavailable for an extended period of time and contingency plans need to be invoked to remain operational
		Critical data might not be recoverable
Medium	2	From a customer's perspective, the impact was nothing more than a nuisance
		There is a workaround but it is very cumbersome and not sustainable for an extended period of time
		Minimal or no loss of customers
		Minimal revenue impact
		Minimal damage to reputation
		Core business process is minimally affected
		Regulatory warning (as opposed to a fine)
		Security breach was addressed with internal resources (who were not able to perform their daily responsibilities for a significant period of time as a result of the breach)
		Critical data is recoverable with significant effort
Low	1	No revenue impact
		Effective workaround
		Ancillary or back-office processes affected, not core business processes
		No impact to customers
		No damage to the reputation of the company
		Affected business process will be phased out or be radically changed in the short term

TABLE 8.2
Assigning Values to Probability

	Score
High	3
Medium	2
Low	1

breach, is extremely subjective but necessary in calculating the potential impact. If the probability of a given vulnerability being exploited is low, this should be considered in the overall risk analysis and when making recommendations. In some cases, if the probability of a particular vulnerability being exploited is low, you may consider accepting the risk and doing nothing about it. Although the probability could have been incorporated into the potential impact, it is important enough to consider separately. In fact, when presenting the findings from a security assessment, one of the questions you might get is — "What are the chances of that happening and how has that been incorporated into the risk analysis?"

Another typical question you get is, "Assuming that a security breach did occur, is there a workaround that can be done so the business process is not disrupted?" For this reason, workarounds are specifically mentioned in the Potential Impact table.

To make this process work, the importance of applying your judgment in a consistent manner cannot be stressed enough. One way to help ensure this is to document your thought process of how you arrived at the values for business impact.

Calculation of Business Impact

To calculate the business impact of a given risk, the scores for the probability and the potential impacts are multiplied. This product of the two items is the overall business impact shown below.

$$\text{Business Impact} = \text{Probability} \times \text{Potential Impact to the Business}$$

This result is then combined with the level of control (discussed in the next section) to determine the priority.

Below is an example of the calculation of business impact:

Scenario: Company X is an online bookstore that sells books where customers can order online or call-in orders on the Internet. During a security assessment, technical security issues were found on critical servers. There were findings related to security patches not being up to date as well as some weak access controls.

Analysis of Business Impact

Probability — Based on the findings and some of the recent exploits, there is a medium chance that a security breach could occur as a result of this finding.

Probability — Medium (2)

Potential Impact to the Business — Based on the findings, the worst-case scenario if a security breach were to occur is that the site would be unavailable for a couple of hours at the most. There would be a minimal loss of revenue, if any, because online sales are not a significant portion of the sales. In addition, customers know that they can call in orders if the Web site is not working. As a result, the potential impact to the business is medium.

TABLE 8.3
Business Impact

		Potential Impact to the Business		
		Low	Medium	High
Probability		1	2	3
High	3	3 — Medium	6 — Medium	9 — High
Medium	2	2 — Low	4 — Medium	6 — Medium
Low	1	1 — Low	2 — Low	3 — Low

Potential Impact to the Business — Medium (2)

Business Impact = Probability × Potential Impact to the Business

$$4 = 2 \times 2$$

The ranges for the overall business impact are as follows:

Business Impact	Range
Low	1 to 3
Medium	4 to 6
High	7 to 9

The overall business impact is then 4, which is a medium-level business impact. This was calculated by multiplying the probability and the potential impact to the business.

To illustrate some variations to the example above, let us assume that the client did not have good management controls and that the lack of security patches could result in credit card numbers being stolen. In addition, let us assume that these vulnerabilities were being exploited frequently. Under these circumstances, both the probability of a security breach and the potential impact to the business are high, resulting in a score of 9, which is a high level of business impact.

Based on the potential business impact scores, there is only one case of a high business impact and that is when both components — probability and the potential impact to the business — are high. This is intentional so as not to dilute the urgency and importance of business impacts classified as "high."

Table 8.3 illustrates the levels of business impact and what the results of various combinations are.

Level of Control

The level of control is the second aspect in determining overall risk score. In the first step of determining the risk score, we determined the following information based on the findings:

- What is the potential impact of a security breach?
- What is the likelihood that the security breach might occur?

Theoretically, the potential impact and the probability are really only half the story. The other half, which is considered in this section, is the controls or security measures in place to mitigate the risks associated with the vulnerability.

Consider the example of company having a business-to-business relationship with a supplier that manages inventory levels of certain items by having access to company's systems to view inventory levels. This relationship can shorten the supply chain by automating the process of replenishing inventory. With this type of a relationship, companies can save money by making the inventory replenishment process more efficient and because certain activities that used to be performed by people are now automated. These relationships, which keep a company competitive, introduce new security risks into the environment. To mitigate these risks, companies might implement the following:

- Strict access controls around who can access inventory information
- Log reviews of business-to-business transactions
- Strong password requirements
- Other controls

These measures to mitigate the risk constitute the "level of control," which is the subject of this section.

The level of control can range from manual internal control processes such as log review to system-enforced security measures such as strong password requirements. Ideally, security measures should be driven by the amount of risk, which is a fundamental concept in the security assessment methodology.

The level of control is the second component in determining risk and is defined as the measures that have been taken by the company to mitigate the risks associated with vulnerabilities. As with the criteria for the business impact, this is also subjective. Also, the criteria can be adjusted based on the client and your judgment — you just need to make sure that you apply your judgment consistently for all findings.

The level of control can be thought of at five levels, which are outlined in Table 8.4. Table 8.4 lists the criteria that should be used in determining the level of control for a given risk. The level of control should be reviewed for each set of findings and associated risks. The numerical values range from 1 to 5 with 1 as the best-case scenario and 5 as the worst-case scenario. The key differences for each level of control are in italics.

Note the differences as you progress from 1 to 5 in the table. The items listed in the criteria represent key aspects of information security, some of which were identified as key components of an information security program (Chapter 3). As with the business impact, you can add items to these criteria or take away items; this is again a judgment call on your part. Remember that you need to justify how you came to your conclusions when you classify these risks.

Some salient points related to the criteria for the level of control that you should be aware of as you proceed are:

TABLE 8.4
Level of Control

Level of Control	Criteria
1	Appropriate security measures in place
	Security procedures consistently followed
	Documented security policy and procedure in place
	Continuous auditing in place to facilitate ongoing enforcement and updates to the process as required
2	Appropriate security measures in place
	Security procedures consistently followed
	Documented security policy and procedure in place
	Mitigating controls in place
	No consistent enforcement
3	Appropriate security measures in place
	Documented security policy and procedure in place
	Security procedures not consistently followed
	Weak mitigating controls in place
	No enforcement
4	Appropriate security measures in place
	Security policy and procedure exist but are not documented
	Security procedures are done on an ad-hoc basis — i.e., when someone feels like doing it
	No mitigating controls
	No enforcement
5	*Nothing is being done to address the security risk*
	No security processes or policies or procedures in place
	No mitigating controls in place

- The score associated with the level of control is higher as the level of control becomes worse.
- The level of control should be determined for each finding and its associated risk.
- When determining the level of control, remember that the criteria above are only guidance to help come up with a score. All of the items listed for each level of control might not be applicable, so some judgment must be exercised.
- One item that is addressed in each level of control is whether appropriate security measures are in place. Related to this, there are two key points to consider:
  - Do not forget about mitigating controls. Although there may not be any security measures in place to directly address the risk, there might be other mitigating controls in place later in the process that can reduce the given risk. This is where having a good understanding of the business process is so essential. Mitigating controls tend to be controls that are detective in nature, i.e., you find out something happened after the fact. Depending on the risk, this might be appropriate.

TABLE 8.5
Risk Score

Business Impact		Level of Control				
		1	2	3	4	5
High	9	9 — Low	18 — Medium	27 — Medium	36 — High	45 — High
	8	8 — Low	16 — Medium	24 — Medium	32 — High	40 — High
	7	7 — Low	14 — Low	21 — Medium	28 — Medium	35 — High
Medium	6	6 — Low	12 — Low	18 — Medium	24 — Medium	30 — Medium
	5	5 — Low	10 — Low	15 — Low	20 — Medium	25 — Medium
	4	4 — Low	8 — Low	12 — Low	16 — Medium	20 — Medium
Low	3	3 — Low	6 — Low	9 — Low	12 — Low	15 — Low
	2	2 — Low	4 — Low	6 — Low	8 — Low	10 — Low
	1	1 — Low	2 — Low	3 — Low	4 — Low	5 — Low

– Note that the wording used in the criterion is "appropriate" security measures. The foundation of this methodology is that security measures must be aligned with business processes and that these security measures should be appropriate and cost effective based on the given risk. As you review what security measures are in place, you may find that too much or too little security is in place, indicating a potentially inefficient use of resources. This might be an opportunity to provide recommendations to make better use of these resources and potentially streamline the security process associated with the risk.

Determination of Risk Score

The risk score is basically a quantification of the risks uncovered during the course of the security assessment. Recall that one of the primary objectives of conducting a security assessment was to provide clients an information security roadmap that contains prioritized security initiatives. The risk score, which quantifies the risk associated with the findings, provides a method to help prioritize the next steps using a consistent and objective methodology.

A risk score should be determined for all of the findings and associated risks identified during the security assessment. It is calculated by multiplying the business impact and the level of control, which were determined in the previous sections.

The risk score is calculated as follows:

$$\text{Risk Score} = \text{Business Impact} \times \text{Level of Control}$$

Once you calculate the risk score, you can review Table 8.5 to determine where it rates on a high, medium, low scale.

The risk score, for simplicity's sake, can be classified as noted in the table below. This table can be used to quickly determine the classification for a given finding and associated risk.

Risk Score	Range
Low	1 to 15
Medium	16 to 30
High	31 to 45

Note that there are only a few scenarios where the risk score is high, indicating findings that are top priority, which should be addressed quickly. This is intentionally done so that "high risk" is not diluted. The "high" risk score scenario is where the business impact is high (i.e., potential impact is high) and where either the level of control is nonexistent or some control exists on an ad-hoc basis. Different clients will look at these risk scores differently. Some clients might want to immediately address situations where there is even a medium risk score because they are very control conscious. Other clients may have a very limited budget and decide to only address the high risk score items and do the rest on a long-term basis. This measurement scheme helps them prioritize the findings and put some perspective around next steps.

To use the risk score effectively, you must educate the client about how it works and how the risk score is derived. Understanding the methodology will help them use this information to make good judgments. In addition, you should be able to talk about any of the findings and be able to show how you reached your conclusions.

FINALIZE FINDINGS AND RISKS

Now that you have done the risk analysis, you need to finalize the wording of the findings and associated risks (Figure 8.2). If you were diligent in documenting them in the report, this should not take much time. As you document the findings and risks, you should try to maintain some consistency in how you present the findings, risks, and recommendations (discussed in the next step) so they have the same "look and feel." The next two sections will provide some guidelines for documenting findings and risks.

FINALIZE WORDING FOR FINDINGS

The first draft of the findings should already be documented, as this was something that was done throughout the assessment. The reason for devoting a separate section to documenting findings is because it is very important how findings are presented to the client. Although you went over the findings with the client during the assessment, the report you are preparing will probably go to a larger audience. In many cases, the final report may go to senior management. When these individuals see the findings, it will probably be for the first time.

With this in mind, you have to be very careful how you word the findings. The same finding worded in different ways can have the same message but affect people differently. For example, let us assume that you find a company where the executives of the company, who deal with highly sensitive information, routinely keep sensitive documents just lying around on their desks. Some of the sensitive documents are kept in locked cabinets, but some are out in the open. These executives have administrative

FIGURE 8.2 Finalize findings and risks.

assistants who watch the offices for the most part, but there are times when the offices are left unattended. In addition, although physical security measures exist upon entering the building, no physical security measures are present once in the building. Because of the sensitivity of the documents that these executives have, this is an issue for the company. This finding can be worded in different ways and each would have a different effect.

First, it can be worded as follows:

- *Version 1:* In offices of key executives, sensitive documents are routinely out in the open on desks. These documents are often not locked in cabinets. Offices are not locked when executives are not present, resulting in anyone being able to gain unauthorized access to sensitive documents.
- *Version 2:* Sensitive documents are not properly locked up in key offices of the company. These offices are often left open where anyone can gain unauthorized access to these documents.
- *Version 3:* In key offices, not all sensitive documents are properly secured in locked cabinets. Although assistants or other support people normally watch these offices, some brief instances occur where the offices are left open and unattended, allowing anyone to walk in and access the sensitive documents. Although physical security exists at the perimeter to control who can enter the building, once in the building, people can walk relatively freely.

Each of the three findings above illustrates the core point that sensitive documents are left exposed. However, each of the findings would probably be received differently. Let us critique each one and note the differences:

- *Version 1* — Although this one communicates the point, it openly singles out a group of people — the ones who are the final audience of the report. It is possible that they probably did not observe the whole company and cannot say definitively that it is only the executives that are guilty of this. In addition, the wording makes it sound as though all of the documents are left out in the open and nothing is locked up, which is not true. Finally, the finding also says that anyone can gain access to these offices and ignores the fact that these offices are mostly watched and that physical security measures control who can enter the building.
- *Version 2* — Like the first finding, this one also communicates the issue of sensitive documents being at risk. This one, however, in the first sentence, acknowledges that it is not all documents that are not locked up. Like the first finding, this wording does not account for the fact that these offices are mostly watched and that physical security measures control access into the building.
- *Version 3* — This is the most appropriately worded of the three. The wording of this finding not only communicates the nature of the finding — that unauthorized individuals can gain access to sensitive documents — it

also acknowledges that security measures are being taken. The finding also acknowledges that not all documents are left out in the open and that the offices are mostly watched except for very brief periods of time. Finally, the finding acknowledges the physical security measures taken to restrict who can enter the building.

The example above is fairly straightforward but illustrates some things to remember when documenting findings for the final report being presented to the client:

- *Try not to single out specific people in findings unless necessary.* Findings can be a criticism of what people are doing. If you can avoid explicitly stating to whom a finding is referring, you should do so. By singling out people or groups of people, you will potentially make people defensive. In addition, you might also be asked why the finding does not apply to all personnel instead of just the group identified. If you cannot answer the question, the finding will appear irresponsible.
- *The severity of the finding should be clear.* Although you will have a criticality for each of the findings, the text of the finding should reflect the severity of the finding. In the example above, you can see the difference in the tone of the three versions of the finding. In version 3, all of the facts are clearly laid out and it is clear, unlike in version 1, where there is no mention of the fact that many paper documents are in fact locked up or that the offices are left unattended for only brief periods of time. Severity is important because it allows the audience to attach a level of importance to the finding. In addition, the eventual recommendation will probably make more sense. In the example above, a recommendation based on the wording in version 1 would probably differ from a recommendation based on the wording in version 3.
- *Existing security measures related to the finding should be acknowledged.* Clients often know where their security weaknesses are and, as a result, have implemented certain security measures or internal controls. Where that is the case, it should be acknowledged. The finding is not accurate if you do not acknowledge what mitigating controls are in place that reduce the risk related to the finding. If you recognize what the client is doing, your finding becomes more accurate and its tone is softened. It is appropriate to give credit where due and clients appreciate it.

These rules for documenting findings are fairly common sense and straightforward. The bottom line is that the approach when conducting security assessments and presenting the results should be consultative. When presenting findings, you should work with the client to determine whether mitigating controls are in place and whether other factors might change the nature of the finding. In the end, the goal with presenting findings is to have all of the relevant facts and present the most accurate picture.

Document Risks and Criticality

After documenting the finding, the next step is to document the risks and the associated criticality based on the risk analysis that was performed in the previous step of the methodology. With documenting risks, the thing to remember is that you must clearly articulate how the finding impacts the business. Clients and in particular the people who make the decisions about what security initiatives are worth spending time and money on want to know the impact to the business. Executive management has many initiatives and projects from many areas of the company (of which information security is only one) to sort through. To even think about committing funds to an initiative, they must see a compelling reason to do so. The risk related to a finding is that reason.

The approach that companies will normally take with information security is to spend what it takes to reduce risk to an acceptable level. One can never fully eliminate security risks, and client management understands this. Clients do, however, have different approaches to risk, and this is something that you must gauge. Some clients are very risk averse and may want to address every single finding you present to them. Other clients, who are willing to accept more risk, might want to immediately address what they perceive as "critical" and make a long-term plan for everything else.

When documenting risk, you must essentially document the thought process you went through in the previous step in this phase when you conducted the risk analysis. The criteria you used to determine the risk score will be articulated to develop the risk.

As with documenting the findings, there are certain things to remember when documenting the risk including:

- *Risk must demonstrate impact to the business.* Assuming the audience for the final report is management, you must ensure that the impact to the business is stated clearly. It is important to understand how a weakness ultimately affects the company from a business perspective. For example, say that you discover personnel are using very weak network passwords. In this case, a risk certainly exists of someone gaining unauthorized access into the network. Some might not see this as a significant risk. However, you can elaborate the risk to say that if these passwords are compromised, someone can gain access into other people's e-mail and to sensitive documents in their home drives. Furthermore, this can lead to unauthorized access to sensitive financial data or competitive research and development data. Now, the impact to the business is much more clear.
- *Quantify the risk whenever possible.* Numbers should always be attached to risk if at all possible. When considering potential impacts in the event of a security incident related to a finding, it is worth quantifying numbers such as potential loss of revenues, cost of remediation, regulatory fines (e.g., HIPAA, GLBA), and other costs. Quantifying a risk makes it objective and measurable rather than subjective.

- *Consider intangible impacts.* Intangible impacts are those that are difficult to quantify but still significant. Some of the more common intangible impacts include damage to reputation, loss of customers, and potential litigation. For example, assume that during a security assessment, you discovered that a company's Web site had some technical vulnerabilities that make defacing it easy. In addition, it was clear that if it was defaced, there was no sure mechanism that would allow the information technology (IT) department to know that it had been defaced. In this case, a risk exists that if the Web site was defaced, the reputation of the company would be damaged. However, the reputation value derived from the Web presence would vary from company to company and is not tangible. Significant judgment and a good knowledge of the business are required when considering intangible impacts. This judgment will eventually drive the recommendation you make relative to the finding.
- *Separate short- and long-term impacts.* Some findings will have both short- and long-term impacts. These should be documented because it will help management determine how to address the finding. For example, take an e-commerce site where you discover vulnerability in the e-commerce application. This vulnerability can bring the Web site down, resulting in the site not being available and customers not being able to make purchases. In this case, both short-term and long-term impacts exist. In the short term, if the site goes down, a loss of revenue will result, the extent of which can be calculated based on historical sales data. In the long term, there is an intangible impact related to loss of customers because some customers will not go back to an e-commerce site after a bad experience. Each of these impacts will have an effect on the recommendation you make and how the client looks at the finding. By breaking up the risk between short- and long-term impacts, you make it clearer and more useful as a basis for decision making.

Once you document the risk, you must also document the risk score calculated in the previous step. At this point, it is good to look at the risk score and make sure that it is in line with how you documented the risk. The bottom line with documenting the risk is that you must show how the risk impacts the business and be able to back up the risk with sound and consistent reasoning. Be prepared for the response, "So what?" (i.e., what does the risk mean to the business) from client personnel when they read the findings, risks, and recommendations.

A good exercise to perform at this point is to put yourself in the client's shoes and see whether the findings and risks make sense and whether you can see the business impact of the risks.

DEVELOP RECOMMENDATIONS AND PREPARE DRAFT REPORT

At this point, you are ready to develop the recommendations and complete the draft deliverable (Figure 8.3). A sample format for the final deliverable was discussed in

FIGURE 8.3 Develop recommendations and prepare draft report.

an earlier chapter. By this point in the assessment, much of the final document should have been completed. The sections of the suggested final deliverable format, as discussed in Chapter 5, are as follows:

- Executive summary
  - High-level description of what was done
  - Business drivers for the assessment
  - Description of key findings
- Scope
- Methodology
- Current state
  - Description of core business processes
  - Significant initiatives that are either underway or planned in the near term
- Findings, risks, and recommendations
- Comprehensive prioritized list of all findings, associated risks, risk scores and recommendations categorized by severity

At this point, you should have completed the whole report except for the recommendations. If any of the sections before the recommendations are not complete, you should go ahead and complete them now. Those sections are fairly self-explanatory. One thing to watch for is that the other sections before the section where the findings, risks, and recommendations are should not be so verbose that they overshadow the findings, risks, and recommendations, which constitute the "meat" of the report.

Once you complete those sections, the only thing left to do in preparing the report is developing the recommendations. Clients are interested in recommendations as much as they are in risk, maybe even more so. In fact, the recommendations are one of the reasons for bringing in another party to do the assessment. The recommendations are your opportunity to really show your expertise as it pertains to information security and securing an environment. One of the terms that has been used frequently in this book is "security roadmap" — recommendations are the security roadmap. Ideally, the company will take your recommendations, and they will become the master list of security initiatives for the short and long term. This will be the baseline project list that is periodically updated and used as the master list for information security initiatives.

In the next section, we will go over some guidelines for developing recommendations. The recommendations are an element of the report that will receive considerable attention and will be heavily scrutinized. Recommendations need to strike the balance between being too general and too specific. Ideally, someone should be able to take a recommendation or a group of similar recommendations and translate it into a project.

DEVELOP AND DOCUMENT RECOMMENDATIONS

Recommendations are the final part of the documentation and a critical part of the security assessment. The recommendations need to be specific enough so that clients can understand what it will take to implement them. The recommendations should be documented in such a way that each recommendation or group of recommendations can be identified as separate initiatives, where costs and resources can be defined. Ideally, the set of recommendations you present in the final report should be used as a master plan for the company's information security program.

In the context of the security assessment methodology, developing recommendations is the final step but something that is happening throughout the assessment as you identify findings. Some findings you discover may be very clear, and as a result, the recommendations might also be very clear. In other cases, the findings might be more complicated, and the recommendation might not be very clear. In these instances, you might start thinking about some options for recommendations. In any case, you probably have some idea of what the recommendations are going to be by the time you get to this phase of the security assessment. Note that in previous phases, recommendations were to be documented to the extent you formulated them. These preliminary recommendations are important because they lay the groundwork for refining and finalizing them in the final phase of the assessment.

Developing recommendations is an iterative process when you are conducting a security assessment because of the way you are gathering information and because of how the business processes and technology are integrated. During Phases 2 through 4 — Initial Research, Business Process Review, and Technology Review — information is gathered and findings are discovered. As these findings are discovered, you will naturally start to think about potential ways to address the given risks. As you gather more information, the previous recommendations might change because of new information. This cycle keeps going during the assessment.

For example, you might discover a security weakness related to a firewall and its configuration. The weakness happens to be related to the firewall rules and how the firewall is set up incorrectly from an architecture perspective. At first glance, the recommendations for changes to the rules and architecture might seem straightforward. Upon meeting with IT management, however, you might learn that there is going to be a server consolidation, and new software including a new firewall is going to be purchased in the next six months. If you originally had significant recommendations regarding the firewall architecture or rule base configuration, this might change. With this new information, you should inquire about the proposed changes to the network and specifically the firewall. At this point, it is not appropriate to spend a lot of time on the current firewall because of the upcoming changes. It is, however, worth looking at what firewall is going to be purchased and the proposed changes to the network. The recommendations will now have a slightly different focus, as they will also reflect the planned changes to the environment.

The iterative process in developing the recommendations helps you sort through the range of potential solutions and determine the best option. Part of this iterative process is receiving input from the client during status meetings. During the regular status meetings with the client, you can discuss recommendations as you develop them. Client feedback during the assessment is very valuable because it can give you an indication of what the client is prepared to do or whether there are things with which the client disagrees. For example, some clients will not deal with certain vendors, or there might be cultural issues that might make some recommendations not feasible. Another example is where you might be proposing a recommendation that the client has already tried. This is all valuable information, and the iterative process involving the client will help surface these issues. It is important to remember, however, that you must still independently advise the client, as you feel necessary. You need to strike the right balance between obtaining the client's input and feedback and still retaining your independence. This is a key concept; the quality of the assessment can be diminished if there is an impression that you are not independent and that you are simply writing based on what the client is telling you. The purpose of client input is so they can provide you with information you might not have uncovered when conducting the assessment — not for them to tell you what they want to see. Remember that the final decision as to how you advise them is yours.

This iterative process is beneficial for both you and the client. From your perspective, you have an opportunity to bounce various options off the client and let the client give you further insight and information that you might not have obtained otherwise. From the client's perspective, they begin to see the types of recommendations that are being generated and have the opportunity to offer their input on them. This is very important for clients because they will ultimately need to get buy-in from their management to implement the recommendations. If your client contact is not comfortable with the recommendations, it will be more difficult for that person to convince his or her own management to implement the recommendations.

Similar to the importance of wording when documenting findings and risks, it is equally important to phrase the recommendations the right way. Several characteristics that you should keep in mind when documenting recommendations are discussed in the next section.

CHARACTERISTICS OF GOOD RECOMMENDATIONS

The importance of good recommendations cannot be overstressed. To clarify, good recommendations are not necessarily the cheapest or easiest solutions nor are they something that the client is necessarily going to be happy with. The recommendations should, however, be what is best for the client based on your judgment and what you learned during the assessment. Every recommendation should:

- Address the risk
- Provide enough detail
- Be cost effective (i.e., show a return on security investment)

Address the Risk

The need for recommendations to address the risk sounds very obvious, but this is not always the case. It is very easy to let discussions go off on tangents and lose focus on what the risk is and what it is you are trying to address. There is often a tendency to start with an idea for a recommendation and let that lead into a discussion of bigger and grander solutions. At that point, if you take a step back, you realize that the recommendation being proposed not only fixes the problem, it also does many other things that the client does not necessarily need. As the solutions become more involved and extensive, they cost more to implement and maintain. Many clients view security as a cost, and their general philosophy is to spend what is necessary and nothing more. One of the ways of adhering to this philosophy is to make sure the recommendation is addressing the risk. The structure of the report facilitates this because you have a separate section for the findings, with a separate risk and recommendation for each finding. With this structure, it is easy to check whether the recommendation makes sense based on the finding and risk. This goes back to the importance of documenting the finding and risk in a clear and concise way.

You should be prepared to talk about any of the recommendations in the final report and specifically, how they address the risks identified. It is highly unlikely that the client will implement recommendations that do not address the risk.

Provide Enough Detail

One of the comments often heard from clients is that security recommendations are so high level that they are useless. This is a legitimate issue that you should be mindful of when writing recommendations. There must be enough detail in the recommendations to allow management to determine the cost, time, and resources that will be required for a given security initiative. If management can do this, the recommendations will have served their purpose as a "security roadmap."

Documenting risks, however, is a balancing act. You need to strike the right balance between providing too much detail and too little detail. If you keep the recommendations too high level, they are of little use to the clients. If you provide too much detail, you are probably going out of the scope of the engagement — i.e., if you are providing step-by-step solutions in a recommendation, you are probably doing too much for a security assessment. You probably do not have the time to do the necessary research to provide in-depth detailed recommendations. You also should not take time away from other parts of the security assessment that require attention. A good rule of thumb to remember when documenting recommendations is that they should convey enough information to determine relevant tasks and the resources required to implement the recommendation.

Cost Effectiveness (Return on Security Investment)

As was stated earlier, security is a cost, and most of the recommendations you make will have some cost associated with them. One of the first questions in the minds of client personnel when you make recommendations is the cost of implementing the recommendations and any costs related to ongoing maintenance. The costs related to security recommendations will face the same level of scrutiny as other expenditures do. Spending decisions for information security or any other initiative are based on the value it will bring to a company. With some security recommendations, the cost justification is easy if it can be tied to revenue. For example, if a company invests money in obtaining a certification to its e-commerce site, that might bring in a sizable number of additional customers. In this case, the justification for such a recommendation is based on potential revenues that will come into the company.

In most cases, however, it is difficult to tie information security spending to incremental revenues — e.g., if I spend $100,000 on implementing an intrusion detection solution, I cannot point to any additional revenues that the company will receive as a result of it. Information security spending is viewed in the same way as spending on insurance, except that insurance is normally required and security is not. Information security initiatives are viewed as planning for something that might happen and not something that necessarily impacts the bottom line. The benefits of investing in security have always been characterized as mushy concepts that live far from the bottom line. Successes like avoiding bad press or not losing productivity to a virus — these are important but they don't translate into profits. The best argument you could make is that you may have prevented an unknowable amount of losses. Think of it this way: If you had to pay $100 for the right to access your seatbelt every time you got in a car, but you never got in an accident, what's your ROSI (Return On Seatbelt Investment)?[1]

For cases where the link cannot be established between information security and profits, it is sometimes very difficult to see the value in it. As a result, it is often difficult to make a business case for information security. For many, the attitude is, "if nothing has happened to me so far, why would anything happen now" or "if its not broken, don't fix it." With this attitude, it is very difficult to convince client management of the value of security. Keep in mind that these decisions regarding whether or not to proceed with a security initiative often rest with individuals outside the security organization. Depending on the potential cost of a security recommendation, the cost could be high enough that chief financial officer (CFO) approval is required. With almost any decision there is potential cost — i.e., external cost (this does not include internal costs where it is just a matter of additional work taken on by employees). Before most executives will approve an expenditure, they want to know the reason for the expense and whether the cost is justified.

Any executive who approves expenditures will ask questions about the ROI (return on investment). In the information security arena, this is referred to as the ROSI or return on security investment. When developing recommendations in a security assessment, it is essential to do a high-level cost-benefit analysis to ensure that the recommendation makes sense for the client. With cost-benefit analysis, there is a rule of thumb that you should always keep in the back of your mind as you make recommendations — the cost to secure an asset should not exceed the value of the asset. This very basic concept can screen out recommendations that are not appropriate, and it is often overlooked.

The question then is how do you do a cost-benefit analysis and demonstrate an acceptable ROSI relative to a recommendation? The first thing is to try to link an information security initiative to revenue-generating activity — i.e., show that information security can help increase revenue. For example, consider a company that performs outsourced services for companies via an application service provider (ASP) model. Imagine that for the outsourcer to continue to do business with this customer, the company must spend on some information security initiatives demanded by the customer. In fact, other customers may demand the same security measures, making the case for the security initiatives even more compelling. Assuming the cost is not exorbitant, the information security initiative will probably be approved to continue doing business with the business partner.

Other cases are more complicated, and convincing client management of the cost benefit of implementing recommendations can be difficult. In these cases, no direct revenue can be tied to the security initiative. With these recommendations, the discussion focuses on the likelihood of a security incident related to the finding, the impact of the security incident, and how much the recommendation mitigates the risk associated with the finding. Essentially, you are trying to predict what might happen and the associated probability and impact. This calculation is the ROSI. Ways to do the cost-benefit analysis and determine the ROSI are explained below.

One of the methodologies for calculating ROSI was developed by a team of Idaho researchers and was published in *CIO* magazine in February 2002.[2] This is a very straightforward calculation that uses the concept of Annual Loss Expectancy, similar to disaster recovery planning. The calculation that was published is documented below and applied to an example of a recommendation proposing the use of intrusion detection.

$$(R - E) + T = ALE$$

T is the cost of the intrusion detection tool.
E is the dollar savings gained by stopping of intrusions through the introduction of an intrusion detection tool.
R is the cost per year to recover from an estimated number of intrusions.

Doing this equation yields the Annual Loss Expectancy (**ALE**).

$$R - ALE = ROSI$$

To determine the return on security investment (**ROSI**) we simply subtract what we expect to lose in a year (**ALE**) from the annual cost of intrusion.

In the calculation above, the formula was intended for intrusion detection, but other security initiatives can be used instead to determine the ROSI for a given security initiative. This is a good formula because it is straightforward and it is something that can be translated into dollars, which is important for decision-making purposes. Although this is a specific formula, some elements in the equations are very subjective. For example, the cost to recover from intrusions (**R**) is a very subjective number, which is what it should be. Intrusions can vary in severity, and the associated cost to recover might range from nothing to something fairly substantial. Similarly, the dollar savings resulting from proactively stopping intrusions (**E**) is also very subjective, as there are many variables in calculating this number. As you can see, there is still a fair amount of subjectivity when calculating ROSI. As difficult as it is, you must work with the client to determine dollar values for these subjective items needed to calculate the ROSI or cost-benefit analysis. Any past experience with security incidents and publicly available statistics can be used to help estimate numbers in this calculation or can be used as a benchmark.

In the formula above, one aspect that is not specifically identified in the calculation that must be addressed is the ongoing cost related to implementing security recommendations. In the calculation, costs related to the ongoing administration of the tool (T) are not addressed. In the intrusion detection example above, there is significant cost related to reviewing logs, incident response, and the ongoing technical maintenance of the intrusion detection system. This is something to keep in mind as you determine ROSI.

When making recommendations, one aspect to think about is how well the recommendation addresses the risk. This is an important concept, and it will be evident when calculating ROSI. For most risks, you can have recommendations that address the risk in different ways. Although it would be nice to have the best solution to address a finding and risk, does the client really need it? For that matter, do they even need something good? It is likely that all they need is a solution that is adequate enough to address the risk. The reason why this is an important concept is that a perfect solution might cost double or triple the amount of the adequate solution — this has a significant impact on ROSI.

Some people do not go through this type of calculation and instead try to demonstrate the cost benefit by utilizing the F.U.D. (Fear, Uncertainty, Doubt) method. The theory with F.U.D. is that management will implement security measures out of sheer fear that something might happen. As people are becoming more knowledgeable about security, F.U.D. is becoming less of a factor when deciding whether or not to implement security measures. Consequently, this is not an advisable method when justifying recommendations.

The bottom line is that cost benefit and ROSI must be considered when making recommendations. For recommendations that require significant outlay of money or resources or significant changes in processes, decision makers will certainly ask questions on the cost benefit and the ROSI of implementing the recommendation. It is really no different than what is done with other major projects. Being able to demonstrate the cost benefit and the ROSI is like making a business case for the investment. As security practitioners, we need to think in financial and business terms to present an accurate picture to management. The trend now is that decision making as it pertains to information security is resting with business unit personnel, not IT. "The Yankee Group expects security budgets to increase in 2004. But companies will no longer spend for security's sake. The enterprise model for security decision making has changed to include line-of-business managers. The biggest discovery in this model is the shift in influence from technology decision-makers to the lines of business."[3] As many of the elements of the ROSI calculation are subjective, the cost-benefit analysis will force you to make certain projections and estimations about the probability of a security incident and the potential impact. It is critical to have a good knowledge of the business to make the estimations required in calculating ROSI. With time and experience, this becomes an easier process.

OTHER GENERAL RECOMMENDATIONS

After the actual security assessment is complete, some other long-term recommendations should be considered. Making these recommendations depends on certain factors such as staffing levels and how much accountability is in the organization. The recommendations include:

- Ongoing assessments
- Managed services
- Service-level agreements

These recommendations do not necessarily address specific risks, but they do address more strategic weaknesses such as lack of proper staff and the desire to focus on core competencies. They are long-term initiatives to strengthen the security posture in a cost-effective manner. These recommendations are not appropriate in every environment, but they are worth considering.

Ongoing Assessment

Once findings are presented and the security assessment is complete, clients should think of how to ensure that their environment is secure on an ongoing basis. Ideally, the security assessment process should be something that is happening all the time. This is especially true for companies with a heavy dependence on technology because technology is changing so rapidly. Reviewing a company's security posture after long periods of time is both expensive and to some extent ineffective for two reasons.

First, a full-blown security assessment after a long period of time is expensive and time consuming. Because the security posture has not been reviewed for a significant time period, everything has to be reviewed — previous knowledge cannot necessarily be leveraged. Because of the time lapse, gathering information for the security assessment is like starting from scratch. This does not mean that security measures have not been taken as the business has changed. However, because no analysis has been done on an ongoing basis, there is little assurance that security measures are commensurate with the associated risks.

Second, companies that look at their security postures after long periods of time might not be making the best decisions from a security perspective because they are not up to speed on the risks facing their organizations. The more frequent reviews allow management to be more in tune with information security requirements for the company and thus make better and more proactive decisions, ultimately resulting in a more secure environment.

A good recommendation to give clients at the conclusion of a security assessment is to use the initial security assessment as a "baseline" and have some type of ongoing assessment. This is similar to what many large companies have with their internal audit function. Many companies have IT audit as a part of the internal audit function, where some IT areas are audited in conjunction with the financial and operational audit. One approach that internal audit departments take is a risk-based approach to auditing the company in which the company's operations are classified based on risk categories. This analysis is then used to determine what will be audited and how often. If this process is already in place for internal audit, information security should be reviewed in a similar manner in conjunction with internal audits. If there is no internal audit function, some type of periodic assessment or audit should be done by internal resources or third-party consultants.

One issue with ongoing assessments is that some small and mid-size companies may feel they are too expensive or unnecessary. These companies might not necessarily see the value in doing ongoing assessments, especially if they have not had any security incidents. With these companies, it is important to point out that taking a proactive approach to information security will ultimately benefit them. One incident, such as computers being infected with viruses or a disgruntled employee doing major damage because his or her access was never revoked, can be far more costly than the cost of having a periodic assessment done. Ongoing security assessments surface information security concerns so that companies can proactively take action and minimize any associated risks.

Managed Security Services

Managed security services are essentially outsourced security services, where a third party manages parts of the security infrastructure. For example, an outsourcer might manage firewalls, routers, or intrusion detection systems. The justifications and arguments for managed security services are similar to those for other types of outsourcing and include:

- Companies should concentrate on their core competencies — i.e., companies should focus on what they are good at and hire experts to handle noncore operations such as IT and security.
- Outsourcing security is a cheaper and better alternative than trying to do it in house.
- Outsourcing security allows the company to stay up to date with current technology related to security.
- Security is managed on a 24/7 basis.

What is the relevance of managed security in a security assessment? As you perform the security assessment and develop the findings and recommendations, one thing to think about is whether the company has the resources to implement the recommendations you are proposing. As part of the assessment, you should be thinking about whether the client's current staff has the expertise and time to implement the recommendations and the time to do the additional administration associated with those recommendations (if any). If they do not, managed security is a potential alternative in certain cases that should be considered to possibly address some areas of security. Some of the managed services being offered in the market today include:

- *Managed vulnerability assessments* — Managed vulnerability assessments are regular scans that are run against a company's network (or some portion of the network) with little human intervention. The scan looks at various system settings and compares them against what are considered best practices. The results of the comparison are reported to the client. It is the client's responsibility to interpret these results and determine which are legitimate and should be fixed and which should not. With managed vulnerability assessments, the critical aspect is having good reports, being able to interpret them, and making the appropriate fixes. The automated vulnerability scan by itself is meaningless unless it is interpreted and acted upon. One potential issue for clients is that they may not have the in-house expertise to interpret the report, in which case some third party should be hired to do so.

- *Managed firewall* — Managed firewall service is when an outsourcer administers the client's firewall. Managing a firewall can be complicated, and although it is an integral part of the security infrastructure, clients do not necessarily have the appropriate expertise. Some of the services that managed firewall vendors will perform include:

  - *Monitoring* — Personnel review traffic passing through the firewall. This can be accomplished by using automated tools to help in the review process.
  - *Rule base changes* — Personnel will make changes to the firewall rule base as business requirements change and different traffic is allowed or not allowed into the network.
  - *Security patches* — Personnel install security patches on firewalls as they are released from the firewall vendor.
  - *Management reporting* — Managed firewall vendors normally have a set of standard reports that are offered with their managed service. These reports are one way of managing the outsourcing vendor and ensuring that service levels are being met.

  Different vendors vary in the way in which they provide the service. Many vendors are limited in what firewalls they support, so some flexibility is lost. As with any service that is outsourced, clients should ensure that the managed firewall vendor is legitimate. Due diligence must be performed before selecting a vendor, and the client must understand that the relationship with the managed firewall vendor is not a turnkey relationship. Because of the criticality of the piece of the security infrastructure managed firewall vendors handle, the client must manage the relationship properly.

- *Managed intrusion detection* — Managed intrusion detection is when a vendor monitors potential intrusions for a company. The services can be for network-based detection, where certain network segments are monitored, or host-based detection, where specific machines are monitored. At a high level, agents are installed on networks or hosts, which watch traffic and determine whether a potential attack is in process. If one is in process, an alert is sent to the console at the managed security provider's location, which operators are constantly monitoring. Operators then classify and send the alert to the client. Note that the attack is not prevented — it is only detected and reported. The basic items that a managed intrusion detection service offers include:

  - *Alert notification* — Alert notification is the main element of the managed intrusion detection service. As attacks are detected, clients are notified of the event. Clients than must decide what action, if any, to take.

- *Attack signature updates* — As new attack patterns are discovered, the intrusion detection system should be updated to ensure it could detect them.
- *Management reporting* — The managed security service should provide some management reports that give the client management a sense for what type of intrusion activity is occurring. The managed security service provider should have some canned standard reports available. The provider might also be able to create other reports as required.
- *Mitigation support* — Once clients are notified of a potential intrusion, they must decide what action (if any) they are going to take. The action, in most cases, is not obvious and requires expertise and some research to determine what to do. Many companies do not have the in-house expertise to do the research and determine a fix. As a result, some Managerial Security Service Providers (MSSP) provide mitigation support, where they give technical assistance with responding to an intrusion. MSSPs will normally have information repositories available to help research how to fix vulnerabilities.

The decision to go with managed security should not be taken lightly because with outsourcing, someone else is managing a critical component of the IT infrastructure and there is a loss of control. Although the MSSP is managing certain elements of security, the company is still ultimately responsible for the security of its information assets. If something goes wrong, the company will feel the impact and be held accountable. As a result, clients must be willing to actively manage the MSSP and hold it accountable for the services for which the business contracted.

If the client makes a decision that managed security is proper for them, you should advise them to look carefully at providers and do a proper due diligence before making a decision. When comparing different MSSPs, it is important to clearly understand what each is offering so fair comparisons and the best decision can be made. You can also refer to the Managed Security Questionnaire for some questions to ask when choosing a managed security provider.

DISCUSS DRAFT REPORT WITH CLIENT

The next step of this phase is to review the draft report with the client (Figure 8.4). At this stage, you should have a good draft of the report, which the client can review. Unlike the previous status meetings where findings were primarily reviewed, risks, recommendations, and the rest of the report are reviewed at this meeting. This meeting should include the people from the client side whom you have been working with throughout the assessment, with the main purpose of giving them the opportunity to provide feedback on the entire report. The structure of this meeting is to walk through the report and obtain feedback from the client. The structure of the final report is something that the client should already have seen. At this time, the

FIGURE 8.4 Discuss draft report with client.

client just has to do a final review of the content in the report and ask any questions to clarify points made in the report.

This preliminary view of the report is also a professional courtesy that should be given to the client. The core group you worked with to conduct the assessment will be the ones questioned when the broader audience, which includes senior management and key stakeholders, reviews the final set of findings and recommendations. The last thing you want is for your key client contacts to be blindsided by the content in the report.

This meeting is beneficial to both you and the client. From your perspective, the feedback provided by the client can be invaluable. Some of the benefits and feedback the client can provide include:

- *Supplemental information* — Information about recommendations (some of this should have been done) and their feasibility — e.g., whether something has been tried before, other factors about which you may have been unaware.
- *Report expectations* — The executives who authorized the security assessment probably have some expectations regarding the type of information they expect to see in the final report. Your client contacts can provide some insight into this. Note, however, that this feedback should not substantively change the content of your report; only the structure should be affected.
- *Buy-in* — During the kickoff meeting, one of the things you discussed was the security assessment methodology, and one of the steps was to have certain client personnel review the draft deliverable before it went to the broader audience. The fact that the report has been reviewed and essentially approved by client personnel creates a level of buy-in from executives.

During this final status meeting, it is essential you maintain your independence. The client's expectation is that you will remain independent; that is one of the reasons to have a separate group perform the security assessment. Ideally, this meeting should have few surprises, as the client should have seen much of what is in the report.

After this review, you should make the final changes to the report. Once that is complete, it is ready for the final step, which is to present it to the client.

PRESENT FINAL REPORT TO MANAGEMENT

Once the final report is complete, you should present it to the broader audience, which includes senior management, the executive sponsor of the assessment, and other key individuals (Figure 8.5). It is important to have these key people in the room, as they will ultimately be the ones approving any security initiatives resulting from the assessment.

When presenting the final report, it is a good idea to do a formal presentation using PowerPoint or similar software rather than go through the report. Because the

FIGURE 8.5 Present final report to management.

report can be very long, it is not worth spending the time to go over the actual document. It is best to pick out the key points from the report and discuss them with the group. The key points that should be covered include:

- Scope
- Methodology
- Findings, risks, and recommendations

The bulk of the time should be spent discussing the findings, risks, and recommendations; this is really what the client is interested in. The reason for going over the scope and methodology is to make sure that everyone is on the same page regarding what was covered in the assessment and how the results were obtained. Because there is a time lapse between the kickoff meeting and the final presentation, it is worth clarifying the scope and methodology for the group.

If you focus on discussion of the findings, risks, and recommendations, client management will have a good sense for the "security roadmap" and the opportunity to ask any questions regarding it. It is important for client management to understand the nature of the findings, the risks facing the organization, and the remedies proposed to address the risks because client management will ultimately make the decisions about what initiatives to pursue.

When developing the presentation for client management, specifically the findings, risks, and recommendations, focus on how they impact the business. Remember that the audience might not fully understand the technical nuances of security and they probably do not care to. They are interested in what risks the company faces from a business perspective.

In delivering the presentation, you should be prepared to answer detailed questions about the findings and risks and specifically on the cost-benefit analysis related to the recommendations. You should be prepared to answer the question "So what?" when discussing a finding. The final presentation is absolutely critical in the security assessment process. As stated several times in this book, when clients purchase security assessment services, they are purchasing expertise. The final report document and the presentation to the client are your main opportunities to show your value.

POTENTIAL CONCERNS DURING THIS PHASE

As with the last two phases of the security assessment, there are some potential concerns during this phase that you should look out for, including the following:

- *Links between findings, risks, and recommendations are not clear.* This is something that might happen when you lose focus and the discussions related to findings, risks, and recommendations go off on tangents. The way to ensure that there is a clear link between findings and risks and recommendations is to take a step back and put yourself in the client's shoes and see if it makes sense. You can also have someone else not connected with the security assessment review the report as if he or she were the client to see if it makes sense. Although the client will review it from this perspective before the report is finalized, it is worth going through this exercise on your own before showing the report to the client in the discussion of the draft deliverable.

- *Revenue and expense numbers used in risk analysis are not accurate.* Quantifying risks can make a very compelling argument. However, verify the numbers you are using, and make sure they are right. The client should validate these numbers before they make it to the report. Using the wrong numbers can create a very embarrassing situation and possibly change the way you view a risk.
- *Key management is not present at final presentation.* When making the final presentation, you should do what you can to ensure that key management is present at the final presentation. Having them there adds significant credibility to the assessment process and helps ensure that the recommendations made will be considered. It also provides management with the opportunity to ask questions about the results of the assessment.

EXECUTIVE SUMMARY

The Risk Analysis and Final Presentation is the final phase of the security assessment. This is also the phase where much of the analysis is done as it relates to determining risks and recommendations. The key steps in this phase include the following:

- *Complete risk analysis and risk score calculation.* Risks must be clearly documented and expressed in terms of potential impacts to the business as they relate to findings that have been discovered. To the extent that risks can be quantified, they should be. Some of the typical quantifications include impact on revenue, as well as costs related to remediation in the event of a security incident. In addition, it is also worth considering the intangible risks such as reputation damage and loss of customers. The risk score is an attempt to make the risk objective. There are several subjective factors, including the potential business impact related to a risk, the likelihood of a security incident, and what security measures are in place to mitigate those risks. The risk score is eventually used to classify a finding as a high, medium, or low risk.
- *Finalize findings and risks.* It is important to ensure that the wordings of the findings and risks are appropriate. The wording must be clear and concise so it clearly articulates the findings and associated risks. The findings should not only include the vulnerability but also any controls that the client has in place that mitigate the risk. As for risks, they must be stated in terms of impact to the business. If the impact can be quantified, it should be done, as that provides the most compelling argument.
- *Develop recommendations and prepare draft report.* Recommendations are the "security roadmap" resulting from the security assessment. It is critical that recommendations specifically address the related risks in a cost-effective manner. Recommendations should be worded so that the

client can easily determine how and what resources will be required to implement them. Ideally, the client should be able to take the list of recommendations and use it as a "security roadmap" for the short and long term. The recommendations along with the risks should be documented in the final report to be discussed with the client.

- *Discuss draft report with the client.* Before sharing the report with the broader audience including senior management, you should review it with the client. This step is beneficial for both you and the client. The client has the opportunity to see the report and be prepared for the final meeting, and the client can provide constructive feedback so you can make any necessary final changes to the report. This step is a win-win situation for all.

- *Present final report to management.* This is the final step of the security assessment, when the results are presented to management. This meeting is critical as it is a culmination of your efforts in conducting the security assessment. This is the main opportunity you have to show the value of the security assessment. To facilitate this meeting, a presentation should be developed in which you discuss the scope, methodology, and findings, risks, and recommendations. Because the main audience is management, the meeting should focus on how the findings and risks discovered affect the business. In addition, recommendations should be discussed in terms of how they address risk from a cost-benefit perspective. It is important that management attend this meeting as that will increase the chance that the recommendations made will be considered.

NOTES

1. *CIO* Magazine — Coming up ROSI, by Scott Berinato; October 26, 2001 — http://www.cio.com/security/edit/a102601_rosi.html
2. *CIO* Magazine, Finally, a Real Return on Security Spending, by Scott Berinato; http://www.cio.com/archive/021502/security_sidebar.html
3. "Security Takes Sides with the Business," by Eric Ogren — February 2004 — http://www.csoonline.com/analyst/report2241.html

9 Information Security Standards

As discussed at various points in this book, standards are important when conducting a security assessment. Standards have typically been developed by a wide range of people and have gone through the scrutiny of practitioners and as a result, have been accepted. Depending on the nature and scope of the security assessment and what the client wants, different standards might be appropriate. This chapter discusses some of the widely known standards in use today.

INTERNATIONAL STANDARDS ORGANIZATION 17799 (ISO 17799)

The ISO 17799 standard started out as British Standards (BS) 7799, which later became ISO 17799 — Information technology — Code of practice for information security management. The original BS 7799 was published in 1995 and was the first major information security best practice standard. After a revision in 1999, the standard was made more flexible, started to gain acceptance, and eventually became an ISO standard.

The purpose of the ISO 17799 standard according to the International Standards Organization is to "provide a common basis for developing organizational security standards and effective security management practice and to provide confidence in inter-organizational dealings."[1] From a practical perspective, the ISO 17799 is a high-level standard for different aspects of information security. The standard is policy oriented in that it provides standards on what should be done, not how it should be done.

When conducting a security assessment, the ISO 17799 is a good benchmark because it represents industry-recognized best practices. Although the standard is not detailed enough to use when evaluating detailed processes, it does provide enough information to perform a high-level review of different areas. The ISO standard is also helpful when evaluating or developing information security policies for a company. Because policies are high-level statements that outline requirements for a given area of security, the ISO standard is a good benchmark in helping to ensure that the policy reflects best practices. Note that when performing a security assessment, the specific business requirements must be considered in addition to standards such as the ISO 17799.

The ISO 17799 is made up of ten areas of security, which are listed next, along with brief descriptions. The information below is taken directly from the ISO 17799 standard document.

- *Security Policy* — Management should support the issuing and maintenance of security policies that effectively communicate the security requirements for the company. This section covers what policies should look like as well as how the policies should be reviewed on a regular basis to ensure that they reflect business requirements.
- *Organizational Security* — The main concept in this section is that of establishing roles and responsibilities for all aspects of information security and establishing a framework for how the information security function is managed. This section discusses the coordination of security between departments. Other specific areas discussed in this section include:
  - *Security of third party access* — Security requirements when third parties access the company's systems and information
  - *Outsourcing* — Protection of information assets when a third party is handling information processing

  There is also a requirement for reviewing the security function on a regular basis.
- *Asset Classification and Control* — The requirements in this section deal with assigning ownership of assets. It then becomes the asset owner's responsibility to ensure that the assets are properly controlled and maintained. With this ownership comes accountability of the assets. Some of the specific areas of asset classification and control that are discussed include the inventory of assets and development of classification guidelines for assets.
- *Personnel Security* — The personnel security section covers all aspects of someone's employment with a company. Guidelines are detailed for the entire process from someone being hired to being terminated. Some of the specific guidelines include:
  - Screening of personnel
  - Inclusion of security in job responsibilities
  - Employment contracts
  - User training
  - Users' responsibility relative to security — e.g., reporting security incidents and security weaknesses
  - Employee disciplinary process
- *Physical and Environmental Security* — This section outlines physical and environmental security measures that should be taken to prevent unauthorized physical access or damage to facilities. The physical security requirements are structured in a layered approach — i.e., there are requirements for everything from securing the perimeter of the premises to securing specific property. The specific sections include (the headings below are directly from the ISO 17799 standard):
  - Physical security perimeter
  - Physical entry controls
  - Securing offices, rooms, and facilities
  - Secure areas

- Isolated delivery and loading areas
- Equipment security
- Security of equipment off premises
- Clear desk and clear screen policy
- *Communications and Operations Management* — The guidelines in this section include processes for securing communications and operating facilities. There are requirements for processes to help ensure that facilities are run in a secure and controlled manner. Some of these processes include (headings below are taken directly from the ISO 17799 standard):
  - Change management
  - Incident management
  - Systems planning and acceptance processes
  - Protection against malicious software
  - Information backup
  - Log review
  - Network management
  - Media handling — e.g., removable computer media, disposal of media
  - Exchange of information and software — e.g., securing media in transit, e-commerce security, security of electronic mail

  Although some of the headings listed above appear to be technical, the ISO standard is focused on policy and on ensuring that there is ownership of the key responsibilities.
- *Access Control* — The access control section defines requirements to control access and prevent unauthorized access to information. The basic concept that drives access control is that employees should be given access only to what they need to do their jobs. The requirements in this section address the need for an access control policy and access at all levels including network, privileged access, and application-level access. In addition, a number of requirements related to proper password management are included. The requirements cover the following topics at a high level (headings listed below are taken directly from the ISO 17799 standard):
  - User access management — Obtaining access, privileged access, password management, periodic review of user access rights, etc.
  - User responsibilities
  - Network access control including secure networking concepts (e.g., use of enforce path, segregation of networks, network routing control)
  - Operating system access control
  - Application access control
  - Monitoring system access
  - Mobile computing and telecommuting
- *Systems Development and Maintenance* — The main purpose of the requirements in this section is to ensure that security is built into information systems. Based on these requirements, security should be built into systems at all levels including the infrastructure, network, operating system, and application level. Some of the specific items in this section include:

- Security in application systems
- Cryptographic controls — (e.g., encryption, digital signatures, non-repudiation)
- Security of system files
- Security in the development and support processes
- *Business Continuity Management* — This section defines guidelines for the complete life cycle of business continuity including the development of the plan, testing, and ongoing updates to the plan. Some of the specific items in this section include the following (information below is taken from the ISO 17799 standard):
  - Business continuity management process
  - Conducting a business impact analysis
  - Testing, maintaining, and reassessing business continuity plans
- *Compliance* — This section defines certain legal and operational requirements with which information security processes must comply. The requirements call for identification of all regulatory, legislative and contractual security-related requirements that are applicable to the company. Specific requirements are defined for ensuring compliance with these requirements. Some of the specific items in this section include (information below is taken directly from the ISO 17799 standard):
  - Compliance with legal requirements (e.g., intellectual property rights, organizational records, evidence handling)
  - Reviews of security policy and technical compliance
  - System audit considerations

USE IN A SECURITY ASSESSMENT

The ISO 17799 is a great reference document when conducting a security assessment. It provides guidance on what elements should exist in an information security program and can be used as a point of comparison when conducting a security assessment. The value of the ISO 17799 is in providing guidance on "what" should exist from an information security perspective. It provides limited guidance on process — i.e., "how" the information security objectives should be achieved.

COMMON CRITERIA (CC)

The Common Criteria (CC) is the name of ISO 15408 and is a standard that "provides the framework for testing the effectiveness of most security systems and individual security solutions."[2] This standard defines certain characteristics or targets that security systems should have. These characteristics can be thought of as minimum security requirements for security systems. The development of the CC is an attempt to define an evaluation system that can be widely used to both develop and evaluate security systems. The origin of the CC was the "Orange Book," which was published in the U.S. in 1985. The Orange Book, like the CC, was a set of security specifications to incorporate into security systems as well as guidelines by which to evaluate security systems. The development of the CC was a result of combining the elements of the Orange Book as well as similar standards from other countries including Canada (Canadian Criteria), Germany (German Criteria), France (French Criteria), and the United Kingdom (UK Confidence Levels). This multinational effort resulted in the publication of the CC. The hope was that the CC would be common basis for evaluating and comparing security systems.

According to the scope of the Common Criteria, "the CC will permit comparability between the results of independent security evaluations ... by providing a common set of requirements for the security functions of IT products and systems and for assurance measures applied to them during a security evaluation."[3] The CC is gaining wide acceptance — e.g., with the U.S. Department of Defense. Since the September 11 attacks in 2001, the National Security Agency (NSA) and the National Institute of Standards and Technology (NIST) have been working together on ensuring that key technologies to be used in federal agencies are secure. The standards are being used to evaluate IT components at all levels including operating systems, databases, and network systems.

STRUCTURE OF THE COMMON CRITERIA

The Common Criteria documentation is divided into three parts including:

- *Part 1 — Introduction and General Model* — Part 1 of the CC is an introduction, which gives general information and familiarizes the user. The document goes over the methodology of the CC and also key terminology that is used in the other two parts. This part also provides a brief history of how the CC was developed.
- *Part 2 — Security Functional Requirements* — Part 2 provides guidance on determining security functional requirements for security systems. This section does not actually provide specific security functional requirements but instead provides a methodology for developing and evaluating security functional requirements for a given security system.
- *Part 3 — Security Assurance Requirements* — Part 3 provides guidance on determining and evaluating the security assurance requirements for security systems. Like Part 2, this section does not define actual requirements. It is more of a methodology to ensure that the assurance requirements make sense based on business requirements.

USE IN A SECURITY ASSESSMENT

Unlike the ISO 17799, the CC does not provide actual standards or guidelines that can be used when evaluating the security posture of a company. The CC provides a detailed methodology for determining whether security measures are adequate, which is similar to the methodology espoused in this book. When conducting a security assessment, the value of the CC is in helping one through the methodology of doing a security assessment as opposed to providing standards by which security can be measured. The value of the CC is that it reinforces the process of thinking in terms of aligning security measures with risks.

COBIT (CONTROL OBJECTIVES FOR INFORMATION [RELATED] TECHNOLOGY)

COBIT was developed by ISACA (Information Systems Audit and Control Association) for IT auditors. COBIT is a framework for evaluating security and controls over information. COBIT does not reference any specific technology and is very process focused. It is actually broader based than information security by itself. COBIT looks at all IT-related processes, and although security is a component, it is more focused on the "bigger picture" of how IT supports the organization. At the core of the COBIT methodology are the 34 high-level control objectives ranging from strategic activities that ensure that sound IT investments are made to strategy execution (e.g., implementation, delivery, and monitoring). As stated in the executive summary of COBIT, the COBIT framework is based on the premise, "In order to provide the information that the organization needs to achieve its objectives, IT resources need to be managed by a set of naturally grouped processes."[4]

COBIT STRUCTURE

The COBIT guidelines contain six documents including:

- *Executive Summary* — The Executive Summary is the shortest of the documents and contains general information about COBIT. This document discusses the overall COBIT methodology and defines key concepts that are used in the rest of the documents.
- *Framework* — The Framework document provides details about the COBIT methodology — i.e., "control in IT is approached by looking at information that is needed to support the business objectives or requirements, and by looking at information as being the result of the combined application of IT-related resources that need to be managed by IT processes."[5] The framework set forth in COBIT is a set of 34 high-level control objectives with specific tasks, which are grouped into one of four areas. The complete set of objectives is grouped in the following categories (based on the COBIT Framework document):
  - *Planning and organization* — There are 11 control objectives in this group, which primarily deals with IT strategy and how it supports the objectives of the business. These objectives range from determining the right type of technology to having the right organization in place to properly support the technology. The control objectives ensure that the planning and organization have been thought through well. This up-front planning significantly increases the chance of success as technology is purchased and implemented.
  - *Acquisition and implementation* — The control objectives related to Acquisition and Implementation move away from the strategic planning to the tactical or the actual execution of the strategy. There are six control objectives in this section, which primarily deal with the acquisition and implementation of IT infrastructure and applications.

In addition, there are also control objectives related to having documented procedures, system accreditation, and change management. The objectives in this domain are the first steps in the execution of the strategy defined in the Planning and Organization domain.
- *Delivery and support* — The Delivery and Support control objectives deal with ensuring that IT systems that were acquired are properly running according to required service levels. The 13 control objectives in this section address the management of IT systems including change, incident, and problem management to help ensure the continuity of IT systems. The control objectives also address user awareness and advising customers.
- *Monitoring* — The Monitoring objectives address how well the IT systems are functioning and whether they are meeting their objectives from a controls perspective. The four control objectives address monitoring and obtaining independent assurance that the systems are functioning as intended.

• *Implementation Tool Set* — One of the challenges that audit and security management constantly face is raising awareness of security and audit concerns. The COBIT Implementation Tool Set was developed to help raise this awareness through the use of tools to help analyze IT controls and security and how they are addressing the risks facing the organization. The two tools in the Implementation Tool Set are:
- IT Governance Self Assessment
- Management's IT Concern Diagnostic

These two tools are essentially questionnaires that help management see the importance of maintaining a sound internal control environment. From the IT perspective, they help in validating that the current security and control measures in place are aligned with the business risks facing the organization. Specific details about the two tools are presented below.

IT Governance Self Assessment

The basis of this assessment is the high-level control objectives used in the Framework. The Self Assessment process asks management to determine the following with regard to each of the high-level control objectives:

- Criticality of the process.
- Whether the process is documented — i.e., are there formal procedures?
- Whether there is ownership of the process — i.e., accountability.
- Whether the process is audited.

These questions force management to think of key processes in a way they probably have not. For example, one of the frequent issues with processes is a lack of accountability because everyone thinks someone else is responsible, with the result that no one is responsible. Another example is documented procedures. Often times, processes are working fine because the person performing them knows the process. However, a problem develops if that person leaves the company or becomes ill and someone else has to do it. The lack of documented procedures makes it difficult for someone to step in and perform the task. This can be a major issue depending on the criticality of the process. These questions eventually cause security and internal control issues to surface and be addressed.

Management's IT Concern Diagnostic

This diagnostic uses the high-level control objectives defined in the COBIT Framework as the basis for determining how well these processes are being performed. There are a number of forms, which are in a checklist format. Managers are to take these forms and essentially assign a rating to internal controls related to each of the 34 high-level control objectives. In each of the forms, managers must rate the importance of the process. The following forms comprise the IT Concern Diagnostics:

- *Prior Audit Work Form* — used to determine whether any prior audit issues exist related to a process and whether they have been addressed
- *Entity Short and Long Forms* — used to rate the performance of a process
- *Risk Assessment Form* — used to rate the level of risk and whether or not documented internal controls exist
- *Responsible Party Form* — documents who is responsible for the process
- *Contract Service/Service Level Agreement Form* — documents whether a service level agreement (SLA) or contract is in place for a given process

Both of these tools are excellent resources to help raise awareness. As with the other components of COBIT, they have a strong focus on the business requirements of the company and a broad view of IT.

Control Objectives

As already discussed, COBIT has 34 control objectives classified in the different domains, which are first introduced in the Framework document. The Control Objectives document takes each of the control objectives to another level of detail. For each of the control objectives, there is documentation that maps the control objectives to high-level business requirements and factors to consider when implementing the control. The high-level control objectives are then broken down into granular ways in which the control objectives can be achieved. For example, the first control objective in the Planning and Organization domain is "Define a Strategic Information Technology Plan." For this control objective, there are eight "detailed control objectives":

- IT as Part of the Organization's Long- and Short-Range Plan
- IT Long-Range Plan
- IT Long-Range Planning — Approach and Structure
- IT Long-Range Plan Changes
- Short-Range Planning for the IT Function

- Communication of IT Plans
- Monitoring and Evaluating of IT Plans
- Assessment of Existing Systems

Similar detailed control objectives exist for each of the 34 high-level control objectives.

Based on the areas listed above, it is clear that the COBIT framework is looking at the entire IT lifecycle from strategically planning for it to acquiring, implementing, managing, and monitoring. Internal controls are a constant theme throughout the control objectives, and a strong focus exists on considering a company's business requirements, as demonstrated by the 11 control objectives related to planning and organization.

Management Guidelines

The Management Guidelines document provides guidance on how to manage and control IT so that it delivers the service required. These guidelines are focused on managing the performance of the IT function and ensuring that appropriate adjustments are made as business requirements change. In developing the guidelines, the developers were trying to address management's concerns. The Management Guidelines basically address four key management concerns listed below (these are taken from the COBIT Management Guidelines Executive Summary):

- *Performance measurement* — What are the indicators of good performance?
- *IT control profiling* — What is important? What are the Critical Success Factors for control?
- *Awareness* — What are the risks of not achieving our objectives?
- *Benchmarking* — What do others do? How do we measure and compare?

In addressing these concerns, a set of four different types of measurements for each of the 34 high-level control objectives was developed. These measurements include (these are taken from the COBIT Management Guidelines Executive Summary):

- *Maturity models* — This is based on the Software Engineering Institute's maturity model and is a way of scoring the IT performance of a company.
- *Critical success factors* — These are critical issues and actions that management should be concerned about — i.e., these issues will drive the success or failure of IT.
- *Key goal indicators* — These are measurements that show whether or not IT processes have met their objectives.
- *Key performance indicators* — These indicators are a measure of overall IT performance.

The Management Guidelines essentially take the detailed control objectives one step further in that they measure how well the IT processes related to a given control are working.

Use in a Security Assessment

The COBIT documents can be very useful in a security assessment. As with the methodology discussed in this book, there is a strong focus on how security measures are aligned to the business requirements of the company. In particular, the Control Objectives and the subsequent details are good resources when defining risks during a security assessment. In addition, the high-level controls listed in the Planning and Organization domain are good topics to help facilitate discussions about the business with customers. The COBIT guidelines also address the governance aspect of IT, which will help you when you are evaluating organizations and how they handle security.

ITIL (IT INFRASTRUCTURE LIBRARY)
SECURITY MANAGEMENT

ITIL is a set of documents focused on best practice processes for IT Service Management. ITIL was developed in the United Kingdom and is gaining acceptance as a worldwide standard for IT processes. Like the other standards discussed so far, ITIL is technology neutral. ITIL is also very focused on process. Unlike the ISO 17799, which described "what" security measures should be in place, the ITIL Security Management describes "how" security measures can be implemented in a company. One of the underpinnings of ITIL is embedding security into everyday processes.

The book has five chapters along with a few annexes at the end of the book. The first two chapters consist of an introduction, a section on the fundamentals of information security, and a section on the links between information security and IT processes. These first two chapters primarily deal with basic security management information including such items as the importance of management commitment and viewing information security as a business enabler instead of a cost. These are all important concepts worthy of reviewing and discussing with customers to help them look at information security from a business perspective and not from a technical product perspective.

The next three chapters discuss security management for a number of key security processes. In the third chapter, there is a discussion about determining the security-related service level requirements for various business processes. These service-level requirements help determine key operational areas that must be in place before effective security management can take place. Some of these operational areas include[6] (these processes are discussed in detail in the ITIL Security Management book):

- Configuration and asset management
- Incident control and help desk
- Problem management
- Change management
- Release management

The final two chapters provide best-practice processes for some key information security areas including:

- Asset classification
- Personnel security
- Communications and operations management
- Access control
- Auditing and evaluation

The list above closely resembles sections of the ISO 17799 (BS 7799) standard. For each of the areas listed above, the ITIL book contains best-practice processes. In the first annex, there is also a table that maps the processes covered by ITIL to the BS 7799 standard.

USE IN A SECURITY ASSESSMENT

The ITIL Security Management standard is a good resource where there is a heavy focus on process, and the customer wants suggestions on ways to make security-related processes more efficient. The ITIL processes can be used in conjunction with the ISO 17799 standard to do a very thorough analysis, with the ISO standard focusing on the security requirements themselves and ITIL focusing on the process of implementing those requirements.

SAS (STATEMENT ON AUDITING STANDARDS) 70

The SAS 70 standard was developed by the AICPA (American Institute of Certified Public Accountants) and is used for auditing service organizations. A service organization for purposes of the SAS 70 is an organization that provides IT services to another company. The SAS 70 audit is an in-depth examination of the service organization's internal control environment related to information technology and any related processes. It must be conducted by a Certified Public Accountant (CPA) with the relevant skill sets to perform such an audit and used to support the internal control requirements related to financial statement audits.

With the SAS 70, there are no defined standards per se. It is up to the service organization to determine what the control objectives are and the steps to take to meet those control objectives. It is the job of the auditor to determine whether the control objectives documented by the service provider are accurate and whether the control processes achieve those objectives. Typically, a SAS 70 is done is to support a financial statement audit for a company that receives services from a third party. For example, a manufacturing company might have its entire IT infrastructure outsourced to a third party — i.e., all of the company's systems are being managed by a third party. For the financial statement audit, the auditors need some assurance that those systems are properly controlled because the numbers in the financial statements come from those systems. To gain this assurance, the outsourcer would provide a copy of the SAS 70 report to the auditors of the manufacturing company. The SAS 70 report becomes particularly useful if the outsourcer provides similar services for multiple companies because the same report could be used to support financial statement audits for the other customers.

USE IN A SECURITY ASSESSMENT

The SAS 70 report can be useful in a security assessment primarily in the initial information gathering process. Although a SAS 70 report is not necessarily going to point out security weaknesses, the report can give clues of where the company might have security weaknesses. If the opinion on a SAS 70 report is that internal controls are inadequate, this should immediately raise questions about the internal control and security environment. At the same time, a favorable opinion on a SAS 70 report should not give confidence that no security weaknesses are present.

AICPA SYSTRUST

SysTrust was designed jointly by the AICPA and the CICA (Canadian Institute of Chartered Accountants) to help CPAs determine the reliability of information systems. As with the SAS 70, only licensed CPAs with the appropriate skill set can perform a SysTrust audit.

With the SysTrust methodology, the reliability of a system is based on four principles (defined by the AICPA/CICA),[7] which focus on ensuring controls are in place to ensure:

- *Availability* — availability of systems and whether it meets SLAs (if they exist)
- *Security* — security measures to prevent unauthorized access
- *Integrity* — completeness and accuracy of system processing
- *Maintainability* — ability to update systems without affecting the availability, security, or integrity of the systems

The SysTrust principles, like the other standards discussed so far, are also technology neutral. For each of the principles listed above, the SysTrust standards contain more granular principles, which can be used almost like a checklist when conducting a SysTrust engagement. The specific questions in the checklist are broad in nature and thus, significant room for interpretation exists. The questions are somewhat open-ended and can spark discussions to provide significant information regarding the security and internal control environment.

USE IN A SECURITY ASSESSMENT

SysTrust can be useful in the context of a security assessment in two ways. First, if your customer has gone through a SysTrust audit, you can have a high degree of confidence that it is secure. Second, the SysTrust criteria and questions, which are freely available on the Internet, can be incorporated into your question sets for a security assessment.

AICPA WEBTRUST

WebTrust is similar to SysTrust except that WebTrust is focused on business-to-consumer electronic commerce conducted over the Web. The main principles in the WebTrust criteria include:

- Business and information privacy practices
- Transaction integrity
- Information protection

As with SysTrust, for each of the principles listed above, more specific criteria are used when conducting the audit.

As stated, WebTrust is focused on business-to-consumer electronic commerce processes. One of the obstacles to growth for companies conducting business over the Internet is consumers' concern about security. To give some confidence, companies can have a WebTrust audit done and if favorable, can have a WebTrust seal on their Web sites. The WebTrust seal means that a qualified person audited the e-commerce processes and gave a favorable opinion on the internal control environment.

USE IN A SECURITY ASSESSMENT

WebTrust is useful in the same way as SysTrust but for companies engaging in business-to-consumer activities. The WebTrust questions can be leveraged when conducting a security assessment for business-to-consumer companies.

RFC 2196 — SITE SECURITY HANDBOOK

RFC 2196 was published in September 1997 and is a security guide to help IT personnel protect their information assets. Although RFC 2196 is technology neutral, the security aspects of many technical concepts related to networking, systems administration, and IT infrastructure are discussed to help develop computer security policies. RFC 2196 takes a holistic approach to security in that its methodology starts with conducting a risk assessment and determining risks and then implementing appropriate security measures. The basic approach as defined in RFC 2196 (Section 1.5) includes the following steps:[8]

1. Identify what you are trying to protect.
2. Determine what you are trying to protect it from.
3. Determine how likely the threats are.
4. Implement measures that will protect your assets in a cost-effective manner.
5. Review the process continuously and make improvements each time a weakness is found.

RFC 2196 discusses methodology as well as providing detailed recommendations on key security topics including the following (listed are the chapter headings from RFC 2196):

- *Security Policies* — e.g., value of security policies
- *Architecture* — e.g., network, firewalls
- *Security Services and Procedures* — e.g., authentication, access, confidentiality
- *Security Incident Handling* — e.g., preparing and handling an incident, roles and responsibilities
- *Tools* — a list of tools that might be useful for security purposes

In each of the areas listed above, RFC 2196 provides best-practice requirements that can be incorporated into an information security program. The requirements range from high-level to fairly technical areas. For example, there are nontechnical sections such as legal considerations related to collection of audit data or the use of one-time passwords.

USE IN A SECURITY ASSESSMENT

RFC 2196 is a good resource for understanding some of the technical aspects of security architecture and key security processes without getting into the specifics of any one vendor's technology. As most security assessments have a technical component, some elements of RFC 2196 can be particularly useful when developing questions and actually conducting a security assessment. The RFC 2196 is a good complement to standards such as the ISO 17799 and the ITIL Security Management standards to achieve a good mix between technical and nontechnical aspects of security.

OTHER RESOURCES

Besides the standards discussed in this chapter, some other resources are worth consulting during the course of a security assessment. Although these are not necessarily standards, they provide good current information and are worth taking into account when conducting a security assessment.

SANS (SYSADMIN, AUDIT, NETWORK, SECURITY)/FBI (FEDERAL BUREAU OF INVESTIGATION) TOP 20 LIST

SANS, a premier provider of security training for security professionals, collaborates with the Federal Bureau of Investigation (FBI) to develop and maintain a list of the top 20 vulnerabilities based on information these organizations receive from a number of resources. This list, located at http://www.sans.org/top20/ on the Internet and updated on a regular basis, contains the top 10 vulnerabilities for both Windows and Unix systems that can be deemed critical, requiring that they be addressed immediately. The list includes information about the nature of the vulnerabilities and step-by-step instructions on how to fix them. The step-by-step instructions contain actual commands as well as links to other Web sites where relevant service packs and patches might be located.

In situations where you have a limited amount of time, this list is an excellent resource in helping to uncover and address significant vulnerabilities. Just ensuring that an organization has addressed these vulnerabilities mitigates a significant amount of risk. This list should be referenced in a security assessment, and customers should be advised to review this list on a regular basis as part of their system administration efforts.

VENDOR BEST PRACTICES

Many of the major vendors, such as Microsoft and Cisco, publish white papers or best-practice guidelines regarding their particular products. From a technical perspective, these guides are excellent resources to use as benchmarks. As an example, the checklists made available by Microsoft on its Technet Web site are excellent technical documents that can be used in the Technology Evaluation portion of a security assessment.

NOTES

1. International Standards Organization Web site — http://www.iso.org/iso/en/prods-services/popstds/informationsecurity.html
2. *Information Security* magazine, March 2002 — Other Security Standards — http://infosecuritymag.techtarget.com/2002/mar/othersecuritystandard.shtml
3. Common Criteria — Part 1 — Introduction and General Model, Page 1 of 56 http://commoncriteria.org/docs/PDF/CCPART1V21.PDF
4. COBIT Framework — Executive Summary, page 5 — http://www.isaca.org/Template.cfm?Section=Obtain_COBIT&CONTENTFILEID=1396&TEMPLATE=/MembersOnly.cfm
5. COBIT Framework document — page 13 — http://www.isaca.org
6. *ITIL and Security Management*, 1999 — page 41
7. AICPA.Org Web site — SysTrust principles — http://www.aicpa.org/assurance/systrust/princip.htm
8. *RFC 2196 — Site Security Handbook,* B. Fraser — Editor, SEI/CMU — http://www.cis.ohio-state.edu/cgi-bin/rfc/rfc2196.html

10 Information Security Legislation

One of the drivers for information security initiatives is legislation. As the U.S. Congress and the legislative bodies of other governments have begun to recognize the need to protect the confidentiality and maintain the integrity of data, various laws either have been passed or are being considered to force organizations to have good information security practices. Much of the legislation is related to protecting the privacy of consumers' information; the Health Insurance Portability and Accountability Act (HIPAA) and the Gramm–Leach–Bliley Act (GLBA) are examples. In addition, other legislation has resulted from specific events; one example is the Sarbanes–Oxley Act, which was a reaction to corporate scandals, specifically the Enron debacle.

Each of these pieces of legislation is an attempt to protect consumers. For example, although a major portion of HIPAA is concerned with standardizing how transactions are performed between health care entities, two sections of the HIPAA law are devoted to privacy and security. The HIPAA security-related requirements primarily deal with the requirement that companies have an information security program consisting of various key elements including security policies and procedures, ongoing risk analysis, certain security technologies, and other provisions. This information security program along with the privacy provisions is there to protect the confidentiality of patients' electronic patient-identifiable information. GLBA is similar to HIPAA and is applicable to the financial services industry.

A closer look at the laws related to information security reveals that they essentially require companies to have good information security practices. For example, many of the HIPAA security requirements really just force health care entities to have good information security programs. Some of these requirements include having a formal security management process and having security assigned to an individual or organization to place a focus on information security. These are all elements of an information security program that we would want to see. The other information security laws are similar in their approach.

RELEVANCE OF LEGISLATION IN SECURITY ASSESSMENTS

As discussed at various points in this book, legislation is a major driver for information security. When conducting a security assessment for a company that is subject to legislation, those laws must be taken into account. Although a company might argue that some elements of security do not make business sense and choose to accept business risk, security requirements driven by legislation do not allow that option. With certain legislation, companies are subject to government audits and potential fines for not being in compliance. From a security assessment perspective, compliance with security requirements that are laws is mandatory and must be considered when performing a security assessment. The only question is how stringently or how loosely the requirements are applied. Noncompliance can result in regulatory penalties and damage to a company's reputation. In some cases, if a company hires a consultant to conduct a security assessment or if the client is using internal resources, knowledge of the legislation the company is subject to should be a part of the criteria when selecting who will do the assessment.

If you are conducting a security assessment for a company that is subject to regulatory requirements, it is critical that you are knowledgeable about the relevant legislation. The questionnaires you use for the assessment as well as the resulting recommendations should reflect the requirements of the legislation. To provide real value to clients, these recommendations should map back to specific requirements of the law. The recommendations you make should explain how to achieve compliance with the law.

As you read about the different laws in this chapter, it will become evident that the requirements are broad and in some cases leave significant room for interpretation. Being able to interpret the regulatory requirements and then translate that into recommendations that ensure regulatory compliance and properly address a given company's security risks is critical in conducting a security assessment for clients subject to regulations. This requires knowledge about the specific requirements and the acceptable ways of ensuring compliance. The gray area is that in most cases, because of the broad nature of the requirements, different ways to achieve compliance exist. Companies should look for consultants who have this knowledge and can recommend the most cost-effective ways to achieve compliance although still having a solid information security program.

This chapter contains a summary and discussion of some of the major information security–related legislation today related to companies having certain information security measures in place. There are other pieces of legislation that impose penalties for criminal behavior related to exploiting security vulnerabilities such as the Computer Fraud and Abuse Act and the Digital Millennium Copyright Act, which are not discussed in this chapter. The focus of this chapter is on legislation that is forcing information security standards on organizations. When conducting a security assessment, you should do the appropriate research and talk to the client about what regulatory requirements the company may be subject to and ensure that they are incorporated into the assessment.

HIPAA (HEALTH INSURANCE PORTABILITY AND ACCOUNTABILITY ACT)

HIPAA was introduced in the mid 1990s and had three main purposes:

- Standardization of health care–related electronic transactions to facilitate efficiencies in health care delivery
- Provision of standards for the privacy of patient information
- Provision of standards for securing patient information in electronic form

The regulations associated with each of the sections above have been issued at different times. The HIPAA Security requirements were issued on February 20, 2003. The compliance date for most health care entities is April 21, 2005. Small health plans have until April 21, 2006 to achieve compliance.

The U.S. government has set significant penalties for noncompliance with HIPAA requirements. Fines for noncompliance include:

- Up to $100 for individual cases of noncompliance with HIPAA provisions
- Up to $25,000 per year for multiple violations of the same HIPAA requirement
- Up to $50,000 and one year in jail for wrongful disclosure of identifiable health information
- Up to $100,000 and five years in jail for wrongful disclosure of individually identifiable health information under false pretenses
- Up to $250,000 and 10 years in jail for wrongful disclosure of individually identifiable health information with intent to sell, transfer, or use for commercial advantage or personal gain

The goal of the HIPAA security requirements is to protect electronically stored health information. As stated earlier, the HIPAA security regulations essentially require health care organizations to have sound information security programs. The requirements include the different phases of the information security life cycle including:

- *Assessment* — e.g., conducting a security assessment to determine security weaknesses
- *Development* — e.g., developing security policies and procedures as the foundation of the information security program
- *Deployment* — e.g., deployment of security technologies such as encryption to protect individually identifiable health care information
- *Monitoring* — e.g., technology and processes for monitoring security

The actual structure of the HIPAA security requirements contains three major areas — Administrative Safeguards, Physical Safeguards, and Technical Safeguards. Below are these major headings with some examples of what areas are covered in each:

- Administrative Safeguards
  - Security management processes
  - Awareness training
  - Business associate contracts
- Physical safeguards
  - Facility access controls
  - Workstation security
  - Device and media controls

- Technical safeguards
  - Access controls
  - Audit controls
  - Transmission security

Although some elements of the HIPAA security requirements are health care specific, the majority of the security requirements are the same measures that any company would take when developing an information security program. Many of the requirements can be mapped back to the ISO 17799 standard. HIPAA security requirements, like the ISO 17799, are not process oriented. HIPAA security requirements define what needs to be done from a security perspective. It is up to companies to implement processes that will achieve compliance with the HIPAA security requirements.

One of the difficulties with HIPAA security requirements is that how compliance will be achieved is not very clear, for two reasons. First, the HIPAA security requirements are broad and leave room for interpretation. Multiple ways to achieve compliance with some of the security requirements exist. Second, because the compliance date for the HIPAA security requirements is not until 2005 for most health care entities, no government audits have been done. As a result, no information exists on what HIPAA security compliance measures the government finds acceptable. HIPAA security is starting to gain more attention, and as we approach the compliance deadline for it, more guidance will inevitably appear.

GLBA (GRAMM–LEACH–BLILEY ACT)

The GLB Act (GLBA) was signed into law in 1999 and was effective as of July 2001. The GLBA security requirements became effective on May 23, 2003. The main purpose of the GLBA was to repeal earlier laws so financial services companies could expand their markets into other areas of financial services such as insurance. The other key element of the GLBA, which is relevant to security assessments, is that these financial service companies must ensure that individuals' personal information is protected.

As with HIPAA, the GLBA security requirements are related to having a comprehensive information security program. With the amount of personal financial information residing on the systems of financial service companies, tremendous risk is associated with the loss or breach of confidentiality of data.

The GLBA requires financial service companies under the jurisdiction of the Federal Trade Commission to have the appropriate level of security to protect the confidentiality of customers' information. The requirements of the GLBA, which are discussed below, are not very specific. As with HIPAA, the GLBA security requirements are focused on the overall information security program and ensuring that the right mechanisms are in place so that customer information is adequately protected. Below are the key GLBA security requirements (information below was obtained from the official 16 CFR Part 314 document at http://www.ftc.gov/os/2002/05/67fr36585.pdf):

- *Information security program* — The entity must have an information security program that is "written in one or more readily accessible parts and contains administrative, technical, and physical safeguards that are appropriate to your size and complexity, the nature and scope of your activities, and the sensitivity of any customer information at issue."[1] This requirement essentially says that the information security program should be aligned to the risks that the company is facing.
- *Coordination of the information security program* — There must be an individual or group of individuals responsible for interfacing with the relevant groups and acting as a coordinator or "single point of contact" for the information security program. This aspect of the GLBA is related to the whole concept of ownership and helps ensure that proper communication takes place between the relevant parties.
- *Regular risk analysis* — An ongoing risk analysis for any company is very important because it is a mechanism to discover any potential security issues for the company.
- *Implementation of controls to mitigate risks discovered in the risk analysis* — One of the results of the risk assessment is the discovery of security risks. Once discovered, the requirement is to implement measures to mitigate these risks and monitor, on a regular basis, that these measures are working as intended.
- *Overseeing of service providers* — Because of the complexity of business today, many companies try to focus on their core competencies. The financial services industry is no exception; companies in this field frequently use third-party service providers for various parts of their operations. The security concern with these providers is that customer information is residing on their systems, and companies using these providers sometimes have no sense of how this information is being secured. This requirement obligates the company to ensure that the service providers have security measures in place to properly safeguard customer information. Companies should perform the appropriate due diligence when selecting a provider and also have the appropriate provisions in the contract with the service provider.
- *Evaluation and adjustment of the information security program* — This requirement is really a byproduct of the requirement related to risk analysis. As new risks are identified, new controls should be implemented to address those risks. In achieving compliance with this requirement, companies should constantly evaluate their information security programs and make adjustments as necessary.

Based on the requirements, it is clear that the objective is for financial services companies to implement and maintain good information security programs, which will ultimately protect customer information.

When conducting a security assessment with a financial services company, it is best to become familiar with the GLBA security requirements and ask the appropriate questions. Because of the broad nature of these requirements, questions can be taken from a number of the questionnaires in the appendices of this book as well as other resources, such as the standards listed in Chapter 9 of this book.

SARBANES–OXLEY ACT

The Sarbanes–Oxley Act was passed largely as a result of the Enron scandal to help restore investor confidence. The legislation makes management and the auditors more accountable for the numbers on financial statements. The first major piece of this legislation was Section 302 — Corporate Responsibility for Financial Reports, which requires chief executive officers (CEOs) and chief financial officers (CFOs) of publicly traded companies to certify that the financial statements are accurate. Technically, management is responsible for the financial statements, but this require-ment brought attention to the fact that management certifies and attests to the accuracy of the financial statements.

The relevant section of Sarbanes–Oxley as it relates to security assessments is Section 404 — Management Assessment of Internal Controls. Most eligible com-panies are required to be in compliance with Section 404 by June 15, 2004. Smaller companies must achieve compliance by April 15, 2005. Specific guidance on deter-mining the compliance date for a company is contained in Section 404-1: Introduction.

This act essentially requires auditors to issue an internal control–related report, which contains two key elements, as part of the annual report:

- Management responsibility for establishing an adequate internal control framework to support accurate financial reporting
- The auditor's assessment of the effectiveness of the internal control structure

To achieve compliance with Sarbanes–Oxley, auditors must have a thorough understanding of the internal control framework. Before Sarbanes–Oxley, auditors may or may not have reviewed internal controls. If these controls were reviewed, one of the main purposes was to determine the amount and nature of substantive or detailed testing that was performed to certify the numbers on the financial statements. If auditors did not have a very high comfort level with the internal control structure, more detailed testing was required on certain numbers in the financial statements to have the required assurance. Auditors could even choose to do minimal internal control review and do a significant amount of detailed testing to certify financial statements. With Sarbanes–Oxley, auditors must understand the internal control framework associated with financial reporting. As a result, auditors must review areas such as application access for certain applications, information flow between systems, and how the integrity of information is maintained. For audit firms, Section 404 increases their work and brings about the need for auditors with different skill sets.

From a security assessment perspective, the internal control report is a good resource when gathering the initial information for a security assessment. The effectiveness of the internal control framework is a significant component of the overall information security program, and this report can provide some good preliminary information before you talk to clients.

To understand the full value of Sarbanes–Oxley, you should fully review the contents of Section 404, which is available at http://www.sarbanes-oxley.com. Some of the other relevant sections of Section 404 worth reviewing include:

- 404-4: Quarterly Evaluations of Internal Control over Financial Reporting
- 404-6: Types of Companies Affected, Transition Period
- 404-9: Cost-Benefit Analysis

The other sections listed above are important and can affect what is done to achieve compliance with Sarbanes–Oxley.

21 CFR PART 11

21 CFR (Code of Federal Regulations) is a regulation by the Food and Drug Administration (FDA) that outlines requirements regarding the use of electronic records and electronic signatures for "any records or signature requirement set forth in the Federal Food, Drug, and Cosmetic Act (the Act), the Public Health Service Act (PHS Act), or any FDA regulation."[2] One of the areas where this rule is significantly applied is the pharmaceutical industry.

21 CFR Part 11 was initially passed in 1997 and was meant to provide rules and regulations pertaining to the use of electronic records to support compliance related to maintaining or submitting information to the FDA. The key components of this legislation are very much focused around security and more specifically, the integrity of electronic records and signatures. Some of the key requirements of 21 CFR Part 11 include (as documented in the 21 CFR Part 11 guidance on the FDA Web site — http://www.fda.gov/cber/gdlns/esigcopies.htm#I):

- Ensuring the authenticity, integrity, and confidentiality of electronic records
- Nonrepudiation of electronic signatures
- Audit trails for electronic signatures

To achieve some of the requirements in 21 CFR Part 11, the company should have a sound information security program in place. These requirements are what one would expect if electronic records were being managed properly and if electronic signatures were in use.

If a security assessment is being conducted for a company subject to 21 CFR Part 11, these requirements should be considered. Although a security assessment cannot ensure that a company is compliant with 21 CFR Part 11, it can uncover some issues that potentially lead to noncompliance. A review to determine compliance with 21 CFR Part 11 requirements should be done by someone with expertise in these requirements.

SAFE HARBOR

The Safe Harbor provision is a result of the European Commission's Directive on Data Protection, which went into effect during October 1998. This directive is comprehensive legislation that describes requirements for ensuring the privacy of data. One of the significant elements of this legislation is that personal data cannot be transmitted between European companies and any non-European company that does not meet the European Commission's standard for privacy. "While the United States and the European Union share the goal of enhancing privacy protection for their citizens, the United States takes a different approach to privacy from that taken by the European Union. The United States uses a sectoral approach that relies on a mix of legislation, regulation, and self-regulation. The European Union, however, relies on comprehensive legislation that, for example, requires creation of government data protection agencies, registration of data bases with those agencies, and in some instances prior approval before personal data processing may begin."[3] As this would affect many U.S. companies, the Safe Harbor was created to ensure that U.S. companies had some minimum standards related to privacy so that they can continue to do business in Europe.

For U.S. companies to take advantage of Safe Harbor, they must go through a process to join, which is handled by the U.S. Department of Commerce (http://www.export.gov/safeharbor/index.html). To join Safe Harbor, companies must have a privacy program and comply with seven specific principles. Two of these principles that have security implications are:

- *Security* — "Organizations must take reasonable precautions to protect personal information from loss, misuse, and unauthorized access, disclosure, alteration and destruction."[4]
- *Data Integrity* — "Personal information must be relevant for the purposes for which it is to be used. An organization should take reasonable steps to ensure that data is reliable for its intended use, accurate, complete, and current."[5]

When conducting a security assessment for companies conducting business in Europe, the Safe Harbor provisions should be investigated — i.e., you should determine whether the company should join Safe Harbor and if it should, whether the appropriate security and data integrity measures are in place.

FEDERAL INFORMATION SECURITY MANAGEMENT ACT (FIMSA)

FISMA was passed in late 2002 as Title III of the 2002 E-Gov Act. The Government Information Security Reform Act (GISRA), which expired in 2002, had many of the same provisions as FISMA. The basic purpose of FISMA is to strengthen information security programs at federal agencies by providing a framework for information security. FISMA itself does not provide any hard standards or guidelines that federal agencies must follow. It is really just mandating having an information security program in place that is aligned with the risks being faced by the agency. Some of the key responsibilities of the agencies under FISMA are summarized below and include (items below are from the FISMA documentation on the Department of Homeland Security's Web site — http://www.fedcirc.gov/library/legislation/FISMA.html):

- Providing information security commensurate with the associated risk
- Performing a risk assessment
- Implementing policies and procedures that reduce information security risks in a cost-effective manner
- Conducting periodic testing of information security measures
- Having a qualified Chief Information Security Officer whose primary responsibility is information security
- Conducting ongoing evaluation and adjustment of the information security program

The requirements above are, for the most part, very similar to those of GISRA. The main difference with FISMA is the integration with National Institute of Standards and Technology (NIST). Under FISMA, federal agencies are to use the standards proposed by NIST to determine information security measures for their operations. Per the legislation, "the Secretary shall make standards [NIST Standards] … compulsory and binding to the extent determined necessary by the Secretary to improve the efficiency of operation or security of federal information systems." Essentially, federal agencies must achieve compliance with NIST standards under FISMA.

In addition to modifying GISRA, FISMA had a number of other effects including:

- Repealing the Computer Security Act of 1987
- Documenting inventory of information systems

Similar to legislation such as HIPAA and GLBA, FISMA is mandating federal agencies to have an information security program that includes the full life cycle of information security including risk assessments, security policies and procedures, use of technology, and ongoing compliance efforts. FISMA also provides some room for agencies to determine what information security measures are best for them.

From a security assessment perspective, FISMA should be reviewed in detail if working with a federal agency.

OTHER LEGISLATIVE ACTION

Information security has become a significant issue with significant dollars associated with it. It is also an issue vital to national security in the U.S. As a result, lawmakers have given and continue to pay significant attention to information security. The federal government is very focused on protecting the nation's critical infrastructure. Due to the interdependencies of different organizations including the government, private companies, and academia, some level of cooperation is needed.

One of the areas receiving more attention lately is cybersecurity. In mid-2003, Congressman William "Mac" Thornberry commented that if companies do not take action in improving the state of cybersecurity, Congress would consider mandating certain information security measures.[6] The other option that would potentially be considered is giving tax incentives to improve the state of security.

For most of these organizations, cost is a major factor in determining to what extent security initiatives are performed. Legislation and regulation are often the drivers for implementing information security measures because they are mandated and companies have no choice. We have seen this already in financial services with GLBA and will see it more with health care companies and HIPAA as the compliance dates draw near. In both of these cases, the information security–related requirements are designed to protect consumers. As other industries are identified as critical to the public, it is possible that the government will consider appropriate legislation.

When conducting a security assessment, it is not only important to know what regulations affect the customer, but what may affect them later. As legislation is considered, it is very valuable to be able to advise clients on future regulatory activity that can affect them and how to effectively plan for this.

NOTES

1. Federal regulations concerning GLB Act — http://www.ftc.gov/os/2002/05/67fr36585.pdf
2. 21 CFR Part 11 — Section 2.1 Applicability — http://www.fda.gov/cber/gdlns/esig-copies.htm
3. Safe Harbor Overview — U.S. Department of Commerce — http://www.export.gov/safeharbor/sh_overview.html
4. Ibid
5. Ibid
6. Congressman: Businesses Must Help Protect Net — *PC World,* August 15, 2003 — by Grant Gross http://www.pcworld.com/news/article/0,aid,112048,00.asp

Appendices

Security Questionnaires and Checklists

In performing security assessments, questionnaires are very helpful to facilitate the information gathering process. The questionnaires in these appendices provide key questions related to common security-related processes to help you determine where potential vulnerabilities might exist. The questionnaires should not be interpreted as a complete list of questions because every company is different and there might be different aspects that are not necessarily covered here. The questionnaires include questions based on best practice standards such as the ISO 17799, industry best practices, and past experience.

The purpose of these checklists is to provide guidance for security practitioners and help in facilitating conversations and meetings with clients when performing a security assessment. Because these questionnaires are meant for a broad range of companies, they are generic in nature and should be considered a starting point when developing question sets for clients. These checklists will not only provide relevant information for the security assessment, but also spark conversation about other business processes, other initiatives, and security issues that are relevant to the assessment. They should be tailored for a given company based on the company's specific business processes.

The final questionnaires used in the assessment should be tailored for a company as much as possible. These generic questionnaires should not be blindly used before they are adequately modified to reflect the client's business. Security consultants should do their homework on a client. When modifying these questionnaires, irrelevant questions should be taken out and other questions should be added as deemed appropriate based on the client's business practices. Credibility is lost if the client is asked questions that should obviously not be asked — i.e., if the consultant had done the proper research, the consultant would already know that the question is irrelevant.

QUESTIONNAIRE STRUCTURE

The questionnaires are essentially divided into two areas: Introduction and Questions. The Introduction provides some basic information about the subject of the questionnaires and why it is important from a security perspective. The Introduction provides basic information for you to familiarize yourself with the topic and educate the client as necessary.

The next section contains the questions. In the majority of the questionnaires, the questions contain four parts:

- *Question* — The questions should be used to spark discussion with clients. In many cases, the questions are intentionally open ended with the goal of generating discussions with clients about their business. These questions will lead to other questions relevant to the security assessment and also help keep the discussion focused on security. As you listen to the client responses, other discussion topics will be generated and new questions will be developed. These questions should be explored to the extent that they are relevant for the security assessment.
- *Guidance* — The Guidance section provides specific information about a given question. This information is useful in understanding the question and why it is important. The guidance can be used in conjunction with your existing knowledge of the company to provide an answer when the client asks, "Why are you asking this question?" It is critical to understand the Guidance sections and ensure that you can explain a question's relevance to clients. Not being able to explain why you are asking something hurts your credibility. The client should not feel as though you are reading from a questionnaire without understanding what is being asked.
- *Risk* — The risk is the impact to the company if there is a potential finding related to a particular question. The risk is the potential consequences of "what if" scenarios related to the question — e.g., what is the impact to the business if I cannot recover data within 24 hours or what is the impact to the business if the company's e-commerce Web site is defaced? Although findings are important, clients are ultimately interested in risk — i.e., "How is the finding going to affect my business?" The risk is important to understand when answering this question and when the client says "So what?" when a finding is presented. Part of the methodology outlined in this book is to determine the risk and calculate a risk score. The risks outlined in the questionnaires will help you go through the thought process of determining risk and calculating the risk score. The risks in the questionnaires are generic in nature and will need to be modified based on the client's business. Note that risks are not documented for all questions

because some questions are there only for information gathering purposes and there is no clear risk. In these cases, risks are marked "not applicable."
- *Client Response* — The Client Response section is a blank area where answers can be documented during client meetings. The idea is that consultants can meet with clients, go through the questionnaires, and document responses as clients provide them. As stated in the methodology, properly documenting the information you gather in meetings is important so you can perform the risk analysis.

These questionnaires are part of an iterative process when learning about the business and performing the security assessment. The responses from these checklists should be used to develop the comprehensive list of findings, risks, and recommendations, i.e., the security roadmap.

COMMON QUESTIONS IN QUESTIONNAIRES

Most of the questionnaires have some common features, which are discussed below. Four key topics addressed in most checklists include:

- *Policy* — One of the key points in this book is that the foundation of an information security program is policies. Policies establish the basic direction of an information security program and provide a basis for assessing and measuring an organization from a security perspective. Policies also establish a basis for enforcing good security practices. When conducting a security assessment, policies can be used as the basis for evaluating the company's information security posture. Consequently, a standard question in most checklists is whether a formal policy exists related to the topic being discussed.
- *Procedure* — Procedures provide detailed step-by-step information on how a process is performed; they are important because:
  - Documented procedures can be used as a basis for evaluating security practices during a security assessment.
  - Documented procedures provide a basis to enforce good security practices.
  - If procedures are documented and kept up to date, there is less dependency on specific people in the organization. If there is turnover, another qualified person can do the same work by following the procedures, which is important from a security perspective.
- *Scope* — Some scope-related question should be asked to determine how important and extensive a given process is. This question helps in determining how much you have to delve into this process, which in turn helps you refine the scope of the assessment. One of the important aspects of this security assessment methodology is to look at the business and related security from a risk perspective — i.e., security should be commensurate with the associated risk and criticality of a process. The scope-related

question should provide some sense of the criticality and associated security risk related to the process.

- *Past security incidents* — Past security incidents are important because they represent a vulnerability that was exploited. All aspects of past security incidents including the vulnerability that was exploited, what the impact was to the business, how the incident was handled, and what steps were taken to fix the vulnerability should be discussed, as they can impact the findings of the security assessment. Past security incidents provide insight into how the business can be impacted and how the company would potentially react to future security incidents. In addition, whether or not the company addressed the security vulnerability that was exploited can give an indication of the company's general attitude about security.

Other parts of the checklists include questions specific to the subject matter and are organized into logical groupings as appropriate. It is critical to understand that these checklists are starting points and that before using them, they should be modified based on knowledge of the specific business practices of the company being assessed.

There are two exceptions to the checklist format discussed above — the Initial Questionnaire and the Health Insurance Portability and Accountability Act (HIPAA) Security Questionnaire. The main difference in the format of these two questionnaires is that the questions do not have associated "risks" identified. The Initial Questionnaire assumes minimal knowledge about the company for which the security assessment is being performed and is for information gathering purposes and thus, no risks were identified. The information from this questionnaire helps in further refining the scope and in determining where to focus the effort in the assessment. The questions in the HIPAA Security Questionnaire follow the HIPAA security regulations directly from the Federal Register. Risks are not identified in this questionnaire because the focus of the checklist is determining compliance with the law.

Appendix A

Preliminary Checklist to Gather Information

This checklist is a preliminary questionnaire designed to obtain general information about a company's operations, organizations, and supporting technologies. This questionnaire can be discussed with a company at the beginning of onsite work or it can be given to clients prior to beginning the face-to-face meetings. If the appropriate members of management and subject matter experts complete the questionnaire, it can provide some excellent information in preparation for meetings with the client during the security assessment. If someone in the client's organization has the time to comprehensively read the questions and answer them, it can be of great assistance. If the client is not able to complete this questionnaire, it can be used at the beginning of the assessment to gather information.

The value of this preliminary questionnaire is that provides a basic understanding of the key business processes and supporting technologies. It is in line with the overall security assessment methodology, which starts with understanding the business and then assessing the security posture based on the risks identified. The answers to this questionnaire along with other preliminary research are enough to prepare for face-to-face meetings with the client.

This questionnaire is a template that should be modified based on any information you might already have about the client. There may be additional questions as a result of research from the Internet, and other questions might not be appropriate based on this same research. The more the questionnaire is tailored to the client, the more valuable it will be.

Note that this questionnaire does not have any risks identified. This is because most of these will be covered in greater detail in later checklists and because the purpose of this questionnaire is to gain initial information regarding the company's operations and supporting technologies.

General Business Information

1. *What are the business drivers for the security assessment and what are you expecting from it?*

   Guidance: This is very important in setting the tone of the assessment and understanding the expectations of the client. The business drivers for a security assessment can vary. Some typical examples of business drivers include:

259

- There was an audit recommendation to do a security assessment.
- There was a security incident and management decided to take a more comprehensive look at security.
- Although a security incident has not taken place, management wants to be proactive and address security concerns before something happens.
- A potential business partner might require a security assessment before working with company.
- Laws (such as the Health Insurance Portability and Accountability Act [HIPAA] or the Gramm–Leach–Bliley Act [GLBA]) might require a security assessment.

Each of the business drivers above will make the focus of the security assessment a little different, and this information will allow you to better tailor your questions in meetings with the client.

Client Response:

---

2. *Describe what the company does.*

Guidance: This should be a high-level description of what the company does — e.g., does it manufacture and sell a product, or is it a services-based company. This question is meant to serve as a starting point for further discussion about the critical operations of the company.

Client Response:

---

3. *What are your mission-critical operations and what are the supporting technologies?*

Guidance: The mission-critical operations will be a point of focus for the assessment, and that will be discussed in Phase 3 — Business Process Review. Depending on the time that is allotted for the security assessment, knowing the mission-critical operations will help in prioritizing the tasks of the security assessment. The technologies supporting the mission-critical operations will help determine where the effort will be focused in Phase 4 — Technology Review.

Client Response:

---

4. *Describe any future business initiatives that may be impacted by technology (e.g., increasing number of employees, adding locations, introducing a new service or product).*

Guidance: This question should provide information about the direction of the company from a business perspective. The future plans may provide some additional areas to review, which might result in recommendations from the security planning perspective. This is of tremendous value to a customer as security is often overlooked in the planning phase of a technology-related project.

Client Response:

5. *Do you have any regulatory requirements that govern your business and if so, what steps have been taken to achieve compliance?*

Guidance: With the amount of security-related legislation, there is a chance that the company is subject to regulatory requirements. Some of the more common information security–related regulations are HIPAA and GLBA. If you already know that the company is subject to a law or regulation, questions can be tailored accordingly.

Client Response:

6. *Have you had any security incidents? If not, how do you know?*

Guidance: This is listed in Question 1 as a potential driver for a security assessment. A security incident will be an eye-opener for companies and might drive them to do a security assessment. If there was an incident, it gives an indication of management's tolerance for risk and an area of vulnerability. The company's reaction to the incident gives an idea of how management views security. If the client answers that there was no incident, they might talk about mechanisms they have in place to detect incidents. In many cases, however, the answer is that they do not really know if they have had a security incident because they have no way of knowing — i.e., they do not have the appropriate software or security monitoring procedures in place.

Client Response:

7. *What security issues are you concerned with (e.g., confidentiality of information, availability of systems, integrity of data, compromise of sensitive information.) What is your expectation for the security assessment?*

Guidance: The security issues in the eye of the client gives an idea of what concerns them from a security perspective. These concerns will probably have some bearing on what they expect from the security assessment. In performing the security assessment, this information also allows you to manage the expectations of the client. In addition, the client may communicate some areas of concern related to security that you may not have known about thus far.

Client Response:

ORGANIZATIONAL INFORMATION

The organizational information questions allow you to gain a sense of the size and structure of the organization and how it potentially impacts security. This questionnaire reviews the organization and roles and responsibilities at a high level. As the business processes are discussed in greater detail in the specific questionnaires, specific roles and responsibilities will be discussed.

8. *How many employees do you have? Break down into business units and locations if information is available.*

Guidance: The size of the organization has impact on several security areas such as user ID administration, as well as security administration and awareness. Based on the how the users are divided into business units, this information can start to provide some indication of how the company is set up organizationally and a high-level understanding of where people are deployed in the organization. This information will be useful when you start planning whom to interview.

Client Response:

9. *Can you provide a high-level view of the organizational structure?*

Guidance: The organizational structure provides the foundation of the roles and responsibilities of the company. One of the key areas to look for is where information technology (IT) and the security function sit in the organization and whether they are centralized or decentralized. Each of these scenarios has different implications from a security perspective. Depending on where IT and security fit into the organization, different questions might be appropriate regarding roles and responsibilities.

Client Response:

---

10. *What are the high-level roles and responsibilities in the IT staff?*

Guidance: The high-level roles and responsibilities will give you an understanding of whether there is ownership of key IT functions. The response to this question will also give you some guidance about whom to interview in the assessment from an IT perspective. This question might also spark discussion about ownership of the security function.

Client Response:

---

11. *Who is responsible for information security?*

Guidance: Where responsibility for information security resides is important information for the security assessment. Potential answers range from having a separate dedicated function with its own budget to where security is a part of the system administrator's job responsibility. Based on this question, the client should provide names of key people to talk to during the assessment. You should also gain some insight about how seriously security is taken at the company.

Client Response:

---

12. *Is there an IT audit function that examines information security?*

Guidance: The audit department is important because it is an independent function reviewing the operations of a company. Because of the detailed review of processes that an audit group performs, they are an excellent source of information about a company. As part of the overall audit group, the IT audit function is good source of information about the security risks the company is facing and what security measures have been implemented to mitigate those risks. Existence of an IT audit function means that there is probably some focus on information security. The audit group's reports, if available, are worth reviewing because they typically identify control and security issues discovered during audits.

Client Response:

---

13. *Is information security a separate item on the budget?*

Guidance: Whether security is budgeted for separately or whether it is included in a general IT or other budget line item may indicate the client's commitment to security. If it is a separate line item, it is more likely that money will be spent on security. If security initiatives are part of another more general budget line item, it will be prioritized against other initiatives. The risk is that in times (like currently) where budgets are being slashed, security might not be a top priority. When compared to other IT initiatives that directly enhance business processes or enable revenue, it can be difficult to justify spending on security.

Client Response:

GENERAL INFORMATION TECHNOLOGY

14. *Describe your current environment.*
   - Number of:
     - Servers by location
     - Desktops by location
     - Other systems by location
   - What operating systems (and versions) are you running?
     - What network operating system (and versions) are you running?
     - Critical applications

Guidance: The answers to the question above provide some demographic information on what the IT environment looks like and an indication of where the significant IT operations might be. This information will demonstrate how up to date the client is on technology, which is an important aspect in assessing risk. If the client is running old systems with known vulnerabilities, this should be a red flag. A related question when drilling down into the details is whether the client has kept up with security patch levels, which is particularly important considering recent virus outbreaks. This information will also help in the determining the specific tasks of the assessment and how to prioritize the work.

Client Response:

15. *Do you have a process for ensuring that security patches are applied to systems on a timely basis?*

   Guidance: Many security vulnerabilities that are exploited today are a result of patches not being kept up to date. This is something that you will probably end up verifying by doing scans during the Technology Review phase.

Client Response:

16. *Do you have standards for hardware and software? Are there standard builds that are used for computers?*

   Guidance: Security systems will have a better chance of being secure with strong hardware and software standards in which security is part of the standard. Also, with similar systems, it is easier to implement security recommendations.

Client Response:

17. *Is there an asset management process in place?*

   Guidance: All IT assets should have assigned owners to ensure that they are accounted for and protected. IT assets should be tied into the personnel hire and termination process to help ensure assets are properly accounted for and returned when an employee is terminated. A good asset management process also facilitates obtaining an accurate inventory of IT assets and is tied into the personnel hire and termination processes.

Client Response:

18. *Describe your remote access environment.*
    - How many remote access users do you have?
    - What percentage are home users and how many travel?
    - How are the users obtaining remote access — e.g., virtual private network (VPN), dial-up
    - What resources are users accessing remotely?
    - Do third parties remotely access your systems?
    - What technology is being used for remote access?
    - Are there any planned changes for remote access?

    Guidance: The workforce is becoming more mobile than ever. Telecommuting is becoming very common, as employees work from home, allowing companies to save money and have some flexibility in their hiring practices. Employees are traveling and remotely accessing internal network resources to do their jobs. Understanding the nature of these other connections and what they are accessing remotely can help scope some of the technical parts of the security assessment. Some security concerns related to remote access are related to:
    - *Availability* — Availability is a major issue because some employees, such as telecommuters, might be totally dependent on remote access to do their jobs.
    - *Access Control* — Similar to access control in a regular network environment, users' access should be limited to what they need to do their jobs.
    At this stage, you may not receive answers to all of the remote access questions, as some of them are a little detailed.

    Client Response:

19. *Do you have any business-to-business (B2B) partner arrangements?*

    Guidance: B2B arrangements pose a whole new set of security risks because other companies are accessing the company's systems. Ensuring that business partners can only access what they need access to is a challenge that requires cooperation between both the client and the business partner. The technology and processes must be in place to ensure the confidentiality and integrity of information and the availability of the B2B connection. If the client is engaged in B2B activities, a separate, more detailed evaluation should be done that reviews the nature of the relationship, supporting IT infrastructure, applications, and any other aspects of the IT environment. There is a separate questionnaire for B2B activities later in Appendix K.

Client Response:

20. *Do you engage in any electronic commerce activities and offer products and services over the Internet? Do you conduct any financial transactions over the Internet?*

    Guidance: E-commerce activities where financial transactions are taking place are a prime target for hackers and the like. Companies engaged in e-commerce are very concerned with guarding consumers' personal information and the availability of the companies' Web sites. Some of the potential risks they face are damage to their reputation and consumers not being able to access their site — both of which can lead to a loss of revenue and a permanent loss of customers. Similar to B2B, if the client is engaged in e-commerce activities, a more detailed evaluation should be done of the supporting IT infrastructure, applications, and other aspects of the IT environment. There is a separate questionnaire later in the Appendices devoted to e-commerce activities.

Client Response:

21. *Do you outsource any of your business functions?*

    Guidance: Many companies outsource various business functions such as payroll, certain accounting functions, and information technology for a number of reasons including cost, to concentrate on core competencies and others. Outsourcing potentially introduces significant security concerns because the function is mostly out of the client's control. The risk will vary based on what is outsourced and the related internal control and security environment. Companies that outsource IT and security need to be very vigilant in ensuring that their information receives an adequate level of security. Regardless of what is outsourced, the company is still ultimately accountable. If the company is outsourcing security functions, you can drill down further using the Managed Security questionnaire in Appendix D.

Client Response:

SECURITY

22. *Do you have any security policies in place and are they readily accessible by employees?*

    Guidance: Security policies are the foundation of any information security program. Policies provide the basis for everything that is done to secure the enterprise. Some companies will have a full set of security policies, but others will have the basic acceptable use or Internet usage policy and nothing else. A lack of security policies has the following effects:
    - It makes it difficult to enforce security; there are no documented security policies to enforce.
    - Security-related roles and responsibilities are not clear; employees do not know what is expected of them in terms of security.
    - There is a risk that security is a set of point solutions that do not necessarily address the risks the company is facing.

    If a client does not have a set of policies, it should be flagged as a finding.

    Client Response:

23. *Do you have security policies for the following at a minimum?*
    - Acceptable use
    - Data classification
    - Data retention
    - User ID administration
    - Obtaining initial access
    - Termination of access
    - Periodic review of user access lists
    - Backup and recovery
    - Incident handling
    - Business continuity and disaster recovery
    - Change management
    - Physical security

    Guidance: The policies listed above are a basic set of policies that most companies should probably have because they address common security processes. If these policies do not exist, it is possible that the client is not performing these processes in a consistently secure manner. As stated in the earlier question, security policies are the foundation of an information security program. It is important to note that clients should be able to show documented policies — not a policy that is verbally known to people. Policies or process in people's heads do not do any good—they must be documented.

Client Response:

24. *Are there any programs that promote security awareness? Are new employees provided with any orientation to make them familiar with security policies? Are there any security awareness campaigns?*

    Guidance: Security policies are more likely to be followed if they are properly communicated so employees are aware of them and understand them. In companies where employees are not aware of company security policies, awareness programs are critical in educating employees and creating a culture where information security is an integral part of the business.

Client Response:

25. *Does someone own the responsibility of updating security policies as the business changes? If so, how are the changes communicated?*

    Guidance: As business changes, so do the risks. Many of these changes could warrant changes to the security policy. When discussing this question, look for whether both business and IT representatives jointly make and approve changes to the policy and whether the cost of implementing a security policy is considered. Having both business and IT personnel involved helps ensure that any changes to policies are feasible from both the technology and the process perspectives. In addition, this collaboration also helps ensure that new security measures are cost effective and aligned with the business requirements.

Client Response:

26. *Describe your security architecture.*
    • Firewall
    • Intrusion detection/prevention
    • Anti-virus
    • Other security architecture — e.g., proxy servers, vulnerability management

    Guidance: The security architecture is a key component in determining the security posture of a company. The items above are only a few examples of the more traditional security technologies in use today. There may be others depending on the client's IT infrastructure. The security architecture can be reviewed from a number of different angles. First, are the security architecture and the technologies appropriate for the environment? Does the architecture require any redesign to provide better security? Second, are the security technologies in place configured according to company security policies and business requirements? The answer to this question will provide the required preliminary information about the security architecture to help in planning the Technology Review phase of the assessment.

Client Response:

---

27. *What security-related logs are enabled — e.g., system-specific logs, firewall logs — and are they reviewed on a regular basis?*

Guidance: Regular log review is an indication that the client takes a proactive approach to security, which is positive. Log review requires manpower, and you may find that companies do not review logs unless something happens, and then the review is after the fact. Some companies use tools that parse the log data and provide reports of events that might require follow up. The answer to this question will provide information on what logs are enabled, which will help in planning the detailed technology review in the Technology Review phase of the assessment. It will also provide some indication of how the client views security, i.e., whether they are proactive or reactive and what type of resources are devoted to security.

Client Response:

Appendix B

Generic Questionnaire for Meetings with Business Process Owners

This questionnaire is for meetings with business process owners. The questions are meant to be specific for the processes in which they are involved. These questions can be supplemented by the additional questionnaires in these Appendices. If you are meeting with someone who has overall responsibility for a particular area where there is a separate questionnaire, you should use that specific questionnaire.

BUSINESS PROCESS–RELATED QUESTIONS

1. *Significant business processes and supporting technologies*
   - Describe how the business process works.
   - What are the critical roles in the process and are there backups in the event that key individuals are not present?
   - What technology supports this business process?
   - Who is responsible for managing the supporting technology?
   - If the supporting technology was unavailable and this business process could not occur, what are the impacts related to revenue, legal or regulatory concerns, and reputation damage?
   - What is the tolerable downtime?
   - Are there any manual or other workarounds that can be done while the technology is unavailable? For how long can the workaround be done?
   - What critical data is generated as a result of this process and where does it reside?

   Guidance: These questions are to be asked about specific business processes. All of these questions should be answered because you will be working with the client's subject matter experts who should know this information.

Client Response:

2. *Integration with other departments.*
   * Dependencies between departments
   * System integration and determination of single points of failure
   * Transmission of information

   Guidance: Integration points are important to understand because they often represent points of weakness. At integration points, roles and responsibilities are not always clear, and as a result, key tasks are not performed, and transitions between departments are not always smooth.

Client Response:

3. *Past security incidents (questions for each incident).*
   * What was the nature of the security incident?
   * How soon did you become aware of the incident? Did you find out because of a documented process or by accident (e.g., happened to be talking to somebody)?
   * What was the reaction?
   * What was the impact of the incident?
   * What has been done to prevent such incidents from happening in the future?

   Guidance: Past security incidents provide a good glimpse of what vulnerabilities exist and how well equipped the company is to handle security-related incidents. This is especially important when considering risks such as those related to terminations and disgruntled employees.

Client Response:

4. *Planned initiatives. Some examples of initiatives that can be asked about include:*
   * Offering services via the Internet — e.g., e-commerce, content
   * Change in location
   * Outsourcing processes and/or technology
   * Use of Application Service Providers for key business processes

- Deployment of a major application
- Will the company be required to comply with certain laws or regulations in the future (Health Insurance Portability and Accountability Act [HIPAA], Gramm–Leach–Bliley Act [GLBA], etc.)?

Guidance: Planned initiatives can change the way you look at findings. Both short-term and long-term planned initiatives will have an impact on how you view the risk and what type of recommendation you make. Some findings may not be as serious if the related business process will drastically change or go away in the short term. One aspect to look for is how definite the schedule for an initiative is. Often, planned initiatives are not necessarily set in stone. For this information, it is worth asking management.

Client Response:

5. *Other interviewee-specific questions — This is a placeholder for additional questions based on the client's specific business requirements.*
   - Questions can be added here that are specific to the business based on what you have learned about the company so far.

SECURITY-RELATED QUESTIONS

Most of the questions below are covered in more detail in other questionnaires in the Appendices. The questions here are high level and are meant to elicit some perspective from business process owners who have limited involvement with these tasks. This perspective also helps validate whether processes are working as intended.

6. *User ID administration: What is your role in users gaining access to systems — e.g., approval authority?*

   Guidance: User ID administration is a process that touches almost everyone in the company. For this reason, it is good to get the perspective of different people in the company to help determine what opportunities exist to improve the user ID administration process.

Client Response:

7. *Employee termination.*
   - What do you do if an employee reporting to you is terminated?
   - What are you accountable for?
   - Is there a documented process for terminations that you follow?

Guidance: Terminations represent a significant risk, especially as related to disgruntled employees. A good termination process requires significant cooperation from several people in an organization. The answer to these questions will give you some perspective from those who are involved in the process but who do not own it.

Client Response:

---

8. *Data retention and classification.*
   - Are you aware of any policies related to data classification or data retention?
   - Are you the "owner" of any data?
   - Do you specify retention or classification requirements for data you are responsible for?

Guidance: Many of the business process owners you interview will be data owners. You will find that many do not do anything with classifying data or ensuring that data is retained for the appropriate period of time. Many data owners think that classification and retention are information technology (IT) issues, which they are not.

Client Response:

---

9. *Backup and recovery.*
   - For data that you own, do you specify any backup requirements for that data?
   - In the event of a disaster, what data would need to be restored for you to become operational?
   - Is that data readily available?

Guidance: Similar to data retention and classification, backup and recovery is something that is often viewed as an IT issue. This answer will help you determine how backups are done and what opportunities for improvement exist. The response to this question will also tell you how aware process owners are about this topic.

Client Response:

---

10. *Business continuity and disaster recovery.*
    - Are you aware of any business continuity and disaster recovery plan?
    - What is your involvement in it?

Guidance: Business continuity and disaster recovery touch everyone in the company and thus, there should be a general awareness of how the plan (if one exists) works. Business process owners should understand what to do in the event of a disaster and how they will become operational in the event of a disaster.

Client Response:

11. *Incident handling.*
    - Do you know what to do in the event of a security incident?
    - To whom would you report an incident?
    - Are you aware of any documented procedures for incident handling?

Guidance: Incident handling is another process that touches most people. Process owners should know to whom to go in the event of a security incident and what the escalation path is. They should also know about procedures to ensure that proper forensics can be done.

Client Response:

12. *Change management.*
    - Do you follow a change management process?
    - Are you aware of a documented process for change management?

Guidance: Many people who do not have overall responsibility for change management can normally initiate the change management process. If the change management process is not done properly from the outset, there is a risk that changes will not follow the change management process. Process owners should understand how change management works, forms that have to be filled out, etc.

Client Response:

13. *Acceptable use of IT resources.*
    - Is there documented Acceptable User policy?
    - Has human resources (HR) or management ever discussed what is considered acceptable use of IT resources?
    - Have you ever signed an Acceptable Use policy?

Guidance: For many people, the concept of Acceptable Use is a matter of common sense. However, many do not know about it or have never seen one in writing. You might see a case where an Acceptable Use policy exists but there is no formal acknowledgment that employees have read it and understand it. For a company to be able to use Acceptable Use as a basis for disciplinary or legal action, they must prove that the employees read the policy. Ideally, this acknowledgment is something that HR should ensure happens and should track with new and existing employees.

Client Response:

14. *Physical security.*
    - What physical security measures are in place for the areas of the facility you access?
    - Do you have any sensitive information in your desk or office and if so, how is it secured?
    - Do you practice a "clean desk" policy when you leave the office?
    - Do you use screensavers on your computer?
    - Do you shred sensitive documents before throwing them away?

Guidance: Physical security measures are something that most employees encounter on a daily basis. The purpose of this question is to get perspective from employees about what physical security measures are in place. The answer to this question will help you validate the more detailed questions related to physical security.

Client Response:

Appendix C

Generic Questionnaire for Meetings with Technology Owners

Similar to the Generic Questionnaire for Business Process Owners, this is a set of questions that can be addressed to any of the technology owners. Additional questions should be added based on your knowledge about the business.

1. *What technology are you responsible for and what business process does it support?*

   Guidance: With your knowledge of the business so far, you should have some perspective on how the technology supports the business. However, the technology owner will be able to give you a different angle on this topic. In some cases, there might not be a specific business process — e.g., a server that handles authentication into the network does not necessarily support a particular business process, it is providing access so users can do their jobs. In other cases, the technology owner might be managing an application that supports a mission-critical business process.

   Client Response:

2. *Where does it fit into the overall architecture?*

   Guidance: Assuming that a network topology diagram is in place, you should be able to see where the technology fits into the IT environment. This is very helpful because it gives you a visual perspective and highlights the relationships with other parts of the IT environment. These relationships will likely generate other questions regarding integration points, transmission of information, and other topics where there are security implications.

Client Response:

3. *What are the key dependencies for the technology you manage?*

Guidance: The key dependencies for any technology are the components that must be functional for the technology in question to work properly. A simple example is business to commerce (B2C). For B2C to be functional, access to the Internet is required. Knowledge of dependencies is important to understand when considering the availability requirements for a given technology.

Client Response:

4. *What are the security requirements related to the systems you manage — e.g., confidentiality, integrity, and availability? Are these requirements being met?*

Guidance: From the discussions with the business process owners, you should have a good sense for what these requirements are. The purpose of this question is to determine whether the technology owner is aware of the security requirements and whether those requirements are being met. One thing to look for here is whether the process and technology owners have the same perspective on security. If not, you can delve further into why the differences exist and whether there is an adequate level of security related to the given system.

Client Response:

5. *How is the technology secured?*

Guidance: This is a follow-up on the previous question. When talking about how it is secured, there are a number of aspects including access controls, physical security, integrity controls, and others. The methods depend on the technology. This question will probably lead to a technical discussion, where it is important to be prepared to talk on a technical level.

Client Response:

---

6. *How is security enforced?*

   Guidance: If security is not enforced, its value is diminished significantly. Enforcement efforts can be automated or manual. To the extent that enforcement can be automated, it should be. Other methods of enforcement include periodic reviews and audits.

Client Response:

---

7. *Does critical data reside on any system you manage? If so, how is it secured?*

   Guidance: From your business process interviews, you should know what critical data exists and where it resides. This is an opportunity to get the perspective of the technology owner, which should hopefully be in line with what you know already. Once you learn how the information is secured, you can determine if there is an appropriate level of security based on the criticality of data.

Client Response:

---

8. *If the systems you manage were not available, how quickly could they be functional?*

   Guidance: With this question, you will have to go through several different scenarios because all system failures are not the same. The goal with this question is to get a range of times for how long the systems can be unavailable and whether these ranges are acceptable based on the availability requirements of the business. This is one of the areas where there is often a disconnect between IT and the business. Availability requirements are often a budgeting issue. For example, consider a company's e-mail functionality. There is a big difference between guaranteeing four-hour maximum downtime and one business day maximum downtime. Many people will tell you that they cannot do any work without e-mail and that half a day is about all they can tolerate. When you start looking at what it costs to meet a half-day maximum downtime requirement, the tolerable downtime will likely change, and other methods of communication such as phones might become more of a viable option.

Client Response:

---

9. *What type of logging and monitoring activities do you perform?*

   Guidance: For key machines or devices, some level of logging and monitoring should take place. For example, for critical servers, does anyone review any of the event logs or any of the other relevant logs? How much log review and monitoring activity occurs provides some indication how proactive or reactive the security measures are. The level of logging and monitoring is often a function of how many people the client has to do the work and the risks they face.

Client Response:

---

10. *Is a formal change management process followed for any changes to the technology?*

    Guidance: Whether or not a change management process is followed is an indicator of how controlled the environment is. If no change management process is followed, it can lead to more questions depending on the technology. At a minimum, a lack of a change management process should be flagged as an issue.

Client Response:

---

11. *Have there been any security incidents with any of the technology you manage?*

    Guidance: This question is the same as what was asked to the process owners. This information is valuable because it provides some clues about what vulnerabilities might exist, what the impacts are, and what management did to ensure that incidents do not recur. If there was an incident, find out the details about it and ask about how it was handled and what subsequent steps were taken to prevent it from happening again.

Client Response:

---

12. *Are there any changes planned for the technology you manage? If so, have the security implications been considered?*

    Guidance: Planned changes can affect your evaluation depending on what they are. Some examples include a major overhaul of the technology, change in architecture, changes in organization, merger or acquisition activity, and outsourcing. If any new initiatives exist, you should find out if security is (was) being considered in the planning process. Any changes that the technology owner is able to talk about are worth discussing because they will affect your evaluation.

Client Response:

Appendix D

Data Classification

Data classification is the basis for determining how data is treated — e.g., how long it is retained, how it is handled (confidential, public, etc.), and how it is protected. It is based on operational, regulatory, and other business requirements and impacts many areas of a company. Some groups that may have significant input in data classification policy include finance, information technology (IT), and human resources. These groups have operational and regulatory requirements with different data including some of the examples listed below:

- Financial records
- Personnel records
- System logs

For example, the finance group has classification requirements driven by operational needs related to financial analysis and regulatory requirements related to taxation and Securities and Exchange Commission (SEC) reporting (if it is a publicly traded company).

Some of the key risks of not having a sound data classification process include:

- Loss of critical data due to inappropriate treatment
- Compromise of confidential data during transmission or destruction due to a lack of appropriate security measures
- Inappropriate disclosure of information as a result of lack of classification or no classification, resulting in fines or damage to a company's reputation or legal exposure

This questionnaire is based on the International Standards Organization (ISO) 17799 standard and past experience and is meant to serve as an initial set of questions. These questions should be asked of people who are significantly involved in the data classification process. This questionnaire should be modified to the extent necessary to reflect the specific client's business based on what you have learned so far.

1. *Is a data classification policy in place?*

   Guidance: A data classification policy is required at the minimum in order to have consistent and enforceable classification practices. It is possible that there is no documented scheme but there is some scheme that personnel generally know about and follow. The policy helps ensure that all personnel are using the same classifications. If there is an "ad-hoc" or unwritten policy in place, it can potentially be leveraged to create the security policy.

Risk: The risks associated with not having a data classification policy include:
- There is a lack of or inconsistent data classifications being used, which can result in data not receiving appropriate treatment relative to operational, legal, and other requirements.
- It is difficult to enforce consistent data classification practices without a formal policy that has been communicated to personnel.

Client Response:

2. *Are any procedures in place to show users how they are to classify information and communicate it to the relevant people in the organization?*

   Guidance: In order for personnel to understand how to implement the data classification policy, a process they can follow should be documented and readily accessible. The procedure should articulate responsibilities (e.g., data owners, IT) and define a process for classifying data and communicating the classification to the appropriate parties. If there is already a process that is working well, it should be formalized into a documented procedure. The documented procedure will make users accountable to a process and help ensure that personnel know about it and that it is done consistently. The other value of procedures is when there is employee turnover. Documented procedures can be used by new employees to quickly come up to speed.

   Risk: Without documented procedures, there is a risk of:
   - Noncompliance with the data classification policy
   - Incorrect or inconsistent data classification processes
   Both of these cases can result in data not being classified properly and not receiving the appropriate treatment.

Client Response:

3. *Does your company have any operational, regulatory, or other requirements that might dictate the need for data classification?*

Guidance: This question should help determine how important data classification is for the company. Some smaller companies might treat all data in the same way and may not have any need for data classification. In larger companies, data classification is probably something to be concerned about, as they are more likely to have those types of requirements.

Risk: Not applicable. This question is to help determine the scope of data classification in the company.

Client Response:

---

4. *Have there been any security incidents recently that could potentially have been prevented if a data classification policy was in place? If so, what steps have been taken to prevent such incidents from happening again?*

Guidance: If an incident has occurred, the nature of the incident, the company's response, and subsequent actions to prevent it from happening again are important to discuss and may lead to findings for the assessment. For example, colleges and universities are always handling sensitive student information — e.g., grades, disciplinary information. The risk related to exposing sensitive student information can be reduced if student information is classified so that it receives the appropriate level of security.

Risk: Not applicable. The purpose of this question is to gather information. There is no associated risk.

Client Response:

---

5. *Do users know the data classification scheme and is it published and easily accessible?*

Guidance: Sometimes a data classification scheme exists but few know about it because it is buried in some obscure intranet site or in some manual, which only a few people have. It is possible that the policy is not with the rest of the security IT policies or operations policies because it was developed by the legal department. Users might want to classify information but if the scheme is not easily accessible, they may not take the time to find out about it and thus may not use it. There may be a need to incorporate data classification into a user awareness program and into existing security policies.

Risk: If users are not aware of the data classification policy and if it is not easily accessible, there is a risk they will not follow it because they do not know about it or are not willing to take the time to find out about it.

Client Response:

---

6. *Does the classification scheme provide enough guidance so users can easily classify information?*

Guidance: When users access the data classification policy, it would be helpful for them to have some criteria or examples to help them classify information and distinguish the differences between the various classifications. As users begin to classify data, real examples, which can be used as reference points by personnel, will become available. One sign of a lack of guidance is that people are not using the existing classification scheme because the meaning of the classifications is unclear. If no guidance exists and personnel are unclear on classifying data, it would be worth incorporating this into a user awareness program and incorporating examples into the classification policy.

Risk: Without some guidance or examples of data for each of the classifications, personnel might not classify data properly. This can lead to inconsistent data classification and data not getting appropriate treatment.

Client Response:

---

7. *Are specific roles and responsibilities defined for data classification — specifically for data owners and system owners?*

Guidance: Data classification, like other areas of security or operations in general, requires clear roles and responsibilities to ensure that key tasks are performed. In the case of data classification, there must be personnel who "own" the data and are thus responsible for classifying it. One thing to look out for is that data classification might be viewed as an IT problem and as a result, IT is responsible for classifying the data. IT should not be making data classification decisions because they do not have the expertise to do so nor do they own the data. The IT group's responsibility should be to provide the necessary level of protection for data based on the classification. In addition, data owners should understand that there are costs related to different classifications — e.g., there are additional costs related to protecting confidential documents versus public documents.

Risk: Without clearly defined roles and responsibilities, there is a risk that data will not be classified properly and will not receive the appropriate treatment.

Client Response:

---

8. *Is the data classification scheme used consistently across the whole organization?*

Guidance: As a best practice, one data classification scheme should be used consistently across an organization. An example of multiple classifications is when a company is classifying confidential data. One group might call it "confidential," but another group might call the same type of data "proprietary and confidential." This will just confuse some personnel and potentially result in the creation of other classifications. In addition, with these rogue classifications, it is difficult to determine what the implications are for the various classifications — i.e., how that data is protected. If other classifications are developed, they should go through the appropriate reviews, and personnel should be provided with some education on them.

Risk: Without a consistent data classification scheme, which has gone through appropriate reviews, there is a risk that data will not receive appropriate treatment as it is unclear what the classifications mean.

Client Response:

---

9. *Does the classification scheme address the following processes for each classification?*
   - Copying and storage of information
   - Retention of data
   - Transmission of data
   - Destruction of information
   - Sensitive information

Guidance: One of the purposes of the classification scheme is to define how data should be handled. Based on how data is classified, the company should have certain guidelines for key data processes such as the ones listed above. If a user classifies data with a certain classification, the user should have an understanding of how the data will be treated and what the financial and process implications might be. For example, when "confidential" information is output, there may be special labeling requirements, which cost money. As users "own" the data, they might have some responsibility related to the cost of protecting it. This element of cost should compel data owners to carefully classify their data.

Risk: If the data classification policy does not address the types of treatment listed above, there is a risk that data will not receive the appropriate treatment based on the classification. This diminishes the value of having a data classification policy.

Client Response:

10. *Is labeling required for all data so that ownership and classification are clear?*

Guidance: Labeling helps ensure that data is handled correctly. There should be a consistent labeling process so that users know how to handle data with the various classifications. This is particularly true with sensitive data where inappropriate disclosure could lead to issues — e.g., legal, damage to reputation. For example, financial information for a publicly traded company is confidential data due to laws related to insider trading. During quarter closes when consolidated financial results are released in a 10Q form and reported to the SEC, it is critical that only those who require access to this information have it — e.g., access to printed financial results must be limited also. Unauthorized access to this information can lead to issues such as insider trading violations.

Risk: Without proper labeling, there is a risk that data might not be handled properly and destroyed or inappropriately disclosed.

Client Response:

11. *Is there any method for enforcing the data classification policy and procedure?*

Guidance: With any aspect of security, enforcement is critical. Security processes are viewed by many as being cumbersome and are often not followed by employees unless they know that that the policies and procedures will be enforced and that there are repercussions for not being compliant. Enforcement is key in ensuring that employees follow the data classification policy. Enforcement efforts might also indicate a need for some education or awareness training so that employees better understand the purpose of data classification and the risks of not following good data classification practices.

Risk: Without enforcement of the data classification policy and procedure, there is a risk of noncompliance with the data classification policy, resulting in inappropriate treatment of data.

Client Response:

Appendix E

Data Retention

Data retention requirements define the retention period for data. These requirements are developed by management and are driven by the needs of the business from various perspectives, which are discussed below. Data retention is intertwined with data classification requirements and is in some ways a subset of the Data Classification policy — i.e., certain retention requirements may be tied into data classifications. Some of the key factors to consider when developing data retention requirements include:

- *Historical* — Historical data is important in analyzing trends in the business over time. Trend analysis can be done for a number of different business functions including finance, manufacturing, and others. For example, a manufacturing company might analyze production data over time for planning purposes and to identify areas of improvement. The amount of historical data retained for these purposes depends on the specific requirements of the business.
- *Legal and regulatory* — Legal and regulatory requirements from governmental bodies mandate retaining records and force companies to ensure that certain processes are in place to accommodate this. An example is the requirements by the Securities and Exchange Commission (SEC) and the Internal Revenue Service (IRS), which require some companies to retain certain financial records for a period of time. Legal and regulatory retention requirements are driven by forces outside the company and thus, you have no control over them. The company's legal counsel should work with the appropriate individuals in the business to ensure that legal- and regulatory-related data retention requirements are properly defined and met.
- *Security and audit* — For both security analysis and audit purposes, certain data is retained from various systems including intrusion detection, firewalls, key servers, etc. Some of this data is used by auditors, and other data is retained for future review in the event of a security incident, system crash, or other problem. These requirements are driven by the information security program and depend largely on how management views security.

A formal data retention policy provides guidance to the business on how long data should be retained to meet operational requirements and be in compliance with regulatory requirements. Although information technology (IT) plays a major role in data retention, the actual requirements must be driven by the business. Therefore, it is critical to involve different groups such as human resources (HR), legal, and finance when reviewing data retention.

This questionnaire is a starting point for what should be asked during a security assessment. These questions should be modified based on the company's specific business requirements.

1. *Is there a formal data retention policy that is easily accessible to employees?*

   Guidance: A formal data retention policy defines the retention requirements. The policy should clearly define categories of data and their retention periods. In a security assessment, the policy should be evaluated to ensure that all critical data is addressed, retention periods are updated, and that ownership of determining the retention period rests with the data owner. The data retention policy should also be readily accessible (e.g., on an intranet site) so personnel can refer to it as they determine the retention period of data they own. If personnel cannot readily access the policy, they might not take the time to find it or ask someone and as a result not be informed about the policy.

   Risk: Without a formal data retention policy, data may not be retained in accordance with operational, legal, or regulatory requirements. If the policy is not accessible, personnel may not know about it or follow it. This will result in a policy that is not enforceable.

   ___

   Client Response:

   ___

2. *Are procedures in place to ensure that data is retained for the required retention period?*

   Guidance: With data retention, its important for organizations to proactively check for compliance, as many of the retention periods are driven by legislation. A documented process of how data is retained for the appropriate retention period will help ensure consistent data retention practices and can be used as a basis for evaluating the retention process.

   Risk: The risks associated with not having procedures in place include:
   • Limited ability to enforce good data retention practices
   • Inconsistent data retention practices
   • Data not being retained for the appropriate periods, which can lead to operational as well as regulatory impacts

   ___

   Client Response:

   ___

3. *Have any incidents occurred related to not retaining data for an appro-*
   priate period of time?

   Guidance: Typical incidents could include the inadvertent destruction of
   electronic files that should have been retained. With these incidents, the
   question is whether defining retention requirements would have minimized
   the chance of that data being destroyed. The specific security incident(s),
   if any, should be evaluated based on that criterion.

   Risk: Not applicable. This question is to gain some knowledge of any incidents and how they were handled.

   Client Response:

   ---

4. *Has the data retention policy been developed or approved by the relevant*
   functional areas of the company including human resources, legal,
   finance, and other departments as appropriate?

   Guidance: Data retention requirements are primarily driven by personnel
   outside the IT department, especially when dealing with regulatory and audit
   requirements. Because of the legal and operational ramifications related to
   data retention, it is critical that all relevant parties have reviewed and approved the policy. At the minimum, the HR, legal, and finance departments
   should be involved in the development and review of the data retention
   policy.

   Risk: If the relevant functional areas did not help develop or approve the
   data retention policy, there is a risk that the data retention policy does not
   meet the legal or regulatory and operational retention requirements of the
   business.

   Client Response:

   ---

5. *What data is currently retained and what would the impact to the business*
   be if the data were not retained?
   * *Operational* — e.g., manufacturing data, financial data
   * *Legal and regulatory* — e.g., financial reporting requirements
   * *Audit* — e.g., system logs

   Guidance: This question is to learn about the extent to which data is
   retained and what the impact would be if it were not retained for the

appropriate period. Out of this conversation, you will probably also learn about what the company does about data retention. In assessing data retention, the data identified based on this question should be compared to the data retention policy (if there is one) to determine whether any critical data has not been addressed. If a data retention policy exists, this comparison will show you whether the existing policy is adequate. The second part of the question regarding the potential impact will give a sense for the criticality and priority as it relates to data retention.

Risk: Not applicable. This question determines the scope and importance of data retention. The potential impacts identified in this question will give an indication of the criticality of data retention in the company. The answer to this question will help formulate recommendations and associated prioritization as they relate to data retention.

Client Response:

---

6. *Are data owners accountable for specifying the data retention period?*

Guidance: Security, like any process, must have clear roles and responsibilities to help ensure that the process is done properly. In the case of data retention, the retention period must be known before steps can be taken to store data for that period. Therefore, data owners must first specify the retention period for their data. Ideally, there should be a mechanism by which data owners inform IT of the retention period for their electronic data. (Physical data will have to be dealt with by another department.) Using this information, IT can then retain the data for the appropriate period. As you assess the process, you may find that IT is completely responsible for retention — i.e., determining the retention period and taking steps to retain the data. It is also possible that IT is making certain assumptions for retention periods or just indefinitely retaining data because they do not know that a data retention policy exists. The company should understand that data owners are ultimately accountable for retention and that it is not an IT issue. Ideally, all data owners should follow a documented data retention policy. In addition, there is cost associated with retention, which should be factored in when determining data retention periods.

Risk: If data owners are not explicitly responsible for specifying the retention period for their data, a risk exists that data might be retained for either too long or too short a time. This can lead to unnecessary costs related to storing data for too long or operational and/or legal concerns related to storing data for too short a time. This issue becomes increasingly significant as more data is generated.

Client Response:

7. *Is data properly destroyed after the retention period?*

Guidance: Data destruction is a significant issue when dealing with sensitive data. After the retention period, data should be destroyed unless there is a good business reason to maintain it. If data is destroyed internally, steps should be taken to ensure proper destruction of data. For electronic data, drives should be overwritten according to best practice standards. If data is destroyed externally using third-party services, you must ensure that due diligence was done in selecting the vendor and that appropriate contracts (approved by legal counsel) are in place with the vendor to help ensure that physical data is appropriately destroyed. Ideally, third parties should provide some proof or verification that data was destroyed. If employees are destroying paper documents, they should be educated to shred documents with sensitive information.

Risk: The risk associated with data not being destroyed properly is the inappropriate disclosure of sensitive or confidential information, which can lead to legal issues or damage to the reputation of the company.

Client Response:

Appendix F

Backup and Recovery

With the use of technology, companies are generating more electronic data than ever before. Many transactions that were paper based at one time are electronic today. As a result, companies are dependent upon a tremendous quantity of electronic data. Being able to back up and recover data is a mission-critical process that can mean the survival of a company. According to one report, 90 percent of companies that lose the data on their computers are out of business within two years. Besides operational concerns, some companies must have good backup and recovery processes to achieve compliance with industry-specific regulations (e.g., health care and financial services).

Like other security practices, backup and recovery requirements should be based on business requirements. More specifically, backup and recovery should be based on data classification and data retention requirements defined by data owners. Roles and responsibilities related to defining backup requirements and performing the backups are critical in ensuring good backup and recovery practices.

This questionnaire is a starting point for what should be asked during a security assessment. These questions should be modified based on the company's specific business backup and recovery requirements.

1. *Is there a formal backup and recovery policy?*

   Guidance: As with other areas of information security, the policy is the foundation for ensuring sound backup and recovery practices. The policy should be easily accessible and should define high-level requirements and roles and responsibilities. The policy also helps the enforcement and audit process. Without a policy, there is no official management position on backup and recovery requirements or who is responsible for them. Some of the key components that you should look for in a backup and recovery policy include:
   - Roles and responsibilities
   - Off-site storage
   - Testing
   - Disposal of media
   - Fulfillment of legal or regulatory requirements (if applicable)

   The above areas are not all inclusive and they will vary with clients.

Risk: Without a backup and recovery policy, the following risks exist:
- Inconsistent backup and recovery processes
- Noncompliance due to lack of knowledge
- Inability to enforce good backup and recovery practices because no official policy exists

---

Client Response:

---

2. *Is the backup and recovery policy linked to the data retention and data classification policies? Are there different backup procedures depending on the type of information?*

   Guidance: The backup and recovery policy should depend on the type of data and the associated significance of data, which is directly tied into its classification and retention. In linking these policies, consider the following:
   - In large companies generating a significant quantity of data, there may be some cost savings if all data does not have to be backed up. Having different backup schedules should be balanced by any additional administration required.
   - In some cases, there may be regulations that drive backing up data for a certain amount of time, which should tie into the data retention and data classification policies.

   For smaller, less complex companies, it might make more sense to take a consistent approach for all backups, as the additional administration associated with multiple backup schedules might not be worth it.

   Risk: If policies for backup and recovery and data retention and classification are not in sync, there is a risk that either too much or too little information is backed up. In addition, there is a risk of noncompliance with regulations if certain data is not backed up for a certain time period.

Client Response:

---

3. *Are there documented procedures for backing up and recovering data?*

   Guidance: Although the policy is "what" should be done, the procedure is "how" the policy translates into specific steps that need to be performed to achieve compliance with the policy requirements. Procedures tend to be more dynamic than policies are, as they can change due to changes in technology, personnel, and the organization structure. Some of the key steps that the backup and recovery procedure should address include:

- Communications from data owners to information technology (IT) regarding backup requirements
- Backup schedules — e.g., incremental, full backups.
- Tape labeling and storage
- Recovery process

There should be enough information so that someone with a little bit of knowledge of backup and recovery can perform the process.

Risk: Without clear procedures for backup and recovery, there are several risks including:

- Backup and recovery processes may be done inconsistently.
- If there is personnel turnover, it will be difficult for someone new to understand the backup and recovery process.

Client Response:

---

4. *Are there clear and documented roles and responsibilities for backup and recovery?*

Guidance: Clear roles and responsibilities are critical in helping to ensure that the process is performed as intended. Clear roles and responsibilities leave no room for doubt about who is responsible for a specific step in the process. For backup and recovery, the two key roles and responsibilities that should be defined are:

- *Data owner* — The data owner should be responsible for defining the backup and recovery requirements. Data owners are knowledgeable about any operational or regulatory requirements with which the company must be in compliance. They should also define how long data should be retained and how much data needs to be on hand so that data can be quickly recovered if necessary.
- *IT department*—A person within the IT organization should be responsible for backing up data according to requirements set forth by the data owner. It is critical that IT does not own the responsibility of defining the requirement because IT does not own the data. IT should also collaborate with data owners regarding backup and recovery strategy based on the defined requirements.

You may also find some companies where all data is backed up and kept indefinitely. Depending on how much data there is, there may be personnel and cost issues related to managing that much data.

Risk: The risk associated with not having clear roles and responsibilities is one of accountability. Without accountability for the different steps in the backup and recovery process, there is a risk that the process will not be completed properly.

Client Response:

---

5. *Have any security incidents related to backups ever occurred?*

   Guidance: Past security incidents provide some insight into the effectiveness of controls related to the backup and recovery process. Some of the potential security incidents include the loss of backup tapes, incomplete backups due to technical issues, tapes being accidentally overwritten, and data not being backed up because requirements were not defined. If any security incidents occurred, it is worth finding out how the company reacted and what they did to ensure that such incidents did not happen again.

   Risk: Not applicable. This question is asked to determine how effective the backup and recovery process and associated controls are.

Client Response:

---

6. *What data is backed up? What data is not backed up and why? How often are files required to be recovered?*

   Guidance: This question is asked to help determine the scope of backup and recovery activities. There is a range of responses for this question ranging from all data being backed up to some data being backed up. You should obtain details on what data is being backed up and the associated backup schedules (daily, weekly, etc.) and determine whether this is adequate based on the company's business requirements. If any data is not being backed up, you should find out why. For example, applications are often not backed up because they can be restored from CDs or some other means. You should determine if this is necessarily feasible. Another example where data might not be backed up is when it is stored on local workstations or laptops. Some companies leave these "local" backup responsibilities to individuals, as they encourage personnel to store all critical data on a network drive that will be backed up. If this is the case, this should be spelled out in the policy, and some related awareness training should occur.

   Risk: Not applicable. This question is used to help determine the complexity and importance of backup and recovery activities.

Client Response:

7. *What would be the impact to the business if any problems developed with the backup and recovery process? Some examples include:*
   - Loss of data
   - Failed backups
   - Inability to recover data from backup tapes

   Guidance: The impact to the business is one of the main components to consider when performing a security assessment. In the case of backup and recovery, impacts can include:
   - Downtime resulting from data not being available
   - Legal issues (e.g., Health Insurance Portability and Accountability Act [HIPAA])
   - Operational issues related to permanent loss of data (in the event backup data cannot be restored)

   Impacts should be quantified to the extent possible. When quantifying the impact, the company should consider short-term as well as long-term losses. Short-term losses might be more quantifiable and measurable, but long-term losses might be more in the form of loss of customers or the cost of instituting new processes to reduce the likelihood of an incident in the future.

   Risk: Not applicable. This question is asked to gain an understanding of the potential impact to help in assessing the importance of backup and recovery processes.

Client Response:

8. *Is the backup strategy in line with the business requirements? Some aspects that should be considered include:*
   - Tape retention schedule
   - Protection based on data classification (e.g., encryption)
   - Media used in backup tapes
   - Other business requirements

   Guidance: The company's backup strategy should correlate with the associated business requirements. You may find a number of scenarios ranging from all data being backed up indefinitely to data not being backed up at all. In some cases, it might be appropriate for all data to be backed up indefinitely if the cost is negligible and having different backup strategies for different data would create more work. Another scenario is where there is no backup strategy and data is not backed up consistently, which is definitely a cause for concern. It is critical that data owners define backup requirements. IT should not be dictating backup requirements. IT should develop a cost-effective backup strategy that fulfills the requirements set forth by the data owners.

Risk: The risk associated with backup and recovery strategies not being aligned with business requirements include:
• Critical data may not be backed up, resulting in legal or operational issues.
• Excessive resources may be spent in backing up too much data.

Client Response:

---

9. *Is your company governed by any regulatory requirements related to backup and recovery?*

Guidance: With regulatory requirements, companies essentially have no choice. For example, there is a specific requirement related to backups in the HIPAA security regulations, with which health care entities must comply. Regulatory requirements are an area where personnel from the business and technology sides must interact. Data owners affected by regulations should stay up to date on requirements and communicate with IT personnel accordingly. As part of the assessment, you should determine whether IT is receiving this information or whether they are expected to know it. One thing to do in preparation for the security assessment is to gain an understanding of the regulations that might affect the client.

Risk: The risk associated with not being compliant with regulatory requirements can include fines or damage to a company's reputation.

Client Response:

---

10. *Are the backup tapes clearly labeled to help ensure a smooth recovery process?*

Guidance: Backup tapes are often needed for restoring anything from single files to multiple directories. Typically, when restorations are required, users want it done immediately, particularly if it affects a mission-critical process. To help ensure this quick turnaround time, tapes should be labeled properly so information can be quickly located. The key benefits related to labeling backup tapes include:

- Turnaround time for restoring files is faster than if not labeled.
- It reduces the dependency on one or few individuals who are the only ones who know the contents of the backup tapes. With labeling, any IT person who knows the restore process can find the right backup tape in the event a restoration is required.

Risk: The risk associated with not clearly labeling backup tapes is potentially not being able to perform restorations on a timely basis. In addition, there is a risk associated with a limited number of people knowing the content of the tapes.

Client Response:

---

11. *Are there Service Level Agreements or Objectives (SLAs or SLOs) related to restoring data for users?*

Guidance: Some organizations have agreements (SLAs or SLOs) for restoring data. The difference between SLAs and SLOs is that the SLAs are more contractual in nature in that penalties exist if the terms of the agreement are not kept. SLOs are objectives for which a servicing organization is striving. With backup and recovery processes, the agreements are between the user community and IT and can specify target metrics for various aspects of backup and recovery. Depending on the organization, these agreements may have financial implications — e.g., if the IT department is charging individual departments of a company for its services, charges may be adjusted if service level requirements are not met. Agreements establish accountability for all parties involved and provide a mechanism to identify processes that are not working properly. In a security assessment, two key aspects of the agreements should be reviewed:

- Are the current processes adequate to achieve the metrics established in the agreements (acceptable time frames for file restoration, tape retention requirements, etc.)?
- Does the company manage to the agreements — i.e., does the company enforce the agreements? Without enforcement, the value of the agreements is significantly diminished.

Risk: Not applicable. A lack of SLAs or SLOs does not necessarily pose any security risk, but the presence of SLAs or SLOs does enhance the overall security posture by adding accountability to the tasks in the information security program.

Client Response:

---

12. *Are users aware of where information should be stored to ensure that their information is backed up? Do they store information locally on their computers, which normally are not backed up?*

    Guidance: Companies typically have several places (directories, drives, etc.) where information can be stored. Users might have a network shared drive, a home directory, and their local hard drives on their personal computers. Not all of these places where a user can store information will be backed up. Local hard drives on users' computers are not typically backed up. However, users are not always aware of this and as a result, they store their critical information on their local machines, which are probably not backed up on a regular basis. For example, sales representatives or consultants may primarily work at customer premises where their work is probably stored on their hard drives. If the hard drive on a computer is corrupted, they can lose all of their information. Consider a research and development person who has significant analysis documentation on his or her personal computer, and the computer crashes or is stolen. In this scenario, some very valuable information can be permanently lost or even worse, proprietary research information can get into the hands of a competitor. In these instances, the value of the information is more than the value of the computer. Users should be made aware of where they must store their information to ensure that it is backed up properly. This can be addressed in an orientation or awareness program.

    Risk: The risk associated with users not being aware of where information must be stored is that valuable information might be permanently lost. Depending on the criticality of the information, significant operational consequences can result.

Client Response:

---

13. *Is off-site storage used for backup tapes? If not, where are backups stored?*

    Guidance: Backup tapes are ultimately used in many cases to restore information. Off-site storage is important in the event that an incident forces the company facilities to be inaccessible. Formal off-site storage might be expensive and not feasible for a company. In some cases (particularly in smaller companies), a person in the IT department or some other person might take backup tapes home, avoiding the cost of off-site storage. In other cases, companies might use their other facilities to store tapes. The main thing to look for is that the tapes are not stored on site, where they might be inaccessible in the event of a disaster. In addition, off-site storage should be addressed in the business continuity plan.

Risk: If tapes are not adequately stored somewhere off site, there is a risk that backup tapes will not be accessible in the event of a disaster, which can potentially result in disruption of operations.

Client Response:

14. *What type of documentation is maintained for off-site tapes?*

Guidance: In the event that restoration of data is required, someone must know where the tapes are, what is contained on what tape, and how to restore from the tape. In addition, there should be documentation on who is authorized to access the tapes, which can be in a procedure for accessing off-site tapes. This is important when information has to be restored or if there is a disaster. Off-site tapes documentation and the related authorization lists should be addressed within a business continuity plan.

Risk: If no documentation exists regarding tapes that are stored off site, there is a risk that tapes will not be easily accessible in the event of a disaster.

Client Response:

15. *Who has access to the backup tapes and how is access managed?*

Guidance: Backup tapes contain sensitive and critical information about a company. As a result, access to the tapes should be limited to only those who need it to do their jobs. Typically, only those who have primary responsibility for file restoration and someone who is a backup should have access. In addition, you may have others who have access for purposes of business continuity and even then, only under special circumstances. In no case should the tapes be easily accessible to the general IT population. In addition, the tapes should be locked up with the appropriate protections. When an authorized individual needs access to the tapes, it should be logged. The person taking the tape and the reason for taking the tape should be documented. There should be appropriate segregation of duties between the person accessing the tapes and the person maintaining the log.

Risk: If access to the tapes is not properly controlled, there are risks related to:
- Unauthorized access to critical company information
- Loss or destruction of the tapes, making restoration of information difficult if not impossible

Client Response:

16. *How do you ensure that backups were successful?*

Guidance: Backups can be done manually or as an automated process where certain batch jobs are run at predefined intervals (daily, weekly, monthly) depending on the company's specific business requirements. For many companies, backups are done as part of automated jobs, which run every night. There should be a process or control in place to ensure that backups are run successfully. At the minimum, there should be a process to ensure that mission-critical data is backed up as required. If backups are not successful, appropriate individuals should be notified.

Risk: If there is no process for ensuring successful backups, there is a risk that file restorations will not be possible due to information not being properly backed up. The risk becomes significantly worse if mission-critical data cannot be restored.

Client Response:

17. *Has a full recovery ever been tested?*

Guidance: A full recovery test is something that is not always performed for a variety of reasons including:
- Full recovery tests can be very time consuming.
- Companies do not always have the staff to do this type of test.
- The recovery test might cause a disruption in operations if not performed properly.
- Companies do not necessarily see the value in doing it because the likelihood that a full restoration is required may seem minimal.

Although these reasons are partially valid, testing is critical. In the event of a disaster, the backups are one of the most critical components required to be up and running again. The potential risk of not being able to recover data even once justifies the value of testing the recovery process. As for testing, the frequency depends on the company and how much the environment changes. One of the mitigating factors that might reduce the risk is if the company routinely does file recoveries and as a result, gains some assurance that the process works.

Risk: Without periodically testing a full recovery or at least having a documented process for how a full recovery would be done, the restoration process might not work properly in the event of a disaster. This can result in not being operational for an unacceptable period of time.

Client Response:

---

18. *What backup measures are being taken for paper-based data where no electronic copies exist?*
    • What is the criticality of the paper-based data?
    • If the paper-based data were destroyed, would the company have a way to recreate the data?
    • What would be the impact to the business if the paper-based data were lost and not recoverable?

Guidance: One of the often-overlooked areas when reviewing backup and recovery is paper-based documents. Hard copy documents can have value for a variety of reasons including:
    • Old documents that predated electronic documents may have historical value
    • Sensitive information that was typed or where electronic copies were not retained (e.g., sensitive personnel information, litigation-related information).
Besides the documents listed above, there may be other paper documents that are of value. Solutions for paper documents include off-site storage, scanning the documents and storing them electronically, some combination of both, and others. As with electronic data, the "owners" of these paper documents must be responsible for defining the requirements related to backups of the paper documents. Paper documents are also addressed when evaluating physical security as well as business continuity and disaster recovery.

Risk: The risk associated with not backing up paper documents is that if these documents are destroyed, it might be impossible to recover them.

Depending on the criticality of the information that is lost, the implications can include disruption in operations or damage to the reputation of the company.

Client Response:

Appendix G

Externally Hosted Services

Companies are increasingly using externally hosted services to obtain services such as hosted Web sites or applications (ASP — Application Service Provider). With externally hosted services, companies are having certain services managed and run on an external service provider's machines. Some of the reasons for this type of arrangement include:

- The company wants to concentrate on its core competency, so they use hosting services for certain operations where they do not have expertise.
- Using external service providers is cheaper than doing it in house.
- The company wishes to use industry-standard applications.
- With certain industry-specific applications, an ASP is more convenient.

One of the effects of this trend is that companies are conducting mission-critical processes through externally hosted services — e.g., services such as Web hosting, where a provider hosts a company's Web site, or an ASP, where the ASP provides an application on its own machines that companies can access over the Internet or some other connection. Typical functions hosted by third-party providers are specialty applications and industry-specific applications. With an externally hosted service, the provider has the application, which a company would connect to and use.

From a security perspective, contracting with third parties results in certain risks that should be given attention before a contract is signed with a third-party provider. Some of the major concerns with external providers include:

- General security of the external provider
- Financial condition of the external provider
- Confidentiality of data on third-party machines
- Availability of services

This questionnaire is focused on the process of using third-party providers — e.g., contracts, conducting due diligence on the provider, and ongoing management of third parties. There is no specific technology aspect to this questionnaire because the specific technical security concerns will depend on what service is being used, the business process being supported, and how the security architecture is set up. From a process perspective, this questionnaire contains some general process questions and some specific questions that address key processes — how user access to the company's information is handled, incident handling, etc. Based on the provider, you should develop additional questions based on other questionnaires as well as your own experience.

For assessing technical security of an external provider, use technical best practice checklists that address the specific environment. As with the other questionnaires, this should be modified based on the specific business requirements of the company.

QUESTIONS

1. *Is there a formal policy governing relationships with external service providers?*

   Guidance: The security policy is the foundation of an overall information security program. With third-party providers, it is important to have a policy that sets standards for what is required of a third-party provider, what type of due diligence is required as part of selecting a provider, and what items need to be addressed in a service-level agreement with a provider. Some of the key areas of the policy include:
   - Roles and responsibilities
   - Security requirements
     - Data access
     - Transmission of information
     - Backup and recovery
     - Audit
     - Incident handling
   - Management reporting
   - Service-level agreement

   Risk: Without clear guidelines governing the relationship between an external provider and the company, a risk exists that the external provider may provide inadequate service resulting in issues related to availability of service, security of information, and other security-related issues.

   Client Response:

   ---

2. *Is there a contract with the provider and does it address security requirements?*

   Guidance: As part of the assessment, the contract with the provider should be reviewed — particularly the security provisions. One issue with these contracts is that they often do not address security. Aside from the operational requirements, the contract should address security issues as outlined in Question 1 as well as any other security issues that may be relevant to the situation. In addition, you should verify that the contract has gone through an attorney review as well as an information technology (IT) review to ensure that the contract is sound and protects the interests of the company. Without security being specifically mentioned in the contract, the legal basis for holding the external provider accountable for having an adequate level of security is diminished significantly.

Risk: If the contract with the external provider does not include security related provisions, there is a risk that security concerns will not be adequately addressed by the external provider. This lack of attention to security can have several negative consequences including:
- Disruption of critical operations leading to loss of revenue or loss of customers
- Compromise of sensitive data
- Noncompliance with regulatory requirements (if operations with regulatory consequences are being supported)
- Others

Client Response:

3. *What business processes does the external service provider support? Is the business process mission critical?*

   Guidance: This is a question to help you understand the importance of the relationship with the external service provider. The criticality of the business process being supported will determine the level of security and control required for the relationship with the external service provider. Based on the criticality of the relationship, it might be worth it to visit or call the external service provider.

   Risk: Not applicable. This question is asked to determine the criticality of the process.

Client Response:

4. *What is the potential impact to the business if a security incident (e.g., compromise of sensitive data, permanent loss of data) with the external service provider occurs or if services from the provider are unavailable?*

Guidance: The potential impact to the business will vary based on the incident. However, it is important to go through some scenarios when asking this question to help determine impacts to the business. Some scenarios to review include:

- Service is unavailable for a period of time — e.g., what is the impact if the service is not available for four hours, eight hours, etc. Impacts might include:
  - Short-term loss of revenue if the business process directly supports the sales process
  - Loss of customers if the business process is e-commerce related
- Loss of data
  - Cost to recreate data
  - Operational impact

Risk: Not applicable. This is information on the potential impact of a security incident, which is another part of understanding the criticality of the business processes being supported by the external service provider and the associated risks.

Client Response:

---

5. *What would be the impact to the company if the information on the third-party provider's systems was compromised?*

Guidance: The impact can vary depending on the severity of the incident. Some of the potential impacts include:

- *Operational* — e.g., loss of customers, services are unavailable, sensitive information is exposed.
- *Legal* — e.g., litigation if customer-related sensitive information is exposed.
- *Damage to reputation* — e.g., incident is significant enough to attract media attention.

In addition to determining the impact, you should also review the contract and the service level agreement (SLA), if one exists, because they may provide information regarding what type of recourse is available to the company.

Risk: Not applicable. This is information on the potential impact of data being compromised, which is another part of understanding the criticality of the relationship with the external provider.

Client Response:

---

6. *Have there been any security-related incidents related to the services from the external provider?*

Guidance: Past security incidents should be reviewed because they provide an indication of potential weaknesses, how the incident was handled, and what was done to prevent similar future incidents. With external service providers, you can also determine how the security incident was addressed in light of the contract and the SLA — i.e., how effective were the contract and SLA in taking recourse and holding the external provider accountable?

Risk: Not applicable. The result of this question can potentially highlight security weaknesses as well as weaknesses in the contract and SLA, resulting in recommendations for amendments to the current contract as well as future contracts.

Client Response:

---

7. *Does the contract provide the company with the ability to audit the external service provider?*

Guidance: The contract with the external provider should be worded so that the client has the ability to conduct audits with a reasonable amount of notice. The company should review key aspects of the provider's operations including internal controls, information technology (IT) areas such as security patch levels on their systems, and physical security. An audit provides the company with a first-hand view of the provider and the chance to determine whether the external provider provides its services in a secure manner. One thing to keep in mind is that the frequency of the audits should be kept to a reasonable number because audits can be involved and take significant time, which might be difficult for the external provider to give.

Risk: Without a provision to audit, there is a risk that the company will not be able to adequately monitor the service being provided or ensure that security requirements per the contract and SLA are being met. This can result in the company receiving services that are less than secure.

Client Response:

---

8. *Overall, what is the quality of service currently being provided?*

   Guidance: This is an open-ended question that can generate conversation about how good the service is from the provider. The discussion related to the quality of the service will lead to further discussion about security, availability, and other issues the client might be having with the provider. The lessons learned from this experience can provide guidance for the next relationship with an external service provider.

   Risk: Not applicable. This question is being asked to obtain an overall judgment of the service being provided.

   Client Response:

   ---

9. *Was any due diligence performed from a security perspective in the process of selecting the external service provider? If so, was someone who represented security part of the due diligence effort?*

   Guidance: External service providers often provide mission-critical services or house very sensitive information on their machines. With this in mind, the selection process should be a rigorous one involving significant due diligence. As part of this effort, someone representing security should be involved. One of the issues seen with external service providers is that security is often an afterthought — i.e., security is considered after the contract is signed. Ideally, security personnel should be constantly interfacing with business unit personnel to ensure that they are involved in the external service provider selection process from the beginning. It is better to discover any security issues sooner rather than later. Once a contract is signed, it becomes much more difficult to change how you do business with an external provider.

   Risk: Without a thorough due diligence process that includes evaluating security, there is a risk that the company will choose a provider that will not adequately secure the company's data.

   Client Response:

   ---

10. *What is the financial condition of the provider?*

    Guidance: In the due diligence process, the financial condition of the provider is one of the most important areas, if not the most important area in

today's economy. If the provider is a publicly traded company, financial information is publicly available (on the Internet). When reviewing the financials, a number of factors should be considered, including:
- Amount of cash on hand
- Amount of debt
- Profit and loss statement trends
- Cash flows

In addition to the above items, the notes to the financial statements, which contain "other" financial information, should be reviewed. Any recent 8K statements should also be reviewed as these contain significant changes to the business. The specific criteria used in reviewing the financial data depend on the company and its tolerance for risk. At the minimum, the provider should have the financial means to stay in business for the duration of the contract. For providers that are not publicly traded, financial information may not be readily available and in these cases, you should talk to the provider as well as do some independent research. For example, if the company is being funded by VC (venture capital), you might be able to see some details on the VC firm's Web site. The importance of the financial condition cannot be overstated. There have been more than a few cases where providers have gone bankrupt or folded. If this were to happen, it would not only be a hassle operationally, there would also be issues relating to retrieving and securing the information on the provider's systems.

Risk: If the external provider is not financially sound, significant risks exist related to disruption of services and the security of information residing on the provider's systems.

Client Response:

---

11. *Does the external provider have any customer references? Do they provide service for companies similar to yours?*

Guidance: Customer references should be checked when looking at an external provider. These can provide great insight into the quality of service given by the external provider. Ideally, customer references from companies similar to the client's are very helpful. An external service provider who services similar companies might have more expertise and thus provide better service. In addition, there might be providers who specialize in customers who are in the same industry as the company's, in which case it might make sense to look at those providers also.

Risk: If the external provider cannot provide solid customer references, there is a risk that they are either not very good or they are just starting out and do not have an adequate level of expertise. This does not mean that providers without solid references should not be considered; it does mean that they should be reviewed thoroughly. Other qualities may make them an attractive choice.

Client Response:

12. *Does the external service provider have any security policies and procedures in place?*
    • Are there procedures that are documented and followed?
    • Are systems used for providing services hardened to the extent possible?

    Guidance: As with the company's own security policies, the provider should also have formal security policies, which are the foundation to their information security program. Ideally, the policies should be reviewed as part of the due diligence process. Whether or not the external service provider has them is an indication of how serious they are about security. With some external providers who are struggling financially, there might be a tendency to cut corners in some areas. Information security is one of those areas that companies will often cut because it typically does not have an obvious and direct link to revenue. In addition, you should determine whether the external service provider has documented procedures for critical processes such as backup and recovery, employee terminations, physical security, and other key processes. A lack of documented procedures could be an indication that these processes are not being performed consistently or not being done in a secure manner.

    Risk: If an external service provider does not have security policies and procedures in place, there is a risk that the provider does not have a sound information security program, resulting in an increased risk of security incidents associated with using the external service provider.

Client Response:

13. *What measures does the third-party provider have in place to physically secure its environment?*

    Guidance: Sometimes, there is a heavy focus on technical security, and physical security is not given much consideration. Remember that sometimes, the best way to gain unauthorized access to systems is to be able to physically have access to them. Physical access to the facilities should be tightly controlled so that only those who need access to do their jobs have access. Physical security for the provider's premises should be comparable to the company's own physical security requirements. For the equipment housing the critical information, strong physical security measures should be in place to protect customer machines and the data on them. This evaluation should be a part of the due diligence process. The physical security of the external service provider's facilities should be a key factor in determining which provider to select.

Risk: If the provider does not have good physical security, there is an increased risk of unauthorized access to their facilities and potentially the systems holding customer data. This can lead to a compromise of sensitive data or the disruption of operations.

Client Response:

---

14. *Does the third-party provider contract call for an independent audit to be performed periodically?*

Guidance: A provider, whether publicly traded or not, should have an audit done by a qualified independent party. An independent audit can validate some of the things learned in the due diligence process and provide some assurance that the provider has good security and controls. The audit can also validate the financial condition as represented by management. One of the audits that is useful is the SAS 70 review, which is sanctioned by the AICPA (American Institute of Certified Public Accountants) and is a review of the internal control environment of a service organization (a detailed discussion of the SAS 70 is included in Chapter 9). The SAS 70 is something that is done typically by certified public accounting (CPA) firms that have appropriately trained individuals and are licensed to provide this service. Besides the SAS 70, there are other standards in use such as the AICPA WebTrust and SysTrust standards, which are also independent audits, based on certain standards (these standards are readily available on the Internet). Besides these, there are several independent audits that can be done. Keep in mind that the key is that these audits must be independent.

Risk: Not applicable. There is no specific risk associated with whether or not an independent audit is done. However, there is significant value in having an independent opinion regarding the external provider's control and security environment.

Client Response:

---

15. *Is there a person or a group of people in the company who are in charge of managing the relationship with the third-party provider?*

    Guidance: Once there is a relationship with the provider, someone from the company should be in charge of managing the relationship, or at a minimum, be a single point of contact. This does not have to be a person for whom this is the sole responsibility. This person's role can vary from being a point of contact to someone with decision-making authority who can manage the relationship and ensure that the contract requirements are met. In addition, having this role in place creates a single point where all communication is funneled through and a mechanism for surfacing any issues in the relationship. The provider should also provide a single point of contact to help ensure proper communication.

    Risk: Without someone being a point of contact and facilitating good communication, there is a risk that the contract requirements, particularly from a security perspective, will not be met. In addition, issue resolution is also more difficult without a point person on both sides who knows what has to be done.

    Client Response:

    ---

16. *How does the external service provider, specifically application service providers (ASPs), secure the company's information on its computers and ensure that the company's information is not commingled with another company's information?*

    Guidance: At a technical level, the data of each company on the external provider's machines should be segregated. Depending on how the architecture is set up, a risk might exist that different companies' data could be commingled. As part of the security assessment, someone with the appropriate technical expertise should review the information flows and determine whether appropriate security measures are in place to protect the confidentiality of the company's information residing on the external service provider's computers and that data from different companies is not commingled.

    Risk: If data from different companies is commingled, there are two potential risks:
    - Other customers of the provider might have unauthorized access to company information.
    - The integrity of the company's data might not be maintained.

Client Response:

---

17. *Does the client's employee termination process address access to external service provider systems?*

    Guidance: Access to company-specific information on the provider's systems is normally granted to certain employees who require it to do their jobs. In many cases, the provider's systems are available through the Internet and access requires a simple user ID and password. The employee termination process should ensure that this access is removed. With these applications, a user can probably access the ASP and information by going directly to the provider's Web site and bypassing the company's network.

    Risk: If access to services by a third-party provider is not discontinued, there is a risk that a user will continue to have access to the company's information after being terminated. This is especially a problem if an employee goes to a competitor after terminating his or her relationship with the company.

Client Response:

---

18. *What steps has the provider taken to ensure the availability of the service? Is this reasonable based on the criticality of the service for the company?*

    Guidance: When asking this question, the company must first consider their tolerance for downtime, which is affected by a number of factors including revenue impact, loss of customers, cost, and whether any alternate procedures can be used in the event the technology is not available. This contract-related information regarding availability could be obtained from the people who initially negotiated the contract. Depending on what is being provided, availability can be a critical issue. For example, in an e-commerce environment, a site being down can mean lost revenues and lost customers — both of which are bad for the business. There are three key items to look for when reviewing availability:
    - Availability requirements related to the external service provider should be aligned with the needs of the business. Availability costs money, so the company should only ask for what is required.
    - Availability should be addressed in the contract or the SLA, and penalties should be attached to not meeting the availability requirement.
    - Specific steps should be taken by the provider to help ensure availability of service.

Risk: If availability requirements have not been well thought through and are not addressed in the contract with the external service provider, a risk exists of disruption of services with limited ability to hold the provider accountable. In addition, if availability is not addressed in the contract, the company has diminished ability to enforce reasonable levels of availability.

Client Response:

19. *Is the transport of information between the company and the third-party provider secure?*

Guidance: Besides protecting the information that is on the provider's machines, the information that is transmitted (if any) from the provider to the company should be secured in some way (e.g., encryption). If information is transmitted in clear text across the Internet, it can be intercepted. If this information contains sensitive information such as personally identifiable data or credit card information, the implications can be severe. The consequences could include legal troubles, reputation damage, and others. A technical person should review this to properly assess the transmission of information.

Risk: If the transmission of information is not secure, there is a risk that the confidentiality of the company's information in transit can be compromised.

Client Response:

20. *If the company's data resides on the external provider's systems, what backup strategy does the provider have?*

Guidance: This is a standard security measure that the provider should take. During the due diligence process, this issue should definitely be raised to understand how data is backed up and whether the measures taken are adequate based on the company's business requirements. Consideration should be given to operational as well as any regulatory requirements related to backups. In addition, all other data backup concerns, such as access control and off-site storage concerns should be addressed (see Backup and Recovery Questionnaire in the appendices for more details). These backup requirements should be addressed in the contract and be enforced. Although the company is ultimately accountable for the data being backed up, they are reliant on the external service provider to ensure backups are done properly.

Risk: If the company's data is not being backed up properly, a risk exists that in the event of any kind of disaster or other event requiring restoration of information, the company will not be able to recover critical data.

Client Response:

---

21. *Is there an incident response process in place whereby the external service provider can inform company personnel in the event there is an incident? Have escalation lists been established?*

Guidance: Incidents must be handled properly to minimize any resulting damage. There should be an incident handling process between the company and the provider. Roles and responsibilities should be clear, and escalation lists should be established. When asking this question, you should determine whether any incidents have occurred in the past, and if so, how the incident was handled. Incident handling is a critical item that should be discussed during the due diligence process. To further review the provider's incident handling process and determine whether it is appropriate, use the Incident Handling Questionnaire contained in Appendix J.

Risk: Without a formal incident handling process in place between the provider and the company, a risk exists that security incidents will not be handled properly. This can potentially have several negative consequences depending on the severity of the incident including:
- Negative publicity if communication with the press is not handled properly
- Slower recovery time from the incident if not handled in an organized fashion
- Loss of revenue, customers, etc.

Client Response:

---

22. *Does the third-party provider have a business continuity plan?*

Guidance: With some of the company's data and operations being handled by another company, what would be the impact to the company if the provider had a disaster? Some issues to be concerned about include:

- Is the provider's business continuity plan robust enough to allow the provider to be operational within a time frame that is acceptable to the company?
- Is the data adequately backed up so that data is not permanently lost?
- Has the business continuity plan been tested?
- Is the plan updated on a regular basis based on changes to the business?
- In the event of a disaster, what priority does the company have relative to other customers serviced by the external provider?

As a part of the assessment, you should review the provider's business continuity plan and determine whether the company's outsourced operations can be recovered in an acceptable time frame.

Risk: If the provider does not have an adequate business continuity plan, there is a risk of long-term disruption of key operations or loss of data.

Client Response:

---

23. *Is there a service level agreement between the company and the provider that specifies the specific services to be provided and the metrics against which it will be measured? Are there any remedies if the provider is not in compliance with the SLA? Some of the items to look for in a SLA include:*
- Site availability
- Reliability
- Quality of service
- Security

Guidance: A client is dependent on the external provider to provide a certain level of service in terms of availability, reliability, security, quality of service, and other factors. The SLA provides details about different aspects of the service including the scope of service, roles and responsibilities, performance metrics, and support. A SLA clearly defines the services being provided and metrics for the provider to meet. The metrics help ensure that the provider understands the level of service required and makes them accountable. When reviewing the metric, two key characteristics to look for include:
- *Metric measurement* — Ideally, the metric should be measured by some automated means, if possible. Automated measurements are more accurate and objective and as a result, less opportunity to dispute the metric exists. Manually generated measures are subject to human error and are not as accurate.
- *Penalties for not meeting the metric* — A metric is much more valuable if penalties are associated with it. Failing to meet the metrics should

result in some sort of financial penalty or some other appropriate penalty depending on the business.

Risk: Without a SLA and associated metrics, an increased risk exists that the appropriate level of service will not be given to the company under the contract, which could negatively impact the business process being supported by the relationship with the external service provider.

Client Response:

24. *Does the contract specifically address confidentiality requirements relative to the company's records?*

Guidance: External providers potentially have a significant amount of information about different clients and their customers, much of which is sensitive. For example, medical information not adequately protected could result in unauthorized access, resulting in potential legal and regulatory issues. In the security assessment, you should determine what information resides on the provider's computers and the related impact if the confidentiality of that information was breached (review Data Classification policy). Depending on the impact, a related provision in the contract might be justified. As with all contract-related matters, ensure that the contract has gone through a legal review.

Risk: If there is no provision in the contract regarding the provider's obligation to protect the confidentiality of information, there is a risk that the company has no basis for recourse against the provider if the confidentiality of the information is breached. Breach of confidentiality related to personal data can result in noncompliance with laws such as the Health Insurance Portability and Accountability Act (HIPAA) or the Gramm–Leach–Bliley Act (GLBA) or with regulatory requirements such as those of the Federal Trade Commission (FTC).

Client Response:

25. *Is access to the company's information limited to only those who need it?*

Guidance: The external provider should be able tell the client which personnel will have the ability to access the client's information. As with all other access, users should only have access to what they need to do their jobs. In addition, procedures should be in place to ensure that as employees from the external provider leave or change positions, access is adjusted as needed. This ties back to the provider's employee termination practices.

Risk: If personnel from the external service provider unnecessarily have access to the company's data, there is an increased risk of unauthorized access to sensitive data and exposure of sensitive information.

Client Response:

Appendix H

Physical Security

Before the electronic age, security was essentially physical security. Although new risks related to electronic security exist today, physical security is still a critical component of an information security program because it is the first line of defense for many companies. Weak physical security can negate many of the other information security measures a company might have in place. If someone can gain unauthorized physical access to company facilities, their chances of doing damage are increased significantly. Some aspects of physical security that should be considered include:

- Physical access to facilities
- Physical access to secure areas within facilities
- Physical access to computing resources (e.g., workstations, laptop computers)
- Physical access to paper records

Each of the areas above and others can be critical for a company depending on the specific risks they face. As with other information security measures, physical security should be based on the specific risks faced by the particular company.

Lack of physical security measures can have significant impacts including:

- Unauthorized access to critical computing resources, which can result in a compromise of sensitive information or malicious activity on critical systems
- Theft of computing resources
- Regulatory fines resulting from not providing adequate protection for sensitive information

ORGANIZATION/POLICY

1. Does the company have a physical security policy?

Guidance: A physical security policy is the foundation of a physical security program. It is the foundation for any physical security measures that are implemented. The policy should outline physical security requirements and high-level roles and responsibilities, which can be translated into specific physical security procedures. The roles and responsibilities can include those of individuals such as facilities personnel, whose job is physical security, as well as regular personnel, who might have some level of responsibility as it relates to physical security — e.g., personnel must ensure that their desks are clean when they leave at the end of the day. The policy should be updated to reflect changing business requirements and enforced via regular audits.

Risk: Without a physical security policy, there are no formal requirements for what is to be done to physically secure the company. As a result, personnel will not necessarily know what to do from a physical security perspective, and it will difficult to enforce good physical security practices at the company.

Client Response:

---

2. *Is someone or some group responsible for physical security of the facilities, e.g., a facilities group?*

Guidance: Someone should own the responsibility of physical security to ensure that accountability exists. Responsibility for physical security can vary and can include:
- Separate department with dedicated personnel
- Part of information technology (IT) security
- Part of facilities management

These groups' responsibilities should be formally documented in the physical security policy. In some cases, such as when the facility is in an office park or building setting, physical security might be handled by a third party that handles security for all companies in the facility. In these cases, someone from the company should be responsible for the relationship with the party providing physical security services. The company will still be responsible for some elements of physical security (e.g., inside offices, file cabinets). Whether internally or externally performed, responsibility for physical security should be clearly defined.

Risk: Without a clearly defined owner of physical security, there is a lack of accountability and a potential that physical security measures will not be implemented as intended by management.

Client Response:

---

3. *Is there any awareness training related to physical security?*

Guidance: To help ensure that physical security is effective, personnel must be made aware of its importance. Some mechanism should be in place to ensure that employees understand physical security and their role in achieving it. In addition to awareness, the policy and any procedures should also be readily accessible, for example on a company intranet. Depending on the organization, there are different ways to provide awareness training to employees including:
- As part of new-hire orientation
- General companywide security awareness training
- Department-level awareness training

Risk: Without an awareness program related to physical security, employees may not know the policy and its requirements and therefore may not follow them, particularly the requirements that pertain to them. Also, as with other security policies, it is difficult to enforce the policy if employees are not aware of it.

Client Response:

DETERMINE SCOPE AND CRITICALITY

4. *Have there been any physical security–related incidents? If so, how was the incident handled and what steps have been taken to prevent it from happening again?*

Guidance: Past incidents are an excellent source of information in a security assessment. The cause of the incident can provide a basis for findings as part of the security assessment. In addition, how the incident was handled can provide insight into the client's incident handling process. If a physical security incident occurred, you should try to quantify the damage and determine whether sensible cost-effective steps were taken to prevent the same thing from happening again.

Risk: Not applicable. This question is to gather information about past security incidents, which can potentially lead to a finding if the cause of the incident was not addressed.

Client Response:

---

5. *What business functions occur at the facility and what is the criticality of these functions?*

   Guidance: The purpose of this question is to gain an understanding of the different functions at the facility (or facilities). Have the client consider the operations that take place at each of the different facilities and their importance to the business. For example, one facility might house the data center, which serves all other facilities and is a critical facility. Another example is a location that is a satellite office with some desk space where some people occasionally work, which is not that important. With this question, you should have a sense for the importance of each facility and where to focus your efforts as it relates to assessing physical security. Based on what you learn, it might also be appropriate to visit a critical site to observe what physical security measures are in place.

   Risk: Not applicable. The purpose of this question is to gain a high-level understanding of what is happening at each location, its criticality, and how critical physical security is at each location.

   Client Response:

6. *How are security incidents handled? Is there an incident handling method or policy that is documented and is part of a security awareness program?*

   Guidance: Incident handling is something that all personnel should be knowledgeable about as any employee can potentially be involved in responding to an incident. In terms of incident handling, there should be clear roles and responsibilities as related to employee communications (should be done through a single point of contact), communication with law enforcement, and communication with the press. Personnel should know to whom to report a physical security incident. In addition, guidelines should exist to help personnel classify the incident in terms of severity. All of this should be documented in an incident handling policy. Incident handling is discussed in more detail in a separate, specific questionnaire (Apendix J).

   Risk: If incidents are not handled properly — i.e., in an organized and controlled manner, there is a risk of increased damage related to an incident.

   Client Response:

7. *What would be the impact to the business if personnel could not access the facility? What is the tolerable downtime?*

   Guidance: Access to some facilities can be critical. Consider the criticality of the operations at a given facility and the related interdependencies. For a manufacturing company, this could be a plant, an office where orders are taken and processed, or a distribution center from which orders are shipped. If any of these facilities were inaccessible, this could seriously impact revenue. On the other hand, a consulting company may not be heavily dependent on any facility if its core operations involve consultants working at client sites or from home. When determining the importance of accessibility to a site, think in terms of tolerable time — i.e., what is the tolerable time frame for which a site can remain inaccessible? When clients answer this question, they should understand that are cost implications associated with the tolerable downtime — e.g., there is difference in cost between four hours and eight hours of tolerable time of inaccessibility. Impact should be quantified to the extent possible (e.g., if a company cannot take orders for a day, potential loss of revenue can be estimated).

   Risk: Not applicable. The purpose of this question is to determine the impact to the business, which will help assess the risks associated with physical security.

   Client Response:

   ---

8. *What physical assets (e.g., computers, equipment, proprietary information) are in the facility and what is their value?*

   Guidance: The value of the physical assets within a facility is another piece of information to help establish the criticality of a facility. The risk associated with physical security at a given facility is largely dependent on the value of the items inside the facility. What is contained in the facilities will help determine the level of physical security required.

   Risk: Not applicable. The purpose of this question is to understand the value of items at each facility to help determine whether physical security measures are adequate.

   Client Response:

   ---

9. *Are any valuable paper documents in the facilities? If so, do electronic copies of the paper documents exist? What would be the impact to the business if the paper documents were either lost or destroyed?*

Guidance: Even with the increased use of technology, companies are still generating quite a bit of paper. There is a tendency to focus on securing electronic information rather than securing physical documents. Aside from the valuable and sensitive paper documents, employees are constantly printing e-mails and files that contain sensitive information. As a result, a slew of sensitive paper documents needs to be protected from unauthorized access. In doing this, the physical security of the facility where the document is stored is an important aspect to consider. For example, many executives are privy to some very sensitive information (e.g., company financial data, personnel records) that is in printed format. When performing an assessment, you should ensure that there are measures to protect both the confidentiality and availability of these paper documents. In regulated environments (health care — Health Insurance Portability and Accountability Act [HIPAA], financial services — Gramm–Leach–Bliley Act [GLBA], education — Family Educational Rights Privacy Act [FERPA]) where companies have certain obligations to protect personally identifiable information, safeguarding paper documents is mandated and a failure to comply can result in financial penalties.

Risk: Not applicable. The purpose of this question is to further understand the criticality and risk associated with physical security.

Client Response:

---

10. *For any sensitive physical documents on site:*
    - How are they protected?
    - What physical access measures have been taken to prevent unauthorized access to paper documents?
    - Are sensitive paper documents shredded before they are thrown away?
    - What would the impact be to the company if unauthorized individuals accessed these documents?

Guidance: As stated previously, paper documents are often overlooked when talking about security. Many people have sensitive paper documents in their possession and do not adequately protect them. If you think about some of the traditional departments and the paper documents in their possession, you will realize that significant risks exist if these documents are lost or destroyed or if their confidentiality is compromised. Examples of departments and sensitive paper documents include:
    - *Finance:* Financial data — For publicly traded companies, financial data should be accessed on a need-to-know basis.

      – **Risk:** Legal exposure if financial data is disclosed in an unauthorized manner prior to being released to the public

- *Human Resources:* Employee salary data and personnel folders.
  - **Risk:** This is highly sensitive information, which includes such things as salary data and sensitive personnel information. There is a legal exposure and potentially, an employee relations nightmare if the confidentiality of this information is compromised.

- *Executive Management:* Sensitive printed electronic mail communications.
  - **Risk:** Many people print electronic mail instead of reading it on their personal computers. Because some of the information is of a very sensitive nature, there is tremendous risk if the wrong people see the information. Although many executives do not use electronic mail for highly confidential or sensitive communications, this issue is worth investigating.

Risk: The risks related to securing sensitive physical documents include:
- Breach of confidentiality of information
- Impact related to having to recreate the information if it is lost or destroyed

---

Client Response:

ACCESS TO PREMISES

11. *What is the process for an employee who needs to gain physical access to facilities? Is physical access restricted to only those individuals who require it?*

Guidance: Employees are generally given physical access to facilities when they first join as part of the new hire process. As responsibilities change, it is possible that the facilities they access may change (this is a moot point in smaller companies where there is only one building). There should be a formal process for providing access to employees, which should include approval from appropriate management and documented business justification for access. In some cases, it may also be appropriate to limit access within a facility depending on the business requirements. For example, a given facility might have general office space and a network operations center that houses systems that support critical operations for the company. In this case, only a small group of employees would have access to the operations center, but all employees would have access to the office space. For any physical access to facilities, there should be a documented process with the appropriate approvals to ensure that access is given only a "need to have" basis.

Risk: Without a formal process for granting physical access to ensure that physical access is granted on a "need to have" basis, persons might gain unauthorized access to facilities. This could lead to theft of information and assets or other malicious activity.

Client Response:

---

12. *How is physical access to facilities controlled for employees, contractors, visitors, etc? What physical security measures exist at the perimeter or when entering the facilities?*

    Guidance: Depending on the environment, the method for gaining physical access can vary. Some of the methods you might see include:
    - Manned desk where someone is checking IDs
    - Visitors required to log in, stating their purpose for the visit and who they are there to see
    - Turnstiles where employees must swipe an ID card to enter the facilities
    - Biometric authentication (e.g., fingerprints used to gain access to a facility)

    You may also see facilities where no controls exist to screen people entering a facility, which is definitely a cause for concern. Based on the importance of the facility, an appropriate level of control for allowing physical access to facilities should exist. Some facilities might justify more stringent controls, but others will require less. You should at least see some type of authentication, whether it is manual (e.g., manned desk) or automated (e.g., scanning badges).

    Risk: If the process for gaining access to physical facilities is not controlled, there is a risk of individuals having unauthorized physical access to facilities, which could lead to theft of information and assets or other malicious activity.

Client Response:

---

13.   *Is there a formal, documented process for granting access for contractors?*

Guidance: Similar to the situation with regular employees, a formal, almost identical process should exist for granting access to contractors — i.e., access should be given on a "need to have" basis with approval from appropriate management and business justification. Some other aspects to consider with contractors include:
- Has the contractor been appropriately screened?
- Access should be given only for the period of time that contractors are working. If they are long term, consider automatically expiring access (e.g., every six months) and then renewing access.

Risk: If physical access to facilities for contractors is not properly controlled, there is a risk of individuals having unauthorized access to physical facilities, which could lead to theft of information and assets or other malicious activity.

Client Response:

14.   *When physically working at a site, do people in the facility (employees, contractors, and visitors) display a badge or something else that identifies them at all times?*

Guidance: Having people display identification is effective, especially in large environments with many employees, where people do not know everyone. It is another layer of security in the event someone gains unauthorized physical access to a facility. For employees and some contractors, badges can be given as part of a new hire orientation process. If badges are used, employees should be made aware that anyone without a badge is potentially not authorized. As part of awareness training, employees should bring it to management's attention if they see someone without any kind of identification. If individuals lose their badges, they should wear temporary ones issued by the appropriate group (e.g., security, facilities).

Risk: Requiring employees to display identification badges helps reduce the risk of individuals gaining unauthorized physical access to a facility.

Client Response:

15. Are visitors required to sign in?
- Are visitors required to have temporary badges that are displayed when in the facility?
- Are visitors required to be escorted by authorized personnel while in the facility?

Guidance: Visitors represent a significant risk to a company if not handled properly. They often just walk right into some facilities without being questioned. A visitor like this with malicious intent can cause significant damage to a company. Ideally, visitors should be required to wear some visible identification (such as a badge) and be escorted by authorized personnel. Visitors should have identification and also be required to sign in to a logbook where they document time in and out, the person they are there to see, and the purpose of their visit. The guard or receptionist who is the first person that a visitor sees when entering the facility should enforce these rules. Being able to "trick" or "finesse" the guard or receptionist into giving physical access is a social engineering technique that can be used to gain unauthorized access to facilities. On this topic, it is worth discussing the process of visitors gaining access, In addition, if badges are used, employees should be aware that everyone in the facility should have some form of identification at all times.

Risk: If visitors are not required to present identification, have a legitimate purpose for their visit, and have some specific person in the company that they are there to see, there is a risk that visitors can gain unauthorized access to facilities and the company's systems and cause damage.

Client Response:

---

16. Does the termination process include discontinuing physical access to company facilities?
- Are identification badges returned?
- If electronic access mechanisms are in place, is terminated employees' access removed?
- Are names of terminated employees removed from the appropriate lists?
- Are terminations proactively communicated to guards so they know about them?

Guidance: Terminated employees represent a very significant risk to companies — especially when the termination involves a disgruntled employee.

Along with revoking systems access, revoking physical access is critical in reducing the risk associated with terminated employees. There should be a termination checklist or some other mechanism to ensure that physical access is revoked and any identification badges are taken back. In addition, as another layer of security, facility security personnel should be made aware that an employee has been terminated.

Risk: If the termination process does not address physical access, a risk exists that terminated employees can continue to have physical access to facilities and gain unauthorized access to company resources. Because of terminated employees' knowledge of the operations of a company, they can use this physical access to do significant damage to the company.

Client Response:

17. *Does a current list of individuals who are authorized to physically access the facilities exist? Is this list periodically reviewed and purged so that any inactive or terminated personnel's access is removed?*

Guidance: Purging is a "catch-all" method of ensuring that only authorized individuals have physical access to facilities. One easy way of purging is to give the managers in a given facility the list of employees who have physical access. It is normally a manager's responsibility to know the people he or she manages and whether or not they should have access to a particular physical site (or a particular area, such as a data center). The value of the purging process is that if access is not removed during the termination process or when an employee changes responsibilities (and no longer needs access to a facility), the purging process will catch it and act as a mitigating control. With larger facilities, purging is more relevant. The frequency of purging depends on the number of employees, the amount of turnover, and how well the process of updating physical access is working — e.g., in larger environments with significant turnover, purging is more critical than in small environments and those with less turnover.

Risk: Without a purging process, an increased risk of unauthorized physical access to facilities exists.

Client Response:

18. *If a data center is on the premises, what additional physical access controls are employed?*

Guidance: Aside from physical access to a building, there should be some additional physical access controls for accessing the data center. Because data centers normally house critical systems that run the business, the access should be strictly limited to personnel who administer those systems. Some additional controls include having the area manned by a guard or having some type of card access where only those individuals who need access actually have it. If there is guard-controlled access to these rooms, look for weaknesses related to social engineering attacks. The guards should have strict guidelines about who is allowed access to the data center room.

Risk: Without strict physical access control over the data center, an increased risk exists of unauthorized access to critical machines that run the business, which if compromised, can cause a significant interruption to the business or breach of confidentiality related to critical data.

Client Response:

PHYSICAL SECURITY OF FACILITIES OR DATA CENTER

19. *Are fire doors periodically tested to ensure the alarm works properly?*

Guidance: Fire doors represent an entry point into the facilities and should be checked on a regular basis. Fire doors are critical in the event of a fire and also represent a security risk because they are an entry point. The alarm capability of fire doors should be checked on a regular basis in case there is a fire and to help prevent unauthorized access to facilities through these doors.

Risk: If fire doors are not tested properly, two risks exist:
- Fire doors may not work properly in the event of a fire by not sounding the alarm when opened.
- Unauthorized individuals can gain access to facilities without anyone noticing and can cause damage, steal, or do something to disrupt operations.

Client Response:

20. *What provisions are in place to deal with a fire?*
    - Are fire extinguishers properly located where personnel can access them?
    - Are fire protection or suppression systems tested on a regular basis?
    - Is there any awareness training for personnel regarding what to do in the event of a fire?

Guidance: Depending on the facilities, appropriate precautions should be taken so that personnel can react appropriately in the event of a fire. The requirements discussed in this question are minimum requirements for any facility. The level of precautions will vary depending on the facility and how critical it is. Fire can cause significant damage to a facility and a significant interruption to the business. Physical items such as alarms, fire extinguishers, and fire suppression systems should be in good working order. In addition, personnel should be aware of what should be done in the event of a fire.

Risk: If a fire is not handled properly, it can cause a safety risk for personnel and a risk of disruption to the business.

Client Response:

21. *If a data center exists in the facility, does it have proper environmental controls?*
    - Air conditioning
    - Uninterrupted power supplies as required
    - Other appropriate controls

Guidance: Data centers need to have certain environmental controls in place to function properly. For companies with a data center, this center is a critical part of the business and should be properly safeguarded. The specific controls will vary by the data center, and the list above is only a start. For detailed analysis of the environmental controls, you will need to learn specifics about the data center you are examining. Depending on the facility, other controls might be appropriate.

Risk: If data centers do not have the appropriate environmental controls, a risk exists of physical damage to critical machines, which can ultimately cause a disruption in the business or the loss of data.

Client Response:

22. *Are any physical security controls (such as closed-circuit television) in place to monitor what is happening in the data center if a 24/7 guard presence is not possible?*

Guidance: Depending on the size and location of the data center, it might not be possible to have people physically man the area. Based on the physical security measures in place and the associated risks, it might be appropriate to have monitoring mechanisms such as closed-circuit television to monitor what is happening in the data center. Closed-circuit television might also be appropriate if the company wants the ability to investigate in the event of a security incident.

Risk: Without some form of security monitoring during off hours, a risk exists of unauthorized access to critical machines which, if compromised, can cause a significant disruption to the business, loss of data, etc.

Client Response:

EQUIPMENT PROTECTION

23. *How are workstations secured?*

Guidance: Workstations are a valuable physical asset for companies. In today's environment, one item that has become popular for thieves is flat panel monitors because of the ease with which they can be taken. Besides the value of the assets, companies also have users who store valuable or sensitive information on their workstations (which they should not do) to the point where the information stored locally on the workstation is more valuable than the workstation itself. If this is the case, the company should consider additional controls such as file encryption, power-on passwords, and backing up the local drives on those computers. Ideally, users should be educated to store important information on the network, if possible. In addition, certain critical workstations as deemed necessary should be physically secured. These workstations might house single-user licenses for specialty applications.

Risk: If workstations are not properly secured, risks exist of theft and of critical information being exposed to unauthorized individuals.

Client Response:

24. *Do users have laptops and if so, how are they secured when they are mobile?*
    - Do users secure their laptops when unattended?
    - Are laptops physically secured with some type of lock?
    - Are laptop users provided any awareness training on securing their laptops and the information on them?
    - Do laptop users encrypt the data on their computer in case the computer is stolen?
    - Do laptop users utilize the power-on password functionality on their laptops?

    Guidance: A significant number of people today travel or work from home and access the company's network remotely. The value of the laptops is often significantly less than the value of the information contained in them. Laptop users should have the equipment to secure laptops and be provided awareness training on securing their machines. Some security measures to consider include encrypting data on the laptop and using power-on passwords, which can significantly reduce the impact in the event the laptop is stolen or lost. When reviewing this question, also consider whether any regulatory requirements exist related to securing information on laptops or whether any of the data residing on the laptop would be subject to regulatory requirements — e.g., personally identifiable information would be subject to the Health Insurance Portability and Accountability Act (HIPAA) or the Gramm–Leach–Bliley Act (GLBA).

    Risk: If laptop computers are not properly secured, a risk exists that the computers will be stolen and confidential information will be lost or exposed to unauthorized individuals.

    Client Response:

25. *What is the impact to the business if a laptop is stolen and the information on it is compromised?*
    - Do mobile users store critical information on the network, locally on the hard drive, or both?
    - If mobile users are storing information on their laptops, is it encrypted or secured some other way?

    Guidance: The level of security applied to laptops is largely a function of what would happen if the laptop was stolen or lost. One of the questions above alludes to whether users store information on the company network or on their laptops. Although it is good practice to not store on the laptop if you do not have to, the majority of users probably store significant amounts of information on their laptops because they are often on the road or away from the office. That being said, the impact to the business if a laptop is stolen can be significant. For example, a salesperson might have sensitive client information, internal pricing data, or proprietary company information, which would have a significant impact if lost or stolen. Impact should be thought of in terms of both confidentiality and availability.

- *Confidentiality* — What is the impact if an unauthorized person gains access to sensitive information? Are there any legal ramifications or potential damage to the reputation of the company?
- *Availability* — If the information on the laptop was not backed up to the company network or on some other media, what is the impact related to recreating the information?

Risk: Not applicable. The purpose of this question is to determine the impact if a laptop computer is lost or stolen.

Client Response:

CLEAN DESK AND SCREEN

26. *Does the company have a clean desk policy and is it followed and enforced? Does any security awareness training address a clean desk policy?*

Guidance: A clean desk policy is something that should be ingrained in companies. Many employees regularly work with sensitive documents, which if just left out in the open on desks, can present a significant risk. For example, human resources personnel often deal with sensitive employee-related matters such as salaries and disciplinary issues. If documents containing this information are left unattended, unauthorized persons such as other employees or facilities maintenance people can access this information. Similar scenarios are possible in other key areas such as finance, operations, and executive management. Companies have an obligation to maintain the confidentiality of this information using a reasonable effort. If they do not, they are exposed to potential embarrassment, legal trouble, etc. A clean desk policy that is enforced can go a long way in reducing this risk.

Risk: Without a clean desk policy, a risk exists of confidential information being exposed to unauthorized individuals, embarrassment for the company, and potential legal troubles.

Client Response:

27. *When unattended, are computers protected with screen saver passwords or other measures? Does any security awareness training address locking down computers and using screen saver passwords?*

Guidance: Using screen saver passwords when computers are left unattended is an easy way to reduce the risk of unauthorized individuals viewing confidential information. Ideally, this should be a part of an overall security awareness program and be something that everyone does. Periodic enforcement of the use of screen saver passwords is also very helpful.

Risk: Without screen saver passwords, there is an increased risk of confidential information being exposed to unauthorizcd individuals.

Client Response:

28. *If sensitive information is printed, is there a process to ensure that these documents are cleared from the printer immediately?*

Guidance: It is very common for personnel to send documents to print and forget to pick them up because something came up. The documents can be taken or just read by any individuals including other employees within a company or even by after hours facilities maintenance personnel. If the documents contain sensitive information, this can be a problem. In some cases, there may be certain printers where this is a more significant issue; some examples include printers where:
- Financial data is printed.
- Executives print documents.
- Human resources prints employee-related information.

The burden of ensuring that documents are picked up from printers falls on the users and this should be incorporated in an awareness agenda. This is also something that can be in a policy, thereby making individual employees accountable for what they print.

Risk: If documents are not picked up from printers in a prompt fashion, a risk of exposure of sensitive or confidential information exists.

Client Response:

Appendix I

Employee Termination

The process of employee[1] termination presents a significant risk to companies primarily because of the damage that a disgruntled employee can potentially do. Stories regularly appear in the media of former employees wreaking havoc on a company by gaining access to the company's network or facilities after they have been terminated. Termination is really part of overall user ID administration, but it has been addressed separately because of the risks associated with not handling termination properly. Some of the main risks associated with weak termination practices include:

- Unauthorized individuals gaining access to the company facilities and information technology (IT) resources
- Existing employees using access that has not been terminated to perform malicious activity
- Disgruntled IT employees gaining access to the company network and causing some type of network outage

The main reason why terminated employees pose such a risk is that many companies do not have a sound process for ensuring that terminated employees' access to systems and physical facilities is removed and all of their outstanding assets are returned. There is often a lack of communication between key departments such as IT, human resources (HR), and business unit personnel when it comes to terminations and as a result, they are not performed properly. In addition, many companies do not have a person or department that "owns" the termination process — i.e., someone who is responsible for ensuring that terminations are handled properly. A strong method for termination requires a structured process that is clear and easy to follow and good communications between the various departments. The key groups that must be involved and their high-level responsibilities include:

- *Department management* — first ones to know about the termination
- *Human resources* — in charge of terminating benefits and fulfilling other employment-related requirements
- *Payroll* — in charge of making the final payment settlement and taking the terminated employee off the payroll
- *Facilities* — in charge of ensuring that physical access is revoked
- *Information technology* — in charge of revoking all access to company systems

QUESTIONS

1. *Do a formal policy and procedure for employee termination exist? Are the policy and procedure communicated and readily accessible?*

   Guidance: A formal policy is critical because it sets the high-level requirements for terminations by which procedures can then be developed. A formal policy also allows enforcement of good termination practices. Some key elements that should be contained in the termination policy include:
   - Roles and responsibilities
   - Involvement of key departments — HR, IT, etc.
   - Compliance and audit requirements

   The policy should be communicated to certain employees, including department managers, IT, HR, and others as appropriate. The policy should be easily accessible so employees can refer to it as needed. One way to accomplish this is to post it on the employee intranet if one is available.

   Risk: Without a formal policy for terminations, the risks include:
   - Difficulty in enforcing good termination processes
   - Terminations not being done properly
   - Lack of ownership of the termination process

   Client Response:

   ---

2. *Is there a documented procedure for terminations with clearly defined roles and responsibilities? Is there a form or checklist that is used to help facilitate the termination process?*

   Guidance: There should be a documented procedure for terminations, with clear roles and responsibilities, and a step-by-step process explaining what to do in the event of a termination. Everyone involved, including managers, human resources, and IT, should know exactly what they are responsible for in the termination process. In addition, someone should own the responsibility of ensuring that the entire process has been completed. Without this overall ownership, there is a chance that the process will not be completely done. One of the reasons why terminations are not always handled properly is that everyone thinks someone else is responsible. Some key responsibilities that should be addressed in the process and have clearly defined owners include:
   - Collecting any assets that the employee has—e.g., laptop computer, personal digital assistant (PDA)
   - Collecting any identifications — e.g., badges to gain access
   - Revoking all access — e.g., network, application, and remote access as well as physical access

- Collecting any company credit cards
- Terminating payroll

Having this process documented will help ensure that personnel are doing the process consistently and will provide a means to hold them account-able. To help facilitate the termination process, a checklist that contains specific tasks that should be performed when a termination occurs is help-ful. The checklist also provides an audit trail of the termination process.

Risk: If there is no documented process, there is a risk that the termination process will not be performed consistently or properly. In addition, with-out clearly defined roles and responsibilities, it is difficult to hold individ-uals accountable.

Client Response:

---

3. *How much turnover does the company experience? What is the turnover rate relative to the total employee population?*

Guidance: This is an open-ended question to gain an understanding of how critical the termination process is. A documented and enforced termi-nation process is very important in larger environments where there is po-tential for significant turnover. In such environments, where many people do not know most of the people working for the company, a formal policy and procedure are critical in ensuring that terminations are processed con-sistently. The policy and procedure along with enforcement help ensure that terminations do not fall below the "radar screen." In smaller environ-ments, the termination process is more manageable because everyone knows everyone and the turnover in many cases is lower than in larger en-vironments. Although it might not be critical to have a formal policy and procedure in smaller environments, it is still a good idea considering the potential risks associated with terminations. Also, once a small environ-ment becomes a large environment, it is more difficult to implement a new policy or procedure. Therefore, it is easier to ingrain certain processes such as terminations.

Risk: Not applicable. The purpose of this question is to understand the sig-nificance of the termination process within the company.

Client Response:

---

4. *Has there ever been a security incident resulting from a terminated employee who was somehow able to gain physical or system access to the company after being terminated? How was it handled?*

    Guidance: Past security incidents related to terminations are a good indication of how good the current process is. If a security incident occurred, you should review how the termination process was performed (or not performed), what actions were taken in reacting to the incident, and what the resulting damage was. In addition, you should also discuss what changes were made to prevent that type of security incident from happening again.

    Risk: Not applicable. The purpose of this question is to determine whether any security incidents related to terminations have occurred. Some findings may result from this discussion if no steps have been taken to prevent this type of an incident from happening again.

    Client Response:

    ---

5. *To facilitate the return of any outstanding company assets possessed by employees when they are terminated, is there an inventory of what company assets the employee has?*

    Guidance: Employees, particularly people who are on the road, will normally have various pieces of company-owned equipment such as laptop computers or PDAs, as well as company credit cards. To ensure that everything is returned, there should be a centralized repository (which a limited number of people have access to) where assets given to employees are inventoried. This inventory can be used in the termination process to help ensure that everything that was given to the employee has been returned. In the event that this documented inventory does not exist, there is a heavy reliance on the employee's manager to know what assets an employee has.

    Risk: If company assets given to employees are not properly recorded, a risk exists that not all assets will be returned when an employee is terminated.

    Client Response:

    ---

6. *If a terminated employee had a job function involving administrator access to critical components of the IT infrastructure or critical applications (assuming that a single account was shared by multiple individuals), would the password be promptly changed after termination?*

Guidance: If the terminated employee had administrator-level access to key components of the IT infrastructure, such as routers, firewalls, or key servers, where a single account was used by all administrators, the termination process should address the changing of these passwords. If the individual had his or her own access, this access should be revoked. If the passwords are not changed, the terminated employee can potentially use that account to do significant damage because of the access that an administrator has and his or her knowledge of the systems. As a best practice, every administrator should have his or her own account for accountability purposes and when an employee leaves, that account should be either terminated or disabled.

Risk: If shared administrator account passwords are not promptly changed when an employee is terminated, a risk exists that the terminated employee can gain unauthorized access and do damage to the company's IT systems.

Client Response:

7. *If a terminated employee dealt with third-party business partners — i.e., business-to-business partners, is there a process to ensure that the business partner is informed? If the terminated employee had access to any business-to-business applications, is that access promptly revoked?*

Guidance: This question is very relevant for companies who are engaged in business-to-business relationships where companies have a view into a business partner's systems for certain functions. A perfect example is where businesses have certain parts of their inventory automatically replenished by vendors who have the ability to go into the business partners' systems via the Web and manage certain portions of their inventory. The problem scenario is if the terminated employee goes to work for a competitor. If the access is not removed, the terminated employee can still potentially access the same information while with a competitor, including information of a sensitive nature (e.g., pricing). For companies engaging in business-to-business activities, this is a major issue as they try to ensure that access is given only to employees that require it.

Risk: If a terminated employee's access to business-to-business applications is not immediately revoked, a risk exists of exposure of confidential data and damage to the relationship between business partners.

Client Response:

8. *If the terminated employee had access to specific applications aside from the standard business applications (e.g., word processing, spreadsheet), are those application owners informed on a timely basis so that the application access can be removed?*

Guidance: Some clients will say that not revoking application-level access is not a major risk as long as access to the network has been revoked because you need network access to get to the application. Although this might have some merit, there are ways to gain unauthorized access to the network. In the case of terminated employees who are technically savvy, we are dealing with insiders who know the network and can potentially gain access because of their knowledge. If they gain access to the network, they can access the applications and cause damage. Depending on what application they access, the damage can be enormous. For example, if they can access order entry systems, fictitious orders can be placed or worse yet, orders can be deleted. If the terminated employee was from HR, that person could potentially gain access to sensitive personnel information. The damage to a company can be significant. Revoking the application access might appear unnecessary, but it is another layer of security that is valuable. Ideally, application access should be specifically addressed in the termination process.

Risk: If a terminated employee's application access is not revoked, a risk exists that the former employee may gain unauthorized access to the application or that some other employee might use the terminated employee's access to access applications and potentially cause damage.

Client Response:

---

9. *Are network access, application access, and facility access lists periodically reviewed and purged to help ensure that terminated users' access has been removed at both the network and application levels?*

Guidance: Periodic review of access lists for the network and key applications is another layer of security that helps ensure that terminated personnel's access has been removed. If an oversight occurred and a terminated employee's access was not revoked, this process should catch such a case. Department heads or application owners should review these access lists to determine whether any access should be removed and ensure that only those who require access have it. The frequency of the process depends on the level of risk associated with the terminations.

Risk: Periodic reviews and purging of access lists reduce the risk of terminated employees having access to the company network, applications, and facilities.

Client Response:

---

10. *Are there any special procedures for terminating disgruntled employees (particularly IT employees) who might pose a threat once terminated — e.g., expediting the communication process of informing the different departments involved?*

Guidance: Disgruntled employees pose a significant threat because they have knowledge of the company and its systems and processes, as well as the motivation to cause damage. Unlike hackers, who probably know very little about a company (from an internal perspective) when they are hacking, a disgruntled employee has intimate knowledge of the company and how things work, which can be used to cause significant damage. IT employees in particular can sabotage systems or leave back doors that can be used later to access the system. Other employees who are disgruntled can potentially destroy information or steal proprietary information. At the discretion of the appropriate manager, disgruntled employees should be handled carefully. With disgruntled employees, the IT department should be involved early in the process. Ideally, system access should be removed before employees even know that they are terminated. Extra care should be given to ensure that all access the terminated employee had is revoked (both system access and physical access). These special procedures require close cooperation between the different departments.

Risk: If a disgruntled employee still has system or physical access to the company after termination, the former employee can use that access to cause significant damage to the company.

Client Response:

---

11. *Are all physical access codes to buildings previously known to the employee changed when an employee is terminated?*

Guidance: Some companies have facilities where physical access is gained by entering a code on a keypad. These keypads may also be used to physically access sensitive areas like the data center. Because everyone uses the same code with these devices, it should be changed when an employee is terminated to prevent terminated employees from using the known code to physically access facilities. A mitigating control and best practice is to periodically change access codes regardless of whether or not terminations have occurred.

Risk: If access codes of facilities are not changed after an employee is terminated, a risk exists that the former employee will gain unauthorized physical access to the facilities.

Client Response:

NOTE

1. For this questionnaire, the term "employees" refers to both employees and contractors.

Appendix J

Incident Handling

Incident handling is the process that should be followed in the event of a security incident. Having an organized and efficient method of reacting to an incident will help minimize its impact and facilitate its investigation. The security breach can involve virtually any aspect of the company and can include:

- Information technology–related incidents
- Physical security–related incidents

Security breaches can vary in severity, with some having no immediate business impact and others resulting in major outages of critical services. Some incidents might require involvement of law enforcement or interaction with the press. As the severity of the incident increases, companies must pay attention to such things as ensuring that evidence is properly handled and that communication with the press comes from a central source within the company. Without an organized and defined way of handling incidents, the response can be as damaging as the incident itself.

This checklist will assess the client's incident handling process. The questions will go through the key phases of incident handling including the following:

- Classification of the incident
- Escalation
- Containment and eradication
- Recovery and post-incident analysis
- Communications with different parties — e.g., employees, press
- Involvement of law enforcement

GENERAL

1. *Is there a documented incident handling policy in place? Is the policy easily accessible for all employees?*

   Guidance: The incident handling policy outlines the requirements, communicates a consistent message of how an incident should be handled, and provides a basis for enforcement of good incident handling practices. New employees should made aware of this policy of as part of an initial orientation. Incident handling should also be a part of a security awareness program. In addition, the policy should be easily accessible to all employees so they can refer to it as necessary (for example, on a company intranet site).

Risk: Without a documented policy, employees will potentially not know what to do in the event of a security incident. They may not follow a structured and consistent approach to incident handling. A risk exists that security incidents will not be handled properly, which can result in a range of consequences, as discussed later in this questionnaire. In addition, if no policy exists, there is no basis for enforcing the proper actions that should be taken when there is an incident.

Client Response:

---

2. *Does the organization provide any awareness training for incident handling? Would the typical user know what to do in the event of an incident? Do personnel understand that they should report a security incident or security weakness as soon as possible to the appropriate individuals?*

Guidance: Awareness training is important considering that personnel need to react quickly if there is an incident. Employees need to have a good idea of what steps to take in the event of an incident. Note that all personnel do not have to go through the same level of awareness training. The majority of personnel need to know how to report an incident and then essentially what they should not do, e.g., speak with the press, tamper with evidence. Other groups, such as managers, executives, and any other individuals identified to have a more significant role in an incident, should go through more detailed awareness training, which discusses all facets of incident handling. Ideally, incident handling should be taught as part of an orientation program for new hires. Existing employees should receive appropriate refreshers periodically (e.g., annually, every two years) depending on changes to the business and employee turnover.

Risk: Without awareness training, personnel may not know what to do in the event of an incident. In the event of an incident, there can be several negative consequences including:
- Evidence being corrupted
- Inappropriate communication with law enforcement or the press
- Increased time in recovering from the incident

Client Response:

---

3. *Does the incident handling policy document specific roles and responsibilities in reacting to a security incident?*

Guidance: Depending on the severity of the incident, the situation can become chaotic. Clear roles and responsibilities enhance a company's ability to react in the event of an incident because personnel know what they need to do. This assumes that personnel have been given the appropriate awareness training. Some of the key responsibilities are handling the evidence, communications, reporting, and a single point of contact who is overseeing all aspects of the incident handling process.

Risk: Without clear roles and responsibilities, a risk exists that the response to an incident will be disorganized and inappropriate — e.g., mishandled evidence, inappropriate communications with the press or law enforcement.

Client Response:

CLASSIFYING AN INCIDENT

4. *If an incident handling policy is in place, does it provide guidance for classifying the incident?*

Guidance: Once the incident is reported, the first step is classifying the incident. The classification is critical because it will dictate what actions need to be taken. If clients do not have a classification scheme, one should be developed in collaboration with employees from key departments. As a security practitioner conducting the security assessment, you can offer a standard framework that can be used as a starting point in developing a classification system. When deciding on classification, clients should think in terms of severity, which is how the incident impacts the company. Questions to guide the client in this process include:
- Does the incident affect the company's ability to perform its core operations — i.e., does the incident affect core systems or processes?
- Will law enforcement need to become involved?
- Can any potential bad press result from the incident?
- Can the incident have legal or regulatory ramifications?

Below are some examples of different severity levels that can be used as a starting point in defining a classification system. This example is meant to generate discussion leading to a classification system tailored for the company's environment.

- Severity 1 — High priority
  - Systems supporting core operations are affected, resulting in core operations being down for an extended period; no reasonable workarounds exist.
  - Incident results in a majority of people in the company not being able to do their jobs for an extended period.
  - Investigators will be called in to examine evidence on affected systems, so care must be taken to preserve it.
  - A system with critical or sensitive data (e.g., research and development [R&D] information, sensitive financial data) was compromised.
  - The incident results in negative publicity — e.g., credit card numbers being stolen.
- Severity 2 — Medium priority
  - Systems supporting core operations are affected, resulting in core operations being down for an extended period; reasonable workarounds can be used.
  - Support or back office operations (e.g., accounting, finance, human resources) are not functional for an extended period.
  - A specific department that does not perform core business functions is not functional for an extended period.
  - Minor theft of equipment has occurred.
  - A noncritical system was compromised.
- Severity 3 — Low priority
  - The incident has no immediate business impact.
  - A small number of individuals are affected.
  - The incident can be dealt with easily.

Risk: Without a classification system, there is no consistent way to prioritize and react to security incidents. The risk is that the company might do too much or too little when reacting.

Client Response:

REPORTING AN INCIDENT

5. *Do personnel know to whom to report an incident once they become aware of one?*

Guidance: This is the initial part of the process of handling a security incident. Typically, personnel should report security incidents to either their direct manager or some other designated person such as a security officer, as documented in the incident handling process. It is important to note that the process should be role driven and not people driven (this is true for any procedure developed) — i.e., if people are referenced in the procedure, the procedure will require updates if that person leaves the company or changes positions. Ideally, companies should have adequate backups in these roles.

Risk: If personnel do not know whom they should go to when reporting an incident, a risk exists that the incident will be reported too late, thereby increasing its potential impact.

Client Response:

---

6. *Are there specific senior level positions designated with the authority to involve law enforcement if necessary and deal with the press?*

Guidance: Dealing with law enforcement or the press can be sensitive and should be handled by qualified individuals. All personnel should understand that there is a point of contact to deal with law enforcement and the press, as there will be cases where either law enforcement or the press will approach general personnel. As part of the awareness training, general personnel should be taught how to deal with these groups. Typically, general personnel should refer them to the appropriate contacts inside the company. The key thing to remember is that personnel are speaking on behalf of the company and it is important that a consistent message be communicated. Therefore, any substantive communication should come from a central source.

Risk: Without a controlled method of communication, inconsistent and potentially incorrect statements can be given to the public or law enforcement, which could result in embarrassment or damage to the reputation of the company.

Client Response:

---

7. *Once an incident occurs, is there a person who is responsible for coordinating the appropriate resources to investigate the incident?*

Guidance: This question speaks to the core process of handling an incident. One effective method of handling the aftermath of a severe security incident is to have a specific role in charge of the response effort. The person in this role should have a good knowledge of the company and be able to review the incident to determine the classification and determine who should be brought in as part of the response effort. This person can be thought of as the "single point of contact" for the incident and is responsible for ensuring that the incident is addressed appropriately. A Security Officer is a good choice for this role, as this person would typically have the knowledge of the company and have relationships with key groups who would be instrumental in handling an incident.

Risk: Without someone in charge, two risks are present. First, the activities in responding to the security incident may not be organized because people may be going off in different directions in reacting to the incident. Second, without someone in charge, little accountability exists in the structure. Someone should "own" the process and make sure things are done; having a single point of contact in charge provides the accountability.

Client Response:

---

8. *When there is a security incident, is communication to employees a coordinated effort, which is controlled by one individual or group to ensure the right information is being communicated to employees?*

Guidance: Depending on the severity of an incident, the state of the company can be chaotic or in a kind of panic mode. At this time, personnel need to be reassured, so communication to them must be handled carefully. Having a centralized communication effort allows the company to review any communications sent out to employees to ensure that they are accurate and appropriate.

Risk: The risk of not having a centralized communication effort is that inaccurate information might be given to personnel, which can potentially lead to an uncontrolled and chaotic situation.

Client Response:

INVESTIGATING AN INCIDENT

9. *Are there processes in place to ensure that evidence is preserved so that it may be used to investigate the cause of the incident or to prosecute (if the situation warrants it)?*

Guidance: When there is a computer-related security breach, the machine itself may contain evidence that might be useful if any legal action is pursued. Procedures should be in place to ensure that the evidence is not corrupted. The dilemma in this situation is whether the company preserves the evidence or just fixes the problem. Company officials are caught between trying to become fully operational as quickly as possible and at the same time, preserving evidence in the event that it is required. The decision will depend on a number of factors including (but not limited to) the severity of the incident, what systems are affected (i.e., do the systems support core operations), and whether any legal ramifications will result from the security incident. Ideally, the company should have some criteria, similar to the classification scheme used in classifying the incident. In addition, it is critical to assemble the right team of people who can quickly come to a sound decision.

Risk: If the company is seeking legal action, the evidence must be carefully preserved. If its not carefully preserved, it has limited value in the legal action.

Client Response:

10. *Depending on the nature of the investigation, does the company engage the appropriate security experts to investigate incidents?*

Guidance: Depending on the company, there may or may not be personnel who are qualified to handle an investigation resulting from a security incident. Larger companies may have someone appropriate on their staff or they may even have a security group that only handles investigations. In smaller companies, this is less likely. In any case, companies should have access to qualified individuals to perform investigations as needed. Sometimes, this might mean calling on external resources.

Risk: Having unqualified people performing the investigation could result in a botched investigation where evidence might be corrupted and recourse might become impossible. Any legal action might also become more difficult.

Client Response:

11. *Is there a process in place for an investigator to obtain administrator access to a machine in a timely fashion if required for an investigation?*

Guidance: In some cases where investigators are engaged, they will require administrator or root access to machines to investigate. With the sensitivity around this type of access, the process for obtaining it can be cumbersome. There should be a process to ensure that investigators receive this access quickly. The access should also be removed once the investigator is finished with the work. If possible, the investigator's activity while accessing the machine with privileged access should be logged. The process for receiving this access should require appropriate approvals and be quick and efficient.

Risk: If investigators do not receive the appropriate access in a timely fashion with proper approvals, the investigation of the incident might suffer as they cannot quickly obtain the information they need.

Client Response:

---

12. *Are security incidents documented? If so, what details are documented?*

Guidance: As part of the process of handling security incidents, ample documentation should occur for audit trail purposes and for "lessons learned." Documenting "what happened" and "how it was fixed" can help in preventing similar incidents from happening again. Based on the documentation, steps can be taken to make the appropriate changes to the relevant business processes or technology. As a best practice, the client should consider documenting the following:
- Incident details — what happened
  - Nature of the incident
  - Classification of the incident
- Impact
  - Business processes
  - Systems
  - People
- Response
  - Results of investigation (if applicable)
  - Remediation steps taken (if any)
  - Groups involved
- Response metrics
  - How long did it take to find out about the incident?
  - How long did it take to assemble a team?
- Lessons learned
  - What could have been done better?

Note that all of the items listed above might not be applicable when documenting a security incident. One thing to remember is that in the midst of an incident, documentation is probably the last thing someone wants to do. It is absolutely critical to have someone who is responsible for documentation. For the last section, "lessons learned," members of the response team should all provide their input. Other information can be documented based on the company's risks. The list above is meant to be a guideline for documentation.

Risk: As is the case with most documentation, a lack of it means that the knowledge is in somebody's head (to the extent they remember the key details). The risks related to not documenting the security incident include the following:
- There might be a tendency to not go back and learn from the incident.
- Needed changes to the environment as a result of the incident are not made.
- If the same type of incident happens in the future, knowledge from the current experience cannot be leveraged to respond to the incident.
- If certain key employees leave, any knowledge associated with the security incident is also gone because it was not documented.

Client Response:

POST-INCIDENT ANALYSIS

13. *Are lessons learned from security incidents incorporated into user awareness programs where appropriate? Are security awareness programs updated as necessary to reflect the experience from security incidents?*

Guidance: Some security incidents result in lessons learned that should be shared with all personnel. One of the ways to share this information is to incorporate it into the security awareness programs offered to personnel. The knowledge resulting from the lessons learned from these security incidents helps in raising awareness and eventually reacting appropriately if a similar incident occurs.

Risk: The risk of not incorporating security incident lessons learned into security awareness programs is that there is a greater chance that any mistakes made might be repeated in future incidents.

Client Response:

---

14. *Are security incidents analyzed on an ongoing basis to identify any trends that might indicate a weakness?*

    Guidance: Ideally, details of security incidents (discussed in an earlier question) are compiled in a database where they can be analyzed. The value of ongoing analysis is in determining whether any relevant trends exist that might indicate a problem with a particular process or system. These trends can then be used to make changes in process, harden certain systems, or take other actions as necessary. This is only possible if the company is diligent in documenting security incidents.

    Risk: The risk of not doing this analysis is that the same types of incidents can keep occurring because trends are not noticed. If the trends are noticed, changes can be made sooner rather than later to help prevent future incidents.

    Client Response:

Appendix K

Business to Business (B2B)

Companies today have business-to-business (B2B) relationships with their trading partners where the companies are linked electronically through various means. These relationships create efficiencies in key business processes (e.g., supply chain) using various methods such as sending transactional data electronically. B2B automates certain transactions and reduces the level of human intervention to achieve these efficiencies. In the past, companies utilized Electronic Data Interchange (EDI) to electronically send transactional information to their trading partners. EDI is still very much in use today, particularly by the Fortune 500 companies. "Industry analysts estimate that 95 percent of Fortune 500 companies use EDI....However, given the complexity and cost of EDI software, most companies only use EDI to communicate with the top 15–20 percent of their trading partners. The remaining 80–85 percent of trading partners need a simpler, less expensive solution that leverages the emerging XML standard for information exchange over the Internet."[1] Many of these less expensive solutions leverage the Internet and secure communications to facilitate B2B relationships. Some of the reasons for B2B relationships include:

- Business process automation
  - Supply chain management
    - Reduction of lead time
    - Improved forecasting
    - Procurement activities
- Sharing information

B2B relationships are continuing to become more prevalent among companies. These relationships can be between two or several companies and may leverage many different technologies including EDI as well as newer eXtensible Markup Language (XML)-based technology. Considering the sensitive and competitive information being transmitted in these B2B relationships, security is a major concern. In some cases, inadequate security may prevent companies from participating in B2B relationships.

One of the challenges with B2B is that it falls into a bit of a gray area when it comes to implementation, support, and ongoing maintenance. In some cases, the internal information technology (IT) group may be doing something very minor, such as opening up a port on a firewall to enable the communication between business partners. The business partner or some other party may handle support issues. However, regardless of who ends up supporting the B2B infrastructure and application, the company is still responsible for ensuring that its information is secure. One of the problems companies face is that they are dependent on the business partner also having certain security standards. Consequently, B2B relationships should be reviewed in detail from a security perspective.

Staying consistent with other questionnaires in these appendices, this questionnaire will be process focused and will not delve into specific technologies such as EDI or vendor-specific technologies as they relates to B2B relationships. Instead, the questionnaire will focus on process-oriented issues relevant to B2B, with some high-level questions regarding technology. When you review B2B in the context of a security assessment, individuals versed in the technology being used should review specific technologies from a technical security perspective. Vendor-issued best practice guidelines as well as independent review should be used to secure the technologies.

GENERAL

1. *Does the company have a security policy governing B2B relationships?*

   Guidance: A security policy should exist that outlines the minimum security requirements for any B2B relationship. The policy should provide guidance for business units as they enter into agreements with business partners. It should outline security requirements as they relate to architecture, transaction processing, and monitoring. The policy should also document what groups should be involved in the process from initial discussions to actual implementation and monitoring. One of the challenges with B2B is that business units who strive for the strong B2B relationships that will help the company are the ones who most often pursue these relationships, and security is not always considered. Having a policy brings awareness and hopefully, involvement from the right IT personnel.

   Risk: Without a security policy, personnel responsible for these relationships will not be clear on the security requirements with which they should comply. It is also difficult to hold personnel accountable for a policy if it is not documented and communicated.

   Client Response:

   ---

2. *Before entering into B2B relationships, is any due diligence performed? If so, is IT or the security group involved in the process to review any security concerns?*

Guidance: Once the business decides that the B2B relationship with a business partner is worth pursuing, some level of due diligence should be done so the company has an opportunity to validate and confirm certain critical information prior to entering into a final agreement. As part of this due diligence, someone who has responsibility for information security should be involved to ensure that the business partner meets certain security requirements based on the nature of the B2B relationship.

Risk: The risk of not having an information security person involved in the due diligence process is that the business partner might not have adequate measures to secure the B2B transactions. Because the business partner will potentially have access to some of the company's data or systems, significant security concerns exist related to confidentiality and integrity of information.

Client Response:

---

3. *As B2B relationships are being implemented, is the internal audit department involved to ensure that all audit and control requirements are met (assuming there is an internal audit or similar function)?*

Guidance: To build on the preceding question related to the due diligence effort, someone from internal audit should be involved in the B2B process from start to finish to help ensure that the company's audit and control requirements are met. Internal audit, because of their knowledge of the company, is in a unique position to provide valuable input into this process.

Risk: The risk of not involving internal audit when forming a B2B relationship is that the final B2B structure may not meet the company's audit and control requirements. Ensuring that the B2B structure is in compliance with audit standards is easier and more efficient during the setup process than after it has been completed.

Client Response:

---

4. *What business process is the B2B relationship supporting and how critical is it to the business?*

Guidance: To understand the importance of the B2B relationship, it is important to understand what business process it is supporting and what the criticality of the process is. Is the B2B structure in place to share information? Are actual transactions, that have revenue and expense impact being performed? The answers will give a sense of the criticality and provide some guidance about how much further testing might be warranted.

Risk: Not applicable. The answer to this question gives an idea of the level of risk associated with the B2B relationship.

Client Response:

---

5. *Does someone in the company have overall ownership of the B2B relationship?*

   Guidance: Once the company has signed the B2B agreement and it is operational, someone in the company should be assigned the responsibility of owning the relationship. The person in this role should ensure that the requirements set forth in the agreement are met, act as the single point of contact with the business partner, and work with relevant groups to manage the relationship. Part of this function should also be to ensure that security requirements are being met.

   Risk: Without someone officially owning the relationship with the B2B partner, a risk exists that it will not be properly managed — i.e., everyone says that another person owns it and in the end, no one ends up owning it. As a result, there is no accountability related to ensuring that the contract requirements are met.

Client Response:

---

6. *Is there a Service Level Agreement (SLA) in place between the company and the B2B partner?*

   Guidance: An SLA is an important element of a B2B relationship. The SLA should outline the scope of the relationship, roles and responsibilities, performance metrics, and other miscellaneous information. If the SLA is enforced, penalties (both financial and nonfinancial) are incurred for not being compliant with the SLA. The company should monitor the relationship with the business partner to ensure that SLA requirements are being met. The SLA should reflect minimum requirements that the B2B partner should have in order for the company to do business with them via a B2B relationship. Many of the items in the SLA will be operation oriented. In addition to those requirements, the SLA should also address security. Some items to look for when reviewing SLAs include the following:

- Tolerable downtime
- Disaster recovery
- Incident handling and related escalation lists
- Notification requirements related to any security incidents
- Backup and recovery of data
- Financial remedies for SLA noncompliance
- Auditing provisions — timing and notification, frequency, etc.
- Security requirements related to hardware and software used in conjunction with B2B transactions
  - Patch application
  - Hardening standards
- Documented encryption standards

Risk: The risk of not having a strong SLA in place is that the business partner may not be accountable to specific service levels required by the company. From a security perspective, there is a risk that the company's information might not receive an adequate level of security. Security requirements also cannot be enforced without the SLA, which obligates the B2B partner to meet those requirements.

Client Response:

7. *Does someone monitor SLAs to ensure they are being met?*

Guidance: Building on the earlier question concerning SLAs, they have limited value if someone is not monitoring them. The person who owns the relationship should work with the appropriate people to monitor the key provisions of the SLA.

Risk: Without monitoring of the SLA, a risk exists that the transactions being facilitated by the SLA and the company's data are not secure because the B2B partner is not meeting security requirements outlined in the SLA.

Client Response:

ARCHITECTURE

8. *What is the method of connection between the company and the B2B partner and what security measures are in place to ensure that the connection is secure? If information is sent across the Internet, how is it secured?*

   Guidance: At one time, EDI was the primary way that B2B transactions were performed. These transactions were secured via the use of a Value Added Network (VAN). Today, the Internet is leveraged for B2B transactions. Virtual Private Networks (VPNs) and other security architectures are used to secure the transactions. In this question, we are concerned with ensuring that the transmittal of information from one business partner to another is secure. This question should give rise to doing a detailed review of the transaction process flow and the architecture to ensure that the transmittal of data is secure. Ideally, security should have been considered up front during the initial architecture design phase as redesigning can become expensive and cause a service disruption. Some architecture-related issues to consider are:

   • *Encryption of information during transport* — Appropriate levels of encryption should be used based on the nature of the connection and the sensitivity of the information being transmitted.
   • *Digital certificates* — Trading partners should agree on architecture details related to encryption and signing. This will enable the senders and receivers to authenticate the trading partner.
   • *Authentication* — Reasonable authentication measures should be used based on the nature of the B2B relationship. Where very sensitive information is being accessed, strong authentication measures should be considered.

   Risk: The risk associated with insecure transmittal of data varies based on the nature of the data being transmitted. If sensitive information, such as competitive pricing information or customer-related information, is not secured during transmission, a risk exists that sensitive information may be compromised and get into the wrong hands.

   _____

   Client Response:

   _____

9. *How are network perimeter security issues handled — i.e., how does the company ensure that the network traffic from the business partner is legitimate? How is B2B traffic authenticated?*

Guidance: From an architecture perspective, once information is transmitted from the business partner, it must enter the company's network. There are security considerations when architecting this that will vary based on the company. For example, certain adjustments may have to be made on the firewall to accommodate B2B traffic. Where the B2B traffic terminates as well as authentication requirements must be reviewed when considering network perimeter security issues. These security considerations must be considered in light of the company's security policy and business requirements.

Risk: Network perimeter security is a critical aspect of B2B security. If these security issues are not dealt with, a risk exists of unauthorized access to sensitive information being transmitted.

Client Response:

10. *What measures does the business partner take to ensure that the company's data is secure?*

Guidance: Depending on the nature of the B2B relationship, the business partner will potentially have the company's data on their machines. Although the data resides on the business partner's systems, the company is ultimately accountable for it. The company must ensure that the business partner is taking reasonable measures to ensure that the data is adequately protected. This is an even more significant issue if personally identifiable or customer-identifiable data is residing on the business partner's machines. For example, if health care companies are in a B2B relationship, personally identifiable health information might reside on the business partner's systems. These issues can be dealt with in the B2B agreement and in the SLA.

Risk: The risks related to sensitive data not being adequately protected can range from minor operational impacts to significant legal impacts related to noncompliance with laws such as the Health Insurance Portability and Accountability Act (HIPAA). The impacts can include fines for violating regulations or damage to the reputation of the company.

Client Response:

11. *What access control measures does the business partner have in place to ensure that access to the company's data and systems is limited to only those individuals who require it?*

Guidance: Access control to data or applications should normally be provided on a "need to have" basis. As it relates to the company's data and the B2B application, the business partner should limit access to only those who require it. This should be part of the B2B agreement. One thing to look out for is personnel from the business partner having "read" access. Although someone with read access cannot perform a transaction, data confidentiality issues still exist — i.e., read access should be limited to only those who need it.

Risk: The risk associated with inadequate access control measures related to the company's data at the business partner's location is unauthorized access to potentially sensitive data. This can eventually result in financial damage or damage to the company's reputation.

Client Response:

12. *Does the company's termination process remove access an employee might have had to B2B applications?*

Guidance: When employees are terminated, their access to the B2B application should be removed along with all other access they have. One issue to look for is where personnel use a common ID and password to use the B2B application (this should not be done in the first place). In this case, the password should be changed immediately because the terminated employee knows the ID and password to use the application. In the scenario where employees have individual access to B2B applications, that access should also be removed. This scenario is particularly a problem because B2B applications are often Web based, which does not necessarily require network access before accessing the B2B application. Therefore, if a terminated employee's access is not removed, that individual can still access the same information as before.

Risk: The risk associated with terminated employees as it relates to B2B applications is the risk of unauthorized access to business partner systems. It can ultimately result in an employee being terminated and then going to a competitor and accessing the same information.

Client Response:

13. Are user IDs periodically purged from B2B applications?

Guidance: The purging process that should be performed for all IDs — network, applications, devices, etc. — should also be performed for IDs on the B2B application. This is a mitigating control in case the IDs were not removed when they should have been. The frequency of this process depends on the level of turnover and the strength of the company's termination process.

Risk: Similar to not terminating IDs, the risk associated with not purging IDs is that ex-employees may still have access to B2B applications. This can result in employees going to competitors and accessing the same information, which could eventually damage the relationship with the business partner.

Client Response:

NOTE

1. *eAI Journal*—"Vitria Acquires XML Solutions," March 27, 2001—http://www.eaijournal.com/News.asp?NewsID=583

Appendix L

Business to Consumer (B2C)

Business to consumer (B2C), for the purpose of this checklist, is the process by which consumers purchase goods or services over the Internet. They can go to vendor Web sites, look through catalogs, find what they want to buy, and then make the purchase by supplying their credit card information and some personal information such as name and address. Before the days of B2C, many companies started by having a presence on the Internet where people could go to learn about the company and what they do. Such Web sites are informational in nature. A significant number of companies now also offer goods and services over the Internet where consumers can make purchases. Some of the better-known sites include Amazon and the common department store chains. This has become very prevalent, and people use it extensively because of convenience and in many cases, price. However, many people do not use it, and one of the major reasons is that they are afraid of divulging sensitive credit card or personal information on the Internet. One can argue that our information is no safer when we shop in stores or go to restaurants and give our credit cards to make a purchase. This is probably correct, but because a store or restaurant is tangible and familiar, the risk does not seem to be as great. On the other hand, with e-commerce activities, the idea of purchasing over the Internet is still an unknown with risks related to the confidentiality of personal information including credit card information. Considering the many publicized stories of hackers gaining access to credit card information and with identity theft becoming a bigger issue, security in the B2C space must be taken very seriously.

In a security assessment, B2C should be reviewed from a process and technology perspective. Some of the key areas to review include:

- Ensuring that consumer information is secure during transmission
- Ensuring that customer information residing on the company's systems is adequately secured
- Integrity of transactions
- Ensuring that the architecture supporting the B2C environment is secure — e.g., Web servers, back-end systems
- Ensuring that the infrastructure supporting the B2C environment can provide the level of availability required

The potential risks associated with B2C can result in significant impact to the business. If the B2C operations are not available or if a breach of security occurs, some of the potential impacts include:

- *Operational* — Depending on how significant B2C is to the company, operations can suffer.
- *Legal* — If a security breach occurs where customers' personal information is stolen, the company can face legal issues.
- *Financial* — If there are security or availability issues, there can be immediate financial impact because customers cannot make purchases, as well as long-term financial impact if a permanent loss of customers occurs.
- *Reputation* — A company's reputation will most certainly be damaged. The degree to which this happens depends on the severity of the incident.

This questionnaire is focused on the processes around B2C operations. Although some references to technology are included, they are conceptual in nature. Specific vendor technologies are not addressed in this questionnaire and should be evaluated from a technical security perspective. Some questions involve technical concepts that may require someone with the appropriate technical expertise to review. These resources should be used in an assessment as necessary. The questionnaire should be modified based on the company's specific business requirements.

QUESTIONS

1. Does a security policy governing B2C processes exist?

Guidance: As noted in the other questionnaires, having a security policy has significant value because the policy outlines the minimum security requirements that must be followed. In the case of B2C, a policy is very useful because it can be used from the outset as B2C operations are being planned so that security is built in to both the process and supporting technologies. In addition, the policy provides a mechanism to enforce good security practices for B2C.

Risk: Risks of not having a security policy related to B2C include:
- The B2C architecture and application will be developed with inadequate security. Addressing security after the fact can be expensive and time consuming,
- No mechanism exists to enforce good security practices as they relate to B2C.

Client Response:

---

2. *How significant are the B2C operations?*
   - What percentage of overall revenues do the B2C operations generate?
   - If the Web site providing B2C services had a security breach (e.g., site defacement, denial-of-service attack), what would be the impact to the company, financial and otherwise?
   - How would a security breach impact the reputation of the company?

Guidance: The purpose of these questions is to understand the significance of the B2C activity and to help determine the extent of the review. Depending on how significant B2C is, detailed system testing may or may not be necessary. Another scenario is that B2C may be insignificant today but plans to grow it are underway, in which case, there may be more of a high-level architecture review to ensure security is properly built in as well as an analysis of what to consider from a security perspective as the site grows. In many cases, B2C operations are important enough to justify further testing. Even if they do not account for significant revenue, the risk of damaging the reputation of the company if a security incident were to happen always exists. For many companies, if B2C is not significant today, it is probably going to become a significant part of the business.

Risk: Not applicable. The purpose of this question is to understand the scope of B2C operations and how the detailed review, if any, will be done.

Client Response:

3. *Has there ever been a security breach related to the B2C operations?*

Guidance: Knowing whether any security breaches have occurred in the past gives an indication of potential impacts and how the company handled the incidents, both of which are important considerations in a security assessment. It is also important to understand what steps the company took to prevent the same type of security incident from happening again.

Risk: Not applicable. The purpose of this question is to gather information about past security incidents, why they happened, and what has been done to ensure that similar incidents do not happen again. This can lead to findings if the security weaknesses were not addressed.

Client Response:

4. *Is someone accountable for the B2C Web site and the related operations?*

Guidance: Ownership is one of the key components of security. In the case of B2C, if no one owns security, there is a good chance that security is not being adequately maintained. Someone should own the B2C operations and be responsible for them. This person should oversee the content on the Web site, ensure that any updates are taking place, and interface with the information technology (IT) and security personnel to ensure that the site is available, functioning properly, and secure. This person may delegate certain portions of these responsibilities to the appropriate people in the organization — e.g., some of the technical pieces can be delegated to IT. However, one person should be ultimately accountable. Ideally, someone on the business side should own the B2C operations because such an individual will have a better understanding of whether the site is working as intended. B2C is a revenue-generating function and thus, someone from the business should be responsible for it.

Risk: Without ownership of the B2C operations, there is no accountability, which is critical because this is a customer-facing revenue-generating activity. Issues with the B2C operations that affect the customer can have significant impact, including lost revenue and lost customers.

Client Response:

5. *Does someone own the database supporting the B2C operations?*

Guidance: In the preceding section, all relevant systems supporting B2C operations were alluded to. The database is highlighted here because of the criticality of the data generated from B2C activity. The database is a critical component of the B2C infrastructure because it contains myriad information. Some of the information potentially contained includes catalog-related information, pricing data, customers' personally identifiable information, and other information, depending on how it was set up. It is important to ensure that this information is adequately secured.

Risk: Without ownership of the database supporting the B2C operations, there is potentially a lack of focus on securing B2C-related data. This can lead to unauthorized access to critical data resulting in issues relating to availability of B2C operations and the integrity of B2C data.

Client Response:

6. *Is access to the database restricted to only those individuals who require it?*

Guidance: Access control is an essential layer in an information security program. Access to the database should be limited to those who need it to perform their jobs. The level of access should depend on the person's job function. As for who has access, there should at least be a database administrator and a backup. Because administrator access has super rights, it should be limited. Besides administrator access, there may also be some individuals who require "read" access to view certain information. In any case, whoever receives access should have some business justification for the access.

Risk: Without strict access controls on the database, the risks include:
- Unauthorized access to sensitive information in the database
- Damage to the integrity of the information in the database

Client Response:

---

7. *If the B2C application was purchased, was any due diligence performed to determine whether it has the appropriate security functionality?*

Guidance: Although functionality of applications is part of the initial analysis when purchasing a COTS (Commercial Off the Shelf) package, security is something that is often overlooked. As part of the security assessment, it is important to review the application and determine whether any associated security risks are present and what mitigating controls are in place to address them. During the review, consider the following:
- *Access control* — Is access given on a "need to have" basis?
- *Information flow* — How is the application interfacing with other systems (e.g., database) and is it secure?

In some cases, you may find that the application has security-related functionality that is not being used. Some things to look for in the application include access control (at the transaction level if possible), controls to ensure the integrity of the data, and integration points with other components of the infrastructure.

Risk: If the application does not have the necessary security features there is a risk of:
- Unauthorized access to the application transactions
- Loss of integrity of B2C data

Client Response:

8. *If the B2C application was developed in house, was security built in from the beginning?*

   Guidance: With application development, security is not always considered during the early phases including gathering business requirements and design. One way to determine whether security was considered is to inquire about the team involved in gathering requirements and designing the application and determine whether any team member considered security. In addition, you should specifically ask what security features were considered during the early stages of the development process. If this information is available, it might be appropriate to verify it. If security was not considered, a more detailed review of the application and its functionality will be required. As application-level security is becoming more important, tools now exist to help developers build security into applications during the development process.

   Risk: The risk of not building in security in the beginning of the development process is twofold. First, there is a risk that the application will not adequately ensure the integrity and confidentiality of information (similar to the risk with commercial applications). Second, potentially significant costs are associated with additional development and potential reengineering of processes when trying to add security to an already-developed application.

Client Response:

9. *Has the Web server where the B2C application resides been hardened and patched according to the vendor best practice standards?*

   Guidance: One of the key aspects of any information security program is the concept of layered information security. As it relates to B2C, hardening the Web server is another layer of security beyond application-level security. The Web server is potentially the first line of defense against someone trying to hack the B2C application. If the Web server is secured, it can help in preventing or making an attack more difficult. Best practices for hardening Web servers can be found on the vendor Web sites as well as other independent information security Web sites. Hardening should be done on an ongoing basis as part of system administration efforts.

Risk: The risk of not hardening the Web server where the B2C application resides is that vulnerabilities in the Web server can be exploited to hack the B2C application. This can lead negative consequences for the Web site (e.g., B2C Web site not available, defacement), which could result in lost revenues and customers and damage to the reputation of the company.

Client Response:

10. *If the Web site were to be defaced or brought down, how would you know and how long would it take before you found out? Are any intrusion management systems running to help detect potential attacks?*

Guidance: The ability to quickly detect whether the B2C Web site is defaced is critical because it is a customer-facing process on the Internet. In protecting this Web presence, consider the following:
- The first step in protecting it is to have the ability to know something has happened in the first place.
- Attacks do not just happen during business hours — they can happen at any time.

Intrusion management systems can help with being able to detect potential attacks on a 24/7 basis. Intrusion management is essentially an alarm that alerts personnel of attacks. Some intrusion management software also has the ability to stop certain attacks in progress. When reviewing intrusion management, determine what is running and whether it is appropriate. Also, you should ensure that appropriate procedures are in place for signature updates (if required), incident handling, and logging and monitoring. If the company is already running intrusion management software, determine whether it is managed properly. Many companies that have deployed intrusion management have not devoted the appropriate resources to manage it properly. Intrusion management is something that needs significant administrative effort for it to be effective. Keep in mind that intrusion management is only as effective as the time that is put into it. If used effectively, it can significantly mitigate risks associated with Web site defacement and other intrusions.

Risk: Without some mechanism for detecting attacks, the company might not know if the B2C Web site has been defaced or is not available. This can lead to loss of revenue and customers as well as damage to the reputation of the company.

Client Response:

11. *Do the B2C application and the database both reside on the same server or is there a "tiered" architecture where the application and the database are on different servers?*

Guidance: Ideally, the database supporting B2C operations should not reside on the same server as the application to better manage risk. Assuming they are on separate systems, if the B2C Web site is attacked or brought down, the database is still safe as it resides on another machine. In a typical architecture, the B2C application is in front of a firewall, which customers can reach via the Internet, and the database is on a separate server, which is protected behind the firewall. With this question, you should review the network topology diagram and determine whether the B2C is set up in a secure manner.

Risk: The risk of having the database and application on the same server is that if the server is attacked or brought down, the database and the application can be compromised, resulting in sensitive information (e.g., customer data, credit card information) being exposed or the permanent loss of information (depending on the backup process).

Client Response:

12. *Are there any firewalls deployed to help secure the B2C infrastructure and are they properly configured?*

Guidance: Part of the B2C infrastructure is a firewall. In many cases, it might be the only security device in place. Although a firewall can be very effective, it can only be effective if it is configured properly. Many companies do not take the time to properly architect the firewall or configure the rule base. When reviewing the firewalls, you should ask for the rationale for how the architecture is set up and what justifications were used in configuring the firewall rule base. Both of these should be documented and if not, this information should be readily known by IT or dedicated security personnel. Based on the risk, it may make sense to review the firewall rule base in detail and determine whether any changes are required.

Risk: The wrong placement of the firewall or a firewall with an incorrectly configured rule base can result in unauthorized traffic into the network. Thus, the B2C system is not protected as intended.

Client Response:

13. *Does the B2C application use cookies to cache any sensitive data?*

Guidance: If certain information such as authentication data is cached or stored, sensitive data can be divulged. Caching can be done with cookies, which are pieces of information stored locally on a machine. This information can include a user's preferences on a Web site or authentication data. The Internet browser uses cached information to speed up performance and bring up Web pages more quickly. System settings related to caching should be reviewed from a technical perspective to determine whether they are appropriate from a security perspective.

Risk: The risk with caching sensitive data is that if a person's authentication data is cached, another person can potentially log on as the preceding person. In an e-commerce setting, this can result in fraudulent activity. To mitigate this risk, clients should not allow authentication data to be cached and should ensure that any cookies expire once the session is over.

Client Response:

14. *Does the B2C application's logout capability work as intended?*

Guidance: B2C applications should have a logout function allowing users to log out of the application. The logout feature does not always work, resulting in users being logged in when they think they have logged out. The other issue is re-entering the session when pressing the back button even though the user has logged out. The only way to determine whether the logout functionality is working is to test some sample scenarios.

Risk: The risk associated with the logout function not working properly is people having unauthorized access to each other's accounts. This can happen in public Internet cafés or kiosks in public places. If the logout function (or lack thereof) can be exploited to gain unauthorized access to a person's account, it could lead to fraudulent activity and a loss of customer confidence.

Client Response:

15. *Does the application, which resides on the Web server, use a secure protocol when sending information across the Internet?*

Guidance: E-commerce transactions generally require some exchange of sensitive information sent over the Internet. These communications should be sent using secure protocols that encrypt any sensitive information. One way to evaluate information flow is to review the network and security architecture and determine how information is flowing and what protocols are in use. To the extent that sensitive customer information is transmitted, adequate measures should be in place to protect the confidentiality of that information. Consumers assume that their information is confidential.

Risk: In an e-commerce transaction, sensitive information such as people's demographic data and credit card information is sent across the Internet. If this information is sent in an insecure manner such as clear text, this information can be intercepted and used to gain unauthorized access to other people's accounts, resulting in fraudulent transactions and the loss of customer confidence.

Client Response:

16. *When someone is using the B2C application, is the password obscured when entered?*

Guidance: Obscuring the password is a feature that B2C applications should have. Although many have this feature, you should not assume it works this way because it is a very important feature.

Risk: The risk associated with the password-obscuring feature not in place is having users' authentication data be accidentally divulged, which can lead to fraudulent activity and a loss of customer confidence.

Client Response:

17. *Does the application enforce strong password rules when users are creating accounts?*

Guidance: Passwords are the first line of defense for consumers. However, consumers will generally not use strong passwords when they create an account on an e-commerce site unless they are forced to. If the B2C application has the capability to force users to create strong passwords, it should be used. Weak passwords are one of the first exploits tried by those seeking to gain unauthorized access. The balance here is to force users to have strong passwords but not so strong that they forget them or paste them onto their monitors.

Risk: The risk of not enforcing strong passwords is that users will have weak passwords that can be exploited to gain unauthorized access to the B2C application.

Client Response:

---

18. *Does the application lock users out automatically after a certain number of failed log-on attempts?*

Guidance: The lockout feature helps prevent malicious users from trying to use brute force techniques to gain unauthorized access. An account is effectively frozen for a period of time after a certain number of failed log-on attempts. It can then be available for that user after a set period of time or it may require the consumer to call and have the password reset. This is a very useful feature that should be used if available. If B2C applications are being developed, this feature should be built in. This feature, along with other password-related security features, should be used for effective password security.

Risk: The risk of not having the lockout feature is that it allows malicious users to use brute force methods gain unauthorized access to B2C applications and potentially conduct fraudulent activity.

Client Response:

---

19. *If a customer requires a password to be reset, what is the process for giving the reset password to the user? Is the customer authenticated before giving that individual the password? Is the password sent to the customer's e-mail address?*

Guidance: Password resets should be communicated to customers once they have been authenticated in some way. Companies should enforce and have documented procedures for communicating password resets, as this is a popular social engineering method used to gain authentication information of users. Ideally, support personnel should ask customers for additional information about themselves to authenticate them. A few methods that can be used include:
- Send the password to the consumer's electronic mail address, which was supplied when the account was created.
- Communicate the password over the phone once the customer is properly authenticated.
- Leave the password on the employee's voice mail.

Risk: The risk with not properly authenticating customers prior to resetting and communicating password information is that the password might be given to the wrong person, who can then use that information to gain unauthorized access to another person's account.

Client Response:

20. *Is administrator access to the Web server limited to only those individuals who require it?*

Guidance: Administrator access to the Web server allows full access rights to the Web server — i.e., an administrator can make any change or see anything on the Web server. This access should not be taken lightly and should be provided to only those individuals who require such access to do their jobs. Ideally, this access should be given to the system administrator who maintains the Web server and a person who serves as the backup. The server should be configured so that administrator activity is tracked, so a security breach related to the Web server can be researched. In addition, the administrator should have a regular account, which is used when not performing administrator activities.

Risk: If administrator access to the Web server where B2C operations resides is not strictly controlled, that access, in the wrong hands, can be used to damage the B2C Web site. This is especially true in the case of disgruntled employees in companies where the termination practices are not effectively performed.

Client Response:

21. *If the application was built in house, do changes go through a change management process before being migrated into production? Is there a development and test environment to facilitate this?*

Guidance: Change management is evaluated closely in another questionnaire but is included here to determine whether it is used for B2C applications. The change management process should always be used when making changes to B2C applications (or any applications), to ensure that changes have been properly tested and that the appropriate individuals have approved the change. Because the B2C application is customer facing and the risks associated with it not functioning can result in lost revenue and customers, proper approval and testing of all changes are critical.

Risk: The risk associated with not having a sound change management process is that vulnerabilities can be introduced into production as a result of untested changes. This could result in a lack of availability of the application or some other security breach.

Client Response:

---

22. *For any products or services being offered on the B2C Web site, what controls are in place to ensure that access to changing item, pricing, or other catalog information is strictly controlled?*

Guidance: This question deals with the process of how the B2C application works. There should be controls in place to ensure that catalog information, especially pricing, is not changed without proper authorization. The ability to make these changes should be limited to specific individuals, and these changes should follow an approval process. In addition, edit lists should be generated and reviewed independently once changes have been made to ensure that changes were approved and correctly made.

Risk: The risk associated with not having these controls in place is that critical catalog information can be changed without proper approvals, which can potentially result in customers seeing and using incorrect information relating to products, pricing, etc. For example, unauthorized or incorrect pricing changes may be made, resulting in customers being charged wrong prices.

Client Response:

---

23. *Is there any ongoing vulnerability assessment of the B2C application? Does the application have any of the Top Ten OWASP (Open Web Application Security Project) vulnerabilities?*

Guidance: OWASP is a project dedicated to application-level security. OWASP has a top ten list of vulnerabilities for which applications should be checked. Tools are available in the marketplace to evaluate application code; they can determine what application security vulnerabilities exist including the OWASP Top Ten. Addressing these vulnerabilities, some of which include cross-site scripting, unvalidated input, buffer overflows, and Structure Query Language (SQL) injection, can significantly reduce the risk with B2C applications. The OWASP Top Ten is available at http://www.owasp.org/documentation/topten.

Risk: Some of the risks associated with the OWASP Top Ten vulnerabilities include the application not being available and unauthorized access to sensitive customer information.

Client Response:

---

24. *Are all relevant logs from the Web server, database server, intrusion detection system, and firewall reviewed?*

Guidance: For the various parts of the B2C infrastructure, logs exist that are worth reviewing on a periodic basis. One of the issues with many companies is that they do not have the time or resources to do these reviews, and as a result, the reviews are not done. Log review tends to be done as a reactive measure when a security incident occurs. One solution is to use automated tools to generate exception reports from the log data so the time required for review is minimized. Another solution is outsourcing. Companies are increasingly looking to Managed Security Service Providers (MSSPs), who provide managed security services at a lower cost than managing it internally. This book includes a separate questionnaire devoted to the use of MSSPs, which should be reviewed if a MSSP is being used.

Risk: The risk associated with not performing proactive log review is that the client might not know about potential security breaches on a timely basis and, as a result, would not be able to take action proactively. Although no guarantee exists that log review will necessarily provide useful information on potential security breaches, periodic review of logs can provide early detection of problems.

Client Response:

Appendix M

Change Management

Change management is the process by which changes are introduced into the information technology (IT) environment. The change management process facilitates the migration of changes to the production environment and helps ensure that all changes are properly tested and that all parties affected by the change have approved it. The other aspect of the change management process is the tracking of changes — i.e., ensuring that changes are properly documented and that an audit trail is associated with all changes that are made.

The main objective of change management is to ensure that any negative impact to the production environment is minimized while required changes are made using a standard methodology. Changes subject to the change management process can include changes to the network infrastructure, specific applications, or devices, as well as other changes. The time that the change management process takes will vary depending on the impact of the change. As an example, for changes that affect many people or groups, the process will require more approvals than for a minor change to an application, which affects a small number of people. The change management process must also consider emergency changes, in which case, testing and obtaining approvals for change need to be performed quickly.

The main risks associated with not having a sound change management policy and process include:

- No audit trail of changes made to the production environment is maintained, making it difficult to recreate the environment if needed.
- Untested changes may introduce a security vulnerability into the production environment.

QUESTIONS

1. Is a change management policy in place that has been communicated and is readily accessible?

Guidance: A change management policy is essential in ensuring that personnel follow good change management practices. As with other security policies, having a change management policy communicates management's expectations and allows enforcement of change management. Although some individuals or groups might understand the value of change management, others might not know. It is very important for all individuals and groups to understand the value of change management because a given change can affect multiple groups. To ensure that changes do not have any adverse effects, all affected parties must understand the implication of changes and approve them. When reviewing the policy, ensure that it at least addresses the following (based on International Standards Organization [ISO] 17799):

- Documentation
- Impact of changes
- Approval of changes
- Communication of changes
- Scope — what changes are covered

Risk: The risks associated with not having a change management policy include:

- It is difficult to enforce change management if no policy exists mandating users to follow it.
- Individuals may follow inconsistent change management practices.

Client Response:

---

2. *Is there a documented procedure in place for change management and is it followed?*

Guidance: The change management policy is "what" should be done and the procedure is the step-by-step explanation of how change management should be done. It is important to have a documented process to ensure that everyone is doing change management consistently. The change management procedure should at least address the following:

- Change control windows for normal and emergency change control.
- Initiation and approval of changes — who can initiate and who can approve changes.
- Testing requirements.
- Documentation requirements — a change management form is useful in facilitating this process.

Other items that can be addressed in the procedure, based on the environment, but the list above is a minimum requirement. The procedure should be readily available (it can be posted on the company intranet) to employees.

Risk: The risk of not having a documented policy is that critical aspects of the change management process may not be done properly or consistently. This can lead to untested and unapproved changes entering the production environment.

Client Response:

---

3. *Is there a form to help facilitate the change management process? If not, how is the process documented?*

Guidance: An important aspect of change management is documentation. The documentation provides an audit trail of key aspects of changes including:
- What was done
- Why it was done
- Impact of the change
- Who approved it
- When the change was made

It is important to capture this information on a consistent basis for all changes. A standard form for change management facilitates the process and ensures that change-related information is documented. The method of documentation can vary and depends on the business requirements. Companies use various methods including manual forms, spreadsheets, sophisticated workflow tools, and others.

Risk: Without a form or some mechanism to track changes, the following risks exist:
- Lack of change documentation, which leads to
  - Lack of accountability for changes
  - Lack of an audit trail, which is an issue if changes have to be recreated
- Inconsistent change documentation

Client Response:

---

4. *What information is required when requesting a change?*

Guidance: Users should be required to gather some minimum information when requesting a change so that approvers have the information necessary to evaluate it. Basic information that should be required includes the following:
- What change is being requested
- Why the change is necessary
- Impacts of the change — e.g., systems, departments, business processes
- Urgency of the change

Risk: The change approval process can be very difficult if the approvers do not have the information necessary to make an informed decision on a change — e.g., whether the change can be put into production, whether all impacts have been considered. This can lead to important changes not being implemented on a timely basis.

Client Response:

---

5. *Are changes tested in a nonproduction environment before being moved into production? Does management enforce this process?*

Guidance: It is critical to test changes before implementing them in the production environment. A test environment that closely resembles the production environment is ideal for testing changes. In some companies, there is an environment set up for production support purposes, which is also good for testing changes. In some cases, a test environment might not be feasible. For example, it is sometimes not feasible to test network infrastructure changes because there is no test environment where it can be done. Testing allows you to see the nature and impact of the change and validate that the change is working as intended.

Risk: The risk of not testing changes can be significant. Untested changes can result in new security vulnerabilities in the production environment. Untested changes may also not work as intended, which can result in other adverse effects in the environment.

Client Response:

---

6. *Who is responsible for ensuring that any changes to the production system follow the change management process?*

Guidance: As with other security-related processes, someone should be responsible for ensuring that changes to production systems follow the change management process. For this to happen, there must be individuals who own the change management process and individuals who have ownership of production systems. Both of these groups must enforce the change management process. Although changes can be initiated from several places, there should be a person (or committee) who is responsible for ensuring that all change requests are funneled through a central mechanism. This will help ensure that changes are made subject to the appropriate scrutiny and subsequent approval.

Risk: Ownership translates into accountability. Without someone or some group owning the change management process, no accountability exists; this can result in untested and unapproved changes being moved into the production environment.

Client Response:

---

7. *If a change control committee exists, does someone in the group represent security?*

   Guidance: Many changes will have security implications. As security is something that is often overlooked, a security representative on the change control committee helps ensure that the security impact of changes is considered during the change review process.

   Risk: If the change control committee does not include security representation, a risk exists that security will not be considered when reviewing changes. This could result in security vulnerabilities being introduced into the production environment.

Client Response:

---

8. *Are there specific change control windows when changes are made? Is this enforced?*

   Guidance: To bring some discipline into the change process, changes should occur during regularly scheduled change-control windows. These windows of time should occur when the potential impact to users is minimal. This is especially important when changes may cause systems to be unavailable for an extended period. In these cases, end users should be informed prior to making changes. The advantage of having change-control windows is that they allow departments to plan for changes and for a formal and structured process to review changes.

   Risk: Without regularly scheduled change-control windows, a risk exists of changes being made in a manner that can be disruptive to users. In addition, the lack of change-control windows can result in users not properly planning changes and trying to force changes through an emergency process.

Client Response:

---

9. *How are emergency changes handled?*

    Guidance: In any environment, some changes will occur that are truly emergencies — i.e., they must be made immediately. The need to make these changes quickly must be balanced with ensuring that all relevant impacts of the changes are considered. In these cases, there should be an emergency change process, which still ensures that the change management process is followed — just in an accelerated manner. Appropriate personnel should review and approve changes, and there should be an audit trail of what changes were made. To help users determine what changes are emergencies, the change management policy or procedure should contain guidelines for what constitutes an emergency change so users know what is and is not an emergency.

    Risk: Without a process for emergency changes, a risk exists that critical changes will not be implemented in production on a timely basis. In addition, untested and unapproved changes may be introduced into the production environment.

    Client Response:

10. *Who can initiate a change? Is there an list of people or roles authorized to initiate a change?*

    Guidance: To ensure that only reasonable changes are considered, there should be some limitations on who can initiate and present changes to the larger group — i.e., a central group of people who are responsible for managing the change process. The members of the change-control committee have other jobs, and their time should not be wasted with reviewing changes that have not gone through any initial screening. This takes time away from discussing the meaningful change requests. One way to limit who can initiate changes is to restrict it to certain titles — e.g., only managers and above can initiate changes. Other methods include having departmental level management doing the initial screening of change requests.

    Risk: The risk of not limiting who can make changes is that trivial or wrong changes might be submitted for review. As a result, meaningful changes will not receive the appropriate time for discussion.

    Client Response:

Appendix N

User ID Administration

The objective of the user ID administration checklist is to determine whether access to the IT resources and information assets of a company is properly controlled. Access control is the first line of defense in information security. Good access control can significantly enhance the overall security posture of a company. The basic principle used when providing access is the "least privilege" rule, which is allowing personnel only the level of access needed to do their jobs.

When reviewing user ID administration, it is important to remember that different levels of access exist, including network, application, and remote access. The principle of least privilege should be applied to all types of access.

In controlling access this way, there needs to be a balance between providing the right level of access and the ongoing administration required to maintain multiple levels of access. In some cases, strict access control may be warranted; in others, however, it may not. The more granular and user-specific the access control, the more time that will be required on administration.

This questionnaire focuses on the user ID administration process, which includes providing, maintaining, and revoking access. The checklist also covers areas such as privileged access and password rules. As with the other questionnaires in this book, this checklist focuses on process and references technology at a conceptual level. When conducting a security assessment, it may be important to bring in resources with technical expertise to do a technical review of access controls on specific systems. As with the other questionnaires, this one should be modified based on the client's specific business requirements.

QUESTIONS

1. *Is a user ID administration policy in place? Has it been communicated and is it readily accessible to all employees?*

   Guidance: A policy for user ID administration is essential for effective access control. The policy, like other security policies, communicates management's expectations and also provides the means for enforcing good ID administration practices.

   Risk: The risks associated with not having a policy include:

- Users do not know the user ID requirements.
- Ensuring user ID administration is being done correctly requires significant enforcement and audit efforts, which are more difficult if no policy can be used to enforce them.

Client Response:

2. *Are procedures in place for the various aspects of ID administration — e.g., gaining initial access, changes in access, termination?*

Guidance: Procedures should be in place to provide guidance to personnel on user ID administration processes. Although the user ID administration policy states the requirements, the procedures provide the step-by-step instructions on how these policies are implemented. Procedures also help promote consistent processes across a company. Some typical procedures that should exist include:
- Obtaining initial access
- Termination
- Obtaining privileged access

The basic elements of these procedures involve having someone in a managerial role approving access and documentation of what access is required for employees to do their jobs. When reviewing procedures, keep in mind that they are very dependent on how the organization is set up (centralized vs. decentralized information technology [IT] organization, number of personnel, etc.). Ideally, access should be given out based on the role of the person.

Risk: The risk associated with not having procedures is that access might not be given properly resulting in users potentially having too much access or too little access. The result is that you may have irate users who do not have the right level of access; others, however, might have unnecessary access to sensitive information. In the case of terminations, the risk is more significant (this is discussed in detail in the termination checklist).

Client Response:

3. *Does the policy or procedure clearly define roles and responsibilities relative to access control?*

Guidance: Roles and responsibilities are critical elements in the policies and procedures. Clearly defined roles and responsibilities establish ownership and accountability for the various tasks. Policies might have higher-level roles, such as at the department level, whereas procedures define roles more specifically by their job titles. Some of the roles that should be defined include:

- Who provides access
- Who approves access
- Who tracks what access a person has
- Who owns the termination process

With ID administration, ownership is critical. In many companies, ownership is not clear, and personnel have different ideas about who does what. This situation can become chaotic depending on the number of personnel and the level of turnover. It is very important that these roles and responsibilities are not defined for specific people but for actual roles. This results in less maintenance and it makes it easier to allocate specific responsibilities to others if needed.

Risk: Without clearly defined roles and responsibilities, there is no ownership or accountability. A risk exists that user ID administration processes will not be completed properly or performed consistently. Taking it one step further, enforcement is also difficult because there is no formal process.

Client Response:

---

4. *Is access to IT resources provided based on what is needed for a particular job and is it approved by a management-level employee?*

Guidance: Typically, when new employees join a company, access is given to certain IT resources so they can do their jobs. The purpose of this question is to determine how this access is given and whether it is based on a person's job description. There is a balance here that should be considered. The more granular a level someone's access is granted, the more administration effort will be required. Ideally, job descriptions should correspond to certain roles, which should correspond to certain access. For example, a profile should exist for the position of accounts receivable clerk that provides certain access, perhaps including edit access to the accounts receivable transactions, read access to other financial information, and other general access such as e-mail and the Internet. Another consideration when reviewing how access is granted is regulatory concerns. For example, access to view consolidated financial information in publicly traded companies should be restricted, as this is sensitive information that can be used for insider trading. In addition, special thought should be given when granting access to sensitive information (e.g., employee salary information, research and development data) or privileged access.

Risk: The risk associated with not granting access based on job descriptions is users having inappropriate access to potentially sensitive areas of the company and to sensitive information, which can be used for malicious purposes.

Client Response:

5. *Are user IDs unique? Are there any cases where IDs are shared?*

Guidance: User IDs should be unique and the system should validate that if possible. With unique IDs, users are accountable for their actions. There may be some cases where IDs are shared by necessity. One example of this is certain manufacturing processes that are controlled by applications. With these applications, if new users had to log on during the production process, the disruption would cause production schedules to slip and ultimately cost the company significant money. In these cases, shared IDs are necessary. However, in most cases, unique IDs should be used. This is especially critical with privileged access, where users have full rights on a system.

Risk: The risk associated with sharing IDs is the lack of accountability if an incident (security or otherwise) occurs.

Client Response:

6. *Do user IDs provide any indication of the access level that an employee has?*

Guidance: Ideally, the user ID should not provide any information about what type of access a person might have. For example, the user ID of a vice president should not contain the official level of the individual or the letters "vp," which indicate vice president. Not having this information makes it a little more difficult for users with malicious intent to determine which user IDs are worth going after and which are not.

Risk: The risk of having IDs that indicate the level of a person is that certain IDs become targets for hackers to use for gaining unauthorized access to the company's IT resources.

Client Response:

7. *Are IDs disabled after a certain period of inactivity?*

Guidance: Disabling IDs after a certain period of inactivity helps mitigate any risks associated with user IDs that have no formal disposition. In some cases, individuals may require access for short periods of time throughout the year. Ideally, this access should be disabled once the user no longer requires it. If the ID administrator failed to disable the ID, this feature automatically disables it. This process is also a mitigating control if the termination process is not being performed effectively. If a terminated employee's access was not revoked, this process at least disables it so it cannot be used.

Risk: The risk associated with not using this feature is that it increases the possibility of having unused accounts that can be used to gain unauthorized access to IT resources.

Client Response:

8. *How are password resets handled? Are reset passwords given to employees in a secure manner?*

Guidance: Password resets are one of the common methods used by social engineers to obtain unauthorized access to a company's systems. Password resets must be handled in a secure manner where users are properly authenticated before being given reset passwords. When reviewing this process, look for documented procedures that help-desk or support personnel must follow when resetting passwords. Ideally, support personnel should authenticate the person by asking for some piece of personal information. Reset passwords can be given after authenticating the person by leaving it on an authenticated system such as voice mail where users can retrieve it after putting in a password.

Risk: The risk of not properly authenticating users when resetting passwords is that it can allow individuals to gain unauthorized access to IT resources, which can lead to accessing potentially sensitive information such as an executives' e-mail, sensitive product information, or competitive data.

Client Response:

9. *Does the user ID administration policy or procedure provide any guidelines about having strong passwords (e.g., minimum password length, use of different types of characters)?*

Guidance: Passwords are a first line of defense in the overall information security program. Having strong passwords can significantly enhance the overall information security posture, but weak passwords can have a detrimental effect. Some commonly known best practices for strong passwords can be used as standards for the organization. What is used really depends on the company and its current practices for passwords — i.e., it might be too much for them to go from very weak passwords (e.g., passwords such as an individual's name, the company name, or the word password) to very strong passwords consisting of upper and lower case letters, numbers, and special characters. When reviewing password strength, consider the following:

- Trying to make users have strong passwords is often a cultural battle, which requires strong management support.
- If changes are made requiring stronger passwords, support calls to the help desk will go up at least temporarily and possibly permanently.
- Enforcing strong passwords is much more feasible if the system automatically enforces strong passwords.

Risk: The risk associated with weak passwords is that they can be guessed and then used to gain unauthorized access to IT resources. Commercial tools as well as freeware, which is readily available on the Internet, can be used to guess weak passwords in a matter of minutes.

Client Response:

---

10. *Does the system have the ability to enforce password controls and if so, is the company taking advantage of it. If not, why not? Some examples of system-level enforcement include:*
    - Validation of password strength
    - Passwords being forced to change at regular intervals
    - Passwords not being recycled within a certain period of time

Guidance: Good password management is almost impossible to enforce manually. You can perform periodic audits to try to force users to have strong passwords that are changed at regular intervals, but this method of enforcement is very ineffective because it affects every user, which you cannot check. The most effective way to enforce good password management practices is to let the system enforce it. If these enforcement features are available, they should be used; if they are not, there should be justification. You may find cases where companies are reluctant to use these features because they are afraid of how users will react or because of the support burden. In these cases, the risks have to be carefully reviewed to determine what the recommendation is — i.e., some aspects of system enforcement might be appropriate, but others might not.

Risk: Without system-level enforcement of good password management, enforcement is difficult. Users will have the tendency to not follow the strong password rules unless they are being forced to do so in an automated fashion.

Client Response:

---

11. *Are employees given any awareness training on user ID administration, which incorporates password management?*

    Guidance: Information security in general requires some level of awareness training to be successful. Password management is one of the areas that should be covered. Users are taught the password policy and given the opportunity to ask any questions they might have. They are also taught the value of having strong passwords. It is likely that many users are not aware of the importance of strong passwords or that they share some accountability if their user ID and weak password are used by malicious users to gain unauthorized access to the company's IT resources.

    Risk: The risk of not having awareness training related to password management is that users will be less likely to follow the rules. They will only follow what the system forces them to.

Client Response:

---

12. *Do the appropriate system or application owners approve access for their systems?*

    Guidance: As part of the access approval process, system and application owners should be in a position to approve or disapprove access to systems or applications they own. This process enforces the idea of ownership and accountability as system and application owners make the decisions regarding access to the systems for which they are responsible. From an assessment perspective, it is important to have owners at least for the mission-critical systems. This process should be documented so there is an audit trail of the approval.

Risk: The risk of not having the system and application owners approve access for their systems is a lack of accountability. This can have negative impacts including:

- Users having inappropriate access
- Access not being removed during the termination process because system and application owners are not involved in the ID administration process

Client Response:

13. *Is privileged access or access to operating system functions restricted to the appropriate administrators? Does a formal approval process for obtaining privileged access exist?*

    Guidance: Privileged access is very powerful because one can do just about anything on a system with that level of access. As such, this access should be limited to only those individuals who require it. In most cases, only system administrators should require this level of access to do their jobs. In other cases, you may find some people need privileged access to perform certain functions for a certain period of time, or they may need administrator rights because of an application they support. For example, if a security incident occurs, an investigator may need privileged access to a system for a short period of time to collect evidence. In these cases, the individuals should provide written justification of why they need the access and how long they need it for, which should be approved by management. This process should be streamlined so privileged access can be granted quickly if required (e.g., the case where an investigator requires access after a security incident).

    Risk: The risk of individuals having privileged access without business justification and proper approval is that the access can be used to do considerable damage or result in a security breach on a given system. This type of access also enables people who damage a system to cover their tracks.

    Client Response:

14. *Do administrators with privileged access also have regular user accounts, which are used for day-to-day nonadministrative responsibilities?*

    Guidance: As a best practice, administrators with privileged access should have regular accounts for day-to-day work. Privileged access should only be used when performing administrative tasks that require having privileged access. Otherwise, regular IDs without privileged access should be used. Those individuals who need privileged access to perform limited functions as part of their jobs should have separate IDs for privileged access. Separate IDs minimize the amount of time privileged access is in use and thus reduce the risk associated with this type of access.

Risk: If administrators use their privileged accounts to do all of their work, they increase the risk of doing something that can have a negative impact on the system. Also, if such an individual is logged in and leaves the computer unattended, someone can potentially do considerable damage to the network.

Client Response:

15. *Is privileged activity logged?*

Guidance: For accountability purposes, privileged access account activity should be logged if the system has the functionality. There is a balance here because logging does require system resources, which could potentially hurt the overall performance of systems. The driving factor determining whether or not privileged activity is logged is based on the environment and culture. As the environment becomes larger and multiple people have privileged access, logging might become more necessary. Two other aspects to consider when reviewing logging of privileged access are:
- To balance logging and potential performance problems, it is helpful to identify what should be logged and if the system supports it, only have certain items logged.
- The company should have adequate resources to review the logs unless they are needed strictly for investigative purposes in case of an incident; in this instance, reviewing logs is something that is done after the fact.

Risk: The risk associated with not logging privileged activity is a potential lack of accountability and ownership. As stated in the earlier question, privileged access is powerful, and a lack of accountability can lead to misuse and an eventual security breach.

Client Response:

16. *As a practice, do users normally use screen savers or do they lock their screens when their personal computers (PCs) are unattended?*

Guidance: Leaving PCs unattended without using screen savers could result in loss of confidentiality of sensitive information. A typical person might have multiple sessions of different applications open at one time. One is bound to be e-mail, and others might be sensitive documents. Anyone can walk by a PC and look at something they should not be seeing. One thing often heard is that internal employees would not look at what is shown on other people's PCs, yet we all know that this certainly happens. Using measures such as screen savers or locking of screens protects the confidentiality of sensitive information and can enhance security. Although the practice of using screen savers can be covered in a policy, it should also be addressed in user awareness training.

Risk: The risk of not using screen savers or other measures to lock down PCs is that unauthorized users may access confidential information on someone else's PC or use someone else's PC to gain access to the network. In addition, they may look at confidential information on that PC if it is left unattended. All of this can lead to potential embarrassment to the company if the security of sensitive information is compromised.

Client Response:

17. *What auditing and logging functions are enabled? Does anyone review the logs?*

    Guidance: To proactively monitor the security of systems, certain auditing and logging functions should be enabled based on the environment and the specific risks. The logs required for auditing and logging use system resources, so clients must be careful when deciding what is to be logged. Ideally, these logs should be reviewed on a regular basis with appropriate follow-ups and actions taken. Clients may also have third-party tools that can parse through log data and provide summary-type information, thereby significantly reducing the time needed for analysis of log data. If clients are not using tools to parse logs and make review and analysis easier, suggesting the use of tools may be a worthwhile recommendation that can potentially save time and provide better security.

    Risk: The risk with not having auditing or logging features enabled includes:
    - A reactive instead of a proactive approach to security is being used.
    - If a security incident occurs, the system may not have the information required to do a proper investigation.

Client Response:

---

18. *How is access to valuable data controlled? Do any special requirements exist for gaining access to this data?*

    Guidance: For any company, some differentiation of the value of data exists. Some data is more valuable than others and as such, requires additional safeguards to protect it. For example, for a pharmaceutical company, research and development data is competitive in nature and requires a higher level of protection than other data does. If the company has data for which confidentiality, integrity, and availability are critical, the company should have strict access control with respect to that data. Theoretically, all access should be given on a "need to have" basis. The reality is that this is not always done. From a risk perspective, critical data at least should have the appropriate level of protection. For example, access to critical data may have special requirements such as executive approval before access is granted. Critical data might also reside on a dedicated server, to which only a few people can access.

    Risk: If critical data is not properly restricted, a risk exists of unauthorized access to it, which can lead to sensitive or competitive data being inappropriately exposed. The severity depends on the data in question.

Client Response:

Appendix O

Managed Security

Although outsourcing information technology (IT) operations has been happening for some time, outsourcing the security function has become more popular recently. In the past, companies have signed significant outsourcing contracts with companies such as IBM and EDS to manage all or part of their entire IT operations. The main drivers for these outsourcing agreements have been:

- *Cost* — There is a clear business case for outsourcing IT. Companies that have done it have achieved substantial reductions in their overall IT costs. Cost reductions are not only seen in IT, but also with all of the support areas such as finance and human resources.
- *Expertise* — As IT became and continues to become more complicated, many companies cannot hire and retain the level of qualified IT personnel needed to effectively run the IT organization. Although many companies do not outsource, most of them are forced to use consultants extensively to get the work done.
- *Concentration on core competencies* — A trend exists where companies are focusing on what they are good at. For example, some banks have made a decision to focus on their core business, which is banking, and outsource other areas where they do not have the expertise.

In the same way that companies concentrate on their core competencies, IT outsourcers are doing the same. Their core competency is running IT operations, and they are able to do it cheaper and better (in some cases) because of economies of scale. For example, it is cheaper for an IT outsourcer to have a big data center where several companies' IT operations can be hosted than for the individual companies to each have separate data centers.

Although this trend continues, IT outsourcing is far from perfect. Companies must go through a thorough due diligence process and develop a solid contract when entering into an agreement with an IT outsourcer. Also, IT outsourcing is not a turnkey operation. Companies must actively manage their outsourcer to ensure that services are delivered as agreed to in the contract.

Security has started to follow a path similar to that of IT outsourcing but with some different drivers. As the typical company's IT environment has become more distributed and the Internet has become a central component of the IT infrastructure, electronic and physical attacks have become more sophisticated. As a result, the security measures required to effectively mitigate risks related to these attacks have also become more sophisticated. Security measures include a focus on internal processes as well as the deployment of security technologies. Managing these security technologies and the security function in general can be a full-time task for several people in an organization. Hiring and retaining individuals who possess expertise in security technologies and how they fit into the organization from a business perspective is very difficult. For this reason and others, which are listed below, managed security is becoming popular:

- *Attacks occur 24/7* — Attacks do not follow the schedule that regular employees keep. They can occur at any time. Managed security services typically provide 24/7 support or off-hours monitoring as required.
- *Cost* — The main costs for security, personnel and technology, can be very expensive and hard to justify. One of the reasons that the cost is hard to justify is that the security personnel may not always be busy even though you are paying for all of their time. On the other hand, with a Managed Security Service Provider (MSSP), the business case for outsourcing security from a cost perspective can easily be made.
- *Technology* — Security, like other technologies, is constantly changing and difficult to keep up with. The evolution of security technologies largely coincides with the evolution of attacks. To ensure good ongoing security, changes in technology must be kept up with. This is another area where a MSSP is in a better position because of their expertise.

For these and other reasons, many companies are turning to MSSPs for their security needs. MSSPs can provide a range of services including (but not limited to) managed firewalls, managed intrusion detection, and managed vulnerability services. Companies should thoroughly evaluate their security requirements to determine what MSSP makes the most sense for them.

Some of the key benefits of using a MSSP include:

- Leveraging the MSSP's security infrastructure and paying for only a portion of it
- Having security staff with subject matter expertise
- Focusing on the company's core competencies and letting the MSSP focus on security

These benefits are not guaranteed, however. The MSSP relationship should not be treated as a turnkey relationship. To get the most out of a MSSP relationship, companies must conduct the proper due diligence during the selection process and monitor the relationship throughout the duration of the contract (just as with general IT operations).

This questionnaire, like the others in this book, focuses on processes relating to selecting and using a MSSP and is technology neutral. The questions try to ascertain whether the right mechanisms are in place to ensure success with the MSSP relationship and to determine whether the current MSSP is performing adequately. The questions are a starting point and should be modified based on the specific business requirements of the company. In addition, depending on the service that the MSSP is providing, you should ask other questions specifically related to the particular service being provided.

QUESTIONS

1. *Does someone "own" the relationship with the MSSP? How is the relationship with the MSSP monitored?*

   Guidance: All relationships with third parties should have a point person who is responsible for the relationship. In the case of managed security, a critical function is being outsourced to a third party. How well the MSSP delivers the services can impact the operations and reputation of the company. Ideally, the person who is responsible should be someone at the management level who is knowledgeable about security and who can effectively deal with the MSSP.

   Risk: The risk of not having someone own the relationship with the MSSP is accountability. No one will be responsible for ensuring that the MSSP is meeting the terms of the service level agreement.

   Client Response:

   ---

2. *What metrics, reports, or other communications are reviewed for purposes of monitoring the relationship?*

   Guidance: Service level agreements (SLAs) with many service providers have documented performance metrics. The relationship with a MSSP should not be treated any differently. As part of the monitoring process, the company should have certain reports or metrics that are reviewed on a regular basis. The company should establish metrics, which should be defined in the service level agreement with the MSSP. These metrics will depend on the type of business and the nature of the relationship with the MSSP. Metrics allow you to baseline the performance of a MSSP and have a better understanding of how well the provider is performing. The metrics allow an objective comparison between how well a MSSP provides security services and how well it was being done internally, thus helping validate the business case for having a MSSP. Metrics are also useful in negotiating future contracts with MSSPs. If possible, the metrics should be based on system-generated information because of the objectivity of the information and the minimal effort required to collect it.

Risk: The risk of not establishing metrics is that it reduces the company's ability to assess how well the MSSP is doing and hold MSSPs accountable for certain service levels.

Client Response:

---

3. *Are there service level agreements (SLAs) with defined metrics that MSSPs must meet? Some of the key items that should be addressed in SLAs include:*
   - Communication requirements
   - Management reporting
   - Penalties for not meeting SLAs
   - Provisions for the client if the MSSP goes out of business
   - Incident handling

Guidance: SLAs are critical when establishing a relationship with a third-party provider, such as a MSSP. The SLA articulates the scope of service, roles and responsibilities, and other key components that define the relationship with the MSSP. In a way, the SLA is a more detailed version of the contract and is focused on the service being provided. The SLA should also include metrics where appropriate (e.g., the metric is system generated) and be referenced in the final contract with the MSSP. The items listed in this question are just some of the areas that should be included in the SLA.

Risk: The risk associated with not having solid SLAs in place include:
   - It is difficult to hold the MSSP accountable for service levels because the required service levels are not documented. Although the contract may have some details, it probably does not have details about service levels.
   - Roles and responsibilities may not be completely clear.

Client Response:

---

4. *Does the contract explicitly define roles and responsibilities for both the MSSP and the client?*

Guidance: It is critical that the roles and responsibilities are clearly defined in the contract with the MSSP. Some of the key roles and responsibilities to look for include:

- MSSP responsibilities:
  - Periodic management reporting that summarizes security events
  - Reporting against established metrics
  - Updating security infrastructure as necessary
  - Communication of security breaches
- Customer responsibilities:
  - Informing the MSSP of any technical changes to the company's environment so that security architecture can be reviewed and updated if necessary
  - Monitoring the service level agreement
  - Communication with outside parties in the event of a security incident

The list above is a starting point and should be modified based on the company and the nature of its relationship with the MSSP.

Risk: The risks related to not establishing clear roles and responsibilities with a MSSP include:

- Confusion may exist over who is responsible for certain tasks, which can lead to the task not being done at all.
- The company might not receive the expected level of service from the MSSP.

Client Response:

---

5. *Has a confidentiality agreement been signed between the company and the MSSP to help ensure the confidentiality of the data to which the MSSP has access?*

   Guidance: a MSSP is a third party with access to some very sensitive information that can be used to learn about the company's environment. This knowledge can be used to potentially gain unauthorized access to the company's IT resources. It is imperative that the MSSP adequately protects this information. In addition, the MSSP is also providing similar services for other customers — some of which may be the company's competitors. It is essential that the MSSP sign a confidentiality agreement with regards to the company's data to help ensure its confidentiality.

   Risk: Without a confidentiality agreement, the company has less ability to take recourse against a MSSP in the event of a breach of confidentiality of sensitive company information. The confidentiality agreement also helps ensure that the MSSP is taking appropriate security measures to protect the confidentiality of the company's data.

Client Response:

---

6. *Is the MSSP's Security Operations Center (SOC) physically secure? Does it meet the client's physical security standards?*

Guidance: The MSSP's SOC should meet certain physical security standards. The best way to determine this is to do a walkthrough of the facilities before signing any contract. If a contract has already been signed, physical security should be audited as part of a regular audit program. Because of the nature of the MSSP's business, the SOC should meet fairly rigorous standards. To put it into perspective, the MSSP's SOC is an extension of the company's network — if the SOC goes down, so does the company's network (potentially). The importance of the MSSP being secure is critical to the well-being of the company's network.

Risk: If the MSSP is not physically secure, a risk exists that the company's information assets are not secure.

Client Response:

7. *Does the MSSP have a tested business continuity/disaster recovery plan? Has the company's own business continuity and disaster recovery plan been updated to reflect the MSSP?*

Guidance: As part of the initial due diligence effort and the ongoing audit process, the company should ensure that the MSSP has a tested business continuity and disaster recovery plan in place. Similar to the earlier question about physical security, the SOC's ability, or lack thereof, to become operational after a disaster is critical to your company. In addition, the company's own business continuity/disaster recovery plan should be updated to reflect that the company is using a MSSP.

Risk: The risk associated with MSSPs not having a business continuity/disaster recovery plan is that the company loses a critical portion of its information security infrastructure in the event that the MSSP suffers a disaster.

Client Response:

8. *Does the client have any data retention requirements as they relate to the security data collected by the MSSP? If so, are they addressed in the contract, and does the MSSP retain the data according to those requirements?*

Guidance: When developing a contract with a MSSP, the company should review its own internal policies to understand the data retention requirements and determine whether any of the data collected by the MSSP are subject to them. For example, companies may have a policy of retaining security-related log data for potential investigations. As part of the monitoring procedures, the company should ensure that data is retained per the contract. This question should tie into the data retention questionnaire earlier in the book as well as any data retention policy the company might have. See the Data Classification and Data Retention appendices (Appendices D and E, respectively) for more detailed questions.

Risk: Without making the appropriate provisions in the LMSSP contract for retention of data, the company may not retain key system-related information per the company's internal requirements.

Client Response:

9. *What is the financial condition of the MSSP? Does it have enough funds and future revenues to sustain operations over the long term?*

Guidance: Documented cases exist of MSSPs that have gone bankrupt and left their customers high and dry. As part of the selection process, it is absolutely critical to ensure that the MSSP has the ability to sustain itself financially for at least the duration of the contract and preferably, even further out. The MSSP should also be financially stable enough to afford quality staff and have a good SOC. When assessing financial viability, look for what type of funding the MSSP has received or, if it is a publicly traded company, look at its financials, which are available on the Internet. In addition, look at the management team leading the MSSP and research what kind of track record they have had with other companies they have led. The financial situation of a MSSP should be reviewed not only during initial selection but also on an ongoing basis as part of the audit process.

Risk: The risk associated with not critically examining the financial condition of a MSSP is that the company may choose a MSSP that is not financially stable. If the MSSP goes out of business or is forced to cut corners due to lack of funds, the security posture of the company can be significantly weakened.

Client Response:

10. *What measures does the MSSP have in place to ensure that their other customers do not have access to the company's data?*

Guidance: Depending on how the MSSP has the service set up, customers might have some level of access into the Security Operations Center. The company must ensure that access controls are set up so that one company cannot see another company's information — e.g., network addresses, general IT architecture–related information. The expectation that the company's data is kept confidential should be formalized, and confidentiality of data should be addressed in the contract. This is a more significant issue if the MSSP has any competitors of the company as customers.

Risk: The risk associated with inadequate access controls in the MSSP is that it can lead to unauthorized access to the company's sensitive information.

Client Response:

---

11. *If the company is subject to any legal or regulatory requirements related to security, is the MSSP meeting those requirements?*

Guidance: There are new regulatory requirements with security implications, which must be adhered to. Laws such as the Health Insurance Portability and Accountability Act (HIPAA) and the Gramm–Leach–Bliley Act (GLBA) have been fully implemented. As security concerns become more prevalent, it is likely that other laws and regulations will spring up. The MSSP should have expertise with regulations and work with the company to ensure that the MSSP contract and services address these requirements. It is important to note that ultimately, the company, whether or not it has a contract with a MSSP, is responsible for ensuring that legal requirements are met. Therefroe, the company should actively work with the MSSP to ensure compliance with relevant requirements.

Risk: The risk associated with the MSSP not addressing legal regulatory requirements is potential fines for the company as well as potential damage to the reputation of the company in the event of a security breach.

Client Response:

---

12. *Does the MSSP have information security policies and procedures?*

Guidance: The MSSP should have an information security program with a foundation of policies and procedures. As part of the due diligence process, the company should have asked to see their policies and procedures. As a follow-on question, the MSSP should be able to answer how it ensures compliance with security policies and procedures — i.e., what type of enforcement takes place. The MSSP should also have a mechanism for ensuring that its policies and procedures are up to date based on new security threats.

Risk: The MSSP should have a top-notch information security program. The risk associated with not having one is that the MSSP may have a less than adequate information security program, which can result in weakened security for the company.

Client Response:

13. *Since the inception of the contract, has any significant turnover occurred at the MSSP and is there a qualified staff to run the MSSP?*

Guidance: A MSSP is as good as the staff that runs it. No matter how good the technology, the quality of the staff ultimately determines the quality of service provided by a MSSP. When determining the quality of staff, some things to look for include certifications such as the Certified Information Systems Security Professional (CISSP) or specific vendor certifications, the experience level of the staff, and the management team. Its important to note that MSSP analysts are not just looking at a monitor and reporting results; they are conducting security analysis and research, which is one of the "value adds" of a MSSP. When reviewing the staff credentials, it is also important to note what type of turnover the MSSP has. A high turnover rate may indicate problems with the MSSP. Relative to turnovers, it is critical for the MSSP to have a strong employee termination process to ensure that employees that leave the MSSP have their access removed. In a MSSP environment, where the analysts are very tech savvy, risks related to disgruntled employees are very significant. Reviewing the staffing with a MSSP should be an ongoing process and not something that is just done at the time of the contract inception.

Risk: The risk if the MSSP has significant turnover and unqualified staff is that the company may receive inadequate security services. In addition, a weak termination process combined with a disgruntled employee can result in a number of negative impacts for the company.

Client Response:

14. *Has the MSSP had a SAS 70 or some other independent review performed? What were the results, and were findings addressed?*

    Guidance: One way to determine the security posture of the MSSP is to see if it has been audited or reviewed by a third party. One popular review is the SAS 70 (Statement of Auditing Standards) which is a standard developed by the AICPA (American Institute of Certified Public Accountants). A SAS 70 review looks at the internal controls that a service organization (in this case, the MSSP) has in place and determines whether these controls mitigate risk as intended. The SAS 70 is an internationally recognized standard that only qualified individuals can perform. Only independent firms with the appropriate credentials can issue a SAS 70 opinion.

    Risk: Not applicable. This question is to determine whether the company has had an independent review done. A clean SAS 70 report is a favorable sign for the MSSP.

Client Response:

15. *Does the MSSP have a change management policy and procedure and are they followed?*

    Guidance: One of the key information security policies that the MSSP should have in place is change management. Having this policy in place and following it indicates that the MSSP is careful about its environment and that only tested and approved changes are allowed in production.

    Risk: Without proper change management, a risk exists that unauthorized and untested changes may be introduced into the production environment, which could result in the MSSP having an unstable environment.

Client Response:

16. *Does the contract with the MSSP address potential termination of the contract and how that would be handled?*

Guidance: For the company's own protection, the contract with the MSSP should have adequate provisions for adjusting or terminating the contract as necessary. There are circumstances where it might be appropriate for the company to either adjust or terminate the contract. For example, if the company was acquired and the acquiring company had a state-of-the-art SOC, it might make sense to leverage the SOC and either reduce the scope of the contract or terminate it altogether. Another example is if a series of security incidents occurred where the MSSP was at fault. In this case, the company should have some form of recourse such as being able to terminate the contract.

Risk: The risk associated with not having a provision in the contract for adjusting or terminating the contract is that as the company's circumstances change or if the MSSP's service is not up to par, the company might have a limited ability to adjust or terminate the MSSP services without incurring a penalty.

Client Response:

Appendix P

Media Handling

As part of most business processes, information is generated and stored on many different types of media including paper documents, computer media (e.g., tapes, compact discs, floppy disks) and others. Much of the information being stored on paper and electronically is critical and can include (among others):

- Mission-critical data
  - Financial information
  - Operational data
- Sensitive information
  - Personnel files

Other questionnaires have covered different aspects of security as it relates to the examples listed above in areas such as backup and recovery and physical security. One aspect of securing this information that has not been covered in any detail is the protection of the media where the information is stored, which is the content of this questionnaire.

The questions below are primarily based on the International Standards Organization (ISO) 17799 information security standard for media handling. The key areas addressed in media handling include:

- Media management
- Media disposal
- Media in transit

The questions below are a starting point in discussing security related to media handling. Other questions should be added based on the client's specific business.

GENERAL

1. Is there a documented policy for media handling?

Guidance: A security policy to communicate management's position on media handling should exist. The policy should outline high-level roles and responsibilities and the requirements as they relate to media handling.

415

The policy should be easily accessible to employees so they can refer to it as necessary. The policy also helps in enforcing good media handling practices.

Risk: The risks associated with not having a policy for media handling include:
- Employees will not be aware of the company's media handling requirements and the related roles and responsibilities.
- It is difficult to enforce good media handling practices without an official policy.

Client Response:

2. *Are there any procedures for media handling?*

Guidance: The procedures for media handling are the step-by-step processes for different media handling scenarios that achieve compliance with the media handling security policy. Examples of scenarios include disposing of media and the use of couriers in sending media. Depending on the associated risk and complexity of the process, it might be appropriate to have documented procedures. Procedures are useful for two reasons. First, when new employees have to learn the process, the documented procedures can facilitate this learning. Second, a documented procedure helps ensure that the process is being performed consistently.

Risk: The risks associated with not having documented procedures include:
- Processes being performed inconsistently.
- Lack of process knowledge if employee turnover occurs; if the media handling processes are not documented and are only known by certain employees and they leave, no one has a good idea of how the media handling processes work.

Client Response:

3. *Does the organization have a data classification and retention policy that is enforced?*

Guidance: One of the dependencies for media handling is data classification and retention. All data does not require the same level of security as it relates to media handling. The appropriate security level is driven by the data classification and retention standards. If data is not classified and if no retention policy exists, it is difficult to determine the level of media handling security required.

Risk: If there is no data classification or retention policy, a risk exists that media handling controls will not be commensurate with the criticality of the information on the media.

Client Response:

4. *Identify the different types of media (paper, computer related, etc.), what information is on them, and the associated criticality.*

Guidance: The purpose of this question is to understand what media there are, what type of information is on the media, how important the information is, and the potential impact if a related security compromise occurs. Based on this question, you should have a high-level idea of the risk associated with media handling and how detailed the review of media handling should be.

Risk: Not applicable. The purpose of this question is to help determine the scope of the media handling activity.

Client Response:

5. *Have any security incidents related to media handling occurred?*

Guidance: Any history of security incidents is important as it might indicate a potential security weakness worth investigating. It is also useful to know what steps management took to address the security breach — i.e., reacting to the incident and taking specific steps to ensure that similar security incidents are prevented in the future. If the cause of the security incident has not been addressed, it may lead to security findings.

Risk: Not applicable. The purpose of this question is to determine whether there were any past security incidents and to obtain related information as outlined in the question.

Client Response:

MEDIA MANAGEMENT

6. *With reusable media, are contents properly erased prior to reuse?*

    Guidance: Reusable media should have information thoroughly erased prior to reuse. The standard for erasing (e.g., number of times information is overwritten) depends on the media. Specific steps should be taken to ensure that the contents are properly erased. This information, regarding specific steps, should be available from the media vendor or on security Web sites on the Internet.

    Risk: If information is not properly erased, a risk exists of unauthorized access to potentially sensitive information if it can be recovered. If the media is reused in the same department, minimal risk exists.

    Client Response:

7. *Is there an audit trail of personnel handling media with critical information (e.g., backup tapes, other stored information)?*

    Guidance: An audit trail of who handles media should be maintained. If a security breach occurs, the audit trail is instrumental in determining who might be responsible. A documented audit trail promotes accountability as it relates to handling media (e.g., tapes). The information should include who took the media, when they took it, for what purpose they took it, and when it was returned.

    Risk: The risk associated with not having an audit trail is a lack of knowledge about who handled the media, when it was taken out, and for what purpose. If a security breach occurs, little information about who handled the media is available. Consequently, there is no accountability, and it is difficult to investigate security incidents.

    Client Response:

8. *Are there controls limiting access to media so that only those who require access to it to do their jobs have it?*

    Guidance: As in other areas of the company, access to resources such as media should be limited to those who need it to perform their jobs. One critical area where this should be strictly followed is for those backup tapes which are mission critical. They are used to restore data on a regular basis and when a disaster occurs. A limited number of people should have access to backup tapes. To further control the tapes, access should be logged. Access control should be used for different media based on the associated risk.

Risk: The risk associated with not limiting access to media is that almost anyone will be able to access media containing potentially sensitive information. This can lead to unauthorized access to sensitive information.

Client Response:

---

9. *How is computer-related media stored? Is it stored according to manufacturers' specifications? Is someone responsible for the proper storage of computer-related media?*

Guidance: To ensure that computer-related media is adequately preserved, someone should be responsible for it. It should be stored according to manufacturers' specifications for the different types of media. In addition, someone's responsibilities should include the storage of media (similar to the concept of ownership in other areas of security).

Risk: The risk associated with not storing media according to manufacturers' specifications is that the media might not last or might lose critical information that resides on it.

Client Response:

---

10. *Are all media containing information appropriately labeled?*

Guidance: All media should be appropriately labeled to ensure that information on the media can be located and that the media receives the appropriate level of security. Labeling also helps ensure that the company data classification and data retention procedures are followed. In addition, labeling also makes it easier to find information. One of the issues you might notice is that media is not properly labeled, but one or two people know what all the media contains. In this case, the company is at risk if they leave. Labeling should follow a standard naming convention, making it easy for anyone to find what he or she needs.

Risk: The risk associated with not having good labeling processes is that data might not receive the right level of security, and in the event that data restoration is required, it may be difficult to find the data because it is unclear what is on the different media.

Client Response:

MEDIA DISPOSAL

11. *Is there a policy that provides guidance to employees on disposing of information based on the type of media and the classification of information?*

Guidance: Disposal of sensitive information can be a significant risk if not performed correctly. In the course of any given day, many paper documents are disposed of — some of these documents are extremely sensitive. These documents can include e-mails, memos, and letters. In addition to paper documents, there is also the issue of disposing of media (e.g., floppy disks, CDs), which requires properly erasing information on that type of media. Users should be aware of what is and is not sensitive based on the data classification policy and some judgment. Shredders should be used to destroy sensitive paper documents, and there should be processes to ensure that electronic information is properly erased.

Risk: The risk associated with not disposing of sensitive information properly is that sensitive information can be inappropriately exposed, resulting in embarrassment or potential legal troubles for the company.

Client Response:

---

12. *Is there a documented process for disposal of media?*
    - Are paper documents containing sensitive information properly shredded?
    - Is disposal of computer media performed so that the possibility of information being recovered is minimal?

Guidance: Until now, this questionnaire has focused on media handling at the policy level. The next step is to have a documented procedure that ensures that personnel know "how" to perform the process — i.e., procedures. The procedures should explain the steps involved in the disposal of media and the specific roles and responsibilities. Procedures help ensure that the processes are performed consistently. If employee turnover takes place, documented processes exist that someone else can follow. In the case of media handling, the procedure should clearly outline the accepted disposal methods based on the data classification. For example, the procedure might say to shred all documents that are considered "confidential."

Risk: The risk associated with not having a documented procedure is that users may not know how to properly dispose of media or it may be done inconsistently. This can result in exposure of sensitive information to unauthorized individuals. In addition, when turnover occurs, it may be difficult for someone else to learn the process.

Client Response:

---

13. *Does a third party handle disposal of media? If so, do appropriate agreements with the vendor exist regarding liability relating to the confidentiality of information?*

Guidance: Some companies use third parties to perform disposal operations such as shredding of documents or disposing of electronic media. Operationally, this makes sense from a productivity and potentially a cost perspective. A business case can be made on the basis that personnel do not have to waste their time on disposal-related activities and that the company will not have to spend money on the equipment required to dispose of media. One area of concern is ensuring that the third party performs the disposal as contracted. The contract should contain specific language regarding confidentiality of information — e.g., the third-party vendor should not be reading sensitive documents that are going to be disposed of. In addition, there should be someone who owns the relationship with the third party to ensure that it is doing the job per the contract. It is important to understand that even though a third party is used, the company is still ultimately responsible for protecting the confidentiality of any sensitive data on the media being disposed of.

Risk: The risk associated with third-party handling media is one of confidentiality. If the third party does not dispose of the media properly, the risk is that sensitive information can be retrieved from the media and be exposed, resulting in damage to the company's reputation and potential legal action (depending on the sensitivity of the information).

Client Response:

MEDIA IN TRANSIT

14. *Who transports media containing sensitive information? Is it handled by reputable organizations? Are there confidentiality agreements with these third parties?*

    Guidance: Similar to third parties handling the disposal of media, having third parties handling transport has the same concerns. These third parties should be adequately screened because this is a critical function that should be handled by a reputable company with the right experience. Typical due diligence such as reference checks and investigation of the condition of the company should be performed when selecting a company. Once selected, comprehensive contracts that address confidentiality should be crafted with the third party to ensure that it is accountable and the company is protected legally.

    Risk: The risk associated with using a less-than-adequate media transport company is that the confidentiality of the information on the media may not be protected. In addition, if the media is destroyed, data might be permanently lost (when media is sent out for repair).

    Client Response:

15. *For any third parties or couriers, are nondisclosure agreements (NDAs) in place?*

    Guidance: NDAs should be considered with any third party that gains access to sensitive company information. These agreements help in taking legal action if third parties inadvertently disclose company information that is meant to be confidential. The NDA essentially holds the third party accountable. When reviewing nondisclosure agreements, ensure that they have been reviewed and approved by the company's legal representatives to ensure that they have the appropriate provisions.

    Risk: The risk associated with not having a NDA is that the company will not have any legal basis for recourse against the third party if it discloses confidential information about the company.

    Client Response:

Appendix Q

HIPAA Security

As discussed earlier in this book, the Health Insurance Portability and Accountability Act (HIPAA) requirements encompass a wide variety of areas including:

- Transactions and codes
- Privacy
- Security

This questionnaire will focus only on the security requirements of HIPAA. The security requirements in HIPAA are very similar to the concepts covered in this book regarding what an information security program should look like. At a high level, the HIPAA security requirements require health care–related companies (those that meet certain criteria) to have sound information security programs that protect electronic patient-identifiable health information. As will become evident in the rest of the questionnaire, the regulations basically require health care companies to have all the elements of an information security program in place — i.e., everything from an initial risk analysis to policies and procedures and certain technologies. The regulation is technology neutral, and the requirements allow some flexibility in implementation. The security requirements are divided into three sections:

- Administrative procedures to guard data confidentiality, integrity, and availability of data
- Physical security to guard data confidentiality, integrity, and availability of data
- Technical security services to guard data confidentiality, integrity, and availability of data

Each of these sections has its own set of requirements, which are discussed in detail below.

USE OF THIS QUESTIONNAIRE

First, it is worth reiterating that this questionnaire is applicable only to the HIPAA Security requirements and not to the Privacy or Technical Code Sets requirements. The primary source for the questionnaire is the actual regulations, which should be reviewed if you have further questions. That said, this questionnaire serves the same purpose as the other questionnaires in this book. Although the questions are basically from the regulations themselves, there is guidance with each of the sections to help you understand why a given question is important. This questionnaire can facilitate a conversation to do much of the initial fact-finding. You obviously must still test and verify based on the client.

There are many software packages now on the market now that automate much of what is being asked here. This questionnaire complements those software packages and each has its place. As you talk with senior or managerial-level individuals at health care organizations, you should be armed with knowledge about the importance of a given regulation, the difference between a "required" specification and an "addressable" specification (discussed in a subsequent section), and how the HIPAA security requirement maps to information security best practices. This questionnaire will help you to become knowledgeable about the HIPAA security regulations and help facilitate the information gathering process for the assessment.

Once you have the initial information, software packages might be appropriate for collecting information in larger environments or to generate reports that are customized for HIPAA security. Tools can save significant time and produce standard reports that are useful for your client.

QUESTIONNAIRE STRUCTURE

The specific sections of the HIPAA security questionnaire are as follows:

- Is the entity subject to the HIPAA security regulations?
- What is the extent of the electronic protected health information?
- HIPAA security requirements
  - Administrative security regulations
  - Physical security regulations
  - Technical security regulations

This HIPAA security questionnaire follows the regulations from the *Federal Register*. Unlike the other questionnaires, the questions contain some guidance information but no risks. One reason for this is that many of these questions have been covered in other questionnaires where the risks have already been identified. In addition, because HIPAA is something that is mandated, companies subject to the regulation must comply.

For the questions in the HIPAA requirements section, the structure contains the following:

- Specification directly from the HIPAA security regulation (as stated in the *Federal Register*).
- For each requirement there are a set of questions to help determine whether a client is in compliance with the requirement. These questions are an initial list and, as with the other questionnaires, you should modify them to fit the requirements of your client. These questions are there to help you determine whether the company is in compliance with the specific HIPAA regulation, so you can use them at your discretion.

In general, this questionnaire is meant to be comprehensive as it covers the entire set of HIPAA security requirements. Although the requirements are fixed, the supporting questions used to determine compliance may vary based on your client.

IS THE ENTITY A "COVERED ENTITY?"

The applicability of HIPAA comes into question when a company provides some form of health care services. By providing health care services, the entity is most likely dealing with some patient records, which may be in electronic format and containing patient–identifiable information. In the *Federal Register*, the HIPAA regulations state that the HIPAA security standards are applicable to "covered entities," which are listed below. Note that further clarification of the regulation can be found on the U.S. Department of Health and Human Services Web site:

- A health plan
- A health care clearinghouse
- A health care provider who transmits health information in electronic form in connection with certain transactions (details provided in the questions below)

1. *Is the entity a health plan?*

   Does the entity provide or pay the cost of medical care? (If so, the entity is a health plan.) Examples of such entities include (from 45 CFR 160.103 Definitions):
   - A group health plan
   - A health insurance issuer
   - A health maintenance organization (HMO)
   - Part A or Part B of the Medicare program
   - The Medicaid program
   - An issuer of a Medicare supplemental policy (as defined in section 1882(g)(1) of the Act, 42 U.S.C. 1395ss(g)(1))
   - An issuer of a long-term care policy, excluding a nursing home fixed-indemnity policy
   - An employee welfare benefit plan or any other arrangement that is established or maintained for the purpose of offering or providing health benefits to the employees of two or more employers
   - The health care program for active military personnel under title 10 of the United States Code
   - The veterans health care program under 38 U.S.C. chapter 17
   - The Civilian Health and Medical Program of the Uniformed Services (CHAMPUS)(as defined in 10 U.S.C. 1072(4))
   - The Indian Health Service program under the Indian Health Care Improvement Act, 25 U.S.C. 1601, et seq.
   - The Federal Employees Health Benefits Program under 5 U.S.C. 8902, et seq.

- An approved State child health plan under title XXI of the Act, providing benefits for child health assistance that meet the requirements of section 2103 of the Act, 42 U.S.C. 1397, et seq.
- The Medicare + Choice program under Part C of title XVIII of the Act, 42 U.S.C. 1395w-21 through 1395w-28
- A high-risk pool that is a mechanism established under State law to provide health insurance coverage or comparable coverage to eligible individuals
- Any other individual or group plan, or combination of individual or group plans, that provides or pays for the cost of medical care (as defined in section 2791(a)(2) of the PHS Act, 42 U.S.C. 300gg-91(a)(2))

Health plan excludes (from 45 CFR 160.103 Definitions):
- A group health plan
- Any policy, plan, or program to the extent that it provides, or pays for the cost of, excepted benefits that are listed in section 2791(c)(1) of the PHS Act, 42 U.S.C. 300gg-91(c)(1); and
- A government-funded program (other than one listed in paragraph (i)-(xvi) of this definition above):
  - Whose principal purpose is other than providing, or paying the cost of, health care; or
  - Whose principal activity is:
    - The direct provision of health care to persons; or
    - The making of grants to fund the direct provision of health care to persons

Guidance: The list above provides guidance to determine whether the entity is a health plan. This guidance is from the original HIPAA regulations.

Client Response:

---

2. *Is the entity a health care clearinghouse?*

Is the entity one of the following (from 45 CFR 160.103 Definitions):
- A billing service?
- A repricing company?
- A community health management information system or community health information system?
- A value-added network and switch?

If the entity is one of the items listed above, does it perform one of the following functions (if so, the entity is a health care clearinghouse):
- Does it process or facilitate the processing of health information received from another entity in a nonstandard format or containing

nonstandard data content into standard *data elements* or a standard transaction?

- Does it receive a standard transaction from another entity and process or facilitate the processing of health information into nonstandard format or nonstandard data content for the receiving entity?

Guidance: This guidance above is also directly from the regulation. To answer the questions to determine applicability as a health care clearinghouse, knowledge of the standard transactions is required. Interaction with those involved with implementation of the standard transaction code sets may be required.

Client Response:

---

3. *Is the entity a health care provider transmitting health information in connection with certain transactions? (from 45 CFR 160.103 Definitions):*

Does the entity transmit information with other parties to carry out financial or administrative activities related to health care where the following types of information are transmitted (If so, entity is a health care provider):
- Health care claims or equivalent encounter information?
- Health care payment and remittance advice?
- Coordination of benefits?
- Health care claim status?
- Enrollment and disenrollment in a health plan?
- Eligibility for a health plan?
- Health plan premium payments?
- Referral certification and authorization?
- First report of injury?
- Health claims attachments?
- Other transactions that the Secretary may prescribe by regulation?

Client Response:

---

4. *Is the entity a "business associate"?*

Guidance: Business associate relationships arise when a person or entity provides services on behalf of a covered entity but is not a member of its workforce. If the work performed involves the handling of protected health information covered under HIPAA. The activities can vary and can include billing, claims processing, data analysis and others.

Client Response:

---

5. *Does the organization work with third-party administrators that handle personally identifiable patient records at their offices or at their satellite offices (or home offices)?*

   Guidance: Based on the HIPAA definition of "covered entities," these third-party administrators are an extension of the company and are thus subject to the HIPAA security regulations.

Client Response:

---

6. *Are there individuals who work from home or remote sites where they handle or transmit personally identifiable health information? What specific processes are these employees performing?*

   Guidance: This is important to understand because the workforce of a "covered entity" includes everyone on site as well as everyone off site — i.e., the security standards must be implemented for all workers. The relevant implication here is that if people are working from home, the "covered entity" is required to ensure that the appropriate security standards are implemented.

Client Response:

If the entity passes one of the criteria listed above, the HIPAA security requirements are applicable and the entity information security program should be assessed against those requirements.

APPLICABLE DATA AND PROCESSES — WHAT IS THE EXTENT OF PROTECTED HEALTH INFORMATION?

The questions in this section are to help in determining the scope of the HIPAA security review. Some of the main drivers of HIPAA security are where electronic protected health information resides and how it is transmitted. The questions below are not part of the actual regulation but are here to help determine which systems will require a detailed review and which types of technology expertise will be required when conducting the assessment. For the questions in this section, as with the others, it is critical to talk to the appropriate business and technology owners.

1. *Critical processes: Describe the processes related to patient records. What applications and systems are used to process patient records? This includes all patient processes including (but not limited to):*
   - Patient appointments
   - Patient diagnosis
   - Transcription services
   - Patient billing
   - Patient collections

   Guidance: This is a general question meant to begin identifying the processes and systems as they pertain to electronic protected health information. All of the processes above and probably some others (depending on the organization) deal with electronic personally identifiable health information being processed and stored. This information will help you drill down into detail about the relevant processes and systems.

   Client Response:

2. *Where is the data? Identify the personally identifiable health information in electronic format and where it is stored.*

   Guidance: This is an extension of the previous question.
   - *Personally identifiable health information:* The HIPAA security requirements are only applicable to *electronic personally identifiable health information.* This includes anything in the patient's records that links a person to health-related information. The HIPAA security regulations *do not* apply to health data that cannot be correlated to specific persons. An example where an organization might have health-related data that is not subject to HIPAA security is research organizations, which collect vast amounts of data for research and analysis purposes.
   - *Information in electronic form:* The HIPAA security regulations are not applicable to any data in *physical form.* In addition to information stored on specific machines, "electronic form" also refers to protected health information on magnetic tape, disks, or other readable media.

   Client Response:

3. *Transmission of data: How is personally identifiable data transmitted and to whom is it transmitted?*

Guidance: Under the HIPAA security regulations, electronic protected health information includes personally identifiable data while in transit, which could be within an internal network or out through the Internet. Although the data that resides on specific machines can be identified by examining what is on the different systems, identifying data in transit will require that you speak to individuals who are familiar with how data flows across the network and how the different applications talk to each other.

Client Response:

4. *Portable devices: Are portable devices such as personal digital assistants (PDAs) used for any processes using personally identifiable health information?*

    Guidance: Under the general term, "workstation," the definition in the HIPAA security standards includes (per the *Federal Register*), "...portable devices...any other devices that performs similar functions, and electronic media stored in its immediate environment." This can include PDAs (personal digital assistants) or other similar devices. If PDAs are in use, you will also have to look at the use of wireless networks at hospitals and what type of associated security measures are in place.

    Client Response:

5. *Telephone and "faxback" systems: Are telephone and faxback systems in use where the entity provides protected health information via fax based on a telephone request? If so, the information faxed back would be considered protected health information.*

    Guidance: In this scenario, only the party that is faxing the information based on a telephone request is obligated to secure the protected health information being faxed as this is in electronic format. The initial request made using the telephone is not subject to HIPAA security regulations because this information is not in electronic form.

    Client Response:

6. *Are there individuals who can access electronic protected health information via a wireless connection?*

> **Guidance:** Wireless is growing very quickly and there is a good chance that the entity being audited is using wireless. Doctors, nurses, etc., can use wireless in a number of different areas. In addition, doctors may also be using wireless at home to access hospital networks, where they may be accessing electronic protected health information or have the ability to do so.

Client Response:

HIPAA SECURITY REQUIREMENTS

This section contains questions regarding the actual HIPAA security requirements. Much of the information is directly from the actual law in the *Federal Register*. The guidance section in some of the questions contains some of the commentary that was given by the public as the law was being reviewed and crafted. As you go through the questions, you should note that many of the requirements imposed in the HIPAA security regulations are simply good security practices. Many of the requirements map back to information security best practices such as the International Standards Organization (ISO) 17799.

Before going through the HIPAA security requirements, it is worth discussing how the HIPAA regulations are set up. The specific requirements are referred to as "standards." For most of the standards, specific instructions for implementation exist, which are either "required" or "addressable." Each of these concepts is discussed in further detail below.

- *Standard* — Standards are the actual HIPAA requirements. They are similar to security policies as they are high-level requirements with which entities must be in compliance. As discussed in earlier chapters, however, these requirements or "policies" should be broken down into procedures to help personnel be compliant with them. The "procedures" in this case are the specifications, which are either "required" or "addressable" (discussed below). In some cases, the standard is very clear and consequently, no specifications exist. In these cases, the standard is supposed to serve as the instructions also. Keep in mind that standards must be complied with.
- *Required* — Covered entities must be in compliance with the "required" specifications — i.e., they have no choice. Essentially, these can be viewed as the minimum requirements with which all covered entities must be in compliance. As will be seen later, although these are minimum requirements, there is flexibility in how these specifications can be accomplished

relative to technology and processes. In the context of a security assessment, security consultants should use their expertise to develop recommendations that address these "required" specifications in a cost-effective manner.

- *Addressable* — With the "addressable" specifications, entities have flexibility. These specifications are essentially suggestions, which entities should implement if they deem it is reasonable for their environment based on a number of factors determining the overall risk. If the measure is deemed reasonable, the entity must implement the "addressable specification." If it is not deemed to be reasonable, the entity can do one of two things:
  - Implement an alternative measure that is more appropriate for their environment and that accomplishes the same goal
  - Implement no measure, accept the associated risk, and document the rationale for not implementing the "addressable specification"

In terms of a security assessment, companies should be advised regarding these "addressable" specifications. Whether or not to implement these specifications comes down to a few considerations:

- *Cost-benefit analysis* — Does the addressable specification make sense based on the risk being mitigated, and are there alternatives that can accomplish the same goal with less cost?
- *Justification* — If no measure is being implemented, can the entity provide a reasonable justification for not implementing the "addressable" specification? Consider the impact to the entity if a security incident results from not having the particular security measure in place.
- *Measure might not be applicable* — The entity might deem that a given measure is just not applicable to its environment and thus not do anything.

In any case, with all HIPAA specifications, the entity must ensure that they document whatever they do. In the case of "addressable" specifications in particular, it is crucial to document the rationale for whatever action the entity finally decides on.

The questionnaire is structured so that the required and addressable specifications are listed separately for each standard. For each set of specifications, some questions and guidance are provided in this questionnaire that could help you discuss them. Some of the guidance and additional questions are based on the comments and questions received from the general public during the period when the public was reviewing the requirements. Note that in some cases, there are no specifications and only a standard. In these cases, the standard is required.

ADMINISTRATIVE PROCEDURES

Below are the questions for the Administrative Safeguards section, which is Section 164.308 in the Federal Register. The Administrative Safeguards are mostly the Security Management–related topics related to HIPAA. These specifications are similar to the "Security Policy" and "Organizational Security" sections of ISO 17799. As stated earlier, many of the HIPAA requirements are recognized information security best practices.

1. STANDARD — SECURITY MANAGEMENT PROCESS

This standard requires that the covered entity "implement policies and procedures to prevent, detect, contain, and correct security violations"[1] This statement basically requires covered entities to have a formal information security program in place. The program requires a foundation of policies and procedures that secures the entity.

a. REQUIRED Implementation Specifications

i. Risk Analysis

"Conduct an accurate and thorough assessment of the potential risks and vulnerabilities to the confidentiality, integrity, and availability of electronic protected health information held by the covered entity."[2]

In determining compliance with this requirement, below are some questions that can be asked. These questions are related to risk analysis and some key aspects that you should look for.

1. *Did the covered entity perform a risk analysis to determine the potential risks to the confidentiality, integrity, and availability of electronic protected health information?*

   Guidance: Look for a risk analysis that is documented and recently performed. The document should contain specific vulnerabilities and risks as well as a mitigation strategy. Because environments from the information technology (IT) and organizational perspectives can change, it is important to understand when the risk analysis was performed and whether any significant changes have occurred since it was done. The risk analysis might have little value if it is too old.

   Client Response:

   ---

2. *Was the risk analysis independently performed?*

   Guidance: The risk analysis can arguably be viewed as the most critical component of the HIPAA security requirement because it defines what security measures need to be enhanced or put in place. An independent risk analysis lends significant credibility to a risk analysis. Independence can mean a third party or an independent internal group such as internal audit. The basic point of this question is to ensure that the analysis was objective.

Client Response:

---

3. *Is the risk analysis documented with risks and recommendations clearly stated?*

   Guidance: The risk analysis should be documented so that evidence exists that it was done and so the findings resulting from it are clearly defined. The risk analysis "deliverable" should map risks and recommendations to help facilitate mitigation activities. Ideally, the risk analysis should basically serve as the roadmap for specific information security initiatives to achieve compliance with HIPAA security requirements.

Client Response:

---

4. *Does the risk analysis clearly define the extent to which electronic protected health information exists?*

   Guidance: From a methodology perspective, the risk analysis should clearly state the extent to which electronic protected health information exists. The risk analysis should have examined all processes and systems where electronic protected health information travels and resides.

Client Response:

---

5. *Does the risk analysis define what the critical systems are (i.e., where the electronic protected health information resides)? In addition, did the risk analysis accomplish the following:*
   - Were the technical security measures in place to protect these systems considered in the risk analysis?
   - Was the network architecture considered?
   - Was the security architecture considered (e.g., firewalls, intrusion detection, host level controls)?
   - Was any hands-on testing performed to validate the security measures in place?
   - Were the logging and monitoring processes considered?

   Guidance: Similar to defining what the electronic protected health information is, the systems on which it resides are equally important. Once these systems are identified, the security architecture protecting these critical systems should have been evaluated and hands-on testing should have been conducted based on the level of risk.

Client Response:

---

6. *Does the risk analysis consider potential impacts of breaches of security related to the confidentiality, integrity, and availability of electronic protected health information?*
   - Were the potential impacts quantified to the extent possible?
   - Were anticipated uses or disclosures of information identified as part of the risk analysis?

Guidance: To properly determine risk, the analysis must determine the potential impacts related to security violations. In this area, it is critical to make sure that individuals from the business side are involved as they will either know or be able to validate the potential impact. The quantification of the impact, if it is possible to determine it, helps determine how to prioritize security recommendations resulting from the risk analysis.

Client Response:

---

7. *Did the risk analysis include meeting with both business process and technology owners?*

Guidance: It is critical to involve both the business process and technology owners in the risk analysis process. Too often, the technology owners take the responsibility for performing the risk analysis and as a result, it is very focused on technology. Because we are concerned about electronic protected health information, where it resides, how it flows, etc., it is critical to involve business process owners. They will typically have more knowledge of the importance of the electronic information and what some of the risks are. In addition, business process owners may be able to tell you more about the process that you would not necessarily know by talking to someone from the technology side.

Client Response:

---

ii. Risk Management

"Implement security measures sufficient to reduce risks and vulnerabilities to a reasonable and appropriate level to comply with"[3] [Section 164.306 — requiring companies to periodically evaluate security measures].

This is effectively the next step after the risk analysis. Covered entities have a significant amount of flexibility in implementing security measures based on how appropriate the level is defined below (based on Code of Federal Regulations section 164.306):

- Ensuring the confidentiality, integrity, and availability of electronic protected health information
- Protecting against any reasonably anticipated threats or hazards to the security or integrity of the electronic protected health information
- Protecting against any reasonably anticipated uses of disclosures of electronic protected health information not permitted

Below are some questions to help determine compliance with this requirement.

1. *Based on the risk analysis, have the risks been mitigated with specific security measures? If not, is a plan in place to ensure that the risks are mitigated?*

   Guidance: To meet this requirement, appropriate security measures must be put in place to mitigate risks identified in the risk analysis. If measures have not been implemented, having a plan in place should help ensure that corrective action is taken. You should verify mitigation steps based on the level of risk involved. Here, you can use a combination of tools and manual procedures to perform testing.

Client Response:

---

iii. Sanction Policy

"Apply appropriate sanctions against workforce members who fail to comply with the security policies and procedures of the covered entity."[4]

The sanction policy is essentially the enforcement component of an information security program. It requires sanctions against individuals for noncompliance relative to the HIPAA security requirements. Below are some questions to help determine compliance with this requirement.

1. *Is there a process in place for detecting noncompliance with HIPAA security requirements?*

   Guidance: Is there a way for the entity to know if a lack of compliance is present? In looking at noncompliance, automated means such as system alerts when noncompliance occurs are the most efficient method of knowing about noncompliance. With certain specifications, the only way to check for compliance is to do it manually. In any case, there should be a process for determining noncompliance with HIPAA security requirements.

   Client Response:

2. *Are there policies and procedures in place so that individuals know what they must comply with?*

   Guidance: There should be some standards or polices that personnel have access to, which state the security requirements that employees must follow. As discussed in earlier chapters, security policies are the foundation of an information security program and are a crucial component of enforcement. Without clear policies that are easily accessible, it is difficult to hold personnel accountable, as compliance standards will not be clear to them.

   Client Response:

3. *Do a noncompliance policy and procedure exist?*

   Guidance: There will be instances where employees will not be able to comply with a requirement for a variety of reasons. To facilitate noncompliance reporting of these cases, a noncompliance policy and procedure, which require employees to report areas of noncompliance to management, should be in place. Along with the policy, a form for noncompliance should be used, where information including what specific policy was not followed, reason for noncompliance, and other mitigating controls is documented. This documentation is required by HIPAA and is a good practice because it creates an audit trail.

   Client Response:

4. Do sanctions for noncompliance exist and are they based on severity?

Guidance: Sanctions are a key component of handling noncompliance issues. Without sanctions, no repercussion exists for personnel who do not follow the policy. Ideally, the sanctions should be based on severity and other relevant circumstances.

Client Response:

---

5. Is an internal audit process in place?

Guidance: Internal audit will be covered later in this checklist; however, it is an important point when discussing sanctions. Audits provide management with a view of where some of the control weaknesses and noncompliance issues are. The audit process is also an excellent way to enforce HIPAA security requirements. Ideally, the internal audit process should audit for many of the HIPAA security requirements to help ensure compliance with HIPAA security.

Client Response:

---

iv. Information Systems Activity Review

"Implement procedures to regularly review records of information system activity, such as audit logs, access reports, and security incident tracking reports."[5]

This specification is a "monitoring" requirement as it pertains to ensuring that information systems and data remain secure. Below are some questions to help determine compliance with this requirement.

1. Do documented procedures detail what reports should be reviewed to effectively monitor the systems (e.g., system logs, audit logs)?

Guidance: Activity review should be a planned activity that is documented. The level of review should be based on the criticality of systems, the level of activity on the relevant systems, and any other relevant factors. Depending on the amount of information generated, it might make sense to recommend that the entity use third-party tools to automate the log review process and provide exception reports. There should also be a process that outlines the frequency and nature of review based on the risk.

Client Response:

---

2. *Are specific people responsible for log review?*

   Guidance: In many organizations, if log review is not assigned to some-one, it is not done or if it is, it is purely reactionary. Although being reactive in some cases may be appropriate, it may not be when it comes to critical systems. Assigning this responsibility to specific individuals and having clear expectations with respect to logging will help ensure that logs are be-ing reviewed appropriately.

Client Response:

---

3. *Who has access to the various logs used to monitor system activity? Can the people who have access to the logs change the information in the logs without being detected?*

   Guidance: Access to the logs and the ability to change them should be closely monitored. Segregation of duties should be considered so that peo-ple cannot perform any malicious activity and hide their tracks. This will especially be a problem in small companies, where the staff is typically very small. In these cases, recommendations for alternative methods pro-viding some mitigating controls should be suggested.

Client Response:

---

b. ADDRESSABLE Implementation Specifications

i. None

2. STANDARD — REQUIRED — Assigned Security Responsibility

"Identify the security official who is responsible for the development and implemen-tation of the policies and procedures required by this subpart for the entity."[6]

This standard requires someone to be identified who owns the responsibility for the development and implementation of the policies and procedures required by HIPAA security standards. This person can have different titles including Chief Security Officer, HIPAA Security Officer, Compliance Officer, etc. Note that this standard does not have any specifications — i.e., the standard serves as both the policy and instructions for implementing. Below are some questions to help determine compliance with this requirement. Note — there are no implementation specifications for this standard.

1. *Does someone in the organization have the responsibility for development and implementation of policies and procedures relative to the HIPAA security standards?*

    Guidance: In the final regulations, the intent was that one person have the ultimate responsibility for security. Even in cases where different divisions of a larger company may assign responsibility at the division level, there still must be one person who has overall ownership for security. This person might have the title "Security Officer" or some other managerial security–type title. The "Security Officer" should ensure that the development and implementation of policies and procedures involve both business and technology representatives. If this is not the case, it should be flagged and a recommendation should be provided. Ideally, the "Security Officer" should be able to facilitate a coordinated effort in developing and implementing security policies and procedures.

    Client Response:

    ---

2. *Does a security awareness program exist to help ensure that implementation of security policies and procedures is successful?*

    Guidance: Awareness is an important part of implementation to help ensure that personnel know and understand security policies and procedures. Once they know about them, they are more likely to follow them, and from management's perspective, they can be held accountable. When evaluating the awareness program, keep in mind that not all personnel have to attend all of the training — i.e., personnel should attend the training they need.

    Client Response:

    ---

3. *Are security policies and procedures readily accessible so that personnel can refer to them as needed?*

    Guidance: Personnel will have questions as they apply the policy in their daily jobs. You should ensure that security policies and procedures reside where personnel can easily access them if they need to. If personnel cannot access these documents, it is difficult to enforce them.

Client Response:

---

4. *Does the "Security Officer" (or whatever that person's title is) ensure that security policies and procedures are updated as the business and IT environment change?*

   Guidance: Maintenance of security measures is a HIPAA requirement. Also, it is critical to ensure that policies and procedures are updated as needed. In addition, there should be a process to communicate updates to personnel. If needed, additional security awareness training might also be necessary.

Client Response:

---

5. *Does the Security Officer (or the person who owns security) have the ability to escalate issues to upper management?*

   Guidance: The Security Officer is something that is new and often, it does not get the visibility that is required for the role to be effective. Security policies and procedures are difficult to implement because people sometimes do not see their value, and they might need to change the way they do things. Aside from the education and awareness that users are provided, the Security Officer needs to have access to upper management to escalate issues and gain resolution.

Client Response:

---

3. STANDARD — WORKFORCE SECURITY

"Implement policies and procedures to ensure that all members of its workforce have appropriate access to electronic protected health information, …and to prevent those workforce members who do not have access, …from obtaining access to electronic protected health information."[7]

This requirement basically states that only those personnel who require access to electronic protected health information should have it and those who do not require access should be prevented from having access. Access should be given on a "need to have" basis. Note that this standard does not have any required specifications. When conducting the HIPAA security review for this standard, you should review the questions from other questionnaires such as User ID Administration and Terminations.

a. REQUIRED Implementation Specifications

i. None

b. ADDRESSABLE Implementation Specifications

i. Authorization and/or Supervision

> "Implement procedures for the authorization and/or supervision of workforce members who work with electronic protected health information or in locations where it might be accessed."[8]

This specification pertains to access control pertaining to electronic protected health information. Access and authorization are at multiple levels including network, application, and database. The process should address these different aspects of access. Below are some questions to help determine compliance with this requirement.

1. *Does a documented process exist for obtaining authorization to access electronic protected health information? If formal authorizations are not granted, does supervision exist for personnel working with electronic protected health information?*

   Guidance: Ideally, a documented process should exist for obtaining authorization, at a minimum. The extent and granularity of the procedure will vary depending on the size and nature of the organization. The standard has given considerable flexibility in making this decision.

   Client Response:

   ---

2. *Is there a form that is filled out or some type of workflow application to facilitate and document the process for obtaining access?*

   Guidance: Depending on the organization, this may be done on paper or via some type of workflow application such as Lotus Notes. The form or workflow process should document what information the individual will be able to access and, in the case of a contractor, how long the access is required. Access should be given once the form goes through the proper approvals. Approvers of the access should understand that the access is to be given on a "least privilege" basis.

Client Response:

---

3. *Can the authorization be controlled so that access is given to only those records that are required for a person to do his or her job?*

   Guidance: If access to the electronic protected health information can be controlled at a granular level, it should be done. Keep in mind that there are maintenance issues associated with that type of access, so when making any related recommendations, make sure you understand the security and operational needs of the client.

Client Response:

---

4. *Is the data owner involved in the approval process?*

   Guidance: The data owner is ultimately responsible for his data. As a result, any process for authorization should involve the data owner. The data owner should at least be informed and ideally, should be one of the individuals who approves access.

Client Response:

---

5. *Is sharing of IDs prohibited?*

   Guidance: If personnel share IDs, accountability is lacking and enforcement becomes difficult. Also, because different people have different levels of access, each should have his or her own ID. If cases exist where it is operationally not feasible to have separate IDs, some form of supervision or logging and review should occur.

Client Response:

---

6. *When users require passwords reset, is this done in a secure manner?*

   Guidance: In an attack scenario, password resets are one of the social engineering tools often used to gain unauthorized access to critical systems and data. Support desks or people handling the support function should properly authenticate people asking for password resets. In a small environment, most people know each other and that knowledge of someone is used to authenticate a person. Although this might be a valid method, it can be a problem in environments where there is significant turnover. It is best to have a secure method for doing password resets regardless of the size of the environment.

Client Response:

---

ii. Workforce Clearance Procedures

"Implement procedures to determine that the access of a workforce member to electronic protected health information is appropriate."[9]

This specification is relevant once it is determined that someone needs access to electronic protected health information. It requires that access to electronic protected health information be given on a "need to have" basis. Below are some questions to help determine compliance with this requirement.

1. *Are roles and responsibilities and job descriptions clearly defined so that access can be provided to personnel on a "need to have" basis?*

   Guidance: Assigning access is dependent on knowing what a person does in the company and what that person will need to access to do his or her job. Roles and responsibilities are not always clearly defined, and this may cause problems when providing access. When performing a security assessment, lack of clear roles and responsibilities should be flagged as a weakness as this has a ripple effect on many other security processes such as user ID administration, incident management, and terminations.

Client Response:

---

2. *How granular is the access control to electronic protected health information? Is this functionality used in providing personnel access to only what is required?*

Guidance: What the system can do in terms of access control is very important because automated system measures are the best way to enforce it. With granular access control, a balance must be maintained between security and the ongoing maintenance of providing very granular access.

Client Response:

3. *Does the data owner (the person responsible for the electronic protected health information records) approve access? If not, is that person made aware?*

   Guidance: The data owner is ultimately responsible for the handling and security of the electronic protected health information, so that individual should approve or at least be aware of who is accessing the data. This helps provide the necessary accountability as it pertains to the safeguarding of the data.

Client Response:

4. *If access cannot be controlled by the system, what mitigating controls are in place to ensure that personnel are accessing only what they need?*

   Guidance: In some cases, there may be systems where there is little or no access control. In these cases, some type of supervision or other mitigating controls should be present. The client may consider log review or reviewing edit reports of key electronic protected health information to help ensure the integrity of the data.

Client Response:

iii. Termination Procedures

"Implement procedures for terminating access to electronic protected health information when the employment of a workforce member ends or as required by determinations made as specified in the Workforce Clearance Procedures paragraph."[10]

The main point of this specification is to ensure that if an employee is terminated or leaves a company, any access that individual had to electronic protected health information should be disabled or deleted. Like other HIPAA security requirements, strong termination procedures are a generally accepted information security best practice. Below are some questions to help determine compliance with this requirement.

1. *Do documented policies and procedures for terminations exist?*

   Guidance: Termination policies and procedures should be documented so that all personnel know their responsibilities in the termination process.

   Client Response:

   ---

2. *As part of the termination process, are specific termination activities performed — e.g., return of items assigned to the individual (such as security badges and keys), change of locks, change of shared account passwords, change any systems where an individual shared access or had privileged access, etc.?*

   Guidance: Ideally, there should be a central repository where information is stored about what items an employee has to ensure that all are returned upon termination.

   Client Response:

   ---

3. *Is access periodically reviewed to ensure that personnel have access only to what they need (relative to electronic protected health information)?*

   Guidance: With access to critical systems, periodic review of access or "purging" is a key control that should be performed periodically as a mitigating control in case access has not been assigned properly or in case terminated employees' access was not properly removed.

   Client Response:

   ---

4. STANDARD — INFORMATION ACCESS MANAGEMENT

"Implement policies and procedures for authorizing access to electronic protected health information."[11]

This standard addresses the process for actually accessing electronic protected health information. This standard is different from the Workforce Security Standard in that this one is more concerned with access to where the electronic protected health information resides, but the other is focused on the people who have the access.

a. REQUIRED Implementation Specifications

i. Isolating Health Care Clearinghouse Functions

"If a health care clearinghouse is part of a larger organization, the clearinghouse must implement policies and procedures that protect the electronic protected health information of the clearinghouse from unauthorized access by the larger organization."

1. *Does the entity qualify as a health care clearinghouse? (See earlier part of checklist).*

   Guidance: Before going further with this set of requirements, it should be confirmed whether the entity is a health care clearinghouse based on the criteria from the first section of this questionnaire.

   Client Response:

2. *If the entity is a health care clearinghouse, are there documented policies and procedures that address access to electronic protected health information?*

   Guidance: Look for documented policies and procedures that address access to electronic protected health information for the health care clearinghouse. The policies should address how authorized access to electronic protected health information is obtained. In addition, all of the other related policies and procedures such as employee terminations should also be included.

   Client Response:

3. *Does anyone from the larger organization have access to the electronic protected health information on the health care clearinghouse systems?*

   Guidance: If someone from the larger organization does have access to the health care clearinghouse systems, is this access authorized and has it gone through the proper approvals? Also, does the covered entity have a way of knowing who uses that access and whether those individuals should have it? This is related to measures such as purging IDs on a regular basis and ensuring that a solid user ID administration policy and procedure are in place.

Client Response:

b. ADDRESSABLE Implementation Specifications

i. Access Authorization

"Implement policies and procedures for granting access to electronic protected health information, for example, through access to a workstation, transaction, program, process, or other mechanism."[12]

This specification addresses access to electronic protected health information wherever it resides.

1. *Do documented policies and procedures for granting access to electronic protected health information exist? Are these policies and procedures readily accessible?*

   Guidance: For this specification, look for the documented policies and procedures. They might just be a part of the overall user ID administration policies and procedures. Situations where this might not be necessary include very small entities, where a limited number of people have access.

Client Response:

2. *Are there specific workstations (or other devices) that are dedicated to certain functions and from which electronic protected health information can be accessed? If so, are there strict access controls to ensure that only those who require access have it?*

   Guidance: In health care facilities, there are often workstations used for certain medical functions where doctors, nurses, etc. can access electronic protected health information about patients. Access to these workstations should be restricted. Also, users should log out of the application after using it so other, unauthorized individuals cannot view sensitive information.

Client Response:

3. *Where systems can facilitate access control to electronic protected health information at the transaction level, is this functionality used?*

Guidance: If the electronic protected health information is accessed via some application, the access control features might allow access to be controlled at the transaction level. This is important because we sometimes tend to think of access at the network or file level. At the application level, features may exist that allow more granular control. Keep in mind, however, that there is maintenance associated with providing this type of access.

Client Response:

ii. Access Establishment and Modification

"Implement policies and procedures that, based upon the entity's access authorization policies, establish, document, review, and modify a user's right of access to a workstation, transaction, program, or process."[13]

This requirement addresses the modification of a user's access based on that individual's job requirements.

1. *Is there a policy and procedure for the establishment and subsequent adjustment or modification of a user's access based on change in positions or other changes in status?*

Guidance: This is very much related to the earlier specification on Access Authorization. The user ID administration policy and procedure should allow for people's jobs to be changed and their access be changed accordingly. Look for human resources (HR), department management, and IT to be involved in this process.

Client Response:

2. *Is users' access reviewed on a regular basis?*

Guidance: Although this is not a required item, it is a good idea in most cases. If the termination process is not effective, reviewing user access is a good mechanism for ensuring, on a regular basis, that only authorized users have access and that the level of access is appropriate. In very small entities, this probably will not be as important because "everyone knows everyone."

Client Response:

5. STANDARD — SECURITY AWARENESS AND TRAINING

"Implement a security awareness and training program for all members of its workforce (including management)."[14]

As discussed in various parts of this book, awareness is a key component in the success of an information security program. This also holds true for HIPAA security requirements. During the initial comment phase of the HIPAA security regulation, some interesting comments, which are worth noting for clarification purposes, were submitted:

- Covered entities are not required to provide training to business associates or anyone else who is not a member of their workforces. Business associates must, however, be made aware of the entity's security policies and procedures.
- Covered entities have significant latitude in how much and what type of training they provide. Training should be based on the specific security risks the entity faces.
- The intention of this requirement is that awareness training is not a one-time process but an evolving one as changes occur in personnel and in the business.

Some general questions that should be asked to assess the level of security awareness include the following. Although these requirements referenced in the questions below have not been specifically stated in the regulations, they help provide a good assessment of the level of awareness:

1. *Are any security awareness programs in place?*

    Guidance: Before going further into the specifications, you should determine whether any security awareness programs are currently in place. Awareness programs do not have to be formal in nature but can include such things as newsletters, security tips sent out over e-mail, etc.

Client Response:

2. *Are security policies and procedures readily accessible by employees?*

Guidance: Having security policies and procedures easily accessible can help promote awareness. Some companies have a central repository on the company's intranet site where employees can easily find them. If a question arises about what should be done from a security perspective, the information is readily accessible.

Client Response:

3. *Does the entity have an orientation program for new employees and does it incorporate security policies and procedures?*

Guidance: Orientation programs for new employees are a very effective way to communicate security policies and procedures. Relative to HIPAA, key provisions affecting employees can be communicated so that new personnel understand their responsibilities relative to security. If there is an orientation that addresses security policies and procedures, employees should formally acknowledge that they were made aware of these policies.

Client Response:

4. *If personnel have questions about policies and procedures, are there people identified to whom they can go?*

Guidance: Security policies and procedures can sometimes be difficult to understand, and it is helpful if employees have the opportunity to ask someone if they do not know what a policy means or whether their implementation of it is compliant. There is a greater likelihood of noncompliance if personnel do not understand and are unable to interpret security policies. This interaction is a very key component of a security program and will help promote compliance.

Client Response:

a. REQUIRED Implementation Specifications

i. None

b. ADDRESSABLE Implementation Specifications

i. Security Reminders

"Implement periodic security updates."[15]

This requirement calls for periodic security reminders for employees.

1. *What type of ongoing security awareness program is in place?*

   Guidance: With security, the more awareness, the better. Often, it takes more than one education session to raise security awareness to the appropriate level. With HIPAA security, awareness is even more important, considering the potential impacts of noncompliance, including fines and damage to the company's reputation. Some of the common ongoing type of "reminder" programs include newsletters, security tips via e-mail, and focused security education sessions.

   _____

   Client Response:

   _____

2. *What is the process for communicating any changes to security policies and procedures?*

   Guidance: There should be a formal process for communicating changes to security policies and procedures. Depending on the complexity of the policy, varying methods such as e-mail and formal education sessions can be used for communicating changes. Someone should be responsible and accountable for making and communicating changes to security policies and procedures. This function should be centralized to the extent possible to ensure that changes are communicated and that there is a common understanding of what changes were made. This communication should include the change and what the implications are for personnel from both the process and technology perspectives.

   _____

   Client Response:

   _____

ii. Protection from Malicious Software

"Implement procedures for guarding against, detecting, and reporting malicious software."[16]

This requirement, before the final draft of the regulations, was related only to computer viruses. The terminology was changed to "malicious software" to include malicious acts such as worms.

1. *Have there been any recent incidents relating to viruses, worms, or other malicious software?*

   Guidance: Recent incidents relating to malicious software and how the entity reacted to it will provide significant information regarding how malicious software is handled. Many of the questions below can be answered as a result of this question.

   Client Response:

   ---

2. *Is anti-virus software in use in the IT environment?*

   Guidance: Anti-virus software should be running where appropriate based on the individual company's business requirements. To the extent possible, anti-virus software should be centrally managed and locked down on PCs, so that employees cannot prevent it from running.

   Client Response:

   ---

3. *Are virus signatures updated on a regular basis?*

   Guidance: Ideally, this should be done automatically with minimal human intervention. Depending on the risk, the company may consider multiple anti-virus vendors to decrease the associated risk.

   Client Response:

   ---

4. *Do users know what to do in the event that they encounter malicious software?*

   Guidance: This question speaks to incident handling, which is a related HIPAA requirement. There should be a documented process for incident handling complete with escalation guidelines, contact names, etc. (see Incident Handling questionnaire for further details)

   Client Response:

---

5. *Do the security risks of the entity justify any type of network- or host-based intrusion management system? If not, what mitigating controls are in place to protect systems with electronic protected health information against malicious software or intrusions? How would the company know if someone was trying to gain unauthorized access to electronic protected health information?*

   Guidance: Depending on the complexity of the environment, how it is managed, and the associated risk, intrusion management might be a viable option for the entity. Within a security assessment, key factors must be considered when recommending intrusion management including monitoring capabilities, risks, and cost. Besides formal intrusion management systems, there are specific logs already on a system, which, if reviewed, can also help mitigate some of the associated risk.

   Client Response:

---

6. *On the systems where electronic protected health information resides, are the following measures taken to reduce the risk of malicious software?*
   - Application of appropriate security and other patches
   - Systems hardened to the extent possible

   Guidance: Earlier in this book, one of the points emphasized was the idea of layered security. System hardening and the application of security patches are two of these layers. During a security assessment, as critical systems are identified, the application of patches and system security should be tested using tools as well as manual procedures. Depending on the system, there are best practice guidelines, which can be used as a benchmark to evaluate how secure it is.

Client Response:

---

iii. Log-In Monitoring

"Implement procedures for monitoring log-in attempts and reporting discrepancies."[17]

This requirement gets into specific measures related to the log-in process. In systems such as Windows 2000, built-in logs readily provide this information. They key impact of this specification is that entities will potentially need to be proactive with regard to log-in monitoring.

1. *Where the relevant systems support the following features, are they used?*
   - Are system controls used to record log-in attempts?
   - Does the system lock users out after a certain number of failed log-in attempts?
   - Are users' logins restricted by other means such as time of day?

   Guidance: Where system features are available for enforcing company security policy, they should be used. If these features are not being used, there is a question as to how logins are being monitored. When recommending the use of system features for user administration security, consider the education and support impacts (from a help desk perspective). These changes require awareness, and there will likely be an increase in help desk calls, which must be addressed.

Client Response:

---

2. *Is there any real-time notification when failed log-in attempts occur on critical machines where electronic protected health information resides?*

   Guidance: Real-time notification is a proactive approach to dealing with intrusions, and this information may be available in the system logs. If no mechanism for notification exists, there might be a need for monitoring on a regular basis.

Client Response:

---

3. *Are the appropriate logs that detail log-in attempts reviewed on a regular basis? Based on logs, are investigations made as needed?*

Guidance: Many systems have logs that record information about log-in attempts, which should be reviewed on a regular basis. The review can either be done manually or by using third-party tools. If anything suspicious is found, an investigation should be initiated.

Client Response:

---

iv. Password Management

"Implement procedures for creating, changing, and safeguarding passwords."[18]

This specification goes into the details of good password management. The HIPAA security regulations recognize the importance of passwords and that they are a first line of defense.

1. *When a new account is created for the network or specific applications that access electronic protected health information, how is the initial password communicated?*

Guidance: Falsely obtaining passwords is a common social engineering technique used by malicious individuals to gain unauthorized access. As a result, communication of initial passwords should be done in a secure manner. Steps should be taken to properly authenticate individuals receiving passwords. In some smaller environments where everyone is familiar with each other, this may not be taken as seriously. This becomes more of an issue as entities grow, where it becomes more difficult to know everyone.

Client Response:

---

2. *Are users encouraged or forced to change their initial passwords?*

Guidance: If possible, the system should be used to force users to change initial passwords. If not forced, may users will not change initial passwords. Depending on the support capabilities, it might be useful (and feasible) to walk users through this process so they understand it. If the system does not support it, the importance of changing the initial password should be taught to users in an education or awareness session.

Client Response:

---

3. *Does the system enforce strong password standards?*

   Guidance: Passwords are the most basic level of protection, and a significant amount of risk related to unauthorized access can be eliminated with strong passwords. If available, the system should force users to have strong passwords. Keep in mind that clients might push back by saying that there will be too many support calls or that users will start placing their passwords on post-it notes stuck to their monitors. In this case, you should provide techniques for users to develop strong passwords such as using the first letters of words in a phrase or substituting certain characters for letters.

Client Response:

---

4. *If the system does not enforce strong passwords, is the strength of passwords audited?*

   Guidance: If the system cannot enforce strong passwords, the strength of passwords should be audited as part of the standard IT audit process. There are third-party tools available for auditing password strength.

Client Response:

---

5. *Are users encouraged or forced to change passwords on a regular basis? Is there a policy on recycling old passwords?*

   Guidance: Passwords should be changed on a regular basis (at least every 45 to 90 days) and there should be a policy on not being able to recycle recent passwords. In addition, users should be discouraged from using passwords such as names of months and other obvious names (the system might be able to enforce this). This should be addressed within a security awareness program.

Client Response:

---

6. *How are password resets handled?*
- When passwords are reset, how are users authenticated?
- Are reset passwords communicated to users in a confidential manner?
- Are users encouraged or forced to change reset passwords?

Guidance: The password-reset process is something commonly used by social engineers to gain unauthorized access to systems. It is imperative that users are properly authenticated and that passwords are communicated in a secure manner. One issue often found is with smaller companies where IT support personnel "know everyone" and do not necessarily authenticate individuals. This practice is a problem because it sets the wrong expectations with users and becomes a problem if turnover occurs or if the entity grows. If the entity grows, it might be difficult to institute this practice. It is better to have a standard process that is always followed.

Client Response:

---

7. *What measures are taken to ensure that users safeguard their passwords?*

Guidance: One of the things seen in many companies is users having passwords on written on yellow sticky notes stuck to their monitors or underneath their keyboards. This should be addressed in a security awareness program and should be part of the IT audit process.

Client Response:

---

6. STANDARD — Security Incident Procedures

"Implement policies and procedures to address security incidents."[19]

The HIPAA regulations define a security incident as "the attempted or successful unauthorized access, use, disclosure, modification, or destruction of information or interference with system operations in an information system."[20]

a. REQUIRED Implementation Specifications

i. Response and Reporting

"Identify and respond to suspected or known security incidents; mitigate, to the extent practicable, harmful effects of security incidents that are known to the covered entity; and document security incidents and their outcomes."[21]

The requirements make up a standard incident handling policy that any entity should have in place as part of its security policies. This is another example of the similarity between HIPAA security regulations and information security best practices. The questions below are based on some of the comments and clarifications to the security incident requirement as documented in the *Federal Register*. In addition to the questions below, the Incident Handling checklist should be used when evaluating this HIPAA requirement.

1. *Is an incident handling policy in place? (See Incident Handling checklist for further best practices related to incident handling.)*

   Guidance: For this requirement, there should be, at the minimum, an Incident Handling policy in place. Like the other security policies, it should be readily accessible by employees and be maintained. With incident management, some entities, particularly the smaller ones, will say that everyone knows what to do in the event of an incident. As with other security policies, this becomes a problem when the number of employees grows or if turnover occurs. In addition, the policy is a requirement for HIPAA purposes so it must be documented and used for handling security incidents.

   Client Response:

2. *As part of the incident handling process, are there any requirements for documenting the details of a security incident?*

   Guidance: Per the HIPAA regulations, there are no specific documentation requirements relative to security incidents. Documentation should be based on the individual entity's business requirements. Specific recommendations for what to document are contained in the Incident Handling questionnaire in the appendices of this book.

   Client Response:

3. *Are there any business or legal requirements related to reporting incidents? If so, are they addressed in the Incident Handling policy?*

   Guidance: Based on the HIPAA security regulations comments and responses as documented in the *Federal Register,* no requirements exist for internal or external reporting. Companies are free to tailor their reporting based on their own business requirements. Keep in mind that an entity might have other reporting requirements that might drive the reporting aspect of its incident handling policy.

Client Response:

---

b. ADDRESSABLE Implementation Specifications

i. None

7. STANDARD — Contingency Plan

"Establish (and implement as needed) policies and procedures for responding to an emergency or other occurrence (for example, fire, vandalism, system failure, and natural disaster) that damages systems that contain electronic protected health information."[22]

Note that this requirement is specific to having a plan only in those cases where electronic protected health information can be lost or compromised. Although comments during the comment period of the HIPAA security legislation process suggested this requirement be removed, it was kept in because in the event of an emergency, the usual security measures might either be ignored or not working. The contingency plan serves as a last resort to ensure the security of electronic protected health information in the event of an emergency. However, in all likelihood, contingency plans related to electronic protected health information (if they exist) are a component of a larger company-wide contingency plan.

a. REQUIRED Implementation Specifications

i. Data Backup Plan

"Establish and implement procedures to create and maintain retrievable exact copies of electronic protected health information."[23]

> **Guidance:** Refer to the Backup and Recovery checklist in this book to evaluate the data backup process. Note that for HIPAA security purposes, the backup requirements are only for the electronic protected health information. However, when performing a security assessment, other data supporting critical operations should be considered.

Client Response:

---

ii. Disaster Recovery Plan

"Establish (and implement as needed) procedures to restore any loss of data."[24]

The questions below address some basic things you should see when looking at a disaster recovery plan.

1. Does the client have a disaster recovery plan in place?

> **Guidance:** Based on this requirement, a formal documented plan should be in place.

Client Response:

---

2. Has the plan been developed using a recognized methodology?

> **Guidance:** The value of developing a plan with a recognized methodology is that risks and business impacts are identified before the plan is developed. Identification of the risks is critical to the success of the disaster recovery plan. In the case of companies subject to HIPAA, you would formally identify electronic protected health information as critical data that must be adequately protected. In addition, using a recognized methodology, such as the one promoted by the Disaster Recovery Institute, provides a good degree of assurance that the plan is thorough.

Client Response:

---

3. What specific measures are taken for electronic protected health information to ensure its confidentiality and security?

> **Guidance:** Because this questionnaire focuses on HIPAA, it is important to identify the specific measures that would be taken for electronic protected health information in the event of a disaster. You should review this and determine whether it is adequate based on the risks facing the company.

Client Response:

---

4. *Is someone responsible for updating the plan as the environment changes?*

   Guidance: Companies are constantly changing and some of the changes might impact the disaster recovery plan. For example, there might be a significant change to the IT environment resulting in critical data being housed on different machines; this can potentially affect the disaster recovery plan. The bottom line is that if the plan is not updated, it can quickly become obsolete. Someone must own this process to ensure that it is properly done.

   Client Response:

5. *Is the plan tested on a regular basis?*

   Guidance: Disaster recovery can be very complicated, and its certainly possible that personnel might not get it right the first time. To minimize the risk of not taking the right steps in the event of a disaster and to ensure that the disaster recovery plan works, the plan should be tested on a periodic basis. The testing can range from a simple tabletop exercise to a full-blown test.

   Client Response:

iii. Emergency Mode Operation Plan

"Establish (and implement as needed) procedures to enable continuation of critical business processes for protection of the security of electronic protected health information while operating in emergency mode."[25]

This requirement is essentially having an emergency plan in place. Each of the questions below addresses a specific element of an emergency plan. Below are some questions to help understand and review emergency plans.

1. *What are the critical business processes that, in the event of a disaster, must continue to protect electronic protected health information? (This is how "emergency mode" is defined in the HIPAA security regulations.)*

   Guidance: The HIPAA security regulations require that certain processes be in place to protect electronic protected health information in the event of a disaster. Although these processes should likely be a part of a disaster recovery plan, this question should be asked to ensure that the processes relevant to HIPAA are identified as critical and that measures are in place to ensure that electronic protected health information is protected.

Client Response:

2. *Are there adequate provisions in the disaster recovery plan to ensure that these processes can continue with minimal disruption in the event of a disaster?*

   Guidance: Related to the question above, part of the HIPAA compliance effort should be to ensure that processes to protect electronic protected health information (identified in the question above) could be continued with minimal effort or interruption.

Client Response:

b. ADDRESSABLE Implementation Specifications

Both of the addressable specifications related to contingency plans are related to updating the contingency plan. Although these are addressable, i.e., they are not specifically required, no real alternatives exist. As a best practice, contingency plans and security practices in general should be evaluated on a regular basis, and adjustments should be made to reflect the current threats and vulnerabilities facing the business.

i. Testing and Revision Procedures

"Implement procedures for periodic testing and revision of contingency plans."[26]

   Guidance: As a best practice, contingency plans should be tested on a regular basis and updated as required. This was made an addressable specification to allow companies to do the level of testing and revision or alternative procedures that are best suited for their environment. The example cited in the *Federal Register* is related to smaller entities, which might not find it reasonable to test as frequently or extensively. For example, a full test might not be feasible, but a certain portion of a contingency plan might be tested or a tabletop exercise might be done. When performing a security assessment, the level of testing and revision should be commensurate with the risk.

Client Response:

ii. Applications and Data Criticality Analysis

"Assess the relative criticality of specific applications and data in support of other contingency plan components."[27]

This requirement is essentially calling for conducting an assessment to determine criticality and risk related to specific applications and data.

> **Guidance:** Although this is listed as a separate specification, the criticality of applications and data should be reviewed when performing the Risk Analysis — one of the first Administrative requirements in the HIPAA security regulations. As a best practice, however, the criticality of applications and data should be evaluated on a regular basis. Often, as new applications are rolled out, security and contingency plans are not always given consideration and are treated as afterthoughts. The person owning the plan should be active in the process of understanding the criticality of data and applications.

Client Response:

---

8. STANDARD — EVALUATION (REQUIRED)

"Perform a periodic technical and non-technical evaluation, based initially upon the standards implemented under this rule and subsequently, in response to environmental or operational changes affecting the security of electronic protected health information, that establishes the extent to which an entity's security policies and procedures meet the requirements of this subpart."[28]

> *1. Does the client perform any type of ongoing security assessment?*

> **Guidance:** This requirement is essentially an ongoing assessment for which the initial risk analysis can be used as a baseline. The goal of this requirement is to ensure that entities do not just implement HIPAA security requirements and then forget about them. The reality is that operations change and as a result, the IT environment changes and the risks change. Notwithstanding HIPAA, ongoing security assessments should be done for any entity to ensure that the information security program is properly aligned with the risks the company is facing. Some ways to comply with this requirement include ongoing IT audits or regular security assessments (using internal or external resources). Some aspects of this requirement, based on the comments received during the comment phase of the HIPAA security legislation process, include:

- Internal or external resources can do ongoing assessments. Entities have the option based on the cost and availability of resources.
- Although HIPAA does not have any "certified" products, entities should monitor the National Institute of Standards and Technology (NIST) for product recommendations.

Client Response:

9. STANDARD — BUSINESS ASSOCIATE CONTRACTS AND OTHER ARRANGEMENTS (REQUIRED)

"A covered entity, in accordance with §164.306 [qualifications for being a 'covered entity'], may permit a business associate to create, receive, maintain, or transmit electronic protected health information on the covered entity's behalf only if the covered entity obtains satisfactory assurances, in accordance with §164.314(a) [business associate contract] that the business associate will appropriately safeguard the Information."[29]

This regulation requires an entity to have assurance that if a "business associate" creates, receives, maintains, or transmits electronic protected health information on behalf of the covered entity, the business associate will appropriately safeguard the information. The business associate requirement does not apply to the following:

- Transmission of electronic protected health information between a covered entity and a health care provider concerning the treatment of an individual
- Transmission of electronic protected health information between a group health plan, HMO, or health insurance issuer to a plan sponsor
- Transmission of electronic protected health information from or to government agencies that are health plans and provide public benefits

1. *Does the client have any business associate relationships and if so, how are they handled as it pertains to the security and privacy of electronic protected health information?*

   Guidance: "Business associate relationships occur in those cases in which the covered entity is disclosing information to someone or some organization that will use the information on behalf of the covered entity."[30] Examples of business associates are professional services such as accounting, law, consulting, and other services.

Client Response:

a. REQUIRED Implementation Specifications

i. Written Contract or Other Arrangement

"A covered entity, in accordance with §164.306 (Security Standard General Rules), may permit a business associate to create, receive, maintain, or transmit electronic protected health information on the covered entity's behalf only if the covered entity obtains satisfactory assurances, in accordance with §164.314(a) (business associate contract regulations) that the business associate will appropriately safeguard the Information."[31]

A covered entity using a business associate should have a written agreement that appropriately safeguards the electronic protected health information in the associate's possession.

1. *Does the client have the appropriate contracts for any business associate working for the client?*

   Guidance: For any business associates, there should be a standard contract that is used. Some of the elements to look for in a contract are those that require business associates to do the following:[32]
   - Not use or further disclose the PHI (Protected Health Information) other than as permitted by the contract or as required by law
   - Use appropriate safeguards to prevent unauthorized use or disclosure of the PHI
   - Report to the covered entity any unauthorized use or disclosure of which it becomes aware
   - Ensure that any agents, including subcontractors, to whom it provides PHI agree to the same restrictions and conditions that apply to the business associate
   - On termination of the contract, return or destroy all PHI in its possession, or, where that is not possible, extend the protections of the contract for as long as the information is retained

---

Client Response:

---

b. ADDRESSABLE Implementation Specifications

i. None

PHYSICAL SAFEGUARDS

The physical safeguards–related requirements are mostly "addressable" specifications. Note that these requirements are separate from the electronic security requirements, which cannot be performed in lieu of the Physical Safeguard controls listed below. There was some confusion over the meaning of "Physical Safeguards" when the HIPAA security requirements were first presented. Based on the *Federal Register*, Physical Safeguards are defined as:

"Security measures to protect a covered entity's electronic information systems and related buildings and equipment, from natural and environmental hazards, and unauthorized intrusion"

1. FACILITY ACCESS CONTROLS

"Entities should have policies and procedures in place to limit physical access to its electronic information systems and the facility or facilities where they are housed, while ensuring that properly authorized access is allowed"[33]

a. REQUIRED Implementation Specifications

i. None

b. ADDRESSABLE Implementation Specifications

i. Contingency Operations

"Implement policies and procedures to limit physical access to its electronic information systems and the facility or facilities in which they are housed, while ensuring that properly authorized access is allowed."[34]

Policies and procedures should be in place to ensure that there is access to facilities to the extent required in restoring data as part of the disaster recovery plan and emergency mode operations. This specification is essentially a complement to the existing disaster recovery plan and emergency mode operations. Some level of access to facilities is required when executing a disaster recovery plan or operating in emergency mode. Keep in mind that this is an addressable specification meaning that covered entities have significant flexibility in how these specifications will be implemented. The flexibility is good for small companies that have limited budget and staff.

1. Do specific policies and procedures to limit access to physical facilities exist?

Guidance: The basic policies and procedures are the foundation for limiting physical access and establishing good physical security controls. This enables personnel to be educated and provides management a basis for enforcement.

Client Response:

2. *Is physical access adequately addressed in the termination policy and procedure?*

   Guidance: Employee termination is a significant risk, and it is critical that physical access is removed as part of the process. If physical access is not removed, former personnel (especially disgruntled ones) can cause significant damage.

   Client Response:

3. *Is the list of people who have physical access periodically reviewed?*

   Guidance: As a mitigating control for the termination process, physical access lists should be periodically reviewed. Any unneeded access should be removed as part of the process. This will vary with the size of the company. In smaller companies, guards and other employees probably know who should or should not be on the premises so the process is not as critical. In larger companies, this is absolutely critical.

   Client Response:

4. *Have facility access requirements been addressed in the disaster recovery plan and emergency mode operation?*

   Guidance: Although the facility access requirements are listed separate from the disaster recovery and emergency mode requirements, they are an integral part of both. If the facility access requirements are not addressed in the disaster recovery or emergency mode operations, where are they addressed? More importantly, are the facility access requirements in sync with the disaster recovery plan and emergency mode operations?

   Client Response:

5. *When the disaster recovery plan is tested, are the people in charge of facility access involved? Are they made aware of updates to the plan?*

   Guidance: Similar to the previous question, the disaster recovery plan should involve those individuals in charge of facility access. The plan test and update process is covered in more detail in the disaster recovery checklist.

Client Response:

---

6. *Are there any awareness programs for the people in charge of facility access?*

   Guidance: Like all security policies and procedures, awareness programs should extend to those individuals in charge of facility access. At the minimum, they should understand and be aware of their roles in the event of a disaster.

Client Response:

---

ii. Facility Security Plan

"Implement policies and procedures to safeguard the facility and the equipment therein from unauthorized physical access, tampering, and theft."[35]

Essentially, this part of the requirement is having physical security policies and procedures in place. Refer to the Physical Security checklist for further questions regarding physical security.

iii. Access Control and Validation Procedures

"Implement procedures to control and validate a person's access to facilities based on their role or function, including visitor control, and control of access to software programs for testing and revision."[36]

Procedures should be in place to control and validate individuals' access to facilities, and their access should be based on their role in the company. This specification also calls for controlling visitors (e.g., logging when they come and go, ensuring visitors walk with authorized personnel). Refer to the Physical Security checklist for questions relevant for this specification.

iv. Maintenance Records

"Implement policies and procedures to document repairs and modifications to the physical components of a facility, which are related to security (for example, hardware, walls, doors, and locks)."[37]

This specification is asking for records to be kept when making any repairs or modifications to security-related components. In addition to the question below, the

Physical Security questionnaire in these appendices should be referenced for other relevant questions.

1. *For any given facility, are the "security-related components" identified so that changes can be appropriately documented?*

   Guidance: To ensure that this HIPAA requirement is met, the specific security components should be identified. Ideally, all significant changes (regardless of whether related to security components or not) should be documented, and these records should be securely kept.

Client Response:

WORKSTATION-RELATED REQUIREMENTS

The next two requirements deal with the use and security of workstations. Before going into the actual requirements, it is worth clarifying the definition of "workstation" as stated in the *Federal Register*:

   Workstation — An electronic computing device, for example, a laptop or desktop computer, or any other device that performs similar functions, and electronic media stored in its immediate environment.

This definition and terminology were a result of comments that the previous terminology "Secure workstation location" (used in the initial drafts of the HIPAA Security regulations) was vague. With the current definition of workstation, this could mean items such as personal digital assistants and other devices.

2. STANDARD — WORKSTATION USE (REQUIRED)

   "Implement policies and procedures that specify the proper functions to be performed, the manner in which those functions are to be performed, and the physical attributes of the surroundings of a specific workstation or class of workstation that can access electronic protected health information."[38]

This specification is meant to ensure that personnel use their workstations in a secure manner.

1. *Identify what workstations as well as other devices can be used to access electronic protected health information.*

   Guidance: Because of the definition of workstation, other computing devices such as personal digital assistants and other wireless devices can be subject to this requirement. This question will help you in determining the scope as well as the associated risk.

Client Response:

---

2. *Does a policy exist that addresses secure workstation use? Some of the things that should be addressed include:*
   - What functions should be performed by the workstation
   - How those functions should be performed
   - What the physical attributes are for the workstation environment

   Guidance: This requirement also calls for having secure practices at the workstation to help ensure that electronic protected health information is protected. For example, the entity might require the use of screen saver passwords so other people cannot see sensitive information when the workstation is unattended. The specific function will vary based on the workstation. As part of this question, you should also ensure that personnel are aware of this policy.

Client Response:

---

3. STANDARD — WORKSTATION SECURITY (REQUIRED)

"Implement physical safeguards for all workstations that access electronic protected health information, to restrict access to authorized users."[39]

One clarification of this specification is that the physical safeguards used are based on the entity's risk analysis process. Consequently, companies have flexibility in implementing this requirement.

1. *Identify what workstations as well as other devices can be used to access electronic protected health information.*

   Guidance: Because of the definition of workstation, other computing devices like personal digital assistants and other wireless devices can be subject to this requirement. This question will help you in determining the scope as well as the associated risk.

Client Response:

---

2. *What physical security measures are taken to protect these devices or machines?*

   Guidance: Once these machines and devices have been identified, they should be secured based on risk. Protection will vary based on the device and can involve such things as locking down laptops with cables or other measures to protect devices such as PDAs.

   Client Response:

3. *Who has access to the physical workstations besides the individual user? Are there facilities people who can potentially access the workstations? If so, what security measures are taken to ensure that these individuals do not gain unauthorized access?*

   Guidance: One of the significant areas of weakness in many companies is that too many people have physical access to machines that access electronic protected health information. Some examples include computers in public areas such as nurses' stations or in cubicles in a typical office. Facilities personnel also have master key access to sensitive areas. Depending on the risk, physical security measures such as locking cables and other devices should be used.

   Client Response:

4. *Were there any workstation security–related findings in the initial risk assessment and if so, were they addressed?*

   Guidance: Workstation security should have been addressed in the initial risk assessment at the start of the HIPAA security compliance process. Any findings should be reviewed to determine whether or not those findings have been addressed.

   Client Response:

4. STANDARD — Device and Media Controls

"Implement policies and procedures that govern the receipt and removal of hardware and electronic media that contain electronic protected health information into and out of a facility, and the movement of these items within the facility."[40]

This specification calls for policies and procedures to help ensure that any media containing electronic protected health information is adequately secured when it leaves or comes back to the facility.

a. REQUIRED Implementation Specifications

i. Disposal

"Implement policies and procedures to address the final disposition of electronic protected health information, and/or the hardware or electronic media on which it is stored."[41]

This can apply to hard drives, backup tapes, etc. where electronic protected health information is stored. Measures such as overwriting disks must be performed to ensure that sensitive electronic protected health information cannot be compromised. The disposal requirement is essentially based on best practices, and nothing is particular just to HIPAA. Questions related to data disposal are documented in the Media Handling questionnaire in the appendices and should be used to evaluate this requirement.

ii. Media Re-Use

"Implement procedures for removal of electronic protected health information from electronic media before the media are made available for re-use."[42]

This requirement is similar to the disposal requirement in the sense that electronic protected health information must be properly destroyed. This will require multiple overwriting to ensure that information cannot be recovered once the electronic media is available for reuse. Like the disposal requirement, there are no aspects that are particular to just HIPAA. As such, questions from the Media Handling questionnaire in the appendices should be used to evaluate compliance with this requirement.

b. ADDRESSABLE Implementation Specifications

i. Accountability

"Maintain a record of the movements of hardware and electronic media and any person responsible therefore."[43]

This specification requires that some type of audit trail be kept of any movement of electronic media and hardware where electronic protected health information resides. One clarification made in the comments section of the regulation is that this specification does not address audit trails within systems or software. The idea here is that because of the sensitive nature of information on the electronic media, it should be secure, and there should be accountability for it.

1. *Are there clear roles and responsibilities for who can handle electronic media?*

    Guidance: Because of the sensitivity of the electronic protected health information and the media where it resides, only certain individuals should be authorized to take it. A policy should identify what roles in the organization are authorized. In a security assessment, one of the main aspects reviewed in virtually any area is roles and responsibilities. Similar to this HIPAA specification, it helps establish accountability.

    Client Response:

2. *When there is movement of electronic media, are there logs of who takes it and when they take and return it?*

    Guidance: This is a process question that maps back to the requirement. There should be a log that records the movement of media. This log should be accessed by a limited number of individuals.

    Client Response:

3. *Is there proper segregation of duties relative to maintaining the log? (The people who are taking the electronic media should not be updating the logs.)*

    Guidance: With any log, segregation of duties is important because it speaks to the quality and integrity of the information contained in it. To achieve accountability, the logs are critical because they establish who had the electronic media and when they had it. If there is even a perception that the information in the log can be altered, the log loses value. The ideal scenario is to ensure that the individuals who take and handle the electronic media do not have access to the logs.

Client Response:

---

4. Is the log kept in a secure manner?

Guidance: Related to the question above, the logs should be kept securely. If electronic, they should have proper access controls (see User ID Administration checklist) and if paper based, they should be properly locked with only a limited number of people having access.

Client Response:

---

ii. Data Backup and Storage

"Create a retrievable, exact copy of electronic protected health information, when needed, before movement of equipment."[44]

The purpose of this specification is to minimize the risk related to electronic protected health information when moving systems and equipment. Like many of the other specifications, entities have considerable latitude in determining what is best for their environment. The comments received on this specification led to a number of clarifications:

- What is backed up (a retrievable and exact copy) is largely dependent on the risk analysis — i.e., where is the risk great enough to require a retrievable and exact copy?
- A guideline that can be used when determining what to back up is — what information would be required by the entity to continue "business as usual"? This information should be available in the analysis done to determine what is required to run in "emergency mode."

For other questions related to this specification, refer to the Backup and Recovery questionnaire in the Appendices.

TECHNICAL SAFEGUARDS

1. STANDARD — Access Control

"Implement technical policies and procedures for electronic information systems that maintain electronic protected health information to allow access only to those persons or software programs that have been granted access rights as specified in § 164.308(a)(4) [Information Access Management standard]."[45]

These policies and procedures should be designed to allow access only to those persons or software that has been granted access rights as specified in the Administrative Safeguards section on Information Access Management. Although the Administrative Safeguards section required entities to have policies and procedures to grant access to systems where electronic protected health information is maintained, this Access Control requirement is essentially requiring that these policies and procedures be translated into technical policies at the technical level. With this requirement, entities should take advantage of the technical capabilities relative to access control to ensure that access is limited to only those who require it. Based on some of the comments received, access control was further clarified to include:

- Context-based access
- Role-based access
- User-based access

a. REQUIRED Implementation Specifications

i. Unique User Identification

"Assign a unique name and/or number for identifying and tracking user identity."[46]

Unique user identification is generally accepted as an information security best practice and is one of the items covered in the user ID administration checklist. The ideas behind this requirement are making users accountable for what they do and enforcing the HIPAA security requirements. One item to note here is that there are several levels of access to be concerned about. Access is at several levels within organizations including network, application, and remote access. This requirement is specifically for access related to electronic information systems containing electronic protected health information.

1. Identify the systems that contain electronic protected health information and how they can be accessed.

Guidance: This information should already be available from the initial analysis but it is a good idea to confirm what systems contain electronic protected health information. In addition, all the different ways the systems can be accessed should be identified.

Client Response:

2. Do individuals accessing the identified systems have unique IDs for access?

Guidance: Systems containing electronic protected health information should be using unique IDs. There may be situations where applications access electronic protected health information and the applications do not have unique IDs for users. One potential issue is people who do not access the systems very often (e.g., a backup person or someone who is temporarily helping) so when they do, they use someone else's ID.

Client Response:

---

3. *Do the systems have any default IDs or guest IDs and if so, 1) are they used? 2) have their default passwords been changed? 3) if not needed, are they (can they be) disabled?*

   Guidance: Default and guest IDs are a significant risk when it comes to unauthorized access to systems. These IDs are usually there out of the box, so if administrators do not change passwords or disable them, they can be used by someone with knowledge of the application or the system to gain unauthorized access. In fact, a malicious user can utilize the Internet to research what the different default IDs and passwords are and use that knowledge to gain unauthorized access. The default or guest ids should be taken care of during the initial deployment if possible.

Client Response:

---

4. *Do these systems have a way of tracking individuals' activities? For example, can specific transactions on these systems such as report generation be tracked to specific individuals? If specific information is accessed, can it be tracked to an individual?*

   Guidance: Tracking someone's activity relating to accessing electronic protected health information is necessary according to this requirement. This tracking can include just accessing specific files or creating and modifying information via an application. At the application level, specific transactions should be tracked as that will provide a record of who made what changes. Besides the built-in mechanisms available in applications and systems, other mechanisms for fulfilling this requirement include tools such as integrity checkers.

Client Response:

---

5. *Who has access to the logs and if the logs were altered, could that be identified?*

> **Guidance:** The foundation of tracking activity is the logs. Access to the logs should be restricted to the extent possible. No one should have any access to modify any information on the logs. Depending on the risk, it might be appropriate to deploy tools to check the integrity of the logs.

Client Response:

---

ii. Emergency Access Procedure

> "Establish (and implement as needed) procedures for obtaining necessary electronic protected health information during an emergency."[47]

This requirement relates to technical measures including backups and the ability to recover. The Backup and Recovery questionnaire in the Appendices and the emergency plan questions from the HIPAA questionnaire should be used to check compliance with this requirement.

b. ADDRESSABLE Implementation Specifications

i. Automatic Logoff

> "Implement electronic procedures that terminate an electronic session after a predetermined time of inactivity."[48]

This was originally a "required" specification, which was changed to addressable because the automatic logoff feature is not always available. Based on the comments and responses documented, some type of equivalent measure based on a specific entity's risk analysis can also be used.

1. *Where available, is the "automatic logoff" mechanism used?*

> **Guidance:** This is a very specific control where you need to verify whether or not the system supports it. If it does support it but is not being used, it might be because the client is not aware of it. If recommending the use of this feature, warn the client that there will be some support issues in the beginning.

Client Response:

---

ii. Encryption and Decryption

"Implement a mechanism to encrypt and decrypt electronic protected health information."[49]

As a form of security, encryption provides confidentiality of information. This became an "addressable" requirement because it was questioned how valuable and feasible it was to encrypt data. The cost of encrypting information and the ongoing maintenance and support can be very expensive for small entities and even some larger entities. Making this specification "addressable" gave entities the option to encrypt data based on their specific risks.

1. Has the client's risk analysis addressed the issue of data encryption?

Guidance: The client's risk analysis should have considered the issue of encryption. Based on the risk analysis, the client should be able to articulate why encryption is or is not being used.

Client Response:

---

2. STANDARD — Audit Controls (Required)

"Implement hardware, software, and/or procedural mechanisms that record and examine activity in information systems that contain or use electronic protected health information."[50]

This standard essentially requires entities to evaluate the systems currently in use and determine if they can record and examine activities of individuals accessing electronic protected health information in the systems. Note that the standard specifically mentions hardware and software. Compliance with this standard may require new systems or custom coding of existing systems. Audit controls, by their nature, are flexible in nature and depend on the level of risk. The comments and subsequent responses as documented in the *Federal Register* clearly state that the audit controls should be based on the entity's own risk analysis. This specification should be analyzed in conjunction with the related Privacy specifications, which require entities to account for disclosures of protected health information to individuals upon request.

1. As part of the risk analysis, has the client reviewed these hardware and software mechanisms for recording activity?

Guidance: This requirement is based on the risk analysis. When determining what is to be reviewed, the client should consider current staffing and how the additional work will be handled (assuming it is not being done already).

Client Response:

---

2. *For cases where activity is to be reviewed, does the client have documented procedures for what has to be reviewed, when logs are generated, etc.?*

   Guidance: The resulting reviews that are instituted to achieve compliance with this requirement are a process that should be documented. There should be minimum requirements for these reviews and there should be some expectation of what the review entails. A procedure is a good place to capture these requirements.

Client Response:

---

3. STANDARD — INTEGRITY

"Implement policies and procedures to protect electronic protected health information from improper alteration or destruction."[51]

Integrity of information is one of the pillars of information security. The point of this standard is that electronic protected health information should not be altered in an unauthorized manner. The integrity standard ties into the earlier requirement that individuals' activities should be tracked to guard against unauthorized alteration of data. There are tools such as "integrity checkers" and intrusion detection systems that claim to do integrity checking. In addition, some systems might have native tools to check integrity. Software as well as existing system mechanisms should be investigated when evaluating compliance with this requirement.

a. REQUIRED Implementation Specifications

i. None

b. ADDRESSABLE Implementation Specifications

i. Mechanism to Authenticate Electronic Protected Health Information

"Implement electronic mechanisms to corroborate that electronic protected health information has not been altered or destroyed in an unauthorized manner."[52]

As alluded to earlier, specific software and potentially existing tools on systems can corroborate that electronic protected health information has not been improperly altered. Examples of built-in data authentication mechanisms include error-correcting memory and magnetic disc storage. In addition, processes that utilize checksums or digital signatures can be considered.

1. *Has the integrity of data been considered in the client's risk analysis?*

   Guidance: Review the risk analysis to determine whether it was considered.

   Client Response:

   ---

2. *Are there any mechanisms such as "integrity checkers" in place?*

   Guidance: Some companies have deployed tools such as Tripwire to ensure the integrity of critical files. If the client does not have something like this in place, determine what tools, if any, are in use.

   Client Response:

   ---

3. *Based on the risk analysis, where (if anywhere) is it appropriate to deploy integrity-checking tools?*

   Guidance: Determine where electronic protected health information resides and where it makes sense to have which integrity checking tools. In different cases, you may be able to deploy cheaper solutions; it all depends on the risk analysis.

   Client Response:

   ---

4. STANDARD — PERSON OR ENTITY AUTHENTICATION

"Implement procedures to verify that a person or entity seeking access to electronic protected health information is the one claimed."[53]

Guidance: This specification builds on the first specification in the Technical Safeguards section requiring users to have unique user IDs. In the initial draft, this specification listed actual technologies that can be used to come into compliance with this requirement. In the final adopted rule, any reference to technology was intentionally omitted to allow companies to use methods that made sense based on their own risk levels. Some of the methods that can be considered when implementing this specification include (as documented in the initial draft):

- A "biometric" identification system
- A "password" system
- A "personal identification" system
- A "telephone callback" system
- Digital signatures
- Soft tokens

1. *When providing support for technologies used in this specification, how are individuals authenticated?*

Guidance: One of the most significant security risks is social engineering. It is critical that users are properly authenticated when they are provided with any support related to gaining access to systems. This is often a problem in smaller companies where the attitude of support personnel is "I know everyone here." Look for specific procedures for authenticating users.

Client Response:

---

5. STANDARD — Transmission Security

"Implement technical security measures to guard against unauthorized access to electronic protected health information that is being transmitted over an electronic communications network."[54]

Guidance: The regulations thus far have been focused on the security of electronic protected health information that is in a system. This requirement focuses on the transmission of that information over an "electronics communication network." To clarify this further, the network is essentially an untrusted network, such as the Internet. To properly evaluate this requirement, a thorough process evaluation of how information is sent should be performed.

1. *Identify all instances where information is sent over a public network (e.g., the Internet).*

Guidance: Examples include: patient information sent electronically to other health care entities, agencies, insurers; billing information sent to insurers. Identifying these instances will define the scope of work required to come into compliance with this requirement. To obtain this information, it is imperative to involve process owners as well as technology owners. Once this list is complete, a risk analysis should be performed to determine what steps to take. As noted below, there are no "required" implementation specifications related to this standard. The specific measures to take are dependent on the level of risk.

Client Response:

2. *Is instant messaging used for communicating electronic protected health information?*

    Guidance: Instant messaging has gone from being used for socializing to being used for business purposes. You should find out if it is being used and what is being transmitted using instant messaging software. There are solutions to secure instant message traffic.

Client Response:

a. REQUIRED Implementation Specifications

i. None

b. ADDRESSABLE Implementation Specifications

i. Integrity Controls
Security measures to ensure that electronically transmitted electronic protected health information is not improperly modified without detection until it is disposed of.

    Guidance: Based on what is being transmitted, the risk analysis should consider the likelihood that electronic protected health information can be altered during transmission. Depending on the risk, different solutions can be implemented including software that can check integrity or other procedures that check to determine whether information has been altered.

Client Response:

ii. Encryption

> 1. *Implement a mechanism to encrypt electronic protected health information as deemed appropriate.*
>
> **Guidance:** Encryption was one of the areas that received comments from the public in the earlier draft of the HIPAA security regulations. For many health care entities, particularly the smaller rural ones, the cost of encrypting communications over public networks can be daunting. As a result, encryption became an "addressable" specification. For example, information communicated over a dial-up line probably would not require encryption because the likelihood that the confidentiality can be compromised is slim. The expectation is that companies should encrypt transmitted information if their risk analysis determines that encryption is warranted.

Client Response:

NOTES

1. *Federal Register*/Vol 68 No. 34/Thursday, February 20, 2003/Rules and regulations pp. 8377
2. Ibid
3. Ibid
4. Ibid
5. Ibid
6. Ibid
7. Ibid
8. Ibid
9. Ibid
10. Ibid
11. Ibid
12. Ibid
13. Ibid
14. Ibid
15. Ibid
16. Ibid
17. Ibid
18. Ibid
19. Ibid
20. *Federal Register*/Vol 68 No. 34/Thursday, February 20, 2003/Rules and Regulations pp. 8376
21. *Federal Register*/Vol 68 No. 34/Thursday, February 20, 2003/Rules and regulations pp. 8377
22. Ibid

23. *Federal Register*/Vol 68 No. 34/Thursday, February 20, 2003/Rules and regulations pp. 8378
24. Ibid
25. Ibid
26. Ibid
27. Ibid
28. Ibid
29. Ibid
30. HIPAA @IT Reference, 2003 Edition, Roy Rada
31. *Federal Register*/Vol 68 No. 34/Thursday, February 20, 2003/Rules and regulations pp. 8378
32. University of Miami — Bioethics Program Privacy/Data Protection — http://privacy.med.miami.edu/glossary/xd_business_associate.htm
33. *Federal Register*/Vol 68 No. 34/Thursday, February 20, 2003/Rules and regulations pp. 8378
34. Ibid
35. Ibid
36. Ibid
37. Ibid
38. Ibid
39. Ibid
40. Ibid
41. Ibid
42. Ibid
43. Ibid
44. Ibid
45. Ibid
46. Ibid
47. Ibid
48. Ibid
49. Ibid
50. Ibid
51. Ibid
52. *Federal Register*/Vol 68 No. 34/Thursday, February 20, 2003/Rules and regulations pp. 8379
53. Ibid
54. Ibid

Index